TEXAS LAWMEN

1835 ✦ 1899

The Good and the Bad

CLIFFORD R. CALDWELL
& RON DELORD

Charleston · London

THE
History
PRESS

Published by The History Press
Charleston, SC 29403
www.historypress.net

Cover images: Front cover photo by Ellen D. Caldwell, Mountain Home, Texas.
Back cover: Members of Company D, Frontier Battalion, Texas Rangers. Taken at Ysleta, Texas, 1895. Photo courtesy of the Nita Stewart Haley Memorial Library, Midland, Texas.

First published 2011

Manufactured in the United States

ISBN 978.1.60949.216.8

Library of Congress Cataloging-in-Publication Data

Caldwell, Clifford R., 1948-
 Texas lawmen, 1835-1899 : the good and the bad / Clifford R. Caldwell and Ronald
DeLord.
   p. cm.
 ISBN 978-1-60949-216-8
 1. Police--Texas--Biography. 2. Criminal justice personnel--Texas--Biography. 3. Peace
officers--Texas--Biography. 4. Law enforcement--Texas--History. I. DeLord, Ron. II. Title.
 HV7911.A1C355 2011
 363.2092'2764--dc22
                              2010050623

"Take it…I shall never be able to use it again"

Said by Texas Ranger private Fountain B. Woodruff, who, while lying mortally wounded, handed his revolver to a fellow ranger.
4 February 1860.

Contents

CONTENTS

Preface

They number more than eight hundred in all, the brave souls who laid down their lives in the service of the State of Texas. They are the Texas lawmen who gave everything they had to give in the service of the citizens of our great state. Here you will find them all—at least all that we know of thus far. The roster includes Texas Ranger captains and privates, sheriffs, deputies, constables, police officers, cattle inspectors, U.S. marshals, jailers and ordinary citizens who volunteered for a day and found it to be their last. While many historians accurately report that the citizens enlisting in ranging companies before 1874 were not officially lawmen, the authors feel that they deserve recognition and are therefore included in this book.

Texas has had its share of lawlessness. Starting in the 1820s, the chief deterrent to crime in this multimillion-acre territory was a small group of lawmen who would later become known as the Texas Rangers. Stephen F. Austin organized two companies in 1823 "for the common defense." In 1835, the provisional government authorized a "ranging company" of twenty-five rangers. Later, that number was increased to a total of three companies consisting of fifty-six men each. Throughout the republic period, ranger units repelled Indian attacks and beat back invasions by bandits from Mexico. Often these companies of rangers were activated for only short periods and disbanded after the crisis.

During the Civil War, thousands of Texans joined the Confederate army. By 1863, ranger companies were mustered into the forces of the Confederate States of America, state militia units and a Regiment of Rangers. After the Civil War, Texas established the Frontier Organization and Minute Men companies modeled on the ranging companies. Between

1871 and 1873, the governor created the Texas State Police to maintain order. In 1874, the Frontier Battalion and Special Forces were established to battle Indian raids and stop lawlessness of the frontier. As counties, towns and villages were formed, local law enforcement agencies were organized to protect the citizens and keep the peace. Many of the local and county law enforcement entities date to as early as Texas independence. After 1846, the United States Marshals Service, which was created on 24 September 1789, often augmented the efforts of Texas state and local law enforcement officials. Altogether, this list of lawmen forms an almost dizzying array of agencies for which brave Texans served in the struggle to enforce the law and keep the peace.

The roster of lawmen in this book includes all of the individuals whom we have been able to identify who died between 1835 and the last day of 1899. Most of the lawmen killed during the Texas Revolution, Civil War and Mexican-American War have been excluded, since those were primarily military actions. However, a few have been included on a case-by-case basis. The war for Texas independence from Mexico officially began on 2 October 1835 and ended on 21 April 1836. This list of lawmen begins just before the war for independence, when Private Benjamin Castleman died from an accidental discharge of a firearm in June 1835 while he was serving with the Washington Volunteers, a ranging company. The seemingly endless list continues through United States Customs Service deputy collector Richard W. "Dick" Wallace, who was killed by smugglers at Presidio on 30 November 1899—the final lawman to be killed in Texas during the nineteenth century. It includes Sheriff Joseph L. Hood of Bexar County, who on 19 March 1840 became the first Texas sheriff to die in the line of duty. You will find the entry for L.B. "Berry" Smith, a Texas Ranger private who was just seventeen years of age when, on 12 June 1875, he gave his life and thus became the youngest lawman known to have been killed in Texas. The list includes a lawman who was killed over a dispute for $1.50 and another who lost his life for something as trivial as disturbing his neighbor on a Sunday morning. Some died in what can only be described as quintessential Old West–style gunfights. Others met their untimely ends when shot by a coward in an ambush.

Throughout the book, the lawmen are listed by the agency for which they served, in chronological order, beginning with the earliest date of death and working down to the most recent. If you are uncertain of the agency for which the lawman you are searching for worked, we suggest that you begin your quest with the index at the end of the book. Early historical records are often less accurate than we would desire them to be. Please keep this in mind, because you may encounter alternate spellings for some surnames and given names. Wherever possible, multiple sources have been used to verify the information contained herein. For a more in-depth study of a particular lawman, we suggest you refer to the bibliography at the end of the book for more thorough reference material.

Throughout the text of this book, you will confront numerous situations in which more than one lawman was killed in the same incident. In those situations, the reader should look to the full description of the incident in an account that generally follows, but may sometimes precede, the entry for the respective lawman.

This book is intended to be a comprehensive reference of the Texas lawmen who died during the 1800s. Due to the volume of entries it contains—and, in many cases, the scarcity of information available—the authors did not intend to offer a complete biography of every man nor an exhaustive summary of the circumstances of each death. Due to space considerations, source citations for each individual biography had to be sacrificed. Including them would have added roughly six hundred pages of additional text. An extensive bibliography section highlights the primary sources. Individuals interested in the details supporting each entry should, and are encouraged to, contact the authors.

For purposes of historical interest, as well as completeness, the book also includes the names of many lawmen whose deaths occurred under circumstances that did not meet the rigorous criteria that have been established by the various memorial organizations for classification as a line-of-duty death. In some cases, an officer's death may have been the result of a personal feud or an accident. It may have occurred after the officer had left his respective agency, or it may have taken place under circumstances for which sufficient information could not be found to meet the criteria for inclusion on the list of those who were killed in the "line of duty."

The officers whose names have been listed on a memorial will have a reference number listed next to their name in the memorial appendix at the back of the book. The reference, or location number, will aid you in finding that name on one of the memorials—either in Austin, Texas, or Washington, D.C.

Acknowledgements

This roster of names, and summary of events, took many years to assemble. It represents thousands of hours of work by numerous volunteers. It is the product of incalculable hours spent by a handful of dedicated individuals, digging through archives in the damp cellars of courthouses all across the state of Texas. Weeks and years were invested sorting through newspaper articles, court records and family history files in an attempt to validate all of these cases. Thousands of miles were spent behind the steering wheel searching for grave markers and headstones. Hours in the hot sun were spent clearing brush in search of a lone grave marker that had long since been forgotten and was hidden from view. Over the years, a mountain of files and correspondence was amassed containing the precious few documents that researchers could find about the lives of these lawmen. Some files are immense and would make sizeable books on their own. Others may contain little more than a handful of documents or a lone piece of paper with a brief newspaper account of the passing of some brave soul.

Who would ever shoulder such a daunting task? Tracking down a thousand lawmen from the 1800s—and, moreover, why? The why is the easy part to answer.

Simply stated: because it needed to be done. Almost all of these men were heroes, in one way or another. Emerson said, "A hero is no braver than an ordinary man, but he is braver five minutes longer." These men were all doing their duty—as they saw it. Perhaps, then, it was their boldness and their sacrifice that sets them apart.

One might criticize the inclusion of lawmen who lost their lives in personal feuds or from criminal misconduct or died as the result of some unfortunate accident. On the other hand, singling out that moment in time, like a snapshot, to narrowly define the motion picture of their service seems shortsighted.

People who serve know about duty. Duty can be a heavy load to shoulder, as is evidenced by the scope of this undertaking. The satisfaction derived by those who have labored so diligently on the research work necessary to assemble this book comes, in large part, from knowing that the passing of some of these obscure lawmen will not go unrecognized. Special recognition is due to Dallas County sheriff's assistant chief deputy Terry Baker (retired), Bexar County sheriff's lieutenant Kyle Coleman, Fort Worth police sergeant Kevin Foster (retired), Harris County sheriff's deputy Doug Hudson (retired) and all of the volunteers who have worked so hard to research the history of these lawmen.

Any author researching a book on the Texas Rangers, or the Texas State Police, knows that the preeminent authority on such matters is Donaly E. Brice, senior research assistant at the Texas State Library and Archives Commission. His support was above and beyond the call of duty.

Many thanks go out to the founders and members of the Officer Down Memorial Page, Inc., including Chris Cosgriff, Mike Schutz and Steve Weiss, who have taken the time to honor our fallen lawmen on their website. Craig Floyd, Caroline Heyliger and Berneta Spence at the National Law Enforcement Officers Memorial Foundation have devoted their lives to researching the deaths of all U.S. officers. Thanks also to Sherlynn Kelly at the Lost Lawmen Memorial of the Sheriff's Association of Texas for memorializing the sacrifices of sheriffs, deputies and jailers. The Texas Peace Officers Memorial is managed by the Texas Commission on Law Enforcement Officers Standards and Education. Executive Director Timothy Braaten and his staff extended every courtesy to the authors during our research.

In the bibliography section at the back of the book, you will find the titles of dozens of well-written books by respected authors and historians whose contributions played a vital role in compiling this anthology. Our thanks go out to all of them, including Stephen Moore, Darren L. Ivey, Mike Cox, Robert DeArment, Leon Metz, Chuck Parsons, Robert W. Stephens, Robert Utley and Walter Prescott Webb. All have done considerable research on Texas lawmen over the years and have contributed mightily to the information we have collected about these fallen officers.

Last but by no means least, we wish to recognize and acknowledge the hundreds of family members, researchers, librarians, staff members of law enforcement agencies and historians who have aided us in collecting the data necessary to produce this book. Without their help, this book could never have been completed.

Chapter 1
County and
Municipal Agencies

Many that live deserve death.
And some die that deserve life.
Can you give it to them?
Then be not too eager to deal out death
in the name of justice, fearing for your own safety.

–J.R.R. Tolkien

ANDERSON COUNTY SHERIFF'S OFFICE

Godley, James Robert
Born circa 1843—Died 13 December 1874
Date of incident: 12 December 1874

Sheriff Ed Davis had deputized James Godley, a man who was a physician by profession. The sheriff ordered Godley and J.F. Henderson to arrest a fellow named Bob Smith. Smith was wanted on a charge of bigamy. When the two deputies attempted to arrest Smith, he shot Godley with a shotgun, mortally wounding him. Godley died the following day. Bob Smith managed to escape in a hail of gunfire.

Smith was arrested several weeks later. According to the poem "The Ballad of Bob Smith," written in the mid-1950s by Lucius Dow Henderson, Bob Smith was lynched in his jail cell at Fosterville. The veracity of this claim has not been verified.

Dr. Godley was survived by his wife, Georgia, and their four children. He is believed to be buried in an unmarked grave in the area of the former town of Fosterville, in northeastern Anderson County.

Rogers, John
Born circa 1863—Died 29 September 1883

Deputy Rogers was shot and killed when he and two other deputies were attempting to arrest an escaped convict named Frank Jackson.

The three lawmen had gone to a small house on the edge of the county where Jackson was said to be hiding. When two of the deputies went around to the back of the house, Jackson attempted to escape through the front. As he fled, he fired at Deputy Rogers, striking him in the chest. The bullet penetrated his lungs, inflicting a fatal wound. Jackson was able to escape the scene but was later captured by a sheriff's posse.

Rogers's place of burial is unknown.

Stafford, James Monroe "Jim"
Born circa 1857—Died 15 June 1899

Deputy Stafford was shot and killed by Palestine city marshal Ed Matthews.

Deputy Stafford was at the county jail with an attorney discussing the previous night's gambling raid. City Marshal Matthews called Stafford out of the jail and began chastising him, telling him to stay out of his business. Stafford argued, claiming that he was just doing his job. Harsh words between the two men soon led to gunfire when Matthews pulled his pistol and shot Stafford.

City Marshal Matthews was convicted of murder and sentenced to twenty-five years in prison.

Deputy Stafford was survived by his wife and eight children. He is buried at the Stafford-Tucker Cemetery.

ANGELINA COUNTY SHERIFF'S OFFICE

McMullen, William Read
Born circa 1819—Died 19 June 1866

Shortly after sundown on 19 June 1866, Sheriff McMullen, along with his son, Foster, left his residence to respond to reports of gunfire near the town square in Homer. Not long after they arrived at the scene of the disturbance, Sheriff McMullen was shot and killed from an ambush. The identity of the killer is unknown.

Once the sheriff had been shot, the gunfire ceased, and those who had been involved fled the scene. Various reports by local newspapers, supported by published historical accounts of the incident, claim that the mysterious shooting may have resulted in the death of as many as five people. The same sources claim that as many as eighteen citizens may have been wounded during the affray.

The killing of Sheriff McMullen occurred shortly after the Civil War had ended, when factions supporting either the North or South were feuding in Angelina County. At the time, members of the Gilley family were fighting with patricians of the Windham family. Locally, this dispute was known as the "Gilley War."

McMullen's assassin was never identified. He was survived by his wife and six children and is buried at Homer Cemetery in Angelina County.

AUSTIN POLICE DEPARTMENT

Fahey, Cornelius L.
Born circa 1840—Died 9 March 1875
Date of incident: 7 March 1875

Between the hours of midnight and 1:00 a.m. on 7 March 1875, Officer Fahey was shot through the abdomen while patrolling an unknown block of Congress Avenue. Fahey's assailant, said to have been a "whiskey-crazed man" named Mark Tiner, fled the scene on horseback and was captured in Hancock's pasture about three and a half miles north of the city.

Fahey was able to identify his killer as being Mark Tiner before dying of his wounds. According to the local press, Officer Fahey was "an efficient officer, and fell while in the discharge of his duty." Fahey was the first Austin police officer to die in the line of duty.

Officer Fahey was a native of Cork, Ireland. He is buried at Oakwood Cemetery in Austin.

Thompson, Benjamin "Ben"
Born 2 November 1843—Died 11 March 1884

Much has been written about Thompson, and those interested in his story are encouraged to read one of the several fascinating book-length accounts of his life referenced in the bibliography section.

In 1880, Thompson was involved in a dispute with San Antonio gamblers Joe Foster, Jack Harris and Bill Simms. The quarrel led to a gunfight in which Thompson killed Harris. On 11 March 1884, Foster and Simms laid a trap for Thompson at the Vaudeville Theater in San Antonio. A volley of shots from two or more hidden gunmen resulted in his death. Thompson was accompanied by the notorious King Fisher, who was a Uvalde County deputy sheriff at the time. Fisher was also killed in the ambush.

Thompson is buried at Oakwood Cemetery in Austin, Texas.

Related case: Uvalde County Sheriff's Office—John King Fisher.

BALLINGER POLICE DEPARTMENT

Hill, John Thomas "Tom"
Born 10 July 1854—Died 8 August 1886
Date of incident: 6 August 1886

John W. Vaden was an undisputedly acrimonious character who became contemptible when drunk. He had killed numerous black men and at least one Union sympathizer. Vaden had also served as a deputy sheriff in Maverick County.

Vaden decided to open a saloon at Ballinger in Runnels County. John Hill, the former city marshal of Abilene, had taken the city marshal's job at Ballinger and left his wife and family in neighboring Taylor County.

On 6 August 1886, Vaden was intoxicated and had armed himself with a Winchester rifle. He shot out the streetlights just outside his own saloon. Next, the intoxicated Vaden went to the neighboring establishment called the Palace Saloon and began creating a disturbance. Marshal Hill attempted to disarm Vaden. Vaden fired his rifle accidentally, hitting Hill in the left foot. The wound was serious. Hill's foot had to be amputated. The surgery was not a success, and Hill died at 6:00 a.m. on 8 August 1886.

Vaden moved to Fort McKavett in Menard County and obtained a deputy commission from the sheriff. On 7 October 1886, Vaden was again inebriated, and this time he was armed with a pike. He confronted Ben Daniels, a bartender who was also commissioned as a deputy sheriff. Daniels shot and killed Vaden. A grand jury decided not to prosecute Daniels for the shooting.

Hill was survived by his wife and three children. He is buried at Abilene City Cemetery.

Related case: Menard County Sheriff's Office—John W. Vaden.

BANDERA COUNTY SHERIFF'S OFFICE

Phillips, Jack
Born (Unknown)—Died 29 December 1876

Deputy Phillips was killed by Indians while leaving Hondo Canyon on official business. He had stopped for dinner at the home of a local rancher named M.C. Click and was leaving the ranch when the attack took place.

Phillips, who lived six miles above Bandera, had headed out alone on an official visit to Sabinal Canyon. Indians attacked him at the Seco Canyon Pass, twenty-two miles southwest of Bandera. Phillips raced for the nearest settlement. When his horse was shot out from under him, he attempted to retreat back to the Click ranch, running for half a mile before being shot through the shoulder and killed. A mail carrier and a couple on their way to the county seat to be married found his body later that day.

Ironically, the Indians involved in the attack had been trailed for many miles by Texas Rangers who had turned back in exhaustion just before Phillips was waylaid. The Indians escaped and were never apprehended.

Phillips, who was referred to as "Captain," was survived by his brother, who was the Bandera County sheriff. Phillips was a Mason and is buried in an unmarked grave at Bandera.

BASTROP COUNTY SHERIFF'S OFFICE

Smythson, William
Born circa 1845—Died 9 December 1877

On 9 December 1877, Deputy Smythson was killed when he was thrown from his saddle horse in Elgin.

Smythson's horse reared, falling backward with the deputy in the saddle. When the animal landed, the horn of the saddle struck Smythson in the stomach, with the full weight of the horse crushing him. Smythson could not speak but is said to have been able to use his hand to motion that he was injured in the stomach and that he was in great pain. The injuries from the fall resulted in his death within a few hours.

Smythson was reported to be a good officer and a young man without family. His place of burial is unknown.

Batts, Charlie A.
Born 10 August 1861—Died 22 April 1879

Jailer Batts was only seventeen years old when he met his untimely end.

Batts was struck by lightning while on duty at the county jail on 22 April 1879. Two other men and a boy were also hit by the same bolt. Batts was killed but the others survived.

Batts is buried at Fairview Cemetery in Bastrop.

Purcell, John
Born circa 1839—Died 1 March 1881
Date of incident: 27 February 1881

On 27 February 1881, Deputy Purcell was mortally injured when he was accidentally thrown from his horse near the town of Elgin. Purcell suffered in great pain and was told that his injuries were fatal. It is said that he attempted to cling to life until his mother could arrive. He wished to have her counsel his young son, who would now have to take over as head of the family after his passing. Purcell is also said to have asked a friend to raise his son. His wife, Lavania Glasscock Purcell, had passed away several years earlier.

Purcell died at 3:00 p.m. on 1 March 1881. He was born in Illinois in 1839 and had moved to Texas in 1854. His place of burial is unknown.

BASTROP POLICE DEPARTMENT

Stallings, Eli
Born circa 1843—Died 12 March 1870

Deputy City Marshal Stallings was asked to preserve the peace at a dance that was primarily attended by black citizens. Some disturbances had reportedly taken place at the affair. Stallings was able to quiet down the commotion, but as he was in the process of taking a seat in the gallery to make certain that his peacekeeping efforts had taken effect, someone fired a shot at him. The gunfire originated from behind where he was seated. The bullet struck Stallings, inflicting an injury that would be fatal.

Stallings was carried home. The city marshal was called and went to the house in which the wounded officer was being attended by a physician. Stallings told the city marshal that he had been shot by a man named Toney Kendall. He died shortly afterward.

The city marshal deputized a group of men and returned to the site of the shooting, finding that the dance was still underway. As the posse reached the gate, Stallings's brother, Jeptha "Jepp" Stallings Jr., joined the group. He was not officially a part of the posse. A man at the dance took Jepp aside and told him that Toney Kendall had shot his brother and that Kendall was inside the building. Jepp immediately rushed headlong into the house. When he spotted Kendall, he shot him with a musket loaded with buckshot. Two pellets entered Kendall's chest, separated and exited through his back about three inches apart. Kendall was killed instantly. Two women, Matilda and Lucy Smith, were also wounded by the same shotgun blast. Both women died from their wounds. Jepp escaped.

There is no evidence that Jepp Stallings was ever prosecuted. He died in 1900 in Orange, Texas.

Very little is known about Eli Stallings. He was in Clarke County, Mississippi, and was about twenty-seven years old at the time of his death. It is not known if he was married. He had numerous siblings. His place of burial is unknown.

BEAUMONT POLICE DEPARTMENT

Patterson, William E.
Born circa 1848—Died 25 September 1881
Date of incident: 24 September 1881

Deputy City Marshal Patterson died of a gunshot wound he received the previous day when he responded to a disturbance at a local house of worship.

When Patterson arrived at the church, he discovered that three persons had broken several windows and were harassing a group of black men and women. While attempting to take the men into custody, one of the trio, Patillo Higgins, drew a concealed handgun and shot Patterson in the abdomen. Although wounded, he managed to get off a shot at Higgins, who was only seventeen. The bullet wounded him in the arm, resulting in a serious injury that eventually required the amputation of the limb.

Higgins claimed self-defense and, in the racially charged climate of the time, was acquitted.

Patterson had served with the Beaumont Police Department for eight years. He is buried at Magnolia Cemetery in Beaumont.

In 1885, Patillo Higgins turned his life around when he attended a Baptist revival. He eventually became a respected local businessman, and in 1900, when oil and gas reserves were discovered on his land, he became wealthy. Higgins became known as the "prophet of Spindletop." He died in 1955.

BELL COUNTY CONSTABLE'S OFFICE

Rice, Darwin P.
Born 23 December 1859—Died 6 August 1886
Date of incident: 5 August 1886

Precinct 6 constable Rice was sent to seize a yoke of oxen from a man named Rufus W. Ledbetter under a writ of attachment. Ledbetter lived in Eddy, on the Bell-Falls county line. Constable Rice did not anticipate trouble in spite of Ledbetter's previous threats to kill him if he tried to arrest him or seize the oxen.

Ledbetter was lying under his plow making a repair when Rice approached and tied his horse to the implement. The constable left his pistol in his saddlebags on his horse. Ledbetter began cursing and threatening to kill

Rice. Ledbetter then grabbed his .56-caliber rifle and shot Rice in the arm. The bullet entered Rice's right side. Rice grabbed the rifle and wrestled it away from Ledbetter. Several witnesses to the incident picked up the wounded Rice and carried him to a nearby haystack. Undeterred, Ledbetter came after Rice again, this time with a knife. He demanded that his rifle be returned to him. One of the witnesses threw the rifle in the field and fled. Ledbetter grabbed the gun and fired at Rice but missed.

Constable Rice died at 9:00 p.m. the next night. Ledbetter was convicted and sentenced to death. Owing to the fact that the constable was outside Bell County by two hundred yards at the time of the incident, Ledbetter appealed; the case was reversed and sent back to the lower court. A second trial was held, and this time Ledbetter was convicted and sentenced to life in prison. He appealed again, and the case was reversed and sent back to the lower court because of improper jury instruction. It is not known if Ledbetter was ever formally convicted of the murder.

Rice is buried at Moffat Cemetery in Bell County. He was only twenty-six years old. Newspaper accounts indicate that Rice may have also been a Bell County deputy sheriff.

Chinn, Cabell Breckenridge
Born 11 July 1853—Died 30 October 1888

On 3 June 1887, R.M. Chinn shot and killed a black man named Doc Lacy. Constable Cabell B. Chinn, brother of the shootist, arrested his brother for the shooting, but the brother managed to escape from the county jail. R.M. Chinn was later arrested, convicted of manslaughter and sentenced to two years in prison.

On 30 October 1888, Precinct 5 constable Chinn was killed by a man named W. Holmes. Holmes claimed that the killing was done in self-defense. The circumstances of his death are unknown at this time.

Constable Chinn was survived by his wife, Rosa Sophie Mourain, and three children: Henry W., Nellie C. and Irene L. He is buried at Hillcrest Cemetery in Temple.

Bell County Sheriff's Office

Venable, Frank W.
Born circa 1852—Died 23 October 1878

While Deputy Venable and another officer were returning a prisoner to his cell, an inmate named Thomas Richardson reached through the bars, grabbed Venable's gun and shot him with it. The gunshot wound was fatal. The other deputy returned fire, killing Richardson.

Deputy Venable is buried at South Belton Cemetery.

Hasley, Samuel L.
Born circa 1844—Died 28 November 1884

Deputy Hasley and another man had been drinking and were creating a disturbance. Hasley was intoxicated and began riding his horse over the sidewalk on Main Street. Belton city marshal Light attempted to arrest the pair, but Hasley drew his pistol, which led to both lawmen commencing fire. About five or six shots were exchanged between the two men. One of Light's bullets struck Hasley in the chest and inflicted a fatal wound.

As was the custom of the time, Light was arrested by Sheriff Fulwiller. It is unknown if any charges were filed.

Hasley is buried at Fort Griffin Cemetery at Little River Academy.

Bells City Marshal's Office

Isbell, James
Born circa 1861—Died 17 January 1891
Date of incident: 14 January 1891

At about 10:00 p.m. on 14 January 1891, a holdup took place in the town of Bells. A man walked into Risenberg's Saloon and demanded that the crowd "shell out." Jim Isbell, the city marshal, was tending bar at Risenberg's at the time. Isbell placed the money from the till on the billiard table, and the robber took it. The thief then ordered a bar patron to take all of the money from the remaining customers. As the robber's attention was diverted, Isbell grabbed his own pistol and fired at the robber one time. The robber calmly fired one shot from his .45-caliber revolver at Isbell. The bullet struck him in the face and exited through his neck. A bystander quickly grabbed the robber, causing the crowd to join in and disarm the man. The patrons considered lynching the thief but decided to place him under guard. The robber identified himself as George Smith, a farmer in Grayson County, and admitted that he had bought the pistol the day before.

City Marshal Isbell succumbed to his wound on 17 January 1891. Although not certain, it is believed that he is buried in an unmarked grave at Old Bells North Cemetery.

Farmer-cum-pistoleer Smith was convicted of murder. He was hanged in Sherman by the Grayson County sheriff on 7 July 1892. As the hangman placed the black hood over his head, Smith uttered, "A fellow can't breathe much in this." Next, Smith commented about the rope, saying, "That is pretty tight."

BELTON POLICE DEPARTMENT

Sweet, Albertus
Born circa 1843—Died 9 December 1881

Albertus Sweet was elected sheriff of Lampasas County on 2 December 1873. He was reelected on 15 February 1876 and served until 5 November 1878.

On 9 December 1881, Sweet was serving as a deputy city marshal at Belton in Bell County. Sweet learned that two men intended to kill City Marshal J.T. Holbert. Holbert, Sweet and two deputized men confronted the two suspects, whose names were Ellis Chalk and Eugene Methvin. The showdown soon escalated into a gunfight. Sweet was shot and killed by Chalk, who used a double-barreled shotgun to commit his crime. City Marshal Holbert was wounded.

Both Chalk and Methvin were eventually apprehended, but both were acquitted at trial. The local newspaper reported that the shooting had been the result of "an intimacy" between Holbert and a female relative of Chalk's.

Sweet was survived by his wife and several children. He is buried at Oak Hill Cemetery in Lampasas.

BEXAR COUNTY SHERIFF'S OFFICE

Hood, Joseph L.
Born circa 1803—Died 19 March 1840

In January 1840, the Republic of Texas demanded the return of all captives held by the Penateka Comanches. Texas officials also insisted that all Comanches leave central Texas, stop interfering with Texan colonization and avoid all white settlements. In response, thirty-three Penateka Comanche chiefs and warriors, accompanied by thirty-two other Comanche tribesmen, arrived in San Antonio on 19 March 1840. Chief Muk-wah-ruh headed the delegation. The Indians had been instructed to bring with them all captured white people who were being held prisoner. They brought only a few, most of whom were Mexican children. They did, however, bring one sixteen-year-old white girl named Matilda Lockhart.

Matilda Lockhart and her sister had been captured in 1838. She claimed that her captors had physically and sexually abused her. Burn scars and mutilation of her nose supported her story. Lockhart also claimed that there were fifteen other white captives remaining in Comanche hands and that the tribe's leaders intended to ransom these hostages one at a time.

Hearing this, the Texan commissioners demanded the release of the other captives, but Muk-wah-ruh claimed that Comanche bands beyond his authority held these prisoners. Texas soldiers entered the Council House where the peace talks were being held. The commissioners informed the assembled chiefs that they were to be held as hostages until the remaining captives were released. Faced with this threat, the Comanche chiefs attempted to escape and called to their fellow tribesmen outside for help. A fight quickly broke out, and in the ensuing melee thirty-five Indians—including chiefs, women and children—were killed. Twenty-seven were held captive. The Texans lost seven men. An additional eight were wounded. Among the casualties was Bexar County sheriff Hood.

A single Comanche woman was freed by Texas authorities and ordered to secure the release of the white captives in exchange for the twenty-seven Comanches who had been captured in the fight. The Penateka leaders refused to respond to that demand. Eventually, most of the Indian captives escaped. Warfare between Texans and the Comanches continued for the next forty years.

Hood was an early settler, businessman and legislator. He was elected sheriff of Bexar County on 4 February 1839 and was the first Texas sheriff known to have been killed in the line of duty.

Stevens, Edward Alexander
Born circa 1827—Died 7 November 1885
Date of incident: 1881

On 7 November 1885, Sheriff Stevens succumbed to complications from a gunshot wound he had received four years earlier. At the time he was shot, Stevens was a deputy sheriff and was attempting to arrest two horse thieves near the town of Luling in Caldwell County. The posse he was riding with became engaged in a furious gunfight with the outlaws. During the encounter, Stevens was shot by a man named Gillespie. He suffered multiple wounds to his left arm so serious in nature that amputation of the limb became necessary. An infection set in following the surgery that eventually led to his death.

Sheriff Stevens was a veteran of the Mexican-American War of 1848. He had been involved in law enforcement for more than twenty-five years, serving with the Bexar County Sheriff's Department, the San Antonio City Marshal's Office and the Texas Rangers.

Stevens was survived by his wife and seven children. He is buried at San Antonio City Cemetery II in San Antonio, Texas.

Sheriff Stevens's son, Charles F. Stevens, served as a Texas Ranger captain and prohibition officer for the United States Bureau of Prohibition (present-day Bureau of Alcohol, Tobacco, Firearms and Explosives, or ATF). Prohibition Officer Stevens was shot and killed on 25 September 1929 at San Antonio while on duty. He and two other officers were returning to San Antonio from a raid in Atascosa County when they were ambushed.

As Stevens and Officer Murphy got out of their vehicle to investigate, shots rang out. Murphy heard Stevens yell, "They got me!" Stevens continued firing at his attackers after he had been struck in the chest by a rifle bullet. After the assailants' ammunition supply had been exhausted, they fled the scene. One of the shooters died from his wounds shortly thereafter. Several had to seek medical attention for gunshot wounds. In total, seven people were charged with the murder.

McClusky (MacCluskey) Daniel "Dan"
Born circa 1859—Died 8 January 1888
Date of incident: 5 January 1888

On the evening of 5 January 1888, Deputy McClusky was shot by Constable Ed Stevens at the Revolving Light Saloon in San Antonio. The fatal shot was fired from Constable Stevens's .45-caliber nickel-plated Colt pistol. The bullet entered the right side of McClusky's neck and imbedded itself in his spinal cord. Constable Stevens was demonstrating the handling of the pistol when it accidentally discharged, striking Deputy McClusky and inflicting the wound that would later become fatal. Constable Ed Stevens was charged with negligent homicide but was not convicted.

Deputy McClusky died at the Santa Rosa hospital on 8 January 1888.

Bitters, W.
Born (Unknown)—Died June or July 1892

While on duty, Deputy Bitters was struck by a streetcar. He died from the injuries he received.

On 2 July, a hearing was held in regards to a citation against motorman S.S. Redford for not having the streetcar under control. Witnesses were called to testify. The hearing concluded with Redford being exonerated of any wrongdoing.

No other information is known about Deputy Bitters at this time.

BOSQUE COUNTY SHERIFF'S OFFICE

Pierson, Jabez C.
Born (Unknown)—Died 9 June 1874

On 9 June 1874, Deputy Pierson was transporting prisoner M.H. "Bud" Galbreath by horse and wagon from Comanche to Meridian, where Galbreath was to be tried for rape. Galbreath was chained. Somehow, during the course of the trip along the banks of the Bosque River, Galbreath was able to gain possession of Deputy Pierson's pistol, which he used to fatally shoot the deputy. Pierson's body was later found in the wagon.

Galbreath (also spelled Gelbrath and Galbraith) was seventeen years old and had been running with the notorious John Wesley Hardin gang when he was arrested by Texas Rangers in Comanche County. After murdering Deputy Pierson, he escaped and fled to Indian Territory (present-day Oklahoma), where he was eventually arrested in 1897. He was brought back to Meridian in 1898 and tried, twenty-four years after the murder of Deputy Pierson. Although the jury found Galbreath guilty of manslaughter, the court discharged Galbreath from all further liability resulting from charge.

Pierson was a Confederate war veteran. He served in Company B, Thirty-first Texas Calvary. While writing about Galbreath in 1875, Bosque County sheriff John A. Biffle penned that "he [Galbreath] killed one of the best men in Texas [Jabez C. Pierson]." Pierson is buried in Section M at Meridian City Cemetery.

Morgan, John
Born circa 1835—Died 2 December 1874

Morgan, Parker
Born circa 1846—Died 2 December 1874

Brothers John and Parker Morgan were deputized to arrest three men from Limestone County who were wanted fugitives. When the two Morgan brothers went to a house where the men were staying to make the arrest, they were both shot and killed. One of the shooters, whose name is not known, was badly wounded and had to have his leg amputated later. The second man, named Crowell, was arrested in June 1875 in Polk County. No information regarding the third man has ever been discovered.

John Morgan was survived by his wife, Mary, and four children. Parker Morgan was not married. No cemetery records or burial information have been found for either John or Parker Morgan.

Conley, Robert M.
Born circa 1876—Died 10 July 1899
Date of incident: 9 July 1899

Deputy Conley succumbed to wounds he received on 9 July 1899 when he was shot at the local train station.

Conley had just returned from Waco on official business and was disembarking from the train when he observed a citizen being threatened by someone with a pistol. Conley drew his own revolver and intervened. The pistol-toting fellow, Ed Burrow, was able to get control of Deputy Conley's revolver and shot him several times.

Deputy Conley is buried at Riverside Cemetery.

Bowie County Sheriff's Office

Morgan, David
Born circa 1852—Died 27 November 1891

On 27 November 1891, Deputy Morgan was in the process of attempting to serve an arrest warrant on a black man named Charley Vines. As he was speaking to Vines, the man picked up an old army musket and fired a shot at Deputy Morgan. The blast struck Morgan in the face, presumably killing him. To make certain that Morgan was dead, and to conceal the body, Charley Vines, his brother William Vines and a third, unnamed black man fastened weights to Morgan's body and threw him into the Red River. Charley Vines fled the scene of the crime and removed himself to the Indian Territory, where he was later apprehended.

It was only with great difficulty that lawmen were able to successfully return Vines to Clarksville without him being summarily lynched by a mob of angry citizens. Vines remained in jail at Clarksville until he was tried on 17 March 1892. He was found guilty and sentenced to be hanged on 28 September 1892. On appeal, Governor James Stephen Hogg granted a two-week extension of the execution on 17 November 1892. Vines's sentence was later reduced to life in prison.

The location of Deputy Morgan's place of burial is not known. Although no conclusive record can be located, Charley Vines is probably buried at Cedar Spring Cemetery.

Nettles, William Lafayette
Born circa 1855—Died 1 March 1892

Deputy Nettles was shot and killed while attempting to disarm an intoxicated man who was shooting a gun into the air. The man, G.T. Moser, turned the weapon on Deputy Nettles and shot him in the chest. The wound was fatal.

Deputy Nettles was survived by his wife and eight children. He is buried in an unmarked grave in Ingersoll.

BRAZOS COUNTY CONSTABLE'S OFFICE

Millican, Marcellus Randall "Pet"
Born circa 1856—Died 14 December 1889

The Millican families were founding members of Brazos County. Marcellus Millican's father, Elliott McNeil Millican, became the first elected sheriff of Brazos County on 1 March 1841. He served until 2 July 1844, when he resigned. Elliot Millican's four other sons also served as Texas lawmen.

On 14 December 1889, Charles "Charlie" Campbell assassinated Precinct 1 constable "Pet" Millican. Two brothers, Zeke and Poker Curd, had enticed Campbell to do the killing. All three were arrested, and Campbell became a state's witness. The jury acquitted the Curd brothers. No reason was determined as to why the Curds wanted to kill the constable.

"Pet" Millican was thirty-three years of age at the time of his death. He had also served as a Texas Ranger. Millican is buried in family plot at the Weaver Cemetery in Millican.

The 1870s were a violent period for the Millican brothers. On 6 February 1870, Brazos County deputy sheriff William Hemphill Millican was killed by Colonel R.C. Myers in a personal dispute. John Earl Millican was the constable of Precinct 1 and a deputy sheriff in Brazos County. He shot and killed Colonel Myers, only to be killed by Myers's son and daughter on 29 August 1872.

Wilbur "Will" Millican was a guard at the convict farm and had reportedly killed several men. He told the Curd brothers to leave the Millican community or he would kill them. Zeke Curd returned, and Will Millican killed him in June 1890. On 15 November 1906, Will was shot and killed in a personal feud by a fellow guard.

Related case: Brazos County Sheriff's Office—William Hemphill Millican and John Earl Millican.

BRAZOS COUNTY SHERIFF'S OFFICE

Millican, William Hemphill
Born circa 1843—Died 6 February 1870

In May 1870, a group of Anglo citizens released several prisoners from the jail. They released only the Anglo prisoners and lynched the lone black convict. Deputy Millican was accused of cooperating with the crowd who had broken into the jail and carried out the hanging. Colonel Robert Myers demanded an investigation. The mob members threatened to kill him. On 6 February 1870, Deputy Millican entered Myers's saloon, reportedly with his pistol in his hand and, by some accounts, in an intoxicated condition. Myers shot Millican with a double-barreled shotgun that was loaded with buckshot. The blast killed Millican instantly. William's brother, Deputy John Millican, shot and killed Colonel Myers.

William Millican's place of burial is unknown, but he is probably buried at Weaver Cemetery in the Millican community.

Related cases: Brazos County Constable's Office—Marcellus Randall "Pet" Millican; Brazos County Sheriff's Office—John Earl Millican.

Millican, John Earl
Born 8 November 1837—Died 29 August 1872

In revenge for the death of their father, Colonel Robert Myers, son Allen and daughter Ms. B.F. "Nannie" Baldridge (Boldridge) shot and killed Deputy John Millican. The two were held on $7,000 bond, but they were never convicted of the murder.

John Millican is buried at Weaver Cemetery.

Related cases: Brazos County Constable's Office—Marcellus Randall "Pet" Millican; and Brazos County Sheriff's Office—William Hemphill Millican.

Coleman, Lafayette
Born (Unknown)—Died 5 or 6 March 1878

Deputy Sheriff Coleman left Bryan on horseback five or six days earlier to serve process papers in the county. His horse was found on 7 March with his overcoat tied to the saddle. The coat had six buckshot holes in it. Blood was found on the saddle and on the horse. A search was initiated, but his body was never recovered. The newspaper reported that foul play was suspected and stated that "Coleman is said to have many enemies in the county." It would seem that those who made that assertion were obviously quite correct.

In May 1878, a warrant was issued for W.N. Dobbs (also reported as "Dabbs"), who was a constable in one of the county precincts, for the murder of Deputy Coleman. Sheriff William B. Forman and a posse of seven men went to Dobbs's house and surrounded it. The sheriff entered alone and engaged in social conversation with Dobbs's brother. Hearing the conversation, the posse thought that the constable had surrendered. As they entered the Dobbs house, posseman George Gentry saw Constable Dobbs with his pistol raised and the muzzle within two feet of his head. Dobbs pulled the trigger. The percussion cap popped, but the pistol did not fire. Gentry fired at Dobbs and missed. Two other possemen entered, and Dobbs fired at them as well. During the exchange, Dobbs was wounded in the thigh, his ear was shot off and his pistol was broken when it was struck by a gunshot. He fled the scene.

A black man was arrested and charged with aiding in Dobbs's escape. It is not known if Dobbs was ever arrested or convicted of the murder.

No personal information about Coleman is known. He may have been James L. Coleman, born about 1852 in Robertson County.

Fletcher, William E.
Born circa 1847—Died 15 January 1883

Burl Burleson was charged with wife beating and assault with a pistol. On 15 January 1883, Brazos County deputy Smith went to arrest him. He deputized two men to assist him. One of the deputies was William Fletcher, a merchant and railroad agent at Wellborn. The identity of the other deputy is unknown.

They found Burleson in his house, but he refused to be taken into custody. Deputy Fletcher began to open the door and was partway inside the residence when Burleson shot him in the heart. The fatally wounded Fletcher fired twice at Burleson, hitting him in the stomach. Incredibly, Fletcher walked a distance of about one hundred yards and then gradually let himself down to the ground and died. Burleson fled but was captured later. He died in the county jail from the effects of the wound he received on 17 January 1883.

Fletcher is buried at Bryan City Cemetery.

BREWSTER COUNTY SHERIFF'S OFFICE

Cook, Thalis Tucker
Born on 10 March 1858 - Died 21 July 1918
Date of incident: 31 January 1891

Thalis Tucker Cook was born in Uvalde County in 1858. The six-foot-tall, wiry-built and already fierce-looking sixteen-year-old was one of the youngest rangers to have ever served in the Frontier Battalion when he joined Captain Neal Coldwell's Company F on 28 February 1874.

On 28 January 1891, Fine Gilliland was working for a large cattle outfit called Dubois and Wentworth near Marathon in Brewster County. A dispute arose with a small rancher named Henry Harrison Powe over an unbranded brindle steer that belonged to Powe. Powe began to drive the steer back toward his ranch, whereupon Gilliland tried to rope the steer and prevent Powe from removing it. Powe then fired a shot from his pistol in the direction of the steer in order to scare it away and prevent Gilliland from roping the animal. No doubt presuming that Powe had fired the shot at him, Gilliland fired and wounded Powe, a one-armed Civil War veteran. Both men faced off and fired at each other. Powe was mortally wounded, staggering only a few feet before he collapsed. Gilliland fled toward the high country, knowing that there were too many witnesses present for him to claim that the shooting had been an accident.

On 31 January, former Texas Ranger and now Brewster County deputy sheriff Thalis T. Cook and Texas Ranger private James M. "Jim" Putman were called on to track down Gilliland. The two lawmen caught up with the killer in the Glass Mountains northwest of Marathon. Nearing Gilliland, Deputy Cook saw that he was attempting to conceal his drawn pistol under a coat that he had thrown across the saddle horn. Just as Deputy Cook turned his horse to identify himself, Gilliland opened fire. Gilliland's first shot hit Deputy Cook in the right kneecap. The impact from the bullet fired at such close range blew him out of the saddle. Cook yelled out to Ranger Putman to shoot the fleeing outlaw's horse. Putman did so, and Gilliland hit the ground and crawled behind his dead horse's body, using it as a makeshift barricade as he continued firing at the pair of lawmen. Ranger Putnam shot Gilliland in the head when he rose to fire again. Gilliland's body was shipped to Snyder for burial.

Cook's ordeal was just beginning, however. His kneecap was shattered. His leg became stiff and straight, so Cook had doctors break his leg and set it slightly bent to allow him to ride a horse. While Cook continued to serve in various law enforcement agencies, his old leg wound continued to give him trouble over the years and ultimately became so painful that he decided to have his crippled right leg amputated. Cook died on the operating table on 21 July 1918, twenty-seven years after he had been wounded. He was buried at Nesbitt Cemetery in Marshall.

Cook was only sixteen years old when he enlisted in the Frontier Battalion of the Texas Rangers under Captain Neal Coldwell's Company F on 28 February 1874 and served until 31 August 1874. He was one of the youngest men to ever serve in the Frontier Battalion. On 16 September 1876, he reenlisted in Company F and served until 30 March 1879. On 25 April 1889, he joined Company D under the command of Captain Frank Jones at Uvalde and served until 30 November 1889. Cook then became a deputy sheriff in Brewster County for Sheriff James Gillett, a former ranger. Cook returned to Company D under Captain John R. Hughes at Ysleta on 24 May 1894 and served until 30 November. He reenlisted on 10 March 1896 and served until 30 November 1898, when he was discharged as a first sergeant. During his breaks between service as a Texas Ranger, Cook also served as a railroad detective, cattle inspector, special ranger and El Paso County deputy sheriff. He was involved in numerous gunfights during his career.

After Cook died, his wife, Ella, remained in Marshall until her death on 6 April 1925. He is buried alongside his wife and son, John, at Nesbitt Cemetery just outside Marshall.

Brown County Constable's Office

Lovell, Jim
Born (Unknown)—Died 8 November 1886

On 8 November 1886, Texas Ranger captain William Scott of Company F laid a trap for fence cutters on the ranch of W.M. Baugh. The ruse worked, and at about 11:00 p.m. three men were caught in the act of cutting fences. A fourth member of the group was holding their horses. Captain Scott called on the men to surrender. His command was obviously neglected, as one of the party opened fire with a pistol. The five rangers, along with several ranchers, returned fire on the group of thieves. During the exchange, Lovell was killed and a man named Roberts was mortally wounded.

Lovell was the constable of the Thrifty Precinct in Brown County. Interestingly, Lovell was also facing charges for fence cutting when he was killed. His surname has been reported by some sources as Lowell.

BROWN COUNTY SHERIFF'S OFFICE

Harris, Jesse Sutton "Sut"
Born circa 1829—Died 6 June 1861
Date of incident: 4 June 1861

After arresting the nephew of former sheriff F.A. Baugh, who had recently resigned to join the Confederate army, a local schoolteacher shot Sheriff Harris with a shotgun. The wounds were fatal, and Harris died two days later. The man fled the county and was never apprehended.

Harris had been appointed sheriff on 2 March 1861 and served only three months.

Webb, Charles M.
Born (Unknown)—Died 26 May 1874

Deputy Webb was shot and killed by the notorious outlaw John Wesley Hardin. At the time of the shooting, Hardin was wanted for murder, robbery and cattle rustling.

Webb encountered Hardin outside a local saloon. Hardin confronted him and asked if Webb had papers for his arrest. Webb reportedly said that he did not. The psychopathic Hardin, in his classic style, became verbally aggressive. It is claimed that both Webb and Hardin went for their guns at the same time. In any case, a gunfight took place. Webb was able to shoot Hardin in the side before he was shot in the left cheek by Hardin. As Webb fell to the ground, two of Hardin's accomplices, Jim Taylor and Bud Dixon, opened fire on Webb and finished the job.

Several years later, Hardin was taken into custody by Texas Rangers outside of Pensacola, Florida, on 23 July 1877. He was sentenced to twenty-five years in prison but was pardoned by the Texas governor after serving only sixteen years. Remarkably, the pardon was extended in spite of the fact that Hardin had, by most reliable accounts, murdered forty-eight people.

Following his release, Hardin became a lawyer. He was shot and killed by El Paso County constable John Selman Sr. on 19 August 1895. Hardin's brother, James Barnett Gipson "Gip" Hardin, killed Kimble County deputy John Turman on 28 March 1898.

Webb had previously served as a Texas Ranger. He is buried at Greenleaf Cemetery in Brownwood.

West, George W.
Born 8 July 1847—Died 12 February 1879
Date of incident: 8 February 1879

On 8 February 1879, a band of armed men called Deputy West out of his house. Brandishing pistols, they forced him to go to the jail and unlock the door. There were several prisoners confined in a cell for which Deputy West did not have a key. His captors, who were intent on freeing the prisoners, began battering the jail door. The noise attracted citizens, who began firing at the men. The men returned fire, wounding West in the leg.

West died from his wound on 12 February 1879. He is buried at Greenleaf Cemetery in Brownwood. West's tombstone indicates his date of death as 28 January 1879.

Bell, Charles
Born circa 1853—Died 23 March 1898

Sheriff Bell and his deputy, George Washington Batton, had gone to the home of a local blacksmith named George Yarber. While upstairs inside the home, Yarber, who was intoxicated at the time, stormed in and shot Sheriff Bell. Deputy Batton returned fire and killed Yarber.

Sheriff Bell was survived by his wife and children.

The once lucky Deputy Batton's good fortune ran out when on 3 June 1922 he was killed in the line of duty while serving as sheriff of Eddy County, New Mexico.

BROWNSVILLE POLICE DEPARTMENT

Allen, (First Name Unknown)
Born (Unknown)—Died 10 January 1867

On 10 January 1867, Anglo U.S. Army troops were drinking in a saloon when some black soldiers entered. Policeman Allen asked to see their passes granting them permission to be off base. Soon an argument arose. A black soldier shot and killed Allen and a citizen.

The U.S. Army transferred the soldiers involved out of Brownsville before any formal charges were made by local police.

Becera, Francisco "Pancho"
Born circa 1853—Died 22 September 1880

Special Officer Becera reportedly drowned while on duty. Nothing further is known of the circumstances surrounding his death. He was reportedly buried in a potter's field.

BRYAN POLICE DEPARTMENT

Hearn, A.G. "Race"
Born (Unknown)—Died 2 February 1870

William McIver of Leon County (also referred to as Bill McKeever) and his father had been drinking excessively. McIver became particularly abusive and violent, causing a great commotion on the streets. Officer Hearn approached him and in a good-natured manner attempted to persuade McIver to control himself and keep order. McIver drew a knife and advanced on Hearn with the obvious intention of cutting him. Hearn, acting in self-defense, struck at McIver with his club. McIver dodged the blow and plunged his knife into Hearn's abdomen, inflicting a mortal wound. The mortally injured Hearn knocked McIver down, planted his knee on his assailant's chest and took his knife and pistol away from him. As he did so, he remarked in a tone of almost unparalleled magnanimity, "I could kill you if I wished, but I won't. I am a dead man."

Officer Hearn lived for only a brief time after the attack. His last words were, "Tell the boys I died, discharging my duty, like a man."

McIver was arrested for the murder of Hearn. He was to have been tried under a writ of habeas corpus on 23 March 1870, but he escaped from a military prison in Calvert on or about 25 March 1870. A writ of habeas corpus means that a person has a right to appear before a judge or magistrate and hear the charges against him. This is to prevent the charging authority from simply throwing people in jail at will or without cause.

McIver was indicted by a Brazos County Grand Jury on 15 April 1870. There is no evidence that he was ever prosecuted for the murder of Hearn.

Virtually nothing is known about A.G. Hearn, who was also referred to as A.J. Hearne, "Race" Hearn and Greene Hearne.

Wiggins, Hugh L.
Born (Unknown)—Died 29 December 1871

Officer Wiggins was shot and killed by a saloonkeeper named Carr on 29 December 1871. Exactly what provoked Carr to shoot Wiggins remains a mystery.

Wiggins served as a Texas state policeman from July 1870 until 30 November 1871. He is buried at Bryan City Cemetery in an unmarked grave.

Although no record exists concerning any charges against Carr, it is possible that he was the same man named A.B. Carr who had a saloon that burned in 1875. There was also a man named A.B. Carr who was city marshal in 1885.

Farmer, James P.
Born circa 1850—Died 16 June 1874

Officer Farmer was shot and killed while speaking with two men inside a telegraph office. Henry Cook, who fired the shot, was arrested. Before Cook could stand trial, a mob of angry citizens stormed the jail, took him out and hanged him in the middle of town. To make absolutely certain that the hanging had taken effect, they shot Cook as well.

Officer Farmer is buried at Bryan City Cemetery.

Smith, Levin P. "Lev," Jr.
Born circa 1861—Died 15 May 1885

On 14 May 1885, forty convicts escaped from a prison work camp. Sixteen of the convicts headed to Bryan to seize the powder magazine. Between one and two o'clock on the afternoon of 15 May, City Marshal A.B. Carr, Deputy City Marshals Levin P. Smith Jr. and Levi Neal, Brazos County deputy sheriff Robert Smith (brother of Levin) and Mr. J.P. Noll stationed themselves about one mile south of the city.

The convicts were all mounted on mules and heavily armed with long guns and pistols. When brought to a halt by the force of lawmen, the convicts immediately began firing. During the exchange of gunfire, Levin Smith was fatally shot. Smith died almost instantly. The bullet entered his right breast and became lodged under the left shoulder. In addition to the fatal wound, a second bullet took off one of his fingers and struck the stock of his pistol. City Marshal Carr was more fortunate. He managed to escape without any physical injury but, upon examination, sustained several bullet holes in his clothing and two through his hat. Three of the convicts were seriously wounded during the gun battle with the lawmen.

Nine of the convicts were indicted for murder. Smith is buried at Wixon Cemetery in Brazos County next to his father, who had died just five weeks earlier.

On 2 December 1888, Smith's brother Robert, who was later elected as a constable, accompanied Bryan city marshal M.M. Wilcox and Deputy City Marshal Levi Neal to serve a warrant. Wilcox was killed. Neal was later killed, on 24 February 1900, while walking a prisoner to the city jail.

Wilcox, Murdock McDuffie
Born circa 1851—Died 2 December 1888

At about 8:00 p.m. on 2 December 1888, City Marshal Wilcox obtained a warrant for the arrest of Earl Knox for burglary. Knox was only seventeen or eighteen at the time. Constable R.H. Smith and Deputy City Marshals John P. Chance, Levi Neal and Laith Lougbridge accompanied Marshal Wilcox on this arrest. Wilcox, Neal and Lougbridge approached the Knox house from the front, while Smith and Chance took positions at various points around the building in an effort to cut off any possible escape. Lougbridge, who was walking in front of the other two lawmen, called for Knox to come outside. Knox fired a Winchester rifle at Wilcox, striking him just above the heart. It was dark at the time, and Knox was able to escape the lawmen.

Wilcox managed to get off several shots at Knox, but given that he was now mortally wounded, his aim was poor and the shots went wild. Wilcox died about 9:00 p.m. after having asked those present to look after his family. The newspapers reported that "[Wilcox] was a brave, kind-hearted man, whose reluctance to use his weapon was well known and, at last, doubtless cost him his life."

Knox was convicted of second-degree murder and sentenced to nine years in prison. He was also sentenced to eight years in prison for burglary and related charges.

Wilcox was survived by his wife and two daughters. He is buried at Seale Family Cemetery in Brazos County.

As a matter of related historical interest, of the five officers involved in this particular arrest attempt during which Marshal Wilcox lost his life two of the surviving four eventually met violent deaths in the line of duty. Brazos County deputy sheriff R.H. Smith (later constable); his brother, Bryan deputy city marshal Levin P. Smith Jr.; and Deputy City Marshal Levi Neal were all involved in a shootout with escaping convicts on 15 May 1885. Levin Smith Jr. was killed during that incident. Bryan deputy city marshal Levi Neal would later be killed while walking a prisoner to jail on 24 February 1900.

BURLESON COUNTY CONSTABLE'S OFFICE

Barbee, William B.M.
Born circa 1822—Died 24 May 1857

Precinct 3 constable John Johnson called on Justice of the Peace William B.M. Barbee, who was at the time acting as a special deputy constable (deputized citizen), to accompany him to arrest John Carroway. Carroway was characterized by the local newspapers as "a notorious thief and outlaw." He was suspected of stealing a mule from the widow of John Nunn. Constable Johnson had a writ for Carroway's arrest.

Johnson and Barbee tracked Carroway to a house on Yegua Creek. Yegua Creek begins about nine miles southwest of Rockdale in southern Milam County. They searched the building and did not find Carroway. Barbee went to search the smokehouse. Unbeknownst to him, Carroway had chosen that place as his hiding spot. While peering between the logs of the outbuilding, he was shot from inside by Carroway. The bullet grazed Barbee's forehead and knocked him down. As Barbee attempted to rise, Carroway fired again. This time, he hit Barbee in the bowels with a shotgun blast of buckshot. Carroway ran from the smokehouse but was shot by Constable Johnson as he did so. It was reported that both Barbee and Carroway died several hours later.

The newspaper reports describe Barbee as a respected citizen who was survived by his wife and a child.

BURLESON COUNTY SHERIFF'S OFFICE

Holmes, James
Born circa 1848—Died February 1876

A posse from Brazos and Burleson Counties was attempting to arrest two brothers, Bird and Redick Fisher. The pair were notorious horse thieves. The brothers resisted arrest, and both were shot and killed by Deputy Holmes. Holmes was wounded in the exchange and reportedly died from his injuries.

On or about 1 March 1876, a mob stormed the Lee County Jail and lynched three men. Two of the men were brothers named Irwin and were cousins of the Fisher brothers. The third man was named Pat Shaw. All three men were allegedly part of the theft ring that included the Fishers.

Deputy Holmes was survived by his wife, Lucy. His place of burial is unknown.

Farr, John P. "Jack"
Born 15 May 1853—Died 8 May 1888

At about 5:00 p.m. on the evening of 8 May 1888, Deputy Farr was in the town of Caldwell when he was shot and killed by a prominent saloon keeper named Ben B. Hunt.

About an hour before the shooting took place, Hunt and Farr had been involved in some sort of misunderstanding that had escalated into a heated quarrel. Friends separated the two and attempted to patch up the differences, but Farr persisted. Farr walked toward Hunt's saloon. Just as he reached the establishment, Hunt fired at Farr with a Winchester shotgun. Amazingly, Hunt's shot missed. He then ran down the street alongside the saloon and into his home. From the window of his residence he fired at Farr again. This time, his errant shot accidentally killed an innocent bystander named Sandy. The determined Hunt fired a third shot. He hit Farr with eleven pellets of buckshot. The blast killed the deputy almost instantly.

Hunt was arrested for the killing of Deputy Farr. Because Hunt was related to the local judge, his case was transferred to the District Court of Burleson County on 7 January 1889. The outcome is unknown.

Farr left behind a wife, Mina J. Anthony. He is buried at Old City Cemetery at Caldwell.

BURNET COUNTY SHERIFF'S OFFICE

Martin, Samuel B.
Born circa 1851—Died 11 September 1876
Date of incident: 7 September 1876

On 7 September 1876, Deputy Martin and a deputized citizen named Wilson Bowntree attempted to arrest Joseph "Joe" Olney for stealing cattle and hogs. Olney had a long record of offenses, including being charged with "exhibiting a Monte bank" when he was only twenty-two years old. A year later, he was charged with gambling and pled guilty to that charge. For those who may not be aware, monte is a gambling card game of Spanish origin. Three or four cards are dealt faceup, and players bet that one of them will be matched before the others as the cards are dealt from the pack one at a time.

Neither one of the deputies knew Olney, so when they went to his residence they were unaware of with whom they were speaking. As the lawmen left Olney's house, he followed them, fired a shot that missed and then hid behind a tree. Martin and Bowntree fired, but both missed the mark. Next, Olney shot Martin in the left arm above the elbow. Martin then told Bowntree to shoot Olney. He attempted to comply; he ran up to Olney with his rifle at the ready and pulled the trigger, but the gun failed to fire. As he tried to draw his pistol, Olney shot him. Olney then shot Martin again and fled. Martin died of gunshot wounds four days later. The wounded Browntree survived.

Martin is buried at Old Burnet Cemetery in Burnet. He was the brother-in-law of Sheriff J.J. Strickland.

Joe Olney was charged with the murder of Martin. He posted a $500 bond and fled Texas in 1877. Olney was also facing an earlier charge from 15 June 1875 for assault on the sheriff of Llano County. He eventually settled in Lincoln County, New Mexico, changed his name to Joseph Hall and allied himself with the James J. Dolan faction, who were pitted against John Tunstall, Alexander McSween and John Chisum during the Lincoln County War. On 11 March 1879, Olney (alias Joseph Hall), along with a long list of his associates, were charged with his complicity in the murder of several McSween faction members. None of the men charged during Colonel N.A.O. Dudley's court of inquiry in Lincoln was ever sentenced—except William Bonney, alias Kid Antrim (and later known as Billy the Kid).

Although some details are inconclusive, it is believed that Olney left New Mexico and moved to Tombstone, Arizona, where he predictably returned to his outlaw ways. He became associated with a gang of badmen known as the Clanton Gang, or "The Cowboys." During his time in Arizona, he became allied with the noted Texas outlaw John "Johnny" Peters Ringo. Olney died on 3 December 1884 when his horse stumbled and fell while driving cattle into a corral.

Miller, Nimrod Johnson
Born circa 1844—Died 1 September 1881

Sheriff Miller was beaten by several men and shot with an arrow while traveling to the Indian Territory to make an arrest. Miller's body was never found. Details of his death were not learned until a prisoner at Fort Smith, Arkansas, confessed that he had witnessed the murder.

Miller was appointed sheriff on 17 January 1878. He was elected on 5 November 1878 and reelected on 2 November 1880. He was survived by his wife and seven children.

BURNET POLICE DEPARTMENT

Wolf, John W.
Born circa 1851—Died 12 May 1892
Date of incident: 10 May 1892

City Marshal Wolf was shot and killed by Constable John Taylor. Taylor was upset with him because Wolf had arrested his son. Constable Taylor came to the marshal's office, and harsh words were exchanged between the two men.

Gunfire soon followed, and Taylor shot Wolf in the leg, severing an artery. He died from the wound two days later.

Before his appointment as Burnet city marshal, Wolf was appointed sheriff of Burnet County on 1 June 1884. He was elected on 4 November 1884 and reelected on 2 November 1886. Wolf served until November 1888. He was survived by his wife and five children. Wolf is buried at Dobyville Cemetery in rural Burnet County.

CALDWELL COUNTY SHERIFF'S OFFICE

Stiner, Granville H.
Born (Unknown)—Died circa 20 March 1852
Date of incident: 6 March 1852

Sheriff Stiner was elected on 5 August 1849 and was the second sheriff of Caldwell County.

Stiner was shot by a man named Thomas Hoskins on 6 March 1852. The incident took place at Stiner's store. He eventually died of his wounds on or about 20 March 1852. His killer, Thomas Hoskins, managed to escape.

No further details concerning this incident have been uncovered. Stiner was survived by his wife, Nancy A. Skinner.

Sullivan, Blackstone B.
Born circa 1852—Died 7 July 1876

Deputy Sullivan was shot and killed while attempting to arrest a man at a local store. As Sullivan struggled to handcuff the man, Dick Allen, he pulled a revolver from his boot and shot Sullivan. Allen was later arrested by the Hays County sheriff and convicted of Sullivan's murder.

Allen was sentenced to hang. When citizens learned that his conviction might be overturned on appeal, they stormed the county jail and lynched him.

Sullivan was survived by his wife. He is buried at Lockhart City Cemetery.

Calhoun County Sheriff's Office

Fulkerson, James Preston
Born circa 1807—Died circa 4 April 1852

Fulkerson was appointed sheriff on 15 November 1851. He was shot and killed while responding to a call about a disturbance. When he arrived at the scene, he confiscated a rifle from the man responsible for the disorder, August Sharkey. Fulkerson told Sharkey to leave town. Relying on the unarmed man to comply, he turned to leave, but Sharkey shot and killed him with a second gun that he had in his possession.

Shortly after killing Fulkerson, Sharkey was lynched by a mob of angry citizens.

Fulkerson was survived by his wife and four children. His place of burial has not been located.

Cameron, County Of

Johnson, Robert L.
Born (Unknown)—Died 28 September 1859

On 13 July 1859, Juan N. Cortina rode into Brownsville. He had nothing more sinister in mind than conducting some routine business. Cortina witnessed Brownsville city marshal Robert Shears pistol-whipping an intoxicated Mexican man who had previously been employed by the Cortina family. Cortina asked the marshal to allow him to take charge of the prisoner, but the marshal cursed Cortina and refused. Enraged by his reply, Cortina shot the marshal in the shoulder and then fled on horseback, taking the prisoner with him.

At daylight on 28 September 1859, Cortina and sixty to one hundred men rode into Brownsville, intent on seeking revenge for numerous grievances. Marshal Shears fled and escaped unharmed. Constable George Morris attempted to run away, but his house was surrounded by Cortina's men. Morris was struck down by one of Cortina's men armed with a sword. His body was riddled with bullets.

Robert Johnson was a county jailer on duty at the time of the assault. The marauders went to the jail and demanded that Johnson unlock the door and release the prisoners. Johnson refused and instead fired at the group, killing one of the raiders. Johnson and a citizen named Viviano Garcia were killed in the fusillade of gunfire that followed.

Very little is known about Johnson. Various accounts report his name as being Johnston and that he was the Brownsville city jailer. He may have been a deputy sheriff. His place of burial is unknown.

Juan N. Cortina was never charged or arrested. He died on 30 October 1894 at the age of seventy. Three of Cortina's followers (called *Cortinistas*) who were involved in the raid—Vincente Garcia, Juan Vela and Florencio Garza—were publicly hanged on 22 June 1866.

Related case: Cameron County Constable's Office—George Morris.

CAMERON COUNTY CONSTABLE'S OFFICE

Morris, George
Born (Unknown)—Died 28 September 1859

Constable Morris was killed in the 28 September 1859 raid on Brownsville by Juan N. Cortina and his men.

After killing Cameron County jailer Robert L. Johnson, the raiders sought out City Marshal Robert Shears. He had already fled the city. Next they found Constable Morris at his house. Morris attempted to escape but was quickly surrounded and struck down by one of Cortina's men armed with a sword. To make certain that he was dead, his body was riddled with bullets. According to various newspaper accounts of the event, Cortina's men hacked Morris's body to pieces. His wife had to gather up the parts in a sack in order to bury him.

Very little is known about Morris. He does not appear in the 1850 census for Cameron County, but in 1858 he applied to establish a pistol gallery. Although no state election records exist, he posted bond as a constable on 20 August 1859.

Related case: City of Cameron—Robert L. Johnson.

Becera, Ramon
Born circa 1847—Died 7 March 1879

Special Officer Becera was reportedly murdered. A "John Doe" indictment was issued, but the circumstances of the murder, or even whether anyone was ever convicted, is unknown at this time. Becera was born in Mexico in 1847 and had come to Texas in the 1850s. He was reportedly buried in a potter's field.

Cobb, Felipe "Philip"
Born circa 1858—Died 5 April 1898

Elections in south Texas often resulted in violence as the various political parties vied for power. On election day, Deputy Sheriff Sam Cobb heard about a disturbance at a voting booth. He went on horseback to investigate. His brother, Precinct 2 constable Felipe "Philip" Cobb, and a Brownsville city policeman followed on foot. Carlos Gullien stepped from an alley and grabbed the horse's bridle. Gullien shot Deputy Cobb. The deputy fired back, wounding Gullien. Both men fell to the ground. As Cobb arrived, Gullien raised up and shot him twice, killing him instantly. Gullien's brother appeared and shot Deputy Cobb again. He died three hours after being shot.

Both of the Gullien brothers fled. Carlos Gullien was arrested and taken into custody. A mob gathered and broke into the jail. Gunfire erupted, and Gullien was shot to death. Members of a mob dragged his body into the street and were going to burn it, but the corpse was eventually return to the jail cell. Gullien had been in numerous shooting scrapes and disliked the Cobbs. Carlos Gullien's brother (given name unknown) was convicted of assault to murder, and the case was on appeal.

Both lawmen are buried at Oddfellows Cemetery in Cameron County.

Related case: Cameron County Sheriff's Office—Samuel Cobb.

CAMERON COUNTY SHERIFF'S OFFICE

Browne, Matthew L.
Born circa 1857—Died 12 April 1892

Browne was elected on 4 November 1890 and served as sheriff for about eighteen months. He was accidentally shot and killed while he and several deputies transported a group of Mexican prisoners from Brownsville to Corpus Christi. The deputies had stopped the wagon for lunch. As Browne sat down, his pistol accidentally discharged. The bullet struck him in the leg just above the knee and severed a major artery. Browne bled to death in a matter of minutes. His deputies took his body back to Brownsville, where he is buried.

Browne was survived by his wife, father, sister and three brothers.

Brito, Santiago A.
Born circa 1873—Died 21 August 1892

Santiago Brito was first elected sheriff of Cameron County, winning that post on 2 November 1880. He served until 4 November 1890, when he was defeated by Matthew L. Browne in a hotly contested election. Brito was then appointed Brownsville city marshal on 1 December 1890. When Sheriff Browne accidentally shot and killed himself on 12 April 1892, the Cameron County Commissioners Court appointed Brito as sheriff to fill out the term for Browne.

Sheriff Brito was assassinated at about 2:30 a.m. on 21 August 1892. The sheriff and two of his sons were returning from a dance in the eastern outskirts of Brownsville. As his open, horse-drawn coach approached the Thirteenth Street crossing of the "Town Resaca," the assassin stepped out from behind the coach and fired two bullets into the back of Sheriff Brito's head.

Despite large rewards offered for information related to the crime, his murderer was never caught. Rumors at the time insinuated that Sheriff Brito's murder was the result of a long-standing resentment of some sort.

Before being elected sheriff, he was the owner of *El Democrata*, a Spanish-language newspaper in Brownsville. He is believed to have been born in the Rio Grande Valley. Brito was married and was the father of five children.

Jacquelin, J. Gustave
Born circa 1866—Died 31 March 1893
Date of incident: 24 February 1893

On the night of 24 February 1893, Deputy Jacquelin was reported to have been drinking heavily at the saloon of Mike Leahy. Jacquelin had a disagreement with a man in the saloon, and Leahy had to separate the pair. The deputy became boisterous and was forcibly ejected from the establishment by Leahy. Now angered from having been forcibly removed from the tavern, Jacquelin soon returned, cutting loose a barrage of insulting language while physically accosting Leahy. Leahy believed, and later claimed, that he thought Jacquelin was going for his pistol, so he reached behind the bar, pulled out his .44-caliber revolver and fired two shots at the drunken man. Jacquelin was hit in the chest. A bullet pierced his lung and became lodged in his back. He died a month later on 31 March 1893.

Jacquelin was a native of Matamoros, Mexico, and is buried at Brownsville. He was survived by his wife, Eulalia Lopez.

Cobb, Samuel
Born circa 1860—Died 5 April 1898

Elections in south Texas have frequently spawned violence; as the various political parties vie for power, heated debates often escalate into vicious confrontations. On election day, Deputy Cobb heard about a disturbance at a voting booth and went on horseback to investigate. His brother, Precinct 2 constable Felipe "Philip" Cobb, and a Brownsville city policeman followed on foot. Carlos Gullien stepped from an alley and grabbed the horse's bridle. Gullien shot Deputy Cobb. The deputy fired back, wounding Gullien. Both men fell to the ground. As Constable Philip Cobb arrived, Gullien raised up and shot him twice, killing him instantly. Gullien's brother appeared and shot Deputy Sam Cobb again. Cobb died three hours later.

Both Gullien brothers fled. Carlos Gullien was arrested and jailed. A mob gathered and broke into the jail. Gunfire erupted and Gullien was shot to death. The members of the unruly crowd dragged his body into the street and were going to burn it, but the corpse was eventually return to the jail cell. Gullien had been in numerous shooting scrapes and disliked the Cobbs. His brother was convicted of assault to murder, and the case was on appeal.

Both lawmen are buried at Oddfellows Cemetery in Cameron County. Constable Cobb left behind a wife, Ann M. Schwarz.

Related case: Cameron County Constable's Office—Felipe "Philip" Cobb.

CASS COUNTY CONSTABLE'S OFFICE

Perdue, Charles F.
Born 21 January 1861—Died 21 January 1889

Charles Perdue was constable of Precinct 4. On 21 January 1889, Deputy Sheriff John Stone intended to serve a warrant on a man named David Farmer for carrying weapons. Stone armed himself with his Winchester and took Constable Perdue with him. The pair proceeded to David Farmer's home to make the arrest. When confronted by the lawmen, Farmer remarked that he would be damned if he would surrender. Making good on his claim, he then drew his pistol and began shooting.

Five or six shots were fired. Perdue was hit. He dropped to his knees and handed Stone his pistol, remarking, "I am a dead man." At that very instant, he fell over and expired. Farmer began to make a run for it, but Stone shot him dead.

Driver, Dave Y.
Born circa 1867—Died 26 November 1898

Driver, James M. "Jim"
Born circa 1839—Died 26 November 1898

A street battle erupted in Hughes Springs that involved Precinct 2 constable James Driver; his son, Deputy Constable Dave Driver; and a man named Ben Boone. Boone killed both lawmen but, in the process, was shot three times and seriously wounded. The shooting was reported to have been the result of a personal feud between Boone and the Drivers. Boone was tried and acquitted.

Both lawmen are buried in unmarked graves at the Old Driver Place Cemetery near Hughes Springs.

CHILDRESS COUNTY SHERIFF'S OFFICE

Matthews, John Pearce
Born 16 March 1857—Died 30 December 1893
Date of incident: 9 December 1893

Sheriff Matthews had a sordid past, having come to Texas from Louisiana, where he had been involved in the killing of a riverboat captain. He shortened his name to John Pearce and is credited with killing a man in the Texas Panhandle. Matthews was also involved in an altercation with two Texas Rangers in 1890 and emerged the underdog. Thereafter he displayed an open hatred of rangers.

Boldly using his true name, he was elected sheriff of Childress County on 4 November 1890 and was reelected on 8 November 1892. Matthews served until his death.

Sheriff Matthews became embroiled in a controversy over the attempted removal of Sheriff Joe Beckham in Motley County. Matthews went to Motely County and arrested Beckham's deputies. Beckham fled to Oklahoma, and Sheriff Matthews went after him. That action led to a conflict with Texas Ranger captain Bill McDonald. That hostility would resurface not long afterward.

Matthews and McDonald became involved in another disagreement concerning Matthews's insistence that McDonald enlist a Childress County deputy in the ranger service. Matthews complained to Governor Hogg about McDonald's handling of the matter, a complaint that resulted in a heated exchange of words during which the two men almost came to blows.

On 9 December, Sheriff Matthews and two of his deputies arrived by train at the town of Quanah in Hardeman County to meet with Sheriff R.P. Coffer concerning various matters. The Beckham case was on the list of subjects to be covered. Captain McDonald happened to be in Quanah at the same time. As might be expected, the old disagreement between the men was soon rekindled.

As Matthews and McDonald argued, a local resident named Dick Crutcher tried to mediate. There were persistent rumors that Sheriff Matthews had threatened to kill Captain McDonald. The matter seemed to have been resolved, but when Captain McDonald, Sheriff Matthews and Sheriff Coffer next crossed paths on the street, the encounter escalated. Both McDonald and Matthews drew their pistols and opened fire. Adding to the confusion, other parties joined in the gun battle. Matthews was shot and mortally wounded during the exchange of gunshots. McDonald was seriously injured.

Matthews died on 30 December. He contracted blood poisoning from the shoulder wound he had received in the gunfight with McDonald. Before he died, Matthews expressed a desire to reconcile his difference with McDonald.

Matthews is buried at Childress Cemetery.

Related cases: Motley County Sheriff's Office—Joe Beckham and G. W. Cook.

CLAY COUNTY CONSTABLE'S OFFICE

Brooks, John McPherson Berrian
Born circa 1848—Died 24 November 1879

On 24 November 1879, a group of cowboys were on a drunken spree and began firing their guns precariously close to the business section of the town. Precinct 4 constable Brooks, hearing the gunfire, walked to where the cowboys were and demanded that they stop shooting. They refused to obey, so he fired his revolver. The group of rowdies then turned and fired at Constable Brooks, shooting him in the back and mortally wounding him. Twenty-five armed citizens started out in pursuit of the shooters and captured four of them. They were returned and lodged in jail. It is unknown at this time whether any of the group was charged or convicted in the death of Constable Brooks.

Brooks was survived by his wife, Nancy Eveline Simmons Brooks, and four children. His place of burial is unknown. The state election records for 5 November 1878 indicate that Precinct 4 had a tie vote. No names were noted. Brooks was apparently appointed as constable for Precinct 4.

COLLIN COUNTY SHERIFF'S OFFICE

Shain, Thomas "Tom"
Born circa 1825—Died 2 July 1860

Deputy Shain was shot and killed while investigating a rash of recent robberies.

Shain had just interviewed a farm owner and was searching the area near the farm. He came upon a man feeding several horses. As he talked with the man, he recognized the brand on one of the animals. Knowing that the animal had been stolen, he attempted to place the man under arrest. The fellow produced a revolver and fatally shot him.

Deputy Shain had served with the Collin County Sheriff's Office for two years. He was survived by his wife and four children. He is buried at Old McKinney Cemetery.

Read, James Lawrence
Born circa 1828—Died 18 May 1864

McReynolds, James Monroe
Born circa 1820—Died 18 May 1864

The only information that is undisputed in this incident is that James Read was elected sheriff of Collin County on 6 August 1860 and was reelected on 4 August 1862 for a term that would have expired in August 1864.

In December 1861, Sheriff Read was recruited by a Confederate army company, but he soon dropped from active military service. He remained a Confederate officer until his death. McReynolds was Sheriff Read's cousin.

William C. Quantrill and his force of four hundred Confederate Partisan Rangers moved into north Texas for winter quarters in October 1863. Sheriff Read and a posse shot and killed two of the four men who had murdered a merchant at the town of Millwood in Kaufman County. The sheriff was acquitted of murder on 20 February 1864.

According to reports, up to sixty renegades from Quantrill's forces went to McKinney to seek revenge against the sheriff for killing their men and, moreover, for Sheriff Read's alleged pro-Union sentiments. The sheriff learned that Quantrill's men were searching for him. He gathered eighteen of his own men and retreated to an abandoned mill. Quantrill's men soon discovered their hideout, and a gunfight erupted. The sheriff's men fled under cover of darkness. Read, Deputy McReynolds and a cousin named J.E. Holcomb borrowed horses and made good their escape.

In what turned out to be a completely unrelated incident, an elderly woman had been beaten and robbed by jayhawkers in Van Zandt County. Jayhawkers were guerrilla fighters who often clashed with proslavery "Border Ruffians." A "Partisan" is a member of an irregular military force formed to oppose control of an area by a foreign power or by an army of occupation. These terms can apply to the field element of resistance movements that opposed rule.

The local militia arrested Read, McReynolds and Holcomb along with a man named Jeff Davis as possible deserters, jayhawkers and horse thieves. The woman identified McReynolds and Read as her attackers. They, of course, denied any involvement in the robbery, having been elsewhere at the time of the incident. The four men were placed in a Confederate stockade at Camp Ford at Tyler in Smith County.

On 18 May 1864, an armed group of about eighty men—reportedly from Van Zandt, Henderson and Kaufman Counties—demanded that the guards turn over the three men to them. The guards did so, and Read, McReynolds and Holcomb were promptly hanged from a nearby tree. Davis was released. A number of prominent citizens in Van Zandt County were later arrested and charged with the lynching. None was convicted.

Sheriff Read is buried at Pecan Grove Cemetery at McKinney. Deputy McReynolds is buried at Kaufman County.

Hall, William C.
Born circa 1832—Died 24 April 1869
Date of incident: 29 March 1869

Deputy Hall was shot and killed as he and several other posse members were attempting to arrest three men on a murder warrant. As the deputies approached the location where the trio were said to be resting, the wanted men opened fire on the lawmen from a place of concealment in the bushes. Hall was struck by a bullet and mortally wounded. Two of the suspected murderers, Penn and Hays, were shot and killed when the deputies returned fire. The third man, also named Hall, escaped.

Deputy Hall had served with the Collin County Sheriff's Office for three years. He was survived by his wife.

COLORADO CITY POLICE DEPARTMENT

Hardeman, Lewis
Born circa 1825—Died June 1885

Deputy City Marshal Hardeman was shot and killed at the Variety Theater in Mitchell County. No other information is known at this time.

Gooch, William Daniel Pomphrey
Born 5 October 1851—Died 4 April 1892

In the evening hours of 2 September 1887, Deputy U.S. Marshal Gooch was reportedly intoxicated and had become verbally abusive to some local citizens. Deputy U.S. Marshal Johnson entered the saloon where Gooch had been drinking and overheard some defamatory remarks directed toward him. Predictably, a gunfight soon followed. According to reports of the day, Gooch is claimed to have gone for his gun first. Johnson told him to stop, but when Gooch continued to draw the weapon Johnson went for his own pistol. The sober Johnson managed to get off a shot just ahead of Gooch. Johnson's shot hit Gooch in the chest, piercing his lung and coming out near his right shoulder.

Next, adding to the drama of the already charged event, the lights in the saloon went out. No matter—several more shots were fired in the darkness. Gooch fired a shot that struck Johnson in the foot, inflicting a very minor injury. Gooch's injury, on the other hand, was far more serious. He did, however, eventually recover.

On the evening of 4 April 1892, as the former deputy U.S. marshal and now city marshal of Colorado City, Gooch was drinking at the Senate Saloon at Colorado City. For some reason, he had drawn his pistol. When two men named Tom Powers and George Bell attempted to disarm him, he opened fire on the pair.

Another wild barroom gunfight broke out, with a total of about a dozen shots being exchanged between the combatants. Two bullets struck Gooch and inflicted a fatal wound. The only other injury that resulted from this barrage of gunfire was to a man called "Happy Jack." Jack suffered a flesh wound to his leg from a stray bullet and was, in all likelihood, no longer called "Happy Jack."

Gooch died of his wounds shortly after the incident. He was survived by a wife and four children. Gooch had been a druggist until about six years earlier, when Deputy U.S. Marshal Johnson had shot him. Since that time, he had served as city marshal. Powers was a well-known local stockman. Bell was a deputy sheriff of Martin County and was running against Gooch for the post of city marshal. Gooch is buried at Colorado City Cemetery.

COLORADO COUNTY CONSTABLE'S OFFICE

Townsend, Thomas Lewis "Tup," Jr.
Born April 1866—Died 26 June 1893
Date of incident: About March 1893

The Townsend family members rank among the earliest residents of Colorado County. Stephen Townsend was the first sheriff of Colorado County, serving from 6 February 1837 until 4 February 1839. Asa Townsend became constable in the early 1890s.

Precinct 4 constable "Tup" Townsend succumbed to the injuries he received three months earlier when his horse fell on him.

Townsend and his brother, A. Morse Townsend, had heard screaming in the distance and were riding out to investigate. They decided to take a shortcut through a wooded area and ran headlong into a barbed wire fence. Both men were thrown from their horses. Tup Townsend's horse landed on him, inflicting serious internal injuries.

Townsend had been with the agency for four years and was survived by his wife, one child, a brother and his parents. He is buried at Odd Fellows Cemetery in Weimar.

Townsend, A. Morse
Born 11 January 1872—Died 18 January 1894

A. Morse Townsend replaced his brother as constable of Precinct 4. Very early on the morning of 18 January 1894, at about 3:00 a.m., an excursion train carrying several coaches and sleeping cars made an unscheduled stop near Weimar. The conductor and one of the brakemen disembarked and asked for a peace officer. Townsend and a night watchman happened to be nearby and responded. The conductor informed them that they had forcibly put an unruly man off the train about two or three miles east of Weimar. The man, who was wearing a large white hat, had thrown a rock through one of the windows at the rear of a sleeper car, shattering the glass. Afterward, he had fired a shot into the car. Fortunately, no one on the train was injured.

Townsend took off in pursuit. He soon came upon two men, one of whom matched the description. Townsend arrested the fellow with the big white hat, a man named DeWitt Braddock of Flatonia, and lodged him in the jail. He also removed a .45-caliber six-shooter from Braddock's possession that held five live cartridges. One cartridge had been recently fired. Weimar city marshal Hatch York recognized the man as being the same person they had arrested recently for carrying a gun and for stealing a ride on an eastbound Southern Pacific passenger train. Braddock had raised suspicion, giving the appearance of someone who was in the process of attempting to rob the train.

At about 6:30 p.m. that evening, Townsend went to the city jail to bring some food and fresh water to the prisoner. As he was in the process of opening the cell door, Braddock became verbally abusive, demanding that the constable turn over his pistol to him. In another account of this incident, it is claimed that Braddock feigned sickness, thereby distracting Townsend. Townsend, thinking that Braddock was not serious, made some casual remark in response. As the door of the jail cell swung slightly open, Braddock leaned out and, without speaking a word, plunged a knife into Townsend's chest. Although mortally wounded, Townsend managed to fire one shot at the fleeing Braddock before he collapsed. Townsend died about three hours later. Braddock fled the jail and escaped.

Constable Townsend was survived by a young wife, an aged father and mother, several siblings and numerous relatives and friends. He is buried at Odd Fellows Cemetery in Weimar.

On the evening of 7 February 1894, a group of lawmen caught up with Braddock at the home of Henry Moore. Involved in the posse were Colorado County sheriff J.L. "Light" Townsend, who was related to Constable Townsend; Wharton County sheriff Hamilton Bass Dickson; and Constable C.W. Hearte. When the group reached the Moore place, Sheriff Dickson, who was in the lead, suddenly came upon Braddock. Braddock immediately fired two shots at Dickson from his Winchester rifle, striking the sheriff with both shots. Sheriff Townsend then fired rapidly at Braddock, killing him instantly. Sheriff Dickson lived only a short time and died at the scene.

Next, Sheriff Townsend and Constable Hearte began their hunt for Moore, who they soon found hiding in a thicket. The lawmen surrounded him. Moore drew his pistol, but Sheriff Townsend was able to beat him to the draw and fire first. Townsend's shot was quickly followed by a second from Constable Hearte. Moore was killed instantly.

Related case: Wharton County Sheriff's Office—Hamilton Bass Dickson.

Sutton, David Ike "Jake"
Born 1 January 1867—Died 19 February 1894

James R. Mitchell was from one of the oldest and most prominent families in Fort Bend County. He married a girl named Lizzie Morris. One month later, in July 1893, they separated over his alleged abuse and abandonment. She moved into Melton Sparks's boardinghouse in Eagle Lake and started supporting herself.

The notoriously bad-tempered Mitchell had reportedly cut a man's throat on a train and nearly killed him because he had taken a seat next to his wife. Precinct 8 constable Sutton arrested him on that occasion. Mitchell sporadically visited his wife at the boardinghouse, but in December 1893 Sparks told him to stay away if he would not support her. Mitchell left the boardinghouse and ran into Constable Sutton. He tried to buy the constable a drink, but Sutton and Mitchell had words over Mitchell's alleged mistreatment of his wife. Mitchell later claimed that Sutton had threatened to kill him during that exchange, but other witnesses denied that any such threats had been made.

On 19 February 1894, the 9:45 p.m. passenger train from Eagle Lake in Colorado County arrived at the Grand Central Depot in Houston. On board were Constable Sutton and several local residents. The constable was transporting witnesses associated with the murder trial of Frank Sparks. The trial was being held in Harris County on a change of venue from Wharton County. The parties looked out of the train window and saw Mitchell waiting on the platform. Sutton told witnesses on the train that he was an officer and was armed, so he would lead them through the depot to a carriage. He also remarked that he expected trouble from Mitchell.

There is disagreement as to whether words were exchanged between the pair and as to who fired the first shot. From some reports, it appears as though Mitchell approached Sutton with a .45-caliber pistol in his hand and initiated the gunfight. Mitchell's first shot struck Sutton in the heart. He died instantly. His second shot struck Melton Sparks in the side, exiting on the opposite side and mortally wounding him. Dan Gleason, an old bus driver who was not involved in the incident, was accidently shot in the heart and killed. Among the wounded in this shooting incident were James Sparks, Mrs. Melton Sparks, her two-year-old daughter and another witness named Mrs. Dow. Mitchell surrendered to Houston police.

The trial of Mitchell for the multiple murders of Sutton, Sparks and Gleason was continued numerous times. On 21 October 1895, Mitchell became involved in an altercation with a man named Cain Neal in a restaurant at Richmond. The argument grew out of the recent trial of Armistead Mitchell, James's brother, involving a homicide he had committed six months earlier. Neal and Armistead Mitchell had been jointly indicted in that slaying, but a severance was granted. Neal's case was dismissed. Armistead Mitchell was convicted based on Neal's testimony. As one might imagine, hard feeling existed between the two men. Both Neal and Mitchell went for their pistols, but Neal was the faster draw and shot Mitchell three times, hitting him once in the neck, once in the chest and once in the temple.

Constable Sutton had recently married and was survived by his young wife. He is buried at Eagle Lake Masonic Cemetery. He was twenty-seven years of age at the time of his death.

Burttschell, Jacob B. "Jake"
Born 5 February 1860—Died 30 April 1894

Precinct 7 constable Burttschell was shot and killed by Tuck Hoover at about 8:00 a.m. on 30 April 1894. The incident took place about three miles east of Weimar. News of the tragedy was brought to town by Hoover, who galloped up to the jail with a pistols in each hand and gave himself up to Sheriff Townsend and City Marshal Reese.

During the inquest, it was learned that Burttschell was sitting in his saloon, unarmed, when Hoover rode up. He dismounted and then walked into the establishment with a cocked revolver in his hand. As he entered the saloon, he pointed the pistol at Burttschell and said, "Jake, I understand you have threatened to kill me." Hoover then fired his pistol at Burttschell. The bullet passed through, or near, Burttschell's heart. As Burttschell fell, Hoover fired again. He then turned and pointed his pistol at Burttschell's clerk, W.H. Dubose, who was also in the saloon. Hoover backed out of the door, keeping Dubose covered with his pistol until he had made it outside. He then mounted his horse, and as he rode by the door of the saloon, he fired again at Burttschell, who was by this time down on the floor mortally wounded and struggling for his life.

Both Burtshell and Hoover had been raised in Alleyton. Burttschell was survived by his wife and several children. He is buried at St. Roch's Cemetery. His death marked the third killing of a constable in Colorado County during 1894.

Wall, Lee
Born circa 1864—Died 6 June 1898

Precinct 4 constable Wall was shot and killed while arresting a man named George Washington for fighting at a local saloon.

Wall had made the arrest of Washington and was walking him to the jail. Washington pulled out a pistol that he had concealed in his belt and shot Wall twice, once in the head and once in the chest. Washington still had four rounds left in his pistol. He threatened witnesses as he fled the scene. A crowd of about forty citizens, many of whom were armed, followed Washington in a running gun battle that continued until the killer had emptied his pistol. The city marshal took custody of Washington, but he was soon met by a mob of about five hundred citizens when he attempted to approach the jail. The crowd seized Washington and lynched him from an electric utility pole. Sheriff Reese arrived afterward and cut Washington down.

Constable Wall had been with the agency for eighteen days and was survived by his wife. He is buried at Odd Fellows Cemetery in Weimar.

Hope, Larkin Secrest
Born 3 January 1855—Died 3 August 1898

Larkin Hope married into the Townsend family. That family group included Sheriff J.L. "Light" Townsend, who served from 1880 to 1894. In 1890, Larkin and his brother, Marion, both served as deputies under their Uncle "Light" Townsend. On 7 July 1890, the Hope brothers arrested the son of Captain Bob Stafford, the wealthiest man in Colorado County. Bob Stafford and his brother John confronted the Hope brothers. An argument took place, and Deputy Larkin Hope shot and killed both of the Stafford brothers. The Hope brothers were never convicted. This shooting affray was the origin of a vendetta between the two families, aptly named the "Stafford-Townsend Feud."

Sam Houston Reese was appointed sheriff on 14 November 1894. Hope was then the Precinct 1 constable and was feuding with Sheriff Reese. When Reese filed for reelection in the November 1898 balloting, Hope ran against him. On 3 August 1898, Constable Hope was shot and killed on the streets of Columbus. The shooting occurred a few minutes after 9:00 p.m. Hope died about an hour later. The killer fired two shots from a shotgun, one taking effect in the bowels and the other in the upper portion of the left thigh. Constable Hope fired his pistol three times during the exchange. Although the streets were occupied at the time, no one claimed to have seen the assassin.

Sheriff Reese later arrested Jim Coleman and charged him with the murder. Coleman was acquitted of the charge. The rumor at the time was that Reese was the instigator of the assassination. This led to Reese being defeated in the election, which started another vendetta, fittingly named the "Reese-Townsend Feud."

Constable Hope is buried at Odd Fellows Cemetery in Columbus.

Sheriff Sam Houston Reese was killed on 16 March 1899 after leaving office. Although the feuds of Texas have received far less general attention and publicity than have the ones that took place in Kentucky, they were perhaps more numerous and bitter. Half a dozen of the worst ones have become fairly well chronicled, but dozens of others, large and small, raged in practically every county in the state. Reading about the complicated and intertwined feuds of this era in Texas calls to mind a low-budget daytime soap opera. All were intense, most were violent and many were fatal.

COLORADO COUNTY SHERIFF'S OFFICE

Reese, Samuel Houston
Born 4 August 1859—Died 16 March 1899

Reese was a well-to-do landowner and was related to the Townsends. He had served as a constable and agreed to be appointed sheriff when J.L. "Light" Townsend resigned. Reese was appointed sheriff on 14 November 1894 and was later elected to that post on 3 November 1896. Sheriff Reese and another Townsend relative, Constable Larkin Hope, had begun quarrelling. Hope ran against the sheriff in the 1898 elections. On 3 August 1898, Constable Hope was assassinated, and Sheriff Reese was suspected of being involved. Another Townsend relative, Will Buford, defeated Reese for the post as sheriff on 8 November 1898.

The bitterness between the Townsend and Reese families came to a head on 16 March 1899. As former sheriff Reese was tying up his horse near the Square, Sheriff Buford's deputies—Marc Townsend, Marion Hope and Willie Clements—opened fire on him. Reese and a farmer named Charles Boehm were killed. A small boy was wounded by stray gunfire. The three deputies were arrested, but the men were never convicted. For a time, the county was an armed camp, and the governor had to send in the Texas Rangers under Captain Bill McDonald to maintain order.

On 18 May 1899, Sam Reese's brother, Dick, and another man were shot and killed by Deputies Step Yates and J.G. Townsend. The pair had been stopped at the bridge into the county on suspicion of carrying a pistol. On 15 January 1900, J.G. "Jim" Townsend was tried at Bastrop on a change of venue for the killing of Dick Reese. Deputy Yates died of tuberculosis before the trial. A motion for continuance was granted. The parties were leaving the courthouse when gunfire erupted. There were three shooters involved: Walter Reese, son of the dead former sheriff; Jim Coleman, who was the alleged killer of Larkin Hope; and Tom Daniels; all opened fire on Deputy Willie Clements. Although Clements was their intended target, they accidently killed Sheriff Buford's son, Arthur.

Reese, Coleman and Daniels were never convicted. On 31 July 1900, Jim Coleman and Walter Reese were involved in another shootout, this time on a train. In this incident, Willie Clements, Marc Townsend, Frank Buford and A.B. Woolridge were involved. On this occasion, both Coleman and Reese were badly wounded. Remarkably, on 30 June 1906, Marion Hope and Herbert Reese were involved in another shooting that resulted in the death of Hiram Clements.

Jim Coleman was later killed in San Antonio. Willie Clements was killed by a blacksmith. Herbert Reese was accidently killed with his own gun when he dropped the pistol, causing it to discharge. Walter Reese died in an automobile accident.

Sheriff Reese is buried at Weimar Cemetery.

COLUMBUS POLICE DEPARTMENT

Goode, Robert
Born (Unknown)—Died 28 June 1868

Marshal Goode was shot and killed while responding to a report of a disturbance involving three men. While attempting to separate the threesome, one of the group, a fellow named John H. Bowen, shot Goode in the heart. The wound proved fatal, and Goode expired several minutes later.

In one more episode of classic Texas vigilante justice "swiftly administered," Bowen was promptly lynched for killing the marshal.

Goode was survived by his wife. His place of burial is unknown.

COMANCHE COUNTY SHERIFF'S OFFICE

Martin, Joe N.
Born (Unknown)—Died 20 June 1885
Date of incident: 15 June 1885

Deputy Martin was shot and killed by a drunken man whom he was attempting to arrest.

Martin was in the process of arresting a physician named R.W. Leach for drunkenness and disorderly conduct. In the process of doing so, Leach pulled a gun and shot Martin several times. Martin lingered for five days before finally succumbing to his wounds. Leach was tried, convicted and sentenced to fourteen years in prison for the crime.

Martin was survived by his wife and five children. He is buried at De Leon Cemetery in Comanche County.

CONCHO COUNTY CONSTABLE'S OFFICE

Pendleton, John H.
Born circa 1855—Died 26 December 1881

On 26 December 1881, Constable John Pendleton was shot through the heart, and killed instantly, while responding to the sound of gunfire emanating from a local saloon.

A gambler named Mike Houston and a bartender named Charles Keens had become involved in a heated quarrel. The fight soon poured into the street, where both men began shooting at each other with their pistols. Constable Pendleton heard the gunfire and was headed toward the door of the saloon when a stray bullet passed through the doorway and struck him in the heart. The bullet traveled through Pendleton and struck another man in the shoulder. Tom Green County sheriff James D. Spears made the arrest and lodged both men in the county jail at Ben Ficklin (seat of Tom Green County until 1882).

Pendleton was married. He was buried by the Odd Fellows, but his place of burial is unknown.

It is not certain whether Pendleton was a constable in Tom Green County or newly organized Concho County (1881).

COOKE COUNTY CONSTABLE'S OFFICE

Nance, Benton
Born (Unknown)—Died 10 March 1878

On 10 March 1878, a Cooke County justice of the peace appointed Benton Nance and William Moran as special deputy constables for Precinct 2. He gave the men a warrant to arrest Ferdinand Lamb. The two deputies located Lamb in the town of Dexter. Lamb resisted arrest and shot Deputy Nance with a double-barreled shotgun. Nance died shortly thereafter.

Lamb was arrested and charged with murder. The disposition of the case is missing from the county records.

No family information concerning Nance has been located. His place of burial is unknown. One newspaper reported that "Mr. Nance, the party killed, was a worthy and respected citizen, and his untimely death is much regretted."

Johnson, J.D.L.
Born circa 1850—Died 14 February 1879

On 14 February 1885, Precinct 5 constable Johnson and Deputy Constables Newton Floyd and John Stewart were attempting to serve a writ of attachment on a team of horses and a wagon owned by J.H. "Old Man" Rainey. Rainey and his son, J.E. "Jim" Rainey, were getting ready to cross the Red River into Indian Territory when the three lawmen confronted them. The elder Rainey resisted the officers and told his son to shoot Constable Johnson. The compliant younger Rainey did so, hitting Constable Johnson in the head and upper body, killing him instantly. He then shot and wounded Deputy Constable Floyd.

Jim Rainey was sentenced to life in prison. The elder Rainey received twenty years in prison.

Constable Johnson is buried at Marysville Cemetery in Cooke County.

Cooke County Sheriff's Office

Knight, M.M. "Meek"
Born circa 1851—Died 30 May 1881

Meredith, Charles "Charley"
Born (Unknown)—Died 30 May 1881

Meredith, Samuel Jackson "Sam"
Born 13 November 1851—Died 30 May 1881

At about noon on Monday, 30 May 1881, Deputy Sheriff M.M. Knight swore in Sam Meredith, Charley Meredith and Jim Dickson, as well as a man named Phipps, to assist him in arresting two men with warrants for carrying concealed weapons.

The five lawmen arrested the first man, a blacksmith, whose name is not known. Two of the deputies, Phipps and Dickson, remained with the blacksmith to guard him, while Deputy Knight and the two Merediths went to arrest the other man, John Thomas (possibly Thompson), who was a gunsmith. As they approached the man's home, Thomas burst forth from behind a counter and opened fire on them with a Winchester rifle. Deputy Sam Meredith was struck in the neck. He fell to the ground in extreme pain. Thomas then shot Deputy Knight in the head. The bullet entered through his mouth and traveled upward, killing him instantly. Deputy Charley Meredith tried to hide behind a tree, but Thomas fired at him as well, killing him instantly. Thomas noticed that Sam Meredith was still alive, so he placed his rifle against the deputy's head and coldly administered the fatal shot. Thomas then proceeded to break the guns of all of the lawmen against a tree in the yard before he eventually left the scene.

Thomas left his family and fled to Indian Territory. It is not known if he was ever arrested or charged with the killings of these three lawmen.

Deputy Knight was survived by his wife and one child. He is buried at North Dexter Cemetery.

Samuel Meredith was survived by a wife and one child. Charles Meredith was not married. Knight and Samuel Meredith are buried at Dexter North Cemetery at Dexter. It is believed that Charles Meredith is buried in an unmarked grave there as well.

Corpus Christi Police Department

Mussett, Elias Tyre, Jr.
Born circa 1845—Died 6 May 1892

Elias Mussett defeated John Parker in the election for city marshal. The defeat resulted in hard feelings between the two men. The Corpus Christi City Council controlled the hiring and appointments to the marshal's office. That unwitting body of politicians recklessly hired the recently defeated Parker as a deputy city marshal under Elias Mussett. When City Marshal Mussett heard that Parker had not acted to quell a disturbance during a festival, he decided to reprimand him. When confronted, Parker drew his pistol and then shot and killed Mussett. Parker rode to the sheriff's office and surrendered. He was convicted of first-degree murder and sentenced to life in prison but was later released. He died in Laredo on 26 August 1936.

Mussett is buried at Rose Hill Cemetery at Corpus Christi. A local historian reported that Elias Mussett Sr. was also a city marshal and was killed in the line of duty in 1873. That incident has not yet been adequately documented.

Corsicana Police Department

Wallace, W.H.
Born (Unknown)—Died 3 December 1872

E. Bennett, a livery stable keeper and citizen of some prominence, was murdered on 3 December 1872 by policeman W.H. Wallace in a dispute involving one dollar for the hire of a horse. Wallace was arrested, but when he tried to escape he was killed by his guard.

Robinson, Augustus W. "Gus"
Born circa 1853—Died 27 December 1886

Gus Robinson is reported to have served as a Corsicana police officer. He also served as a Texas Ranger in Company C under the command of Captain J.C. Sparks, having enlisted on 30 November 1876 and again on 28 February 1877.

Gus Robinson had taken up the profession of well drilling. On 27 December 1886, former officer Robinson went to the home of an acquaintance named Jack Garrett in McGregor to borrow a lye kettle. It is unclear from the reports if he had permission to do so or was just going to help himself to the cauldron. When Robinson was confronted by Garrett concerning his proposed use of the kettle, he responded with a barrage of insulting language. Garrett then told Robinson to leave his property, which he did. Garrett presumed that the matter had been settled. It was not.

At about 9:00 a.m., Garrett was at Stephenson & Smith's store engaged in the repair of a sewing machine. Gus Robinson and his brother William came into the store and attacked Garrett. During the struggle, Garrett drew a pocketknife and cut Robinson in the back and side. The injuries were fatal, and Robinson died in about two hours.

City Marshal S.K. Lindsey brought Garrett to Waco and confined him to the jail. Garrett went to trial on 19 May 1872. Based on the fact that there was insufficient evidence, Judge Williams instructed the jury to find a verdict of not guilty. They dutifully complied.

Both men were well respected in the community. Robinson was survived by his wife, Roshe. His place of burial is unknown.

CUERO POLICE DEPARTMENT

Brown, Reuben "Rube"
Born 28 November 1851—Died 17 November 1875

In the early 1870s, Rube Brown was considered a leader of the Sutton-Tumlinson party. The Sutton-Tumlinson faction was fighting the Taylor-Pidgen families. On 12 August 1873, the parties signed a peace treaty, of which Brown was a signatory. The treaty collapsed on 11 March 1874 when William E. Sutton and Gabriel Webster Slaughter were killed by Bill and Jim Taylor on board the steamer *Clinton* while it was docked at Indianola. Brown was the city marshal of Cuero in DeWitt County at the time and had arrested Bill Taylor and received a $500 reward. Brown resigned as city marshal on 8 June 1874. Bill Taylor escaped from jail during the aftermath of a hurricane and sent Brown a message that he would kill him.

About 8:00 p.m. on 17 November 1875, a man walked into a saloon in Cuero and found Brown playing cards. The man stared at Brown and left. Soon after, five men entered the bar and opened fire. The men dragged

Brown outside and continued shooting him. Brown's body was riddled with bullets. The saloon was filled with patrons at the time. A man named Tom Freeman was also killed, and another man was wounded during this wild exchange of gunfire. As the killers escaped, it is claimed that one of them said that they "got their man." No one was ever tried for the murder of Brown. Bill and Jim Taylor, Mason Arnold and A.R. Hendricks were allegedly the gunmen.

Brown had never married and is buried at Epperson Cemetery near Clinton.

On 27 December 1875, Jim Taylor, Arnold and Hendricks were killed by a posse in Clinton in DeWitt County.

The frequently overused phrase "riddled with bullets" means to pierce with numerous holes, or perforate. Writers of the era often used this somewhat sensational term to describe a shooting incident in which the victim received multiple bullet wounds. Rarely was a shooting victim's body actually "riddled with bullet holes." However, it was not at all uncommon for victims of gunshot wounds before the advent of more powerful gunpowder at the turn of the last century to have been shot numerous times before succumbing to their injuries. Also, in situations in which there were multiple assailants, or mob violence, numerous bullet wounds were not uncommon.

Related cases: DeWitt County Sheriff's Office—Martin V. King and William E. "Bill" Sutton; Texas Rangers—A.R. Hendricks.

Martindale, John E.
Born circa 1862—Died 25 October 1887

City Marshal Martindale accidentally shot himself when his revolver fell from its holster and struck the hammer on the ground, causing the gun to discharge. The bullet entered his stomach a little left of his navel, turning upward and passing entirely through his body before exiting below his left shoulder blade. Martindale died at 9:30 p.m. on 25 October 1887. The newspaper described him as "an energetic young man and a good officer, faultlessly filling his position."

Martindale is buried at Hillside Cemetery in Cuero in DeWitt County.

Dallas, City of

Daniels, Charles A.
Born (Unknown)—Died 13 August 1899

Mounted Police Officer Albert Parks Rawlins was shot and killed by Special Policeman Daniels during a duel that took place on the streets of Dallas.

In classic Old West fashion, the pair faced off over a personal disagreement. From a distance of three paces they fired their large-caliber single-action revolvers at each other. This unwise move resulted in the death of both officers, thereby settling their disagreement for all time.

Related case: Dallas Police Department—Albert Parks Rawlins.

Dallas County Constable's Office

Burnett, W. Riley
Born circa 1859—Died 2 August 1893

Precinct 8 constable Burnett was shot and killed while serving an arrest warrant on Alfred Miers. Miers asked Burnett if he could go into his brother-in-law's home to get his hat. Burnett agreed. Apparently Miers had other plans, because he soon emerged from the building hatless but also firing a Winchester rifle. Shots from Miers's Winchester struck Constable Burnett in the lung and face. Miers was apprehended and sentenced to twenty-five years.

Constable Burnett was survived by his wife and children.

Dallas County Sheriff's Office

McMahan, James
Born circa 1844—Died 16 January 1871

Nichols, Charles H.
Born circa 1840—Died 20 January 1871
Date of incident: 16 January 1871

Deputies McMahan and Nichols were shot and killed while attempting to arrest John Younger.

Younger had been trying to shoot a pipe out of an elderly man's mouth the preceding day. The elderly man told the sheriff that Younger was trying to kill him, so the sheriff sent the two deputies to make the arrest. They found Younger eating breakfast in the local saloon with a friend named Tom McDaniels. Younger asked that he be allowed to finish his breakfast before being arrested. The two lawmen agreed and left the saloon. Once the lawmen had left, Younger and McDaniels abandoned their meal and went to the local livery stable to retrieve their horses. Nichols and McMahan were already at the stable. While the deputies attempted to handcuff Younger, he produced a handgun and shot both officers. Younger was wounded in the arm. Both he and McDaniels mounted their horses and fled.

Deputy McMahan had served with the agency for one day. He was survived by his wife. His place of burial is unknown.

Deputy Nichols is buried at Masonic Cemetery in Dallas.

The Younger Gang later shot and killed Deputy Sheriff Edwin Daniels of St. Clair County, Missouri, on 17 March 1874. The Youngers were also connected to the death of Bureau of Indian Affairs police officer Frank West on 17 December 1886.

Vise, George V.
Born 13 January 1841—Died 8 June 1878

In some accounts of this tragic accident, the reader may find George V. Vise's surname spelled as Vice.

At about 10:00 a.m. on Wednesday, 5 June 1878, Deputy Vise was returning to Hutchins in Dallas County after an all-night search for a convict named Frank Weaver. Weaver was a horse thief who had escaped from prison. Vise had been assisted by five or six posse members, all of whom spent the preceding night in a thicket exposed to a terrible rainstorm that was accompanied by high winds. The following morning, Vise was ill and started back to Hutchins. A witness reported that Vise had attempted to cross the rain-swollen Cottonwood Creek and that his horse bucked him off. Vise became entangled in some vines and drowned. His body was removed from the stream about an hour later.

Vise was survived by his wife, Sarah Jane Flowers, and two sons, George and William.

Pate, Addison C.
Born circa 1866—Died 9 September 1895

Deputy Pate was shot and killed by a man whom he was attempting to arrest for robbing a food store clerk. When Pate approached the hatless and shoeless fellow to arrest him, the man, Loraine Cady, shot him several times. The wounds were fatal.

Cady was later arrested in Oklahoma. He was transported to Paris, Texas, by 30 October 1895, where he was positively identified by Bynum Witherspoon of Midlothian as the man who killed Deputy Pate. Cady was recovering from an arm wound that, according to reports of the day, may have required amputation.

DALLAS POLICE DEPARTMENT

Pegues, Albert G.
Born circa 1856—Died 7 April 1892
Date of incident: 26 March 1892

Detective Pegues, one of the most respected and faithful officers on the force, had been shot a year earlier when his partner's gun discharged accidentally, striking him in the fleshy part of his right leg. He fully recovered from that injury, but in a subsequent mishap he would not be so fortunate.

While running to overtake a streetcar near the Windsor Hotel on the evening of 7 April 1892, Detective Pegues met with a fatal accident. His pistol fell from his pocket and discharged when it hit the ground. The bullet struck him in the ribs on his right side and then ranged upward, breaking his right shoulder blade. He was taken to his home on Grand Avenue, where the wound was dressed. Although the doctor did not consider the injury to be serious at the time, blood poisoning set in and Pegues eventually died from the effects of the wound on 7 April 1892.

Pegues, who was thirty-eight years old at his death, had been a member of the police force since August 1888 and had been promoted to the rank of detective two years earlier. He was a native of Longview. Pegues left behind a wife and three children.

Brewer, C.O.
Born circa 1850—Died 24 May 1892

Officer Brewer was shot and killed at the Union Depot station while attempting to arrest Henry Miller for slander. While talking to the man, Miller pulled out a large-caliber handgun and began firing, fatally striking Brewer. Miller was later apprehended and on 28 July 1893 was hanged for the murder.

Brewer had been with the agency for three years. He was survived by his wife and children. He is buried at Greenwood Cemetery in Dallas.

Riddle (Riddell), William H.
Born circa 1837—Died 17 June 1892

Officer Riddell was shot and killed while he and his partner attempted to serve a warrant. The convicted killer, Frank P. Miller, was sentenced to be hanged. That sentence was later commuted to life. Miller was pardoned thirteen years later on Christmas Day 1905.

Officer Riddell had been with the agency for three years and was survived by his wife and seven children. He is buried at Grove Hill Cemetery in Dallas.

McDuff, William
Born circa 1833—Died 24 December 1896

Officer McDuff was shot and killed by two youths he had arrested earlier in the day. Jim Barclay and Homer Stone had come to his home and were standing outside, yelling at him. When he went out to tell them to stop, they shot him with a shotgun, killing him instantly. Barclay was sentenced to ten years in prison and Stone to twenty-five years.

Officer McDuff had been born in the Indian Territory and was the first black officer with the Dallas Police Department to be killed in the line of duty. He had been with the agency for two months and was sixty-three years of age at the time of his death.

McDuff is buried at the cemetery near the Christian Methodist Episcopal Church in Dallas (which had been called the Colored Methodist Episcopal Church at the time of his death).

Rawlins, Albert Parks
Born 16 February 1863—Died 13 August 1899

Mounted Police Officer Rawlins was shot and killed by Special Policeman Charles A. Daniels over a personal disagreement. Their quarrel resulted in a most unusual spectacle, which unfolded on the streets of Dallas.

Not unlike a scene from a classic western movie, the pair faced off at a distance of three paces. Both men fired their large-caliber single-action revolvers at each other. Predictably, the confrontation resulted in the deaths of both officers.

Related case: Dallas, City of—Charles A. Daniels.

DENISON POLICE DEPARTMENT

Day, John Sherman
Born 22 April 1844—Died 5 February 1874

At about 10:00 p.m. on 5 February 1874, Officer Day heard a loud disturbance coming from the Eldorado Saloon on Skiddy Street. Day entered the bar and tried to calm the commotion. While attempting to arrest several men who were the cause of the uproar, someone in the crowd shot him in the head. It is believed that one of the unruly men he was attempting to arrest did the shooting.

Day died instantly. Officer Barney Daniels, who had come to Day's aid, was shot in the arm and hand by a member of the same group of rowdies. All of the men involved in the disturbance escaped.

A man called "Cherokee Jake," who was suspected of being the killer of Day, was arrested in Indian Territory a month later and was taken to the county jail in Sherman, Texas. No further information has been found concerning the status of any charges against "Cherokee Jake."

Day is believed to have been a Union soldier during the Civil War, having served as a corporal with the Sixth Minnesota Infantry, Company D. He was survived by his wife, Mary Hanna. Day is buried at Oakwood Cemetery at Denison.

Patman, Charles
Born circa 1839—Died 2 May 1875

At about 1:30 a.m. on 2 May 1875, Officers Patman and Barney Daniels were called out to the Grand Southern Saloon to investigate a report of a man carrying a concealed weapon. Two men, named Charles Sherman and S.A. Doran (or Major Dorn), had been drinking and causing trouble at the saloon for several hours before the officers were called. Daniels attempted to search Sherman but he resisted. Patman came to assist Daniels. When he did so, Doran shot Patman in the face. Patman died instantly. Doran then shot Daniels in the arm.

Both Doran and Sherman fled the scene but were later apprehended and charged with murder.

Officer Patman was survived by his wife and three children. His place of burial is not known at this time.

The now twice-lucky Officer Daniels, who had also been shot in the arm a year previous when his partner John Day was killed, survived his wounds.

Johnson, Joseph E.
Born (Unknown)—Died 30 October 1879

At about 9:00 a.m. on Thursday 30 October 1879, Officer Johnson and Constable J.F. Spence went to arrest a man named Frank Porter (alias Charles Henry and Charles Johnson). Porter was accused of stealing a coat. The officers went to Porter's residence. Porter had been sleeping but lit a lamp and spoke with the officers. During the conversation, he gave the lawmen several aliases. Next Porter arose from bed, extinguished the lights and commenced shooting, firing twice at the officers. One shot struck Johnson, wounding him fatally. He managed to stagger out of the house but was later found dead in the front yard of Porter's residence.

Porter stole a horse and escaped. He was later apprehended in the Indian Territory by City Marshal Hardwick and brought back to the Sherman jail. Johnson was described by the local newspaper as being "an efficient officer and very popular." Regrettably, neither of those positive attributes will stop a bullet.

Officer Johnson was survived by his young wife. The couple had been married only six weeks.

DENTON COUNTY CONSTABLE'S OFFICE

Griffin, George Elbert
Born circa 1865—Died 10 December 1898

On 10 December 1898, three men were drinking in Lewisville when they decided to "paint the town red." For entertainment, the threesome began riding their horses down the sidewalks while, at the same time, randomly discharging their pistols. Precinct 3 constable Griffin and a man named Harrison obtained a buggy and went after the revelers. Two of the would-be merrymakers were riding double, and the third man was riding his own horse. The single rider rode away. The constable ordered one of the remaining two men off the horse and searched him. He found a knife and an axe, which he then returned to the individual. As he began to search the second man, the first man struck him with the axe that the constable had just returned to him. The blow hit Griffin just above his kidneys, penetrating into the hollow of the body. Griffin fell, mortally injured. The two men fled. Harrison took the constable back to Lewisville, where he later died.

It is unknown if any of the three men involved in the gruesome murder of Constable Griffin were ever apprehended and brought to justice.

DENTON COUNTY SHERIFF'S OFFICE

Coberly, Floyd
Born circa 1862—Died 23 February 1897

Jailer Coberly was making his rounds when he was attacked by an inmate who was in the process of attempting an escape. The inmate, George Henry, beat Coberly with a blunt object and killed him. Henry was charged with the murder and convicted. He was hanged for the crime on 18 February 1898.

Coberly was thirty-five years old and had served for only ten days at the time of his death. He is buried at Little Elm Cemetery in Frisco.

DeWitt County Sheriff's Office

Faust, Edward
Born circa 1839—Died 18 October 1869

Woods, Henry Gonzalvo
Born circa 1816—Died 29 November 1869
Date of incident: 18 October 1869

Deputy Faust and a posse that included Henry Gonzalvo Woods went to the homestead of John Kerlick in DeWitt County, near Yorktown. The posse was sent there to arrest Christopher Kerlick for the stabbing death of Thomas Lockhart. That killing had occurred several weeks earlier, on 24 September 1869, in Harris County.

When the posse reached the residence, they were told that Kerlick was not at home. There are several inconsistent accounts as to what triggered the gunfight that followed that day, but the interpretation of the local newspaper claimed that after the members of the posse had searched the house and were preparing to leave, several members of the Kerlick family opened fire on them. The shooting left Deputy Faust dead and posseman Henry Woods mortally wounded. At least one other posseman was also injured in this exchange.

The following day, the sheriff organized a posse and returned to the Kerlick house to arrest Christopher and William F. Kerlick. Not long after the group started back toward Clinton, the two young men attempted to escape and were shot by the guard. Both were killed.

The tragic irony of this story is that two days before this incident the Harris County Grand Jury had determined that it did not have sufficient evidence to charge Christopher Kerlick and had, to use a legal term, "no billed" him. This information had not yet reached the lawmen. The communication delay, or failure, cost the lives of two lawmen and two citizens.

Faust was reported to have been thirty years old and a native of Germany. His place of burial has not been located. It is unknown if he had any surviving family members.

Woods was fifty-three years old and a former captain in the Confederate army. He was survived by his wife. Woods is buried at Woods Cemetery at Yorktown in DeWitt County.

Morgan, James B.
Born (Unknown)—Died 16 April 1873

One account alleges that Morgan was the chief deputy sheriff under Sheriff Jack Helm and that he had been directed to arrest the notorious John Wesley Hardin. Another account claims that Morgan was an Irish stonemason who may or may not have been a deputy at the time of the incident.

In any case, on 16 April 1873, Morgan confronted Hardin inside a saloon in Cuero and insisted that Hardin buy him a drink. Hardin went outside and was followed by Morgan. Morgan attempted to pull his pistol, but Hardin, the notorious pistoleer, was quicker on the draw. Hardin's bullet struck Morgan over the left eye and killed him instantly.

In 1877, the DeWitt County Grand Jury indicted Hardin for the murder.

While in prison in 1898 for the murder of Brown County deputy sheriff Charles Bell, Hardin wanted a pardon. He decided to plead guilty to manslaughter for killing Morgan and received a two-year concurrent sentence.

Christman, John W.S. "Jake"
Born 26 December 1836—Died 15 May 1873

Cox, James W. "Jim"
Born 1823—Died 15 May 1873

Jack Helm and Jim Cox were two of the original four state police captains appointed when the Texas State Police organization was created on 1 July 1870. Both men were aligned with the Sutton faction during the Sutton-Taylor Feud. Helm was also the sheriff of DeWitt County, and Cox rode with Helm's "Regulators." The infamous outlaw John Wesley Hardin was a member of the opposing Taylor faction.

One account claimed that on 15 May 1873, a DeWitt County posse of five deputies led by Joe Tumlinson was ambushed by about forty men from the Taylor faction. It was claimed that Hardin and Jim Taylor had organized the attack. It is unknown if Hardin was present. Another account indicated that Cox was returning from Helena, where he had gone to answer an indictment, and that Tumlinson, Christman and an another man had ridden along with him. What is known for certain is that Christman was killed outright, and Cox was wounded and fell from his horse. Cox allegedly had his throat cut by one of the killers. On 17 May 1873, members of the Taylor faction were successful in their efforts to kill Sheriff Helm.

Christman was married and had two children. Cox was a widower with five children.

Helm, John Marshall "Jack"
Born circa 1839—Died 17 May 1873

Without question, Jack Helm was a highly controversial character. Those interested in the story of Helm should consult the bibliography section for books about Helm and the Sutton-Taylor Feud.

In June 1869, General J.J. Reynolds, the military commander of Texas during Reconstruction, appointed C.S. Bell and Helm as special officers to deal with outlaw bands, including the "Taylor Party." Helm went to Austin and became the leading figure in the band of special officers known as the "Regulators." Throughout July and August 1869, the Regulators carried out a reign of terror in Bee, San Patricio, Wilson, DeWitt and Goliad Counties. It was reported that they killed twenty-one people in two months, turning over only ten to the civil authorities.

On 23 August 1869, Bell and Helm arranged a second attack on Taylor's ranch near Noxville during which Hays Taylor was killed and "Doboy" Taylor was wounded.

On 3 December 1869, Helm was elected sheriff of DeWitt County. He was appointed on 23 March 1870 by General J.J. Reynolds and served until his death. After the founding of the Texas State Police on 1 July 1870, Jack Helm was appointed one of the four captains. On 26 August 1870, his detachment arrested Henry and Will Kelly, of the Taylor faction, on a trivial charge. Helm killed both of them. He was suspended in October and subsequently dismissed in December. He continued to be a menace while serving as sheriff during and after his tenure as captain of state police.

On 17 May 1873, Sheriff Helm was shot and killed by Jim Taylor and John Wesley Hardin. The killing was the result of years of feuding during the Regulator-Moderator War and the Sutton-Taylor Feud. His misdeeds had finally caught up with him.

Helm is buried at McCraken Cemetery in DeWitt County.

Sutton, William E. "Bill"
Born 20 October 1846—Died 11 March 1874

On occasion, Bill Sutton served as a DeWitt County deputy sheriff. In March 1868, he led a posse of citizens to Bastrop to locate thieves who had stolen a saddle and some livestock. When they tried to arrest the men, Charley Taylor and James Sharp, a shootout erupted during which Taylor and a bystander were killed. En route back to DeWitt County, the posse shot and killed Sharp near Lockhart and left his body along the roadside.

Murder charges were filed in Bastrop County, but no one was ever tried. On 24 December, Buck Taylor and his cousin, Dick Chisholm, got into a gun battle with Sutton at a saloon in Clinton. That fight resulted in the deaths of both Taylor and Chisholm. Once again, no charges were pursued against Sutton. The often violent animosity between the Sutton and Taylor factions resulted in another famous Texas feud, appropriately called the Sutton-Taylor Feud. This vendetta eventually led to many more deaths.

In August 1870, Texas State Police captain Jack Helm deputized Sutton and three other men to arrest the four Kelly brothers for a shooting disturbance in Lavaca County. The Kelly brothers were related to the Taylors. William and Henry Kelly were arrested, and while en route to Lavaca County both were shot and killed by possemen. Sutton, "Doc" White and C.C. Simmons were indicted for the murders. All were found not guilty at a trial in October 1871. Sutton continued as a deputy sheriff under Sheriff Jack Helm when Helm took over that office after having resigned from the state police. Jim Taylor attempted to kill Sutton at a saloon in Cuero, but the wounds were not fatal. On 4 April 1873, Jim Taylor and John Wesley Hardin killed Sheriff Helm.

The end came for Sutton on 11 March 1874 in Indianola. Sutton, his wife and some friends were boarding a steamer when Jim and Bill Taylor opened fire on them, killing Sutton and Gabe Slaughter. Both men were buried at Evergreen Cemetery in Victoria. Sutton's wife was pregnant at the time of his death.

On 26 May 1874, John Wesley Hardin killed Brown County deputy sheriff Charles M. Webb in Comanche. Bill Taylor was convicted and sentenced to ten years in prison for the murder of Slaughter. When he was standing trial for the murder of Sutton, a hurricane struck Indianola and he escaped. On 18 November 1875, Jim and Bill Taylor, along with A.R. Hendricks and Mason Arnold, shot and killed former Cuero City marshal Rueben "Rube" Brown in revenge for his support of the Sutton faction. On 27 December

1875, a posse led by DeWitt County deputy Dick Hudson, a Sutton supporter, confronted Jim Taylor, Arnold and Hendricks in Clinton and killed all three outlaws. Bill Taylor was eventually arrested on a rape charge in 1882 but was acquitted and quickly disappeared. He was reportedly killed in Oklahoma in 1895. One author claimed that he died in the line of duty as a peace officer, but no evidence can be found to substantiate that allegation.

Related cases: Brown County Sheriff's Office—Charles M. Brown; Cuero City Marshal's Office—Reuben "Rube" Brown; DeWitt County Sheriff's Office—Jack Helm; and Texas Rangers—A.R. Hendricks.

Lampley, Judge Edward
Born circa 1855—Died 28 February 1876

Henderson County deputy Goethry called on Sheriff Weisiger of DeWitt County for assistance in the arrest of a man named Joseph Allen. Allen was wanted for killing a man in Henderson County.

J. Agee, a DeWitt County citizen, was deputized by Sheriff Weisiger to take a posse and assist Deputy Goethry in the arrest. The posse also included a young man named Judge Edward Lampley, who was not a lawyer or magistrate.

On 28 February 1876, the posse approached the house of Allen and demanded that he surrender. Deputy Agee found Allen hiding in the house. Allen sprung from concealment and fired at Agee, grazing his forehead. At that point, several people in the house, along with members of the posse, all began shooting. Agee was shot in the leg with a load of buckshot. Allen was wounded several times. After being shot, Allen was dragged back into the residence amid a hail of gunfire. It was during this exchange of fire that Lampley was killed. It is unknown exactly who shot him.

Lampley was twenty-one years old at the time of his death. He was not married. Lampley is buried at Old Clinton Cemetery.

King, Martin V.
Born circa 1835—Died 2 October 1876

On 27 December 1875, Jim Taylor, Mason Arnold and A.R. Hendricks were in the town of Clinton and had just stabled their horses at King's Livery. The men were wanted for killing former Cuero city marshal Reuben "Rube"

Brown. A posse confronted the outlaws at the livery. When they tried to flee, they found that the stable doors had been locked. A shootout soon began, and all three men were killed by the posse.

On 2 October 1876, jailer Martin King, owner of King's Livery and a blacksmith by trade, was shot and killed while playing cards. After discovering that he had been cheated at a card game, he rose from the table and began to walk out of the saloon. At that point, someone shot him in the back, wounding him mortally. Another man was wounded in the same incident. There were rumors that King was killed because he had indirectly caused the killing of Taylor, Arnold and Henricks when he had locked the stable doors a year earlier.

Jailer King was survived by his wife, Margaret, and five children.

Related cases: Cuero City Marshal's Office—Reuben "Rube" Brown; Texas Rangers—A.R. Hendricks.

DIMMITT COUNTY SHERIFF'S OFFICE

Marshal, William
Born circa 1861—Died February 1885

Marshal was a member of a posse involved in the pursuit of some Mexican bandits who had stolen about 150 head of horses from the San Palo Ranch in Dimmitt County on 30 December 1884. The posse, which was led by Sheriff Joseph Tumlinson, crossed the border and pursued the bandits about two miles into Mexico, where they ultimately overtook the thieves. The bandits fired at the posse, killing one horse. The posse camped by the old Alaminta Crossing and sent word back to Texas that they needed reinforcements. Ranger captains Hays and Shelley responded and were eventually involved in this battle with the bandits. During the ensuing shootout, posseman Marshal was hit by gunfire and died from his wounds.

Marshal is believed to have been unmarried. His burial records have not been located.

Donley County Constable's Office

Green, James Frederick
Born circa 1859—Died 5 July 1892

By means of background, James Green was a Donley County deputy sheriff and a former Texas Ranger. He was not an inexperienced gunfighter. On 26 May 1888, four years before his death, Ranger Sterling Price and his friend James Green were at a bordello in Quanah in Hardeman County. Price got into an argument over a woman with a cowboy named Tom Ferguson. Ferguson left but returned with a Winchester. Price and Green shot and killed Ferguson.

On 5 July 1892, the train arrived in Clarendon in Donley County with James F. Green, who was now a Donley County constable. He was accompanied by G.B. Grissom, who was an inspector for the Stock Raisers' Association of North-West Texas (present-day Texas & Southwestern Cattle Raisers Association), and a man named D.A. Peel. The three men went into a saloon. Potter County sheriff R.M. Worden was also in the barroom but was unarmed. Coincidentally, the Bell brothers, R.W. "Bob" and Eugene, were in the same drinking establishment at the time. Green had arrested one of the Bell clan and had sent the man to prison for cattle rustling. As a result, a feud existed between Green and the Bells. Bob Bell spotted Green and opened fire on him. A stray bullet hit Inspector Grissom and killed him. Bell continued to shoot, hitting Constable Green and delivering a mortal wound. Green fired several times at the Bell brothers. He managed to kill Bob Bell before dying from his wounds. Eugene Bell was arrested. It is unknown if he was ever convicted of any charge.

Green was elected constable for Precinct 2 in Donley County on 4 November 1890. The newspaper reported that Green had killed a black man six weeks earlier in Clarendon while attempting to arrest him. Green enlisted in the Texas Rangers on 1 September 1881 and served until 10 October 1887. He served under Captain G.W. Arrington in Company G and Captain S.H. McMurry in Company B. He was reportedly buried at Donley County, but the grave site has not been located.

Related case: Texas & Southwestern Cattle Raisers Association—George Bingham Grissom.

DUVAL COUNTY CONSTABLE'S OFFICE

Reyna, Clemente Benavides
Born circa 1850—Died 6 February 1893

Hayes Dix and Andrew Valls were involved, or were about to be involved, in a fistfight at a bar in Benadives in Duval County. Constable Reyna, an amputee with only one arm, stepped up and attempted to grab Dix and separate the pair. Dix pushed Constable Reyna away. He lost his balance and fell to the ground. While being shoved backward, Constable Reyna drew his pistol. A man named E.A. Glover, who was also in the barroom at the time with Dix and Valls, spoke to Reyna several times, demanding him to stop pressing the matter and allow the men to settle their differences. Glover persisted, attempting to prevent the constable from shooting. As Constable Reyna raised his gun to fire, Glover shot him in the head with a double-barreled shotgun. The blast killed him instantly.

Glover was indicted in the District Court of Duval County for the murder of Constable Reyna. The venue was changed to the District Court of Webb County. Glover was found guilty of manslaughter. He was sentenced to two years in the penitentiary. The case was appealed and on 25 April 1894 and was reversed and remanded.

Reyna was elected Precinct 2 constable on 8 November 1892. He took office on 1 January 1893 and remained in that office until his death. No burial or family information on Constable Reyna has been located.

EL PASO COUNTY CONSTABLE'S OFFICE

Krempkau, Gus
Born circa 1856—Died 14 April 1881

A Texas Ranger and a group of armed cowhands from a Mexican ranchero went to the El Paso County ranch of John Hale. There they found three stolen cattle. Two Mexican cowhands remained behind to continue the search for additional stolen livestock. On 14 April 1881, seventy-five armed Mexican cowboys rode into El Paso looking for the two missing vaqueros. Constable Krempkau accompanied the Mexican cowboys to the Hale ranch, where they located the bodies of their two companions. Ranger Fitch arrested two of Hale's cowboys, who were bragging about killing the Mexicans.

The bodies were brought into town, and an inquest was held. A large crowd gathered, including John Hale and his friends. There was a great deal of animosity among Anglos about the armed Mexicans being in the city. The bilingual Constable Krempkau was asked to interpret for the judge. At noon, the court decided to recess and let the crowd disperse. Former El Paso city marshal George W. Campbell confronted Krempkau and accused him of favoring the Mexicans. Hale approached Krempkau and shot him once in the chest. Krempkau slumped against a saloon door but had enough strength left to pull his own gun.

City Marshal Dallas Stoudenmire came running toward Hale. He fired one quick shot at him but accidentally hit and killed a bystander named Jose Perez, who was a peanut vendor from San Elizario. Both Krempkau and Stoudenmire now began shooting at Hale. One bullet hit Hale in the head, killing him. Campbell, who did not want any part in the fight, had pulled his own gun. Krempkau, who was dying, shot Campbell in the gun hand and in the foot. Stoudenmire shot Campbell in the body. Campbell dropped in the street. He died the next day. In total, four men died as a result of this shootout. The incident had lasted less than one minute.

Very little can be confirmed about Krempkau. He was evidently appointed constable when a candidate failed to make bond after the November 1880 election. He is believed to have been from San Antonio and to have served as a Texas Ranger under Captain Baylor. His father also served as a Texas Ranger in 1852–53.

Krempkau is buried at El Paso but is believed to have been reburied in San Antonio. No records of his grave site have been located.

Related case: El Paso Police Department—George W. Campbell.

Conlova, Jesus
Born (Unknown)—Died 11 July 1890

For some months, ill feelings had existed between rival political factions at Ysleta in El Paso County. The discord had grown out of differences in the recent municipal elections. The Republican incumbent, J.G. Goal, was defeated for mayor by the Democrat Beanigro Alderette. Goal refused to give up his office. Alderette sued and won, but the strife continued. Goal sent armed men to stop some of Alderette's men from working. Alderette swore out a warrant against Goal. On 11 July 1890, Constable Bryant and

City Marshal Carbojal attempted to serve the warrant on Goal. Goal and his men were confronted and refused to surrender. A fight broke out during which one of the constable's possemen, Jesus Conlova, was shot and killed. Several men on both sides were wounded in the exchange of gunfire. Sheriff James White arrested Goal, George Allen and fifteen other men. Goal was charged with murder.

No personal information is known about Jesus Conlova at this time.

Chavez, Leon
Born circa 1858—Died 9 December 1894

On 9 December 1894, a man named Antonio Aquirre, who worked at Judge Richardson's dairy, found the dead body of Deputy Constable Chavez lying in an arroyo behind the cow barn. Chavez was reported to have been the deputy constable at Towne, which is an El Paso suburb.

Chavez had been stabbed under the fifth rib. The knife had penetrated his heart. A blood trail led to the saloon of Aquirre Mendoza. Blood was found on the door and inside the saloon. Evidence indicated that Chavez was stabbed as he entered the saloon. Blood was also found on the shoes and coat of Jesus Aquirre, a bartender. The bartender admitted that Chavez was in the saloon that night but left at 9:30 p.m. in the company of a number of Mexicans. The bartender claimed that he closed the bar at that time, but witnesses said that it was open past midnight.

Mendoza, Aquirre and five other men were arrested. It is not known if anyone was ever convicted of the murder. The motive for this crime is also unknown. One newspaper account stated that Chavez had resigned as a deputy constable several days earlier over concerns about his safety.

Chavez's place of burial is unknown. He was survived by his wife, Ignacia Garcia, and daughter, Felipa.

Selman, John Henry, Sr.
Born 16 November 1839—Died 6 April 1896

Over the years, a great deal has been written about John Selman and his son. It would be impractical to attempt to cover his entire life story in this brief biographical sketch. Interested readers should review the bibliography section for more information on Selman.

John Selman was an outlaw and a lawman, oftentimes simultaneously. He served as a deputy for Shackelford County sheriff John M. Larn. The two controlled the vigilantes, rustled cattle and often terrorized the county until the vigilantes shot Larn to death in a jail cell. Selman fled to Lincoln County, New Mexico, and organized the "Selman Scouts," a band of desperadoes accused of murder and rape during the late 1870s. In 1880, Selman headed to Fort Davis in Jeff Davis County, where he was involved with outlaw Jessie Evans in a cattle rustling and butchering operation. Texas Rangers captured him and took him to Shackelford County for trial. He escaped, however, and fled to Chihuahua, Mexico, where he lived until 1888, when the charges were dropped.

Selman moved to El Paso and lived mostly as a gambler and constable for Precinct 1. On 5 April 1894, he killed Deputy U.S. Marshal and former Texas Ranger sergeant Baz Outlaw during a wild brawl outside Tillie Howard's sporting house. Outlaw was stopped by Texas Ranger Joe McKidrick. Outlaw in turn shot McKidrick and killed him. Constable Selman shot and killed Outlaw but was seriously wounded in the affray.

John Selman killed the famous gunman John Wesley Hardin from ambush on 19 August 1895 by putting three bullets in him as he rolled dice at the Acme Saloon. Selman was tried for the murder of Hardin, but a hung jury resulted in him being released on bond.

Late one night, after leaving the Wigwam Saloon, Selman met Deputy U.S. Marshal George Scarborough. The two fought. During an exchange of gunfire, Scarborough shot Selman four times. Selman died on the operating table on 6 April 1896. Scarborough resigned as a deputy U.S. marshal and was acquitted of the murder. On 5 April 1900, he was working as a detective for a cattle raisers association in New Mexico when he was shot and mortally wounded chasing train robbers.

John Selman is buried at El Paso's Concordia Cemetery in the Catholic section, but his grave is unmarked. All attempts to locate it have been unsuccessful.

Related cases: Shackelford County Sheriff's Office—John Larn; Texas Rangers—Joe McKidrick; and U.S. Marshals Service—Baz Outlaw.

Karr, Samuel M. "Sam," Sr.
Born (Unknown)—Died 7 March 1899

On 7 March 1899, Constable Sam Karr and R.G. McGonagill went to a saloon and dance hall. Karr was in a bad mood and was complaining that the city police were monopolizing all of the petty business and were depriving him of his fees. Karr met El Paso policeman John Denniston and asked him to have a drink. Karr became intoxicated and launched into a verbal assault about the police force. Next he threatened to slap Officer Denniston. Denniston wisely decided to remove himself from the situation and started to leave. Karr pulled his pistol. McGonagill attempted to disarm him. Karr threatened to kill any officer who tried to arrest him. In spite of that warning, Denniston approached Karr and told him he was under arrest.

By this point, both men had their guns drawn and at the ready. Karr reached around McGonagill and fired, striking Denniston in the chest. In a remarkable twist of fate, the officer's whistle stopped Karr's bullet from penetrating his body. The stunned but not seriously injured Denniston fired back three times. His first bullet struck Karr in the jaw. The bullet ranged upward to his brain. Karr fired again, this time striking Denniston in the left hand and wounding a bystander named Alex Cooper. Denniston fired once more, this time striking Karr in the forehead and killing him.

Karr had been in El Paso six to eight years and had previously served as a customs guard and deputy sheriff of Martin County. He is buried at Evergreen Alameda Cemetery in El Paso.

EL PASO COUNTY SHERIFF'S OFFICE

Ellis, Charles E.
Born circa 1835—Died 12 December 1877

Ellis was appointed sheriff on 26 May 1871 and served until 2 December 1873.

The El Paso Salt War began in the late 1860s. It was a political struggle between Anglo entrepreneurs desiring to acquire title to the salt deposits at the foot of Guadalupe Peak (one hundred miles east of El Paso) and Tejano citizens wanting the salt flats to remain open to the public. Feelings between the two groups erupted into open warfare in 1870. In 1872, Charles Howard tried to claim ownership of the salt flats, an act that outraged local citizens, who seized Howard and released him on bond only upon the promise that he would leave the state.

On 10 October 1877, Howard returned and killed a rival political leader. On 11 November 1877, Lieutenant John B. Tays took command of newly organized ranger detachment of Company C. Howard was arraigned for the murder and freed pending trial.

Howard was guarded at an adobe house the rangers used as quarters in San Elizario. The Tejanos gathered, roped Howard's associate and former El Paso County sheriff, Charles Ellis, and dragged him through the streets, slashing him to death with knives and mutilating his corpse.

Sheriff Ellis had held his office since 1869. A native of Maine and a California veteran, he settled after the war in San Elizario, where he became a general merchant. He wed Teodora Alarcon in 1870—according to El Paso historian C.L. Sonnichsen, she "was large and stately and gracious, like her house." Their hacienda, the old Casa Ronquillo, was grand by any standard. According to the 1870 Census, the Ellises were the wealthiest residents in San Elizario.

Mortimer and McBride have their own sections in this text. We have shortened this Salt War story here after Ellis is killed because the full story is located in the Texas Rangers section.

Related cases: Texas Rangers—C.E. Mortimer and John E. McBride.

EL PASO POLICE DEPARTMENT

Campbell, George Washington
Born 23 December 1850—Died 15 April 1881
Date of incident: 14 April 1881

Campbell served as a deputy sheriff in Clay County from 1876 to 1880. He drifted to New Mexico and may have served as a deputy sheriff or cattle raisers association detective. On 1 December 1880, Campbell became the city marshal of El Paso. He was known to frequent sporting houses and was friendly with the Manning brothers, who ran several local saloons. Campbell resigned at the end of December 1880.

On 14 April, seventy-five armed Mexican cowboys rode into El Paso looking for two missing vaqueros. Constable Krempkau accompanied the Mexican cowboys to the nearby Hale ranch, where they located the bodies of their two companions. On 14 April, Ranger Fitch arrested two cowhands from the John Hale ranch who had been bragging about having killed the Mexicans.

The bodies were brought into town, and an inquest was held. A large crowd gathered, including John Hale and his friends. There was a great deal of animosity among Anglos about the armed Mexicans being in the city. The bilingual Constable Krempkau was asked to interpret for the judge. At noon, the judge called a recess to let the crowd disperse. During the interlude, Campbell confronted Krempkau, accusing him of favoring the Mexicans. Hale approached Krempkau and shot him once in the chest. Krempkau slumped against a saloon door but had enough strength left to pull his own gun.

City Marshal Dallas Stoudenmire came running toward Hale. He fired one quick shot at Hale but accidentally hit and killed a peanut vendor named Jose Perez, who was an innocent bystander and happened to be visiting from a nearby town. Seeing the incident, both Krempkau and Stoudenmire opened fire at Hale. One shot struck Hale in the head, killing him almost instantly. Campbell, who did not want any part in the fight, had also pulled his gun. Krempkau, mortally wounded from Hale's earlier assault, shot Campbell in the gun hand and in the foot. Stoudenmire shot Campbell, inflicting a serious wound that resulted in Campbell's death the following day.

In total, four men died during this celebrated shootout that lasted less than one minute.

Related case: El Paso County Constable's Office—Gus Krempkau.

Cummings, Samuel M. "Doc"
Born (Unknown)—Died 14 February 1882

Cummings was the brother-in-law of El Paso city marshal Dallas Stoudenmire. Stoudenmire was out of town getting married, and Chief Deputy James Gillett was ill. Cummings had little experience and had mainly been in charge of feeding the prisoners.

On the night of 14 February 1882, Cummings was drinking heavily at the Globe Restaurant and Variety Theater. Cummings asked Jim Manning to drink with him and brought up the previous year's shooting, when Manning had been accused of hiring an assassin to kill Stoudenmire. Manning denied the accusations, but Cummings cursed him as a liar. The bartender, David King, asked the men to leave and take their disagreement to the street and settle it there. They did so but soon returned to the bar, where Cummings continued to berate Manning relentlessly. In the act of going for his drink, Cummings instead went for his revolver. He was a bit late. Manning fired first, and Cummings was hit twice.

In an interesting twist, upon examination after the incident, Manning's revolver was found to have had but one empty chamber, giving rise to the belief that David King, the bartender, may have fired the second shot that killed Cummings.

Moad, Thomas P.
Born (Unknown)—Died 11 July 1883

On 11 July 1883, Nicholas Biddee, Howard H. Doughty, Dr. Wear and two other men attended the National Theater. Apparently, the production didn't suit them, because Doughty became drunk, insulted one of the actors and then threw a whiskey glass at him.

Next, the erstwhile theatergoers went to a sporting house and initiated another disturbance during which Howard Doughty broke a panel in the door. As the group left the first establishment and started along their way to a second bordello, they were followed by a policeman. The parties had reached their destination, where Doughty was reclining on a sofa, as Assistant City Marshal Moad entered with his pistol drawn. Seeing the officer, Doughty drew his pistol and shot Moad through both lungs and the heart, killing him almost instantly.

Doughty fled to Mexico but was eventually apprehended. He was convicted and served five years in prison.

Moad is buried at the cemetery on Fort Bliss Boulevard in El Paso. He was a private in Company C of the Frontier Battalion of the Texas Rangers under Lieutenant John Tays from about December 1878 to September 1879. His name has been mistakenly reported as "Mode."

ELLIS, COUNTY OF

Cain, Charlie D.
Born 28 February 1869—Died 9 July 1891

During this era in Texas history, many counties operated "poor farms" and "convict farms." These were correctional facilities at which the inmates were required to work off their sentence, fines or debts. The county, and not the sheriff, employed the armed guards. Ellis County operated a poor farm from 1883 until the early 1960s.

In the late afternoon of 9 July 1891, Charlie Cain was returning with the convicts who had been working in the fields all day. Cain stepped on a watering or feeding trough and stumbled. He was carrying his shotgun by his side. During the fall, he apparently struck the hammer in some manner, causing the weapon to discharge accidentally. The load of shot passed through his right hand and entered just beneath the right jawbone, traveling upward. He died in two to three hours.

The newspaper reported that he was a young man of good standing in the community and was the brother-in-law of the manager of the poor farm. He is buried at Waxahachie City Cemetery.

ENNIS POLICE DEPARTMENT

Bullard, Joseph C.R.
Born circa 1850—Died 19 August 1880

City Marshal Bullard was shot and killed by a man named Sid Alexander. Alexander had been arrested the previous day for public intoxication and disorderly conduct. When he was released from custody, he immediately proceeded to shoot and kill Marshal Bullard.

Alexander was arrested and later convicted of murder. He was sentenced to life in prison.

Marshal Bullard is buried at Waxahachie City Cemetery.

ERATH COUNTY CONSTABLE'S OFFICE

Adams, John A.
Born 18 October 1845—Died 18 December 1897

Adams had come to Texas from Louisiana about ten years after the end of the Civil War. He became the Precinct 2 constable in about 1879. During the course of his tenure as constable, Adams had a disagreement with a local man named Thomas A. Wright, also known as "Little Tom." Wright was a known bootlegger and, on at least one occasion, an arsonist.

On 18 December 1897, the quarrel between the two men came to a deadly conclusion. Some time earlier, Constable Adams had threatened to shoot Wright, armed or unarmed, if he saw him in town again. Wright was intoxicated and had borrowed a gun from a man named Tom Leslie when he came to town. Wright ambushed Constable Adams. The first shots from Wright's gun hit Adams in the back of the head. Adams immediately fell to the ground. With Adams already lying on the ground, suffering from the effects of the first two gunshot wounds to the head, Wright fired again at the fallen man. This time the bullets hit him in the body.

Two other men, Dick McCain and a man named McCarty, were implicated of complicity with Tom Leslie in this crime. Wright was arrested, convicted and sentenced to death for the murder. On 11 November 1899, he was hanged at the county jail in Stephenville.

Constable Adams was survived by his wife and three children. He is buried at Old Dublin Memorial Park Cemetery in Dublin.

Erath County Sheriff's Office

Mastin, James
Born circa 1837—Died 25 June 1877

Sheriff Mastin was shot and killed when he and Deputies Handsel and Cozby went to the Wolfe farm three miles from Stephenville to arrest a horse thief named Bonaparte "Bone" Wilson from Palo Pinto County. After the lawmen had searched the Wolfe house, they went outside to examine the area. Wilson suddenly stepped out from behind a tree and opened fire on the officers, mortally wounding Sheriff Mastin. The deputy returned fire, wounding Wilson.

Wilson escaped, but on 15 September 1877, a posse of Texas Rangers led by Captain John Sparks caught up with him near Snyder and killed him in a shootout.

Mastin is buried in an unmarked grave. He was elected sheriff on 15 February 1876 and served until his death.

Robertson, Marion David
Born circa 1853—Died 29 March 1879

Ross, John T.
Born circa 1850—Died 29 March 1879

Erath County deputy sheriff W.H. King deputized John T. Ross, Marion Robertson and Eli Keith to assist him in serving a warrant on a man named John Russell "Russ" Holloway for a forged bill of sale for a horse and for unlawfully carrying a pistol. When the lawmen arrived at Holloway's farm near Stephenville on the evening of 29 March 1879, they discovered that members of the family were holding a prayer meeting. Deputy King approached Holloway, shook hands and announced that he had a warrant for his arrest. King asked Holloway if he was armed. He replied, "Yes, but none of your sort will get them" as he stepped back and threw open his coat.

One of Russ Holloway's brothers, Joe, grabbed a pistol from Russ. John Ross threw up his hands and asked for peace. A shootout commenced. Russ fired one shot and then dashed to the other side of the house, with Robertson following him. A bullet struck Robertson, who staggered and collapsed. Another Holloway brother, Jim, took a gun from over the fireplace and fired a shot. Keith, who was outside the house, saw Ross fall, stand and attempt to return fire.

During the gunfight, Deputies Robertson and Ross were both killed. Two members of the family were said to have been wounded.

Three men in the family were charged with murdering the deputies. Russ and Joe Holloway were acquitted. Jim Holloway was sentenced to thirty-five years. A fourth member of the family turned himself in forty-eight years later to face charges of murder.

Robertson and Ross had both been deputized that day to assist with the arrest. Both are buried at Old Dublin Memorial Park. Robertson's surname is listed as "Roberson" in several references. It is unclear which is correct; however, given that his name is inscribed as "Robertson" on his tombstone, the authors have chosen that rendering.

Falls County Constable's Office

Sharp, Henry
Born (Unknown)—Died 14 September 1878

Constable Sharp was reportedly a man of desperate disposition when he was drinking.

On the evening of 14 September 1878, Sharp, who was up for reelection in November, approached a man named Cato Woods at the town of Reagan and asked him for his vote. Sharp had been drinking that day, and during his conversation with Woods something was said that displeased Woods. Woods broke and ran, with Constable Sharp in close pursuit, brandishing his drawn pistol. He shot Woods, wounding him mortally. After the shooting, Sharp became more desperate and swore that he would "take the town." Deputy Sheriff M.M. Coleman, hearing the disturbance, attempted to arrest Sharp. Sharp then fired at him. Coleman shot Sharp twice. He died of his wounds.

On 18 September 1905, M.M. Coleman was serving as the city marshal of Marlin when he was shot and killed in the line of duty.

Loftin, Thomas H.
Born circa 1868—Died 25 December 1894

Deputy Constable Loftin of Precinct 7 was accidentally shot and killed when he responded to a disturbance at a local bar. When he pulled out his weapon, someone struck his arm, causing the firearm to accidently discharge. The bullet from the gun struck him in the neck, killing him.

Loftin was born in Alabama in 1868 and had been living in Hardin County with his brother and family. His place of burial has not been located.

Breeland, Samuel S.
Born circa 1857—Died 7 June 1899

Precinct 6 constable Breeland was shot from ambush while leaving the courthouse to serve several warrants. His wounds were fatal. The main suspect in the shooting turned himself in, but he was later acquitted due to a lack of evidence.

Constable Breeland had served with the agency for eight months. He was survived by his wife and nine children.

Breeland is buried at Calvary Cemetery in Marlin.

FALLS COUNTY SHERIFF'S OFFICE

Tubbs, J.C.
Born (Unknown)—Died 4 January 1887

J.C. Tubbs was reported to have been the former sheriff of Falls County. There is no record of him having served as sherriff, so it is presumed that he had been a deputy.

At 10:00 p.m. on 4 January 1887, Tubbs was called from his residence to visit a neighbor who was said to be dying. When he had traveled only about three hundred yards from his home, he was attacked by three assailants and shot through the body. A bullet entered near his left nipple, and the wound proved fatal.

Although the assassins were not identified, the newspaper accounts of the day claimed that they were men whom Tubbs had previously arrested.

FANNIN COUNTY CONSTABLE'S OFFICE

Hill, Russell B.
Born 3 April 1850—Died 15 December 1887

On 15 December 1887, Precinct 4 constable Hill was shot accidentally by a man named Peck near the town of Ladonia. Hill was killed instantly. Constable Hill and Mr. Peck were out hog hunting at the time the accident occurred.

Hill is buried at Ladonia Cemetery.

Dunn, Morris T.
Born 8 February 1850—Died 26 May 1888

By means of background, on 11 May 1885, Fannin County sheriff Thomas A. Ragsdale and Deputy Joseph R. Buchanan were shot and killed by the four Dyer brothers. Eli and Sam Dyer were lynched by an angry mob. Jim and Joe Dyer managed to escape.

On 26 May 1888, Precinct 7 deputy constable Dunn left Bonham with a posse of men in pursuit of the Dyer brothers' gang. They located the group at a log cabin on the Diamond Ranch in Indian Territory, just over the Red River about seven miles north of Elwood. During the encounter, Deputy Dunn was shot and killed by one of the outlaws. His death was not discovered until daylight the following morning. A posseman returned to Bonham for reinforcements, who were promptly dispatched and led by Sheriff Evans. Joe and Jim Dyer, along with a third man named Thomas Hughes, gave the posse the slip and managed to escape. They ultimately surrendered to Deputy U.S. Marshal Andy J. Fryer of the Oklahoma Territory several days later on 31 May near Fort Smith, Arkansas. The gang claimed that Deputy Dunn had forced the fight on them and that they had acted in self-defense.

On 16 March 1889, the trial of Jim and Joe Dyer and Thomas Hughes was concluded at Fort Smith, Arkansas. The three were found innocent on the grounds that Dunn's posse had no authority or jurisdiction to pursue the men into Indian Territory. The trio contended that the posse's objective was to bring them back to Texas and lynch them for their complicity in the killing of Sheriff Ragsdale, an allegation that was probably quite accurate. Jim Dyer was later shot to death by John McHenry near Island Bayou in Indian Territory.

Deputy Dunn is buried in an unmarked grave in Fannin County. He was survived by his wife and three children.

Related case: Fannin County Sheriff's Office—Thomas A. Ragsdale and Joseph R. Buchanan.

Milstead, Thomas E.
Born circa 1858—Died 14 February 1898
Date of incident: 10 February 1898

Precinct 1 constable Milstead, along with Fannin County deputy sheriffs C.B. "Charley" Bridge, Dailey Parish and June Riddling, went to the community of Mulberry in northern Fannin County to arrest Will Green and Bob Hunter. The men were wanted for selling illegal whiskey and carrying pistols.

Constable Milstead and Deputy Sheriff Bridge knocked on the front door of the home where the two men were reportedly staying. When Green opened the door, they advised him that they had a warrant for his arrest. Green immediately drew a pistol and began firing at the officers. Milstead was struck in the face by the gunfire but still managed to draw his gun and charge into the house. In the process, he killed Green. The constable then engaged in a desperate struggle with Hunter. Milstead, who was by then weak from the loss of blood, was thrown down on a bed by Hunter, who was trying to shoot him. Bridge came to Milstead's rescue and shot and killed Hunter.

Milstead's wounds were fatal, he having been shot five times during this episode. He died four days later. Bridge was seriously wounded by the gunfire but did not die.

Constable Milstead was survived by his wife. He is buried at Willow Wild Cemetery at Bonham in Fannin County.

Fannin County Sheriff's Office

Ragsdale, Thomas A.
Born circa 1840—Died 11 May 1885

Buchanan, Joseph R.
Born circa 1831—Died 12 May 1885
Date of incident: 11 May 1885

Sheriff Ragsdale and Deputy Buchanan were shot and killed as they attempted to serve warrants on a pair of suspected horse thieves.

As the officers approached the home of the two horse thieves, brothers named Sam and Eli Dyer, the pair opened fire on them, killing the sheriff and mortally wounding the deputy. Deputy Buchanan died the next day. The Dyer brothers were arrested, but angry local citizens saved the county the time and expense of trial by lynching the pair before they could be brought to trial.

Ragsdale was elected sheriff on 4 November 1884 and served until his death. He was survived by his wife. He is buried at Elizabeth Grove Cemetery in Savoy.

Deputy Buchanan was survived by his wife. He is buried at Buchanan Cemetery at Randolph.

Related case: Fannin County Constable's Office—Morris Dunn.

Douglass, W.K.
Born circa 1864—Died 16 April 1886

On 15 April 1886, Special Deputy Douglass arrived at Atlanta in Cass County. He was searching for some persons wanted in Fannin County for horse and cattle theft.

Douglass went to Mrs. White's boardinghouse, where he shared a room with Marshal Parker. He retired to bed. At 5:00 a.m. on 16 April, he arose, dressed and washed. He asked Parker where his pistol was and was told that it was under his pillow. As Douglass picked up the gun, it discharged accidentally. The bullet entered Douglass's right cheek and came out through the back of his head. He fell dead without uttering a word.

An inquest was held, and the death was determined to be accidental. Douglass is believed to have been born in Arkansas and to have come to Texas in about 1880, living there with the Sears family in Fannin County. He is buried near Whitewright in Grayson County.

Holland, Benjamin F.
Born circa 1833—Died 6 February 1892

When Deputy Holland arrived on the scene in the town of Laconia, about fifteen miles from Bonham, he found a man named Tom Mitchell holding a gun on a deputy sheriff. Mitchell was a local black schoolteacher. When Holland attempted to arrest Mitchell, he shot him in the left side.

Mitchell was brought to Bonham by way of the railroad. Deputies stopped the train some distance from the depot and took Mitchell directly to the jail so as to avoid the possibility of a lynching, which had been threatened by local citizens after hearing the news of this incident.

Mitchell was tried and convicted of the killing and received a sentence of ten years in prison for the crime.

Holland is buried at English Cemetery in Bonham. He was survived by his wife and one child.

Haskins, Richard "Dick"
Born circa 1851—Died 19 January 1898

Dick Haskins and J.W. McKee were both employed as jailers and assigned to the county lockup in Bonham.

The two men became engaged in a quarrel, the point of which has long since been lost to history. The argument escalated, and McKee shot Haskins one time in the nose. The bullet exited the back of his head, inflicting a fatal wound. McKee had been the former constable.

FAYETTE COUNTY CONSTABLE'S OFFICE

Pivoda, John
Born 7 July 1866—Died 31 August 1894
Date of incident: 30 August 1894

On 30 August 1894, Constable Pivoda was acting as the Schulenburg city marshal in the absence of City Marshal Henry Ellers.

Constable Pivoda had received a writ from Luling in Caldwell County to arrest a man. At about 10:00 p.m., he went to the freight depot to look for the wanted person, and from the suspicious sounds emanating from a box car he speculated that several men were inside gambling. Pivoda walked up to the car, stuck his head through the door and asked who was in there. Someone replied, "Who are you?" An instant later, a shot was fired. The bullet struck Constable Pivoda about three inches below the left nipple, ranging downward and inflicting a fatal wound. The constable managed to fire one shot and then collapsed.

The men in the boxcar fled. The mortally wounded constable was taken home, where he expired at 9:00 a.m. the following day. In his dying statement, he identified a man named Rhine (or Ryan) Stewart as his assassin.

Stewart was a local gambler. A $200 reward was issued for his arrest, and in February 1895 the sheriff obtained extradition papers on Stewart, who was reported to be hiding in Mexico. It is unknown at this time if Stewart was ever arrested and tried for the murder of Constable Pivoda.

Pivoda was born at Herrnitz, Germany. He was elected the constable for Precinct 8 on 8 November 1892. Pivoda is buried at St. Rose of Lima Catholic Cemetery in Schulenburg.

Null, Charles Henderickson
Born 15 August 1848—Died 8 August 1896

By means of background, Bunk Stagner had been among the largest cattle raisers in the county, but he had fallen on hard times. Stagner was suspected of being involved in cattle rustling. Local cattle raisers hired a detective agency to identify the thieves, and in July 1891 Bunk's oldest son, Charles, was charged with eight counts of cattle theft. He was never brought to trial. In 1894, Bunk's son William was shot and killed by a neighbor while hunting stray cows. In 1895, Charles Stagner was again arrested in Bastrop County, convicted and sentenced to four years in prison.

In December 1892, Null was elected constable in Precinct 5 at Muldoon. On 8 August 1896, Constable Null was ambushed and assassinated by several men while he was riding to the precinct courthouse to obtain a warrant for the arrest of Bunk Stagner. Null was shot three times and, while on the ground, was shot in the back of the head. Several days earlier, Null had said that he had evidence against one of the rustlers who was in prison. He is also quoted as having said, "My life is in danger and I expect to be killed."

On 10 September 1896, the constable's sons, Will and George, along with the neighbor who had killed Bunk's son William, caught up with Bunk. Bunk tried to explain everything, but Will Null shot him with both barrels of a shotgun.

Will Null was tried for the murder of Bunk but was never convicted. Several years later, the sheriff interrogated Jim Nite while he was in the state prison. He admitted that he and his now deceased brother Jud were paid $500 by Bunk to kill the constable.

Constable Null was survived by his wife, Rebecca, and five children. He is buried at Byler Cemetery in Muldoon.

FAYETTE COUNTY SHERIFF'S OFFICE

Gardenier, Aaron A.
Born (Unknown)—Died June 1845

Sheriff Gardenier was elected on 30 October 1843 and served until his death. He was shot and killed in a duel that had grown out of a disagreement over the results of an election to a convention.

Menn, Otto
Born circa 1867—Died 9 November 1898
Date of incident: 8 November 1898

Menn was the resident deputy sheriff at Carmine. On election day, some of the young men of the city were creating a disturbance, and Deputy Menn warned them to be quiet. Harsh words followed, and one of the men, Albert Brau, stabbed Menn in the abdomen. Menn died the next day. Brau was arrested, but the disposition of the case is unknown at this time.

Menn is buried at Carmine Cemetery. He was survived by his wife, Marie; his daughter, Olga, who was just one month old; his parents; and at least eight brothers and sisters.

FISHER COUNTY SHERIFF'S OFFICE

Mitchell, William L. "Brack"
Born 8 January 1829—Died 23 April 1899

At about 2:00 p.m. on 23 April 1899, Deputy Mitchell arrested Frank Anderson and Will Simpson near Eskota. Eskota is in Fisher County and is located about ten miles from Sweetwater. He was transporting the prisoners in a buggy to the county jail in Roby when Anderson made an escape attempt by grabbing his pistol. The two men started struggling and fell from the buggy. Not surprisingly, the twenty-five-year-old Anderson overpowered the seventy-year-old Mitchell and then shot the officer in the top of the head. The wound was fatal. Anderson turned the pistol on Simpson, who knocked the gun away and shot Anderson. Simpson called the sheriff and said that he would remain at Eskota until authorities arrived.

Mitchell was also the elected constable for Precinct 5. He is buried at Sweetwater Cemetery in Nolan County.

FOARD COUNTY CONSTABLE'S OFFICE

Beverly, Andrew Young
Born 31 October 1867—Died 24 December 1893
Date of incident: 23 December 1893

On 23 December 1893, Sheriff S.J. Moore and Precinct 1 constable Beverly were arguing over some papers that had been sent to Collin County to be served. Sheriff Moore shot and fatally wounded Constable Beverly. Beverly, in turn, shot and wounded Moore in the thigh. Beverly died the following morning.

Constable Beverly is buried at Old Plano Cemetery in Collin County.

FORT BEND COUNTY SHERIFF'S OFFICE

Morton, John V.
Born circa 1805—Died 7 February 1843

Sheriff Morton was killed by his deputy, George W. Pleasants, at Richmond in what is said to have been a personal disagreement.

He was survived by his wife, Elizabeth Shipman, and three children.

Blakely, Jacob W. "Jake"
Born circa 1839—Died 16 August 1889

Garvey, James Thomas "Tom"
Born circa 1860—Died 16 August 1889

The Reconstruction period in the South may have officially ended in 1877, but the Republican Party had gained a stronghold in many counties with the support of freed black voters. Congress removed the civilian governments in the South in 1867 and put the former Confederacy under the rule of the U.S. Army. The army now conducted all elections. Freed slaves could vote, while white men who had held leading positions under the Confederacy were denied that right. They were also banned from running for public office.

In ten states, including Texas, coalitions of freedmen, recent arrivals from the North (carpetbaggers) and white southerners who supported Reconstruction (scalawags) cooperated to form the Republican state governments that introduced various Reconstruction programs that were often marred by widespread corruption. Violent opposition emerged in numerous localities. Democrats calling themselves "Redeemers" regained control state by state, sometimes using fraud and violence to control state elections.

A feud broke out in Fort Bend County in 1888 between wealthy white Democrats called "Jaybirds" and Republicans called "Woodpeckers." The Woodpeckers had held power since Reconstruction. The feud crossed racial, social and politics lines. Assassinations and violence had become commonplace. Sheriff Garvey was a leader of Woodpeckers and opposed the efforts of the Jaybirds to return to power through violence. The town was an armed camp. The governor sent Texas Rangers to maintain order.

On 16 August 1889, the Jaybirds faced off against the Woodpeckers in front of the courthouse. Sheriff Garvey and a crowd of armed men warned the Texas Rangers to get out of the way, claiming that the fight was none of their business. Ranger sergeant Ira Aten and four privates on horseback tried to block the two sides from fighting. Nonetheless, a gun battle ultimately erupted during which Sheriff Garvey was killed. Two Jaybird leaders— Garvey's uncle and former sheriff J.W. Blakely and H.H. Frost—were killed. An innocent bystander was also killed. Numerous participants were wounded. Ranger private Frank Schmid Jr. was critically wounded and later died from his injuries on 17 June 1893.

Garvey was appointed sheriff in October 1886 and was elected on 2 November 1886. He was reelected on 6 November 1888. Ranger sergeant Ira Aten, who was trying to maintain order that day, was appointed sheriff on 21 August 1889.

Blakely was appointed sheriff on 25 September 1876 and was elected on 5 November 1878. He served until 2 November 1880. His son, Thomas M. Blakely, was elected on 2 November 1880 and was reelected on 7 November 1882 and again on 4 November 1884. He served until October 1886, when he resigned.

Hoffman, Heinrich Wilhelm
Born circa 1867—Died 19 February 1893
Date of incident: 17 February 1893

Deputy Hoffman was shot and killed after being "set up" by patrons of a local saloon who were not fond of him.

It seems that Deputy Hoffman had a notoriously bad temperament and was disliked for the fact that he had arrested some of the saloon's patrons in the past. On 17 February 1893, a group of locals managed to get a man named Jody Wade drunk. They then called Deputy Hoffman to come and arrest him. The men did so knowing that the chances of a shootout were highly probable. When Deputy Hoffman arrived at the saloon, Wade drew his weapon and shot Hoffman. Hoffman returned the fire, killing Wade. Hoffman died two days later.

Hoffman was survived by his wife and two sons.

FORT WORTH POLICE DEPARTMENT

Fitzgerald, Columbus C.
Born circa 1842—Died 26 August 1877

Deputy Marshal Fitzgerald was shot and killed while attempting to settle a dispute over a horse racing bet.

Fitzgerald was in the process of trying to break up a fight between two men who were arguing over the bet. He was shot and killed by one of them. He managed to return fire and fatally shoot his murderer before dying from his wounds.

Fitzgerald had served with the agency for five years. He was survived by his wife and two children. Fitzgerald is buried at Pioneer Rest Cemetery in Fort Worth.

White, George H.
Born (Unknown)—Died 8 August 1879
Date of incident: 2 August 1879

Deputy Marshal White died from a gunshot wound he received six days earlier when he was ambushed by the family of a man named George Alford.

White had traveled to Arlington with a man who claimed he had bought a horse that had been sold to him illegally by a man named Alford. While in Arlington, Deputy Marshal White arrested Alford for selling the horse and started back toward the city with the prisoner. During the course of the journey back to Fort Worth, Alford's family ambushed them, opening fire and hitting White with a blast from a shotgun. White was able to return fire. He killed one of his assailants and wounded another.

Alford was apprehended and sentenced to five years in prison. The conviction was eventually overturned on an appeal due to a technicality regarding Deputy Marshal White's swearing in.

White is buried at Pioneer Rest Cemetery in Fort Worth.

Wise, W.T.
Born circa 1862—Died 2 October 1884

Deputy Marshal Wise was shot and killed in Oxford, Mississippi, while working undercover in an effort to apprehend two men who were wanted for murder in Texas.

Wise had gone to Oxford to return a prisoner to the local sheriff. While in town, the sheriff requested Wise's assistance in capturing two men. Wise returned to Fort Worth, where he was given permission by the city marshal to return to Oxford and help with the investigation.

Upon his return to Mississippi, Wise disguised himself as a cattle buyer and made contact with a man who was close to the suspects. The man agreed to help Wise in exchange for part of the reward money. Wise devised a plan to slip the man a "Mickey Finn." A Mickey Finn, or simply a "Mickey," involved secretly mixing a drug such as chloral hydrate with whiskey and then giving it to the unsuspecting recipient. Once the drug took effect, Wise planned on taking the man into custody. The informant betrayed Wise, however, and told the man about the plan. As Wise approached the suspect's home, he was ambushed. The man shot him with a shotgun and a pistol and then hastily buried his body on the side of the road, where it was not discovered until the following day by a search team.

Three men were eventually apprehended. Two of the men were acquitted. The third man, Doc Bishop, was found guilty and was eventually hanged in Pittsboro, Mississippi, on 3 July 1886.

Wise had been with the agency for eighteen months and was survived by his wife. He is buried at the Serepta, Mississippi cemetery.

Waller, C. Lee
Born circa 1874—Died 30 June 1892
Date of incident: 28 June 1892

Officer Waller died from gunshot wounds he received two days earlier when he and his partner were shot by three men at Twelfth and Rusk Street.

The two officers were on foot patrol in the Acre section of the city, a notoriously rough part of town. By some reports they were "on the prod" and were looking for the two individuals they eventually encountered. A disturbance took place, and harsh words were exchanged. One of the men, a fellow named Burris, left the scene and obtained a pistol. Burris then recruited two friends, one of whom was Jim Toots, to help him even the score. Later in the evening, Burris and his colleagues waylaid the two officers. During the ambush, Burris shot Officer Waller four times.

Burris was apprehended in Big Spring and convicted of capital murder. He was sentenced to death, but the sentence was commuted to life in 1895. He received a full pardon in 1902. His two colleagues died in the penitentiary.

Waller had been with the Fort Worth Police Department for two years. He is buried at Hico Cemetery in Hamilton County.

Franklin County Constable's Office

Tedder, William
Born circa 1867—Died 3 December 1892

Precinct 3 constable Tedder was shot and killed while attempting to settle a rent dispute.

Tedder and a property owner went to the residence of a tenant regarding nonpayment of rent. While at the residence the tenant, Alexander Spencer, prepared coffee and went to a neighbor's house on the pretense of borrowing coffee cups. Although Spencer returned without the cups, he had used the interlude to arm himself with a Winchester. In lieu of coffee, Spencer turned the gun on Tedder, killing him instantly.

Spencer was convicted of murder and sentenced to life in prison.

Tedder had served as constable for three weeks. He is buried at Greyrock Cemetery.

Franklin County Sheriff's Office

Morgan, Robert
Born (Unknown)—Died 5 April 1879

Deputy Morgan relieved the sheriff at the county jail so he could eat a meal. After Morgan had taken his post, the prisoners—Ed Murphy, M.J. Allen, Sam Wilson, John Blake, Emanuel Daniel and John Red—staged a jailbreak in an attempt to free one of the men. Apparently, one or more of the prisoners had somehow obtained pistols, because Deputy Morgan was shot and killed in a gun battle that took place with the would-be fugitives. He was, however, able to wound one of the men during the exchange of fire.

All of the prisoners were later apprehended. All were charged with burglary, and two were charged with murder.

Deputy Morgan is buried at Mount Vernon City Cemetery.

Freestone County Sheriff's Office

Rogers, James Bonner
Born 27 November 1836—Died 3 April 1872
Date of incident: 30 March 1872

Early on 30 March 1872, three men—the first identified only as "Garrett," the second as George Storey and the third as Jesse Dove—arrived in Fairfield. Sheriff Rogers suspected that they were horse thieves and went to speak with them at the Planter's Hotel. A man identified by some sources as Wood, but who was more likely Deputy Blood Noland, accompanied the sheriff.

The three suspected horse thieves were sitting in front of the establishment having a conversation. Sheriff Rogers asked the three men to go inside the hotel with him. When they refused, he told them to consider themselves under arrest. At that point, Storey drew his army six-shooter and shot Sheriff Rogers. The bullet entered through his back and came out under his left breast. Deputy Noland, who had either accompanied the sheriff or joined the group in the meantime, drew his revolver and shot Storey, killing him instantly. Dove and Garrett fled the scene. According to witnesses, Deputy Noland would have killed the remaining two men had it not been for the darkness.

Rogers lingered until 3 April, when he finally died from his wounds. He was elected sheriff on 3 December 1869. Rogers was survived by his wife and four children and is buried at Fairfield Cemetery.

Dove was quickly apprehended near Thornton Depot. On 10 April 1872, a group of unknown persons overpowered the guards and removed Dove from jail. Neither Dove nor the group of jailbreakers were ever located. The third fellow, the man named Garrett, escaped and was never found.

Galveston County Sheriff's Office

Kelly, Patrick William
Born circa 1840—Died 20 July 1891
Date of incident: 14 July 1891

On 14 July 1891, a mentally ill inmate at the Galveston County Jail brutally beat jailer Kelly. The inmate attacked him, striking and kicking him repeatedly. The assailant then pulled Kelly into a cell, where he continued to thrash him mercilessly, stomping on his chest and stomach. The prisoner had to be forcibly restrained in order for Kelly to be rescued and receive medical attention. Kelly died six days after the vicious attack.

Kelly had served with the sheriff's office for five years and was survived by his wife and three children. He is buried at Old Catholic Cemetery in Galveston.

GALVESTON POLICE DEPARTMENT

Israel, D.C.
Born circa 1835—Died 3 December 1868

Israel, who was a native of Connecticut, had come to Texas from Opelousas, Louisiana. He was reported to have been a former Galveston policeman who traveled to El Paso to serve as a juror in the District Court of the United States. He left for the interior of Texas mounted on a Mexican horse and accompanied by a guide. His body was found near the *Laguna of Tio Cano* (Lagoon of the White Uncle). He had been beaten to death and robbed of all of his possessions.

Ferguson, John T.
Born circa 1843—Died 6 April 1873

Officer Ferguson was killed while responding to a report of a mentally deranged man who was stabbing citizens. When Ferguson approached the man, James B. Helm, he thrust his knife into the officer's heart, killing him instantly.

At Helm's trial, Ferguson's distraught son shot and killed his father's murderer in the courtroom.

Ferguson had been with the agency for five years and was survived by his wife and two children. He is buried at Old Catholic Cemetery at Galveston.

Giddings Police Department

McKeown, Hugh
Born 21 January 1841—Died 4 May 1877

City Marshal McKeown had a long-standing feud with Lee County sheriff James M. Brown. At about 6:00 p.m. on 4 May 1877, their quarrel came to a fatal end when Sheriff Brown shot and killed McKeown. Brown was arrested but was later released on $1,500 bail.

Brown was apparently not convicted, because he continued to serve as sheriff until 1884. On 11 October 1878, Sheriff Brown performed the first legal hanging in Lee County when he executed the infamous outlaw William Preston "Bill" Longley.

McKeown is buried at Giddings City Cemetery.

Goliad County Sheriff's Office

Jacobs, Andrew Jackson
Born circa 1819—Died 5 June 1869

Jacobs was appointed sheriff by U.S. Army general J.J. Reynolds on 15 July 1868. On 27 March 1869, Sheriff Jacobs wrote to federal military authorities about the lack of law and order in Goliad and asked for assistance. General Reynolds issued an order removing Jacobs as sheriff on 3 June 1869, but it does not appear that the order reached him before his death. On 5 June, two brothers, James Madison "Matt" and Christopher "Chris" Peace, shot and killed Sheriff Jacobs.

The Peace brothers were arrested and indicted on 25 August 1869. The pair had murdered Jacobs because they felt he "showed partiality in making arrests." After being released to await trial, the two men left the area. Matt Peace died in 1872. Chris Peace was tried and acquitted on 19 April 1878.

Sheriff Jacobs's son, William "Will" Jacobs, became an outlaw and was involved in the killing of Guadalupe County deputy sheriff Richard "Texas" McCoy, Deputy U.S. Marshal Frank Rhodes and Milam County deputy sheriff Gabriel Leander "Lee" Pool.

Jacobs was buried in Goliad and was survived by his wife and several children.

GONZALES COUNTY SHERIFF'S OFFICE

Stinnett, Claiborne
Born (Unknown)—Died March 1838

Claiborne Stinnett was the second sheriff of Gonzales County, elected on 27 January 1838. He followed the famed Matthew Caldwell, who was first sheriff of the county.

There are conflicting reports concerning Sheriff Stinnett's death. One report asserts that he was killed by Indians. Another account of his death alleges that it was two runaway slaves who killed him and that the pair later fled to Mexico. Although the exact date is unknown, he was killed in March 1838.

Claiborne Stinnett was the third husband of Sarah Creath. Indians killed her first husband, John McSherry, in 1828 and her second husband, John Hibbens, in 1836. She and her two children were captured. The Indians killed the infant child. She managed to escape from her captors. Soon after, Texas Rangers recaptured the second child. Sarah married her third husband, Stinnett, in 1838. As cited earlier, the unlucky Stinnett was killed the same year. In 1840, she married her fourth husband, Phillip Howard. This time her fate, and that of her husband, changed. Sarah died in 1876, after nearly forty years of marriage to Howard. Phillip Howard outlived Sarah and finally died on 6 April 1894.

Little, Albert
Born circa 1854—Died 8 February 1888
Date of incident: 6 February 1888

Deputy Albert Little died from a gunshot wound he received on 6 February 1888 while attempting to arrest a man named Charles Jackson, alias Hicks, on a warrant for theft.

Deputy Little had gone to Jackson's home with a posse and knocked on the door of the cabin. When Jackson asked who was calling, Little responded that he was "an officer." Jackson immediately fired three shots through the door. One bullet struck Little in the abdomen.

A member of Little's posse carried him to a nearby home and summoned a doctor. A local constable led a posse back to the Jackson home and forced their way into the cabin. Jackson opened fire on the constable. The constable returned fire and mortally wounded Jackson.

Little was survived by his wife. He is said to be buried in an unmarked grave at Coe Valley Cemetery.

Coleman, Robert R.
Born circa 1853—Died 4 November 1896
Date of incident: 3 November 1896

Deputy Coleman was apparently involved in a feud with the Rhodes family. He had previously arrested Claud Rhodes for gambling, much to the displeasure of the family.

On 3 November 1896, which was election day in the town of Waelder, Ed Rhodes pulled his hat off, waved it around above his head and said, "Hurrah for Bryan and free silver by God!" Coleman reportedly approached Ed Rhodes, grabbed hold of him and said, "If you don't be quiet, I will put you in the calaboose." Bill Rhodes then walked up to Coleman and said, "Coleman, you are no officer, and can't arrest anybody." Coleman replied, "Sheriff Jones requested me to preserve the peace, and I will arrest him if he cuts up." Bill Rhodes then cursed Coleman. Coleman immediately drew his pistol and struck Bill Rhodes with it. The blow knocked him to the ground, inflicting a severe wound to his head that bled profusely. Another member of the Rhodes clan, Claud Rhodes, got a pistol and gave it to Bill.

Bill Rhodes charged at Coleman with gun drawn. Colemen drew his revolver, and both men fired until they had emptied their guns. Now out of ammunition, they continued the fight by hitting each other with their now empty guns. The gruesome spectacle continued as the exhausted men took to the street. Ed Rhodes hit Coleman in the head with a billiard cue. Yearby Rhodes tried to stab Coleman but was held back by the crowd.

Coleman died from the effects of two gunshot wounds he had received during the exchange, one of which had entered his right side and traveled through his body, breaking the breastbone. The other entered above and to the right of the left nipple and became lodged against the skin near the backbone. He lived until the next day. Bill Rhodes lived about a week and died from the effects of the wounds he had received.

Ed Rhodes was convicted of murder in the second degree. His punishment was assessed at confinement in the penitentiary for a term of seven years. He appealed, and the case was reversed and remanded for improper jury charge.

The comment "Hurrah for Bryan and free silver by God" made by Ed Rhodes refers to William Jennings Bryan (1860–1925), who was a congressman from Nebraska, three-time presidential candidate (1896, 1900 and 1908) and, later, secretary of state under President Woodrow Wilson. In 1896, Bryan faced an uphill battle as the Democratic and Populist nominee. Democrats held the White House for the previous four years and were widely blamed for the severe economic depression of 1893. Furthermore, sitting President Grover Cleveland disapproved of Bryan's nomination. Many Democrats abandoned the party to form the Gold Democrats or to vote for McKinley.

DeLeon, Lallero "Laddie"
Born (Unknown)—Died 27 January 1898

At about 10:00 a.m. on 27 January 1898, Deputy DeLeon, who lived on the Henry Caldwell ranch, came to Gonzales and notified Sheriff Glover that a gang of horse thieves were hiding in the county. An informant had advised him that the men intended to raid a pasture that night and steal some horses. The sheriff and his deputies were tied up with criminal court and could not assist. The sheriff told DeLeon to find some men to assist him and to capture, or kill, the thieves.

DeLeon located three assistants and waited for the would-be horse thieves. About midnight, the expected perpetrators arrived near where DeLeon had positioned himself. He ordered them to halt and surrender, but instead they opened fire. A heated gun battle quickly commenced. DeLeon was shot through the heart with a bullet from a Winchester. He died instantly.

It was reported that a posse later surrounded the rustlers in Wilson County. Refugio Garcia, who later fled to Mexico to avoid prosecution, was reported to be the killer of DeLeon.

GRAYSON COUNTY CONSTABLE'S OFFICE

Archer, Jack B.
Born circa 1834—Died 12 July 1871

Special Deputy Constable Archer was serving in the place of Precinct 1 constable J.L. Hall, who was transferring prisoners from Grayson County to the Texas State Prison in Huntsville.

Several days earlier, Deputy Archer had arrested Harvey Adams for carrying pistols. On 12 July, Archer was attempting to arrest a man named Corhorne for interfering in the earlier arrest of Adams. Adams came to assist Corhorne and shot and killed Archer. Archer had lost his right arm serving for the Confederacy in the Civil War and was unable to defend himself.

Deputy Caywood and a posse of about thirty citizens followed Adams. They caught up with him a few miles south of Cleburne in Johnson County. Adams refused to surrender and was shot and killed by a member of Sheriff Caywood's posse.

Archer was survived by his wife. No cemetery records have been located.

Stark, John
Born circa 1832—Died 20 February 1873

Precinct 5 deputy Stark was shot and killed when he and another deputy constable went to arrest suspected horse thieves. While the deputies were mounting their horses, someone opened fire on them from concealment. One of the bullets struck Stark in the head.

Stark had been with the agency for ten years and was survived by his wife and three children.

Nelms, James A.
Born circa 1843—Died 4 July 1879

Precinct 2 constable Nelms was shot and killed when he responded to a report of two drunken men fighting at a saloon. When he attempted to intervene, he was shot and killed by one of them.

Constable Nelms was survived by his wife and four children. No cemetery records have been located.

Hodges, Dallas
Born circa 1846—Died 5 May 1881

A desperado named Jim Lee and his companion, whose name was probably Bob Mallory, rode into Gordonsville on 5 May 1881. As Precinct 7 constable Hodges was attempting to question the men, they opened fire on him, killing him instantly. Two months later, on 8 July 1881, the same two men shot and killed Deputy Reuben Coleman of the Grayson County Sheriff's Office as he attempted to arrest them for Constable Hodges's murder.

Constable Hodges had been with the agency for two years. He was survived by his wife and nine children.

Related case: Grayson County Sheriff's Office—Reuben Coleman.

GRAYSON COUNTY SHERIFF'S OFFICE

Coleman, Reuben D.
Born circa 1852—Died 8 July 1881

Deputy Coleman was shot and killed as he and other deputies attempted to take a man into custody. The man was wanted in the murder of Grayson County constable Dallas Hodges, which had taken place two months earlier. Another outlaw subsequently murdered one of the suspected killers.

Coleman had been with the agency for three years. He was survived by his wife and three children.

Related case: Grayson County Constable's Office—Dallas Hodges.

May, Robert L. "Bob"
Born circa 1842—Died 26 May 1889

Two first cousins named Mandrew and Benjamin Isom arrived from Kentucky to stay with relatives in the village of Howe. The young men were lying about and drinking. They purchased firearms in Sherman and returned to Howe, where they became involved in a dispute at a saloon. The pair fled, with the city marshal in pursuit. Sheriff May along with Deputies Scott Creager and James May, brother of the sheriff, went to Howe to arrest the cousins.

The lawmen found the two Isoms, along with three other men, in the woods and ordered them to surrender. The Isoms each fired a Winchester at the sheriff. The sheriff managed to get off one shot in reply. The deputies later found the sheriff dead.

Mandrew Isom turned himself in and received forty years in prison. Benjamin Isom was captured and sentenced to life in prison.

Bob May had been elected sheriff on 2 November 1886 and was reelected on 6 November 1888. He is buried at Allison Cemetery in Gordonville.

GRIMES COUNTY CONSTABLE'S OFFICE

Hall, Joseph A. "Joe"
Born circa 1871—Died 16 April 1898
Date of incident: 15 April 1898

On 15 April 1898, a debating society met at the schoolhouse in Bedias. After the event had concluded, Precinct 7 constable Hall and others were standing by the side of the house, talking. Witnesses heard the sound of loud voices coming from the direction of the graveyard, in or near the public road. They called this to Hall's attention. Hall, who was unarmed at the time, got on his horse and started down the road in the direction of the disturbance. Shots were heard, and Hall was later found lying in the road, severely wounded. A physician was brought to the scene to treat his wounds.

Hall was suffering a great deal of pain and asked the doctor if he thought he would live. The physician told him that he did not think that he would. Hall agreed. He said that at the time of the shooting he had ridden up to a man and put his hand on his shoulder and said, "Consider yourself under arrest, brother." At that point, the man shot him. Hall was unable to identify his killer. He died from his wounds the next day.

A.H. Montgomery was indicted for the murder of Constable Hall in the District Court of Grimes County. Montgomery was convicted and sentenced to three years in prison. He appealed, alleging that Hall never identified himself as an officer. The appeals court reversed its decision and sent the case back to the lower court in Brazos County for a new trial. Montgomery was convicted a second time and sentenced to two years in prison. He appealed again, but the conviction was affirmed.

Hall is buried at Bedias Methodist Cemetery. He was survived by his wife, Stella, and three children: Edwin, Mariah and Joseph.

GRIMES COUNTY SHERIFF'S OFFICE

Smith, John
Born circa 1848—Died 14 December 1868

On 14 December 1868, Acting Deputy Smith was shot and killed by L. Adkins at the town of Anderson. The two men had had been involved in a scuffle earlier, during which Adkins cut Smith on the head and right side. Smith left and returned with a shotgun but fell over from exhaustion before he could fire the weapon at Adkins. Adkins then shot Smith five times using Smith's own gun while the deputy was lying on the ground dying.

GUADALUPE COUNTY SHERIFF'S OFFICE

McCoy, Richard "Texas"
Born circa 1830—Died 16 May 1881

Deputy McCoy was shot and killed in LaSalle County while searching for cattle thieves.

McCoy was riding with several Texas Rangers and cattlemen when they came upon about one hundred head of stolen cattle. The group rounded up the cows and took them to a nearby home to temporarily pen them up. Unbeknownst to McCoy, a notorious cattle thief named Will Hill owned that house. As McCoy asked Hill's wife if he could pen the cattle there, Hill and his friends were busy setting up an ambush. As McCoy opened the corral gate, Hill and several other men opened fire, killing McCoy. The assailants were Will Hill, James Wright and Will Jacobs.

Hill and one of his friends were charged with McCoy's murder. Because the informant was a known horse thief, his testimony was not enough to convict Hill. The charges against Will Hill were dropped in May 1882.

Will Jacobs was the son of Goliad County sheriff Andrew Jacobs, who was killed in the line of duty on 5 June 1869. Will was also involved in the killing of Deputy U.S. Marshal Frank Rhodes on 11 April 1885 and Milam County deputy sheriff Lee Pool on 7 April 1887.

Deputy McCoy was a veteran of the Confederate army. He had previously served as a Texas Ranger for one year. McCoy is buried at Sandies Chapel Cemetery in Belmont.

HAMILTON COUNTY SHERIFF'S OFFICE

Poe, James Dudley
Born circa 1855—Died 4 May 1886

James Poe was born in Tennessee in about 1855. The most reliable account of Poe's death claims that on 4 May 1886 he was shot and mortally wounded by William Dennis "Bill" Payne. Poe was apparently involved in an altercation with Payne, or a heated verbal exchange of some sort, over the treatment or ownership of a horse. Some accounts allege that Poe was shot in the back.

Poe is buried at Evergreen Cemetery, which is located about eleven miles east of Hamilton, near Whiteway. The precise location of his grave—which was unmarked, according to his family—has been lost to antiquity.

Deaton, Thomas J.
Born circa 1860—Died 8 December 1893

Deputy Thomas Deaton was shot and killed while he and a posse member were attempting to serve a warrant on a man who was wanted for several crimes.

The man, Jim Jones, saw the posse approaching his house and opened fire. Deaton was struck in the head and died from his wounds. Jones was arrested and convicted of killing Deaton. He later fled Texas with his brother, John. Both were killed in a train robbery in Colorado.

Deaton had been with the agency for ten years and was survived by his wife and three children. He had three brothers, all of whom were lawmen. Bill Deaton was killed while serving as a Montana ranger. Dave Deaton was sheriff of Erath County, and Thomas Deaton was sheriff of Comanche County.

HARRIS COUNTY SHERIFF'S OFFICE

Courts, Carl F.
Born circa 1858—Died 30 November 1895

Deputy Courts was shot from ambush while he was speaking with a store owner during a routine patrol in the town of Chaneyville. His wounds were fatal. The gunfire came from someone outside the store.

Several men were arrested, but none was charged with the shooting. Courts had served with the sheriff's department for five years. He had also been a constable. He was survived by his wife and one child.

HARRISON COUNTY SHERIFF'S OFFICE

Campbell, John B.
Born (Unknown)—Died 23 January 1841

By means of background, the "East Texas Regulator-Moderator War" was a feud that took place in Harrison and Shelby Counties between 1839 and 1844. The Regulators were organized to control cattle rustling and crime by means of vigilante justice. The Moderators were organized to restrain the vigilante actions of the Regulators. George May became the first elected sheriff of Harrison County on 12 February 1840. He resigned in late 1840. John B. Campbell, a medical doctor, was appointed to replace him.

William Pinckney Rose was the leader of the Regulators in Harrison County. Although he served as a private under Andrew Jackson at New Orleans, he was referred to as "Captain Rose." George W. Rembert and Isaac Hughes organized a Regulator posse to capture two thieves who were allegedly hiding in a cabin. It turned out to be a trap that had been set by Moderators, and Rembert was shot and killed.

Shortly afterward, a posse led by Sheriff Campbell found Hughes and ordered him to surrender. Hughes refused, and Campbell ordered the posse to fire. Hughes was killed in the exchange of gunfire. Hughes's brother sought revenge and was assisted by Rose. On 23 January 1841, Campbell was assassinated in Port Caddo by Hughes's brother. It is believed that Rose may also have been involved.

Robert Potter was the leader of the Moderators and saw the chance to get rid of his Regulator enemies. He charged Rose with the murder of Campbell and two other men. On 15 November 1842, President Mirabeau B. Lamar put a reward out on Rose in the amount of $500 for murdering Sheriff Campbell while he was discharging his official duties. On 1 March 1842, Potter formed a posse and attempted to arrest Rose and collect the reward. Rose was hidden by his slaves and evaded capture. On 2 March 1842, Rose formed a posse and surrounded Potter's cabin. Potter was shot and killed while attempting to escape across the lake. Potter's wife filed charges against Rose and nine posse members. The cases were dismissed in 1843.

Some accounts report that Campbell was the sheriff of Panola County, meaning the judicial county of Panola, which had been created from the eastern end of Harrison County. Judicial counties were held to be unconstitutional in 1842.

No other personal information is known about John B. Campbell except that he was a medical doctor and had moved to Texas in 1839. His place of burial and family history is unknown.

DeLisle, Leonard C.
Born circa 1834—Died 27 May 1869

Sheriff DeLisle went to a residence outside of Marshall to arrest a man named Stephen Lott. The sheriff was accompanied by another man on this trip. Lott had a history of mental illness and was wanted on a peace warrant. (A peace warrant is a written complaint, submitted under oath, from a person who fears that their life or property is under threat from another person. A peace officer, judge or mayor can issue a warrant for arrest, and the sheriff can bring the accused before a hearing judge to respond.)

When the sheriff and his companion arrived at the residence, they called Lott outside. Lott approached the fence, and Sheriff DeLisle told him that he was under arrest. Lott stated that he would not, and could not, be arrested. Lott then started back to the house. DeLisle stood up in his buggy and fired, striking Lott in the thigh. Lott then fired one shot, striking DeLisle in the head, killing him instantly. Lott died the next day from the gunshot wound to his thigh.

DeLisle had been appointed sheriff by the military authorities on 3 May 1869. He had served only twenty-four days in office when he was killed. He is buried at Marshall Cemetery, on East Grand Avenue in Marshall.

Harwood City Marshal's Office

Fly, James Milton
Born 12 February 1860—Died 21 October 1887

Harwood is located in Gonzales County. City Marshal Fly and a man named J.G. Booth had a dispute over a bill. On the evening of 21 October 1887, Fly went to Booth's son's store and an argument began. The quarrel escalated and eventually led to Booth shooting and killing Fly. Both men were well known and had many friends. Booth surrendered to the sheriff's office.

The disposition of the case is unknown at this time. Fly is buried at Gonzales Masonic Cemetery.

HAYS COUNTY SHERIFF'S OFFICE

Banks, Henry C.
Born circa 1852—Died 16 November 1873

H.C. Banks had resided for a few months in Stringtown and had been in the employment of Hays County sheriff Zachariah P. Bugg during the week preceding his death. On 16 November 1873, Deputy Banks was on his way to San Marcos when he passed the house of L.M. Dugger. A former slave was there named Mathew Burnham, who had been employed by Dugger for the preceding twelve months and had returned to the premises after an absence of about four days. Burnham packed his clothes in a blanket and, as he left the house, complained to Mrs. Dugger that he had not been treated well. Angry words were exchanged between the two.

At the time of the incident, Mr. Dugger was speaking to Deputy Banks and asked him for assistance. As Burnham reached the gate, he was met by Mr. Dugger. They exchanged harsh words. Banks dismounted and told Burnham, "Old man, you are drinking...you had better put down your bundle and wait until tomorrow before you go." Burnham replied, "And who are you?" Banks responded by saying, "I will show you who I am."

Banks drew his revolver. Burnham sprang forward and grabbed the pistol. As the men struggled for control of the revolver, Banks called out to Mr. Dugger for assistance. The conflict continued and the gun discharged. The bullet struck Banks near the base of his neck. Mr. Dugger fired at Burnham as he was stooping down to shoot the already wounded Banks in the side of the head as he lay on the ground. Dugger fired two more times and Burnham fled.

Burnham was eventually captured. He was brought before a grand jury and indicted on 18 November 1873. Burnham was convicted of first-degree murder and was sentenced to death. The Texas Supreme Court overturned his conviction in 1875.

Burnham was shot and killed by an unknown person in Austin in December 1875.

H.C. Banks was about twenty-two years of age. His mother and family resided in Alabama. Banks's place of burial was reported to have been initially in Hays County, with his remains having later been shipped to Alabama for final interment.

HEARNE POLICE DEPARTMENT

Bishop, Albert
Born 7 August 1848—Died 8 November 1883

By means of background, City Marshal Bishop was said to have been a dangerous person. He had killed several men during his time as a law enforcement officer, including a man named John Brown in June 1882. Bishop was convicted of that crime in February 1883 and sentenced to serve seven years in prison. After being acquitted, he ran again for city marshal and was elected on 21 August 1883 by a wide margin.

On 8 November 1883, City Marshal Bishop was shot and killed by a local lawyer named Oscar D. Cannon. It was claimed that there was a conspiracy on the part of Bishop to kill Cannon and that hard feelings existed between the two men. If so, Cannon beat Bishop to the punch.

Cannon was tried on 2 July 1884 and found not guilty.

Bishop was survived by his wife, Emma Jordan, and two sons, Elbert and Lawrence. He is buried at Hearne Norwood Cemetery.

HEMPHILL COUNTY SHERIFF'S OFFICE

McGee, Thomas T. "Tom"
Born 13 September 1848—Died 24 November 1894

McGee was the first elected sheriff of Hemphill County, having taken office on 5 July 1887. He was reelected on 6 November 1888, 4 November 1890, 8 November 1892 and 6 November 1894.

On 24 November 1894, there was a large shipment of cash scheduled to arrive from Wells Fargo at the train station in the town of Canadian. While responding to a call of suspicious activity at the train yard, Sheriff McGee was shot and killed as he entered the station.

One man named George Isaacs, who was suspected of being involved in the shooting, was convicted of murder and sentenced to life in prison. Somehow he was able to forge a pardon and was released. He fled to Mexico and was never captured.

McGee is buried at Canadian Cemetery.

HEMPSTEAD POLICE DEPARTMENT

Adams, John Howell
Born circa 1838—Died 6 November 1880

Deputy Marshal Adams was shot and killed while responding to a domestic disturbance. The man who was causing the problem was Peter Moore, an intoxicated ex-convict. While Adams was taking Moore into custody, Moore drew a handgun and shot him. The wound was fatal.

Adams had served with the city marshal's office for ten years and was survived by his wife and two children.

HENDERSON COUNTY CONSTABLE'S OFFICE

Rhodes, John E.
Born (Unknown)—Died 24 December 1898
Date of incident: 23 December 1898

On 23 December 1898, Precinct 6 constable Rhodes was shot and killed while attempting to arrest George, John and James Humphries, who were all wanted for stealing hogs. Rhodes spotted one of the men trying to hide behind some bushes alongside a road. When he ordered the man to come out, he opened fire with a rifle, mortally wounding Rhodes.

All three men were lynched by local citizens. James Patterson and five other mob members who were involved in the hanging went to prison for the lynching.

Rhodes had served with the agency for three years. His place of burial has not been located.

HENDERSON COUNTY SHERIFF'S OFFICE

Day, Rufus H.
Born circa 1839—Died 24 December 1879

Deputy Day and an assistant were transporting three prisoners whom they had arrested in the Indian Territory. The men—two brothers named Owens and a fellow named Henry Smith, who was a Baptist preacher—had been indicted in Henderson County for horse theft.

Day and his prisoners were on their way back to Henderson County when the group stopped at a farmhouse in Van Zandt County to spend the night. Smith somehow got possession of Day's pistol and then shot and killed him. Preacher Smith and the two Owens brothers escaped but were soon captured.

In May 1883, Smith was tried in Van Zandt County and sentenced to life in prison for the murder of Day. In October 1880, Elmer Owens was tried in Henderson County and sentenced to five years in prison for horse theft.

Day was survived by his wife and children. He is buried at Athens City Cemetery.

HIDALGO COUNTY CONSTABLE'S OFFICE

Guzman, Genovevo
Born circa 1855—Died 15 September 1895

At 6:00 p.m. on 15 September 1895, Constable Guzman was shot and killed along the banks of the Rio Grande River roughly twenty-two miles below Hidalgo. His assassin was a man named Zeferino Dominquez.

Guzman had a warrant for the arrest of Dominguez. He was going to make the arrest with another deputy named Zamora. The two lawmen met Dominguez on the public road. He was traveling with his brother, Felix, and a group of friends. Guzman attempted to make the arrest, but Dominguez resisted and went for his gun. During the exchange of fire that followed, Guzman was shot and killed and Zamora's horse was shot by Felix Dominguez.

The Dominguez brothers were arrested by troops of the Mexican army under the command of Colonel Mainero at Rosario, Mexico. During that gunfight, Zeferino was seriously wounded and Felix slightly wounded.

The disposition of the cases against the Dominguez brothers is unknown at this time.

Guzman was elected constable of Precinct 1 on 28 November 1894. He was survived by his wife, Francisca, and daughter, San Juan.

HILL COUNTY CONSTABLE'S OFFICE

Owens, Thomas "Tom"
Born circa 1857—Died 20 March 1875

Tom Owens was formerly a deputy sheriff. On 20 March 1875, Constable Owens and his brother Doug, along with another man named Franklin, were in the local post office. An argument of some sort took place between Owens and a group of three men that included John Warren. The disagreement was apparently regarding tobacco.

Soon a struggle between Warren and Owens began, during which Owens was severely stabbed in the neck and chest and shot several times in the buttock. Owens fell to the ground and drew his pistol. Someone in Warren's group wrenched the gun from the constable's hand and shot him in the head.

Warren and his two colleagues were arrested. The disposition of any charges is unknown.

HILL COUNTY SHERIFF'S OFFICE

Snead, John Carroll
Born 15 June 1834—Died 22 July 1869

Snead was appointed sheriff on 21 January 1867 and served until 20 May 1869, when he was disqualified. Former sheriff Snead was shot and killed at Mount Calm by an alleged horse thief named Alex Bell.

Snead was survived by his wife, Sarah Ann Webb, daughters Mary and Ella and son John. He is buried at Hillsboro Old City Cemetery.

HOOD COUNTY SHERIFF'S OFFICE

Truitt, James M.
Born circa 1840—Died 20 July 1886

James Truitt was shot and killed out of retaliation over an event that had taken place while he was a jailer more than a decade earlier in 1875.

By means of background, on 4 October 1875 Jailer Truitt shot and killed a man named Jeff Mitchell. Jeff Mitchell was trying to assist his seventy-six-year-old father Nelson in escaping from jail. The youngest of the Mitchell boys, twenty-three-year-old Bill, vowed revenge. Truitt resigned in 1886 and moved to Shelby County, but Bill Mitchell tracked him down and lived up to his earlier promise of mortal retaliation.

Truitt was shot and killed in the presence of his family and at his own home. Bill Mitchell was sentenced to life in prison.

Truitt had served with the agency for ten years. He was survived by his wife and six children.

HOUSTON COUNTY CONSTABLE'S OFFICE

Craig, T.C.
Born circa 1818—Died 27 April 1875

On the evening of 27 April 1875, a man named David Land stole a horse from M.C. Depuy at Colonel Tharps's place, located about eighteen miles from Crockett. Mr. Depuy and Precinct 3 constable Craig pursued Land, eventually overtaking him after a chase of about seven miles.

It was already dark by the time the men reached Land. He had already concealed himself in the bushes and fired several shots at Craig and Depuy. One shot struck Craig, killing him instantly. Another shot hit Depuy, seriously wounding him. One horse was also killed during the exchange of gunfire. Land emerged unscathed from the encounter and escaped.

On 1 May 1875, Land was captured by a group of men while asleep at a friend's house. He was bound to a horse by his feet and neck and taken ten miles away. The men said that they offered Land the ominous choice of "jail or death." They claimed that Land chose death over confinement in jail, so the group obliged and promptly shot him. His body was found riddled with buckshot and left in the woods.

A related and unfortunate incident occurred on 1 May at Phelps Station. Several citizens arrested a man who fit the general description of Land. When a deputy sheriff and constable arrived to investigate, they discovered that the man was named Tobe Morris. Morris was at Land's house the morning after the murder and saw Constable Craig's friends loading his body in a buggy. The lawmen decided to arrest Morris, but the citizens who had arrested him were intoxicated and demanded the $500 reward. A scuffle occurred during which a man named Arthur Davis shot and killed another citizen named J.H. Patrick.

Craig's place of burial is unknown. The state election records do not show that Craig was ever elected constable, but all newspaper articles refer to him as such. He may have been appointed to fill a vacancy, which was commonplace at the time.

Craig served in the Confederate army in Texas as a sergeant in Company A of the Eleventh (Spaight's) Battalion of Texas Volunteers. The regiment name was expanded to Eleventh Battalion, Texas Volunteers, Cavalry and Infantry.

HOUSTON COUNTY SHERIFF'S OFFICE

Lathrop, James W.
Born circa 1855—Died 9 January 1884

On the night of 9 January 1884, Sheriff F.H. Payne organized a posse to arrest a desperado named Sandy Robinson. Robinson, a black man, was found hiding in a cabin at the Bannerman plantation on the Trinity River in Leon County. As posseman Lathrop entered the cabin through the door, Robinson shot and killed him. He then grabbed Lathrop's weapon and fled. Robinson was later arrested and placed in the Houston County Jail in Crockett.

Sheriff Payne received information concerning a possible lynching attempt of Robinson and summoned a guard of ten or more men to stay at the jail. Only about six men and the sheriff were present when a mob of between seventy-five and one hundred masked citizens on horseback arrived at 1:00 a.m. on 3 February 1884. The sheriff begged the men not to take the prisoner out, but they overpowered him and took his keys. The sheriff succeeded in drawing his pistol, which discharged by accident during the scuffle. No one was injured. There were about ten prisoners in the jail at the time, but none of them was molested. The mob took only Robinson. The vigilantes promptly lynched him near the graveyard.

Lathrop was a farmer and was survived by his wife, at least one daughter and a stepson. His place of burial is unknown.

HOUSTON POLICE DEPARTMENT

Foley, C. Edward
Born (Unknown)—Died 10 March 1860

Officer Foley was shot and killed by a man named Michael Floeck. Officer Foley was patrolling in the market area when Floeck approached him and, for reasons unknown, attempted to interfere with his duties. Foley struck Floeck. Floeck then fled the scene, but he returned later in the day with a double-barreled shotgun and killed Foley.

Floeck was arrested, and his bail was set at $8,000. He was indicted for murder, but the case never came to trial. Floeck was from a prominent family. He died in 1891.

Foley's place of burial and family history are unknown.

Hager, Abraham L.
Born circa 1842—Died 22 February 1873

Officer Hager and a twenty-year-old printer named James A. Thompson became involved in some sort of dispute. The reason for the quarrel remains unknown. Hager pulled his pistol and told Thompson that he "meant business." Apparently, Thompson did as well, since he pulled his own pistol and shot the officer, delivering a fatal wound.

Thompson was arrested and held without bail. The final disposition of the case is unknown. Not surprisingly, the newspaper reported that public opinion favored Thompson.

Hager was a former Union soldier who had served with the Fifth Regiment of Vermont Infantry. He was buried by the Odd Fellows. The place of burial is unknown.

Snow, Richard
Born (Unknown)—Died 17 March 1882

On 17 March 1882, Officer Snow was at the home of a black man. He was keeping the peace at a church function being held there. A crowd had gathered, and at about 10:30 p.m. Snow believed that some trouble was about to take place, so he called for assistance. When Snow questioned a man named Henry Campbell, the man assaulted him. Campbell drew a pistol, and Snow attempted to take control of the weapon. Snow drew his pistol, but he was grabbed by the crowd; in the process, his gun accidentally discharged. The bullet struck a small girl. Campbell then shot Snow above the eye with a .38-caliber pistol. Officer Snow staggered into the yard and died. His body was found there by other officers some time later.

Campbell was arrested. He was convicted and sentenced to death. The governor commuted the sentence to life in prison.

Williams, Henry
Born (Unknown)—Died 8 February 1886

Kyle Terry, a member of a prominent Fort Bend County family, had been drinking heavily and was arrested by Officer Williams. Terry was carrying a pistol and was also charged with that offense. He was released on bail, and a court date was set for the next day.

Terry arrived early at court and discovered that the session time had been moved to later that day. He decided to get a drink and, while doing so, ran into Officer Williams on Preston Street near Market Square. After some harsh words were exchanged between the pair, Terry pulled out a pistol and opened fire, striking Williams. Terry shot the officer again after he had fallen to the ground.

Terry was convicted of the murder on 30 December 1886 and was sentenced to two years in prison. He appealed the case. Terry returned to Fort Bend County and killed a political rival on 21 June 1889 during the Jaybird-Woodpecker War. On 21 January 1890, Terry went to trial for that murder in Galveston and was killed by his victim's brother.

Williams is buried at Glenwood Cemetery. He was survived by his wife and two (or perhaps three) children.

The Jaybird-Woodpecker War was a feud between two political factions for the control of Fort Bend County. The Jaybird faction represented most of the wealth and about 90 percent of the white population. They were the regular Democrats who sought to rid the county of the Republican government that had gained control during Reconstruction. The Woodpeckers, numbering about forty persons, also claimed to be Democrats but also were the officials and former officials who held office as a result of the black vote for the Republican ticket. In this unfortunate feud, former friends, neighbors and relatives became bitter enemies.

Fenn, James E.
Born circa 1859—Died 15 March 1891
Date of incident: 14 March 1891

Officer Fenn was assigned to work at a black dance hall. He observed a man named Henry McGee who was known to carry a gun. As he approached McGee, the man shot him in the stomach with a .44-caliber Bulldog revolver, inflicting a mortal wound. Fenn died at 1:30 a.m. the following day.

McGee was identified as the killer. He had made threats against Fenn stemming from prior arrests. McGee was arrested and finally convicted after two trials. He was sentenced to death for the murder and was hanged on 12 August 1892.

Fenn is buried at Washington Cemetery in Houston. He was survived by his wife and three children.

Ellison, Clifton T. "Cliff"
Born circa 1861—Died 27 April 1899

Ellison had been a Houston police detective for two years. For the nine months preceding his death, he had also carried a commission as a Special Texas Ranger, doing investigative work for the Wells Fargo Express Agency.

At about 7:00 p.m. on 27 April 1899, Detective Ellison had just left the police station when he became involved in an argument with Patrolman Gus Albers over an arrest that had taken place three weeks earlier. Ellison slapped Albers. Albers slapped him back and kicked him in the side. Ellison put his hand to his hip as if to draw his weapon. Officer McClanahan then stepped in and pulled Ellison back. Ellison somehow lost his footing. Albers pulled his pistol and began firing. Ellison was struck in the right breast and died within ten minutes. Albers turned and walked toward the police station, all the while looking back at Ellison. He quickly mounted his horse and went home.

Albers was arrested for the murder and released on a $5,000 bond. More than a year and a half later, in July 1900, Albers was still making arrests as a Houston policeman. The final disposition of his case is unknown.

Ellison was a former Harris County sheriff's deputy. His father was a judge in Colorado County. He was survived by his wife and two-year-old son.

HUNT COUNTY SHERIFF'S OFFICE

Mason, William Walker
Born 3 March 1845—Died circa 1874–1880

Deputy William Mason was reportedly shot and killed by a known horse thief named Ed Goff (or Ed Gee). A posse tracked down Goff and hung him from a tree not far from the location where he shot Mason. Goff's body was left hanging for a week as a warning to other horse thieves and criminals.

Mason's exact date of death is still unknown, but it is believed to have been after 1 January 1874 and before the 1880 census was taken.

William Mason's father, John Mason, served as sheriff of Hopkins County from 6 August 1860 until 1 August 1864. John Mason also served as sheriff of Hunt County from 25 June 1866 to 6 April 1869. William's brother S.J. Mason served as sheriff of Hunt County from 2 November 1886 to 8 November 1892 and again from 6 November 1894 to 3 November 1896.

Mason was survived by his wife, Margaret Kelly. He is buried at East Mount Cemetery in an unmarked grave.

Hagood, Robert F.
Born circa 1847—Died 14 October 1874

Deputy Hagood had followed horse thief James Glass to Marion and Cass Counties in east Texas. Hagood was subsequently killed when he attempted to arrest the man.

On 19 October 1874, the Hunt County Commissioners Court offered a $500 reward for the arrest of Glass in connection with the murder of Hagood. On 2 December 1875, the Hunt County Commissioners Court ordered the payment of the $500 reward to three men who had arrested and delivered Glass to Sheriff N.J. Ross. No records were found as to the disposition of the murder charge.

Hagood's place of burial is also unknown.

Adair, John William Benjamin
Born circa 1849—Died 1 September 1886
Date of incident: 28 August 1886

Deputy Adair was stabbed to death while escorting six escapees back to the Hunt County Jail. As he traveled back to the jail, one of the inmates attempted to escape. Adair gave his pistol to a passing citizen and told him to go after the inmate. While Deputy Adair was guarding the remaining prisoners, they attacked him, cut his throat and wrist and then cut him from his shoulder to his waist.

Adair succumbed to his injuries and died four days later.

Brigham, Joe
Born (Unknown)—Died 18 December 1892

Deputy Brigham was shot and killed while attempting to arrest a burglar who was hiding in a coal car. The highly unfortunate Brigham had been deputized by the sheriff that day in order to help capture the burglar.

Brigham was survived by his wife.

JACK COUNTY SHERIFF'S OFFICE

Ward, Isaac
Born circa 1825—Died 23 May 1867

Deputy Isaac Ward was shot and killed while attempting to arrest a man on a warrant for horse theft. During the arrest, the man produced a handgun and fatally shot Ward.

The killer, Hudson "Hut" Farmer, escaped and wasn't apprehended until twenty-six years later. He was returned to Jack County, where he was tried and acquitted of Deputy Ward's murder.

Ward was survived by his expectant wife and seven children. He is buried at Oakwood Cemetery in Jacksboro.

King, William Meredith
Born circa 1844—Died 17 July 1885

By means of background, King was elected sheriff on 2 November 1880 and reelected on 7 November 1882. He served until 1884, when his term of office ended and the new sheriff, John D. Rains, took over on 4 November. On 13 March 1884, during the term of Sheriff King, Deputy J.E. Richardson shot and killed a man named Caleb "Cale" Parrott.

On Friday, 17 July 1885, the former sheriff King was riding his horse on the street in front of former sheriff Leroy Ladd Crutchfield's saloon in Jacksboro. Floyd Parrott and Trammell Hickman stepped out of the saloon. Parrott drew his pistol and shot King, killing him instantly.

Parrott was apparently still upset about the death of his brother and shot King in revenge. Sheriff King did not arrest Richardson at the time of the shooting, but Richardson was later indicted and tried in Young County on a change of venue for the killing of Cale Parrott. The court records have since been lost.

Parrott and Hickman were indicted for the murder of King. In January 1886, Parrott was found not guilty by a Jack County jury. The charges against Hickman were dismissed at the request of the district attorney for lack of sufficient evidence.

King was survived by his wife, Paradine. They had eight children. King and his wife are buried at King Cemetery in Jack County.

Rains, John D.
Born 8 December 1830—Died 14 June 1888

John Rains was elected sheriff of Jack County on 4 November 1884. He was reelected on 2 November 1886 and served until his death on 13 June 1888. Sheriff Rains was shot and killed by his brother-in-law, W.W. Terrell, in a personal feud.

At about 8:00 p.m. on 14 June 1888, Sheriff Rains and his son were both shot and killed by Terrell. The killings took place shortly after harsh words and blows had been exchanged between the parties.

Terrell was unarmed during the verbal exchange and episode of fisticuffs that preceded the shooting, which occurred near the town square. Afterward, he went home to get his Winchester. Sheriff Rains and his son went to a nearby livery stable and procured a Winchester to augment their six-shooters. The gunfire between the factions commenced near the southwest corner of the courthouse and the public square, with both parties advancing toward each other as they fired. Much like a classic Wild West showdown, the men continued firing as they closed the distance, finally emptying their weapons in a hail of gunfire and a cloud of acrid gray smoke. Terrell shot and killed Rains and his son with the last two bullets from his six-shooter. During the gunfight, Terrell sustained wounds to his left leg, left arm and both thighs. According to reports of the day, he was expected to recover. The *Galveston Daily News* of 15 June 1888 reported that the cause of the shooting was a long-standing family feud.

Rains is buried at Oakwood Cemetery in Jacksboro.

Hoskins, H.M.
Born 23 December 1856—Died 9 June 1891
Date of incident: 31 May 1891

Sheriff Hoskins was shot and killed by a man who had been drinking all day. As Hoskins pursued the man, he eventually overtook him and suddenly found himself face to face with the man, Bryan Cope, who fired at the sheriff and missed him. Hoskins drew his weapon and shot Cope in the chest. Cope, in turn, shot Hoskins in the stomach. As he lay on the ground, Hoskins was able to shoot Cope again, this time killing him. Hoskins died from his own wounds ten days later.

Hoskins was elected sheriff on 4 November 1890 and served until his death. He was survived by his wife and three children. He is buried at Oakwood Cemetery in Jack County.

Jackson County Sheriff's Office

McIver, John
Born circa 1808—Died 1 May 1871

Sheriff John McIver was in Morales on business and decided to spend the night at the house of a man named N.B. Thompson. Thompson lived by himself, except for a black woman and child who lived in the kitchen area of the dwelling. During the night, six men in red flannel masks came to the home and asked the woman if anyone was home. She advised them that Sheriff McIver was in the house. They inquired as to which room he was in and also asked where Thompson kept his money. After they entered the house, she heard a pistol shot, followed by Thompson begging for his life and saying that he would give them all of his money and that he wanted time to pray. The woman heard another pistol shot and then heard nothing further from Thompson. The men set the house on fire. The bones of McIver and Thompson were found the next morning. Thompson was reportedly about seventy-five years of age.

McIver was appointed sheriff on 1 November 1867 by General J.J. Reynolds's Special Order No. 195; he was subsequently elected to the post on 3 December 1869 and served until his death. McIver was survived by his wife. His place of burial is unknown.

A public safety committee was formed in Jackson County on 6 May 1871 and issued a preamble and resolutions, which were adopted. The resolutions condemned the murders and called on the military and civil authorities to find and arrest the guilty parties. The committee concluded that the outrage was committed for the purpose of obtaining money that was supposedly in the possession of N.B. Thompson. A reward of $500 was offered. The killers were never found.

Jacksonville Police Department

Clark, William A.
Born circa 1844—Died 30 August 1883
Date of incident: 28 August 1883

City Marshal Clark observed B.F. Temple (also referred to as Nick Temple) carrying a pistol, which was in violation of a city ordinances. Clark confronted Temple, who had the pistol in his hand, and demanded that he surrender the gun. Temple refused, cocked the pistol and told Clark not to approach him. Temple then crossed the street. Clark unwisely followed. Temple then fired twice at Clark. The second shot struck Clark in the bowels. The battle was on, and both men emptied their .44-caliber pistols at each other. Clark started walking down the street and told the gathering crowd that he had been killed. Temple went to his father's house, got a shotgun and came back after Clark. Temple was arrested before he could shoot Clark again with the shotgun.

Clark died on 30 August 1883. He gave a dying declaration and said goodbye to his wife and friends.

Temple was convicted of manslaughter in the death of Clark and was sentenced to four years in prison. He appealed, and the case was reversed due to a technicality—the state had never established the date and time of the homicide nor the county. Temple was tried a second time for the crime in June 1885 and sentenced to just two years in prison.

Clark was survived by his wife and two children. He is buried at Jacksonville City Cemetery in Cherokee County.

JEFFERSON CITY POLICE DEPARTMENT

Sanford, William Daniel "Dan"
Born circa 1836—Died 20 November 1868

At about 2:00 p.m. on 20 November 1868, Marshal Sanford was shot and killed when he was ambushed while eating at a local restaurant.

The shooter, an intoxicated man named W.E. Rose, approached Sanford and shot him without saying a word. The newspaper said that Rose was a "Ku Klux'er of the viler sort" and had attempted murder several times in the past three months. Rose was later apprehended by the military. Fearing a mob, Rose surrendered to military authorities.

JOHNSON COUNTY SHERIFF'S OFFICE

Wilson, Albert J.
Born circa 1855—Died 24 December 1879

Jailer Wilson was shot and killed while trying to enter a sporting house on Christmas Eve. The unusual circumstances of his death leave open speculation as to whether he was chasing a suspect into the house, shot by someone at the brothel or was himself a patron of the establishment. No other information is known at this time.

Albert Wilson left behind a wife, Mahala Madison, who had come to Texas from Missouri. The couple had been married in Cherokee County on 25 March 1871. Wilson had two daughters, Florence and Mollie, and a ten-month-old son named James. His place of burial is unknown.

JONES COUNTY SHERIFF'S OFFICE

Buck, (First Name Unknown)
Born (Unknown)—Died April 1885

In April 1885, Deputy Buck was pursuing cattle thieves in the Panhandle when he was killed. His murderer escaped into the Indian Territory. The gang's leader was reported to have been the notorious Bill Williams, who had his headquarters located in the thickets bordering the Clear Fork of the Brazos River. No other information is known about this incident.

Glazner, William C.M.
Born 30 April 1855—Died 5 September 1886
Date of incident: 31 August 1886

Sheriff George A. Scarborough and his deputy were out of town transporting a prisoner and had left jailer Glazner in charge of three other "guests of the county" who were confined at the jail. At about 8:00 or 9:00 p.m. on the night of 31 August 1886, witnesses heard loud cries coming from the jailhouse. The distressed sounds were thought to be those of Glazner. The pleading voice was saying, "Help, boys, help." Witness looked through the jail window and saw a man striking Glazner. They heard the man say, "Boys, I have done him up."

Upon entering the jail, it was discovered that prisoner A.B. "Add" Cannon had escaped. Prisoners Ben Kirby and Joe Brown were still locked in their cell. Glazner was lying on the floor in the corridor of the jail and had been beaten bloody and senseless. He was groaning and uttering unintelligible sounds. The door leading to the corridor where the cells were located was open. Glazner had been beaten with an iron bar. He died on 5 September 1886.

Prisoner Kirby was indicted and tried for the murder. He was found guilty of second-degree murder and sentenced to twenty-three years in the penitentiary. Kirby appealed, arguing that he did not kill Glazner. However, his statement to the justice of the peace at the inquest was enough to convict him of being a part of the conspiracy to escape, in spite of the fact that he had not intended to injure the jailer. His sentence was affirmed. Brown was reportedly not tried for the murder. Cannon was never apprehended.

Jailer Glazner is buried at Mount Hope Cemetery in Jones County. He was reported to have had six children and a pregnant wife.

Jones County sheriff George Scarborough left office on 6 November 1888 and later became a deputy U.S. marshal. On 6 April 1896, Scarborough shot and killed El Paso County constable John Selman Sr., who was awaiting trial for killing John Wesley Hardin.

Scarborough resigned as a deputy U.S. marshal and was acquitted of the murder. On 5 April 1900, he was working as a detective for a cattle raisers association in New Mexico when he was shot and mortally wounded while chasing train robbers.

KARNES COUNTY SHERIFF'S OFFICE

Littleton, John
Born circa 1825—Died 3 December 1868

Littleton was elected sheriff on 12 September 1857. He was reelected on 2 August 1858 and served until 3 April 1860. While serving as sheriff, he joined the Texas Rangers, serving in Captain William G. Tobin's Mounted Volunteers. Littleton enlisted during the Cortina War in 1859 and served until 1863. He was eventually promoted to the rank of captain. Littleton then joined John S. "Rip" Ford's battalion to fight against Federal troops in the Civil War. He was elected sheriff again on 23 January 1866 and reportedly served until 25 June 1866.

Littleton became involved in a dispute that aligned him against the Taylor faction. On 3 December 1868, Littleton and William Stannard were returning from San Antonio in a buggy when they were attacked by a group of men. Both Littleton and Stannard were shot numerous times and killed.

Littleton and Stannard were buried in unmarked graves at Old Masonic Cemetery in Helena in Karnes County. A witness identified six men as the killers, two of whom were the Taylor brothers. This incident was the start of the deadly Sutton-Taylor Feud.

Leary, Edgar
Born circa 1850—Died 26 December 1884

On 26 December 1884, Emmett Butler and Hugh McDonald returned to Helena after a night of drinking and creating a disturbance in a neighboring town. Butler, the son of a wealthy cattleman, was only nineteen years old at the time. McDonald was twenty-two.

Butler and McDonald made some disparaging remarks that were directed at former Karnes County sheriff I.M. Reisinger. Hearing the young men's offensive dialogue, the unarmed Reisinger left to retrieve a weapon. He soon returned "well heeled," and the disagreement picked up where it had left off. McDonald attempted to grab Reisinger, but the former sheriff struck him in the face. Both men pointed guns at each other, but the gathering crowd quickly intervened and separated the angry pair. Butler and McDonald, still carrying their weapons, continued terrorizing the town.

Sheriff Leary had been out of town. When he heard of the disturbance, he went in search of the two rowdy and intoxicated young men. At about 3:00 p.m., Leary found Butler and McDonald drinking at a bar. When Butler saw Leary, he reached for his Winchester but was disarmed by Deputy Joe Manning. Butler was released and walked from the saloon into the street, where he drew a pistol that was concealed under his coat. Leary observed this and started walking toward Butler. Butler fired at the sheriff, striking him near the heart. As the sheriff fell backward, he was heard to say, "Shoot him, boys, he has just killed me." Just before dying, Leary raised up and fired at Butler, but his shot missed the mark.

Butler held the crowd off by pointing his six-shooter at them. He recovered his horse and fired another shot into the dead body of Leary. He also fired at Deputy Manning but missed, just grazing his coat.

Members of the crowd fired several shots at Butler as he ran behind a tree. Butler then mounted his horse, and as he rode away he fired at Reisinger. By then the crowd had started firing at Butler. Butler was shot in the leg and in the back of the head. He managed to ride another fifty feet before falling from the saddle. He lived until the next morning, when he died of his wounds. No one knew who had fired the shot that killed him.

Leary was survived by his wife, Fannie, a son and a daughter. He had been appointed sheriff on 14 July 1884 to fill the term of Sheriff Reisinger. He was elected on 4 November 1884 and served until his death. He was the first of two Karnes County sheriffs to be shot and killed in the line of duty by members or friends of the Butler family. Sheriff Leary is buried at Helena Cemetery.

Elder, Isham Lafayette "Fate"
Born 23 December 1851—Died 6 September 1886

Elder, James J. "Bud"
Born 6 June 1862—Died 6 September 1886

Bailey, John Melville "Jack"
Born 31 March 1851—Died 7 September 1886
Date of incident: 6 September 1886

Sheriff Elder was sitting outside a polling place at Daileyville shortly before noon on 6 September 1886. He observed Juan Coy and Epitacio Garza ride into town. Coy was wanted in connection with a murder that had taken place at Floresville in Wilson County. Coy and Garza dismounted, and each took their Winchester rifles from their saddle scabbards. It was violation of the law to be carrying firearms within half a mile of a polling place by anyone except lawmen.

William G. Butler, a wealthy local rancher, employed Coy and Garza. Butler and Sheriff Fate Elder had some hard feelings between them that had resulted from the shooting death of Butler's son. The shooting had occurred after the younger Butler had killed Sheriff Leary two years earlier.

Coy and Garza began firing at Sheriff Elder. The sheriff drew his pistol and attempted to shoot, but the gun misfired. Sykes C. Butler approached from behind the sheriff and fired a shot into the back of his head. Elder fell dead to the floor. Deputy Bud Elder was fired on by Coy and Garza and was seriously wounded. Bud managed to get off a shot that wounded William Butler. An unknown person then walked up to Bud Elder and shot him in the head, killing him instantly.

Deputy Bailey realized the bad situation he was in and ran for cover in a yard near the store. As he reached the yard, someone shot him as well. He fell to the ground, seriously wounded. As Bailey was lying faceup on the ground, he was shot two more times. It was later determined that he never even had an opportunity to draw his gun and fire.

Bailey had been shot in the right leg, and his knee was shattered. Doctors had to amputate his leg. The surgery was unsuccessful, and he died the following day on 7 September. This tragic shooting incident became known as "the Daileyville Riot."

Garza and Coy fled to Mexico, where Garza disappeared into the interior of the country. Coy stayed near the border in Nuevo Laredo. On 10 October

1886, a Bexar County sheriff's deputy took the drunken Coy back across the border to be arrested. Various charges were filed against the participants in "the Daileyville Riot." Some were convicted of minor charges. William Butler was convicted and fined $100 for unlawfully carrying a firearm and pled guilty to aggravated assault. He was never convicted of murder. Butler provided Coy with seven lawyers, and his case ended in a hung jury. The widows of Fate Elder, Bud Elder and Jack Bailey sued William Bulter and lost.

Sheriff Fate Elder was married to Elizabeth Jane Robuck. He is buried at Helena Cemetery in an unmarked grave.

Deputy Bud Elder was married to Prudence Scoggins. He was the younger brother of Sheriff Fate Elder. He is buried at Helena Cemetery, and his grave has a marker.

Deputy Bailey was married to Maggie Bailey and had six children. He is buried at Helena Cemetery in an unmarked grave.

On 25 January 1892, Juan Coy entered a saloon partially intoxicated. Henry Krempkau was the bartender, and Coy started an argument. Coy drew his knife, and Krempkau shot and killed him. At the time of his death, Coy was a Wilson County deputy sheriff, hired by Sheriff Lee Hall, who was a former Texas Ranger captain, to guard railway property.

KAUFMAN COUNTY CONSTABLE'S OFFICE

James, J.D. "Dave"
Born 1 January 1859—Died 22 December 1897

At about 3:00 p.m. on 22 December 1897, Precinct 8 constable Dave James and Justice of the Peace W.H. Cariker were seen having a conversation in downtown Terrell. Witnesses heard James tell Cariker that he owed him $3.00. Cariker replied that the amount was only $1.50. James said that he wanted his fees. Harsh words were exchanged between the two men. Cariker drew his pistol and shot James in the right side of the face. He died instantly. James's pistol was still in his holster.

James had been killed over a disagreement involving just a few dollars. He left behind a wife, Lucy N., and four children. James was buried in Terrell by the Odd Fellows.

KERR COUNTY SHERIFF'S OFFICE

Nelson, John D.
Born circa 1842—Died 12 November 1882

Nelson served for the Confederacy during the Civil War. After discharge, he returned to Texas and enlisted on 4 June 1874 in Company F of the Frontier Battalion of the Texas Rangers. He served under Captain Neil Coldwell. Later, Nelson requested a transfer to Captain McNelly's Company A of the Frontier Battalion. He resigned his ranger commission to become a deputy sheriff.

Reportedly, hard feelings had existed for some time between Nelson and a local man named Tom Baker. On the night of 11 November 1882, Nelson and Baker had differences that escalated to a point where they had to be separated by bystanders. About 6:00 a.m. the following morning, Baker armed himself with a Winchester and approached Deputy Nelson in front of the Schreiner's Store at the corner of Water and Mountain Streets (present-day Earl Garrett Street). He walked up within twenty paces of Deputy Nelson before he saw him coming. Baker fired a shot that passed diagonally through Nelson's lungs. Nelson fell to the ground as Baker advanced and fired again, this time breaking Nelson's left arm. He was about to fire a third time when Nelson exclaimed, "You have killed me, don't shoot anymore." Nelson died of the wounds at about 10:15 a.m. on 12 November 1882.

After the shooting, Baker immediately fled the scene. Sheriff Buck Hamilton of Bandera County was in town on business, and although out of his jurisdiction, he caught up with Baker at the edge of town. Hamilton fired three shots at long range, missing Baker. After hearing what had happened, Baker's father gave chase immediately. He caught up with his son, dismounted and gave his son his horse so that he could make good his escape. Baker was eventually arrested and convicted for the murder of Deputy Nelson. He was sentenced to twenty-five years in prison.

Deputy Nelson was not married. No record of his burial can be located.

KIMBLE COUNTY SHERIFF'S OFFICE

Gorman, Newton Samuel
Born 5 May 1846—Died 8 March 1878

Major J.T. Wright was involved in a lawsuit with two cousins, Button and Pete Brazier. The claim involved a yoke of oxen.

On 8 March 1878, Wright encountered the Braziers in front of the county courthouse in Junction City. A quarrel took place. Wright was armed with a shotgun, as was Pete Brazier. Button Brazier was armed with a six-shooter. Button struck Wright in the head with the pistol. Facing a two-on-one fight, Wright exclaimed that he was double-teamed but to go ahead and shoot if they felt like it. Deputy Smith, who was watching the disturbance unfold from the courthouse, summoned Deputy Gorman, Marcellus Denman and West Johnson to help him get the situation under control. Gorman told the men to drop their weapons. He then repeated the command and added "or I would shoot." At that point, Gorman and Button threw down on each other and began firing.

Both men were shot in the initial exchange. Button, who was wounded, turned and fired at Wright, hitting him two or three times. Gorman continued firing until both of the Braziers as well as Wright were lying dead in the street. It was later claimed that both Braziers had been drinking heavily, adding greatly to the occurrence of the incident.

Gorman was married to Sara Crisswell. He is buried at Gorman Family Cemetery in Junction.

Turman, John Martin Calhoun
Born 25 May 1857—Died 28 March 1898

On the evening of 28 March 1898, James Barnett Gibson "Gip" Hardin, the brother of the notorious outlaw John Wesley Hardin, had gone to the Turman Hotel in Junction City for supper. The Turman Hotel was owned and operated by Deputy Sheriff Turman. Hardin and a man named W.A. Taylor seated themselves at a table already occupied by Tom Morse and Will Haley. Haley's father was being tried for murder at the time. Hardin made some disparaging comments about the elder Mr. Haley. His remarks were accompanied by foul language, causing Haley to get up and leave the table. Turman asked Hardin and Taylor to leave the hotel, which they ultimately proceeded to do.

The men continued their vulgar language as they exited the establishment. Turman announced that he would have to place them under arrest, calling out to a local man named Trimble to assist him. Turman and Trimble followed Hardin out the door. They grabbed Hardin and pulled him backward in an attempt to place him in custody. Hardin jerked away from Turman, and immediately the shooting began. There were six shots fired, two by Turman and four by Hardin. Turman was hit in three places in the arm and once through the body, all entering on the right side and exiting through the left. Neither of Turmans's two shots hit Hardin. Turman clung to life for a brief time before dying in front of his own hotel.

Deputy Turman is buried at Old Junction Cemetery. Gip Hardin argued at his trial, and on appeal, that he had not heard Turman place him under arrest. He further claimed that Turman had fired at him first. He was initially convicted of second-degree murder and sentenced to thirty-five years in prison. Hardin appealed and won both a new trial and a lighter sentence. In 1918, Gip Hardin was crushed to death in Florida by shifting boxcars.

KINNEY COUNTY SHERIFF'S OFFICE

Fries, John P.
Born circa 1850—Died 25 October 1873

John Fries was appointed sheriff on 15 July 1870 and was elected on 8 November 1870. He served until 30 May 1870, when he resigned. State election records do not show anyone serving as sheriff until 8 April 1874, when Warren Allen was elected. Apparently, Fries was reappointed sheriff and was also serving as a deputy U.S. marshal for the Western District of Texas under U.S. Marshal Thomas Parnell.

On 25 October 1873, Fries was in Brackettville serving a warrant for desertion on a man named McWebber and a warrant for murder and escape on a man named Mansfield. While speaking to several men, an assassin fired one shot through the window at Fries, killing him instantly. No one saw the killer, but the men believed that it was McWebber.

Kinney County offered a $1,000 reward. Governor Ed Davis offered an additional $800 reward. In December 1873, the Grand Jury of Kinney County failed to indict any of the suspects who were charged with the murder of the sheriff. Fries' killer has never been identified.

Fries was born between 1849 and 1850 and was about twenty years old when first elected sheriff. He was survived by his father, John Fries, and at least eight siblings. His place of burial is unknown.

Cave, John
Born circa 1844—Died 18 May 1878

Very little information is known about this incident. On 18 May 1878, Patrick Grecian, a soldier at the time and a member of the Fourth Cavalry, shot and killed Deputy Cave. Grecian was quickly apprehended and locked up at the military jail at Brackett (now called Brackettville). On 1 June, Grecian and another soldier named William Goggin, who was serving fifteen years for mutiny, escaped from the cells by making a hole through the ceiling of the guardhouse. Fifteen or twenty shots were fired at the escaping pair, but they managed to get away.

Ronquilla, Thomas
Born (Unknown)—Died 25 July 1879

On 25 July 1879, a great disturbance took place at Fort Clark that drew the attention of jailer Thomas Ronquilla. Ronquilla arrested the man involved, whose name was Pedro Garcia. While transporting Garcia to jail, the man stabbed Ronquilla in the chest. The knife blade struck his heart and inflicted a fatal injury. Another Mexican man came to assist Ronquilla in the arrest, but he was cut across the face by Garcia. Garcia escaped and is believed to have fled to Mexico.

KYLE POLICE DEPARTMENT

Hodges, E.P.
Born circa 1862—Died 13 July 1898

Marshal Hodges was involved in a heated personal feud with a man named Frank Martin. Martin had experienced a difficult period during his youth. He had been abandoned by his father, who later moved to Texas and married without bothering to divorce his first wife. One of the elder Martin daughters had married Marshal Hodges, and thus the two men were related.

The dispute centered on the estate of the late Mr. Martin. Before this incident, Marshal Hodges had reportedly assaulted Martin and publicly marched him to jail. At about 6:30 p.m. on the evening of 13 July 1898, Hodges came onto the property of Martin. He was asked to leave by Martin's wife. An argument began, during which Hodges used abusive language. Martin heard this, grabbed his rifle and ran to the corner of the house. He then shot and killed Hodges.

No further information has been found concerning the disposition of any charges against Frank Martin.

Lamar County Sheriff's Office

Green, Mat
Born (Unknown)—Died March 1867

In March 1867, Deputy Green went to levy an attachment on property belonging to Robert B. Anderson. Anderson armed himself with a six-gun and then shot and killed Deputy Green. Anderson escaped the scene by crossing the Red River into the Indian Territory.

In 1878, Anderson was found in the mountains of northern Arkansas. Attorney Fred W. Minter of Paris wrote a letter to the governor of Texas requesting that a reward be offered for Anderson's arrest. The governor responded by offering a $400 reward. Lamar County deputies Hansley and Barnett arrested Anderson and returned him to Lamar County to be tried for the murder of Deputy Green.

On 21 March 1916, much of the town of Paris was destroyed by fire. The fire also struck the Lamar County Courthouse and the newspaper office. In what locals would later call "the Great Fire," all of the county district clerk records that may have revealed the outcome of Anderson's trial were lost.

No family information, burial records nor the exact day of the month of Green's death have been located.

Black, James H.
Born circa 1850—Died 16 November 1884

On 4 November 1884, James Black won a hotly contested election for sheriff against the incumbent, G.M. Crook. Sheriff Crook and two of his deputies, James Yates and Newt Harris, helped a prisoner by the name of John Middleton escape with the understanding that the prisoner would kill sheriff-elect Black. Middleton made good on his promise and promptly went to Black's home, where he shot and killed him.

Crook was tried in Sherman on a change of venue and found not guilty. Yates and Harris were charged with murder and sentenced to prison. Yates and Louis Holman turned state's evidence. The escapee Middleton was later found dead, having drowned in Arkansas while riding a stolen horse across a river.

Black is buried at Blossom Cemetery.

Harris was a former jailer. Yates was a former deputy under Crook. Louis Holman, who was a deputy under Crook, was arrested in Topeka, Kansas.

Davis, Henry Clay
Born circa 1858—Died 27 December 1885

Deputy Davis was shot and killed while serving an arrest warrant on a man named Garrett. Garrett was wanted for disturbing the peace. Davis allowed the man to go to his room to retrieve more clothing. Instead of coming back with garments, Garrett returned with a rifle and shot Deputy Davis.

Garrett was arrested and lynched by an angry mob from the Springhill community.

Davis is buried at Springhill Cemetery.

Caston, William B. "Billy"
Born (Unknown)—Died 8 October 1891

On the night of 8 October 1891, Sam Morris and Deputy Caston were both murdered in Morris's Saloon in Arthur City.

Arthur City is a border town and lies on the boundary of Texas and the Indian Territory. Morris was found behind the bar with four bullet wounds. Caston was found in Morris's bedroom with three bullet wounds.

Deputy U.S. Marshals Joe Everidge and Joe McKee investigated this crime. It seems that four black men (Tom Johnson, Jeff Shoales, Tom Beatty and Sam Burrell) from the Indian Territory had decided to buy some alcohol from Morris's Saloon on credit—or take it if credit was not extended. The group had decided that Johnson would take the liquor and leave, while the others dealt with any protest from the proprietor.

One of the three men, believed to have been Shoales, fired at Morris first. He shot from across the bar, hitting him with a .38–.40-caliber Winchester rifle that he had brought with him. Next, Burrell and Beatty, both armed with Winchester .44–.40 rifles, went to the bedroom of Morris, where Caston was sleeping. Caston, by some reports, was intoxicated. They shot him as he slept. Seven shots in all were fired at the two men: four at the body of Morris and three at Caston. Both were killed instantly.

Shoales had taken an ivory-handled pistol from Morris, and Burrell had taken a gun from Caston. Johnson, Beatty and Burrell were taken into custody and charged with the crime.

Shoales had already been incarcerated in the federal penitentiary in Detroit, Michigan, under a five-year sentence for assault to commit murder. Beatty and Burrell were ultimately tried for the murders of Caston and Morris. The trial concluded on 4 January 1892 with Burrell remanded to jail and Beatty freed on a $4,500 bond pending sentencing. The outcome of Beatty's sentencing is unknown.

LAMPASAS COUNTY SHERIFF'S OFFICE

Doolittle, George M.
Born circa 1851—Died 8 January 1879

Deputy Doolittle was in the vicinity of the town of Lexington in the Indian Territory attempting to arrest Bluford "Blu" Cox. Cox was from Lampasas County and was wanted for the 1871 murder of Thomas Gardner of Williamson County.

As Doolittle attempted to arrest Cox, Cox shot and killed him. Cox escaped, and it is unknown if he was ever apprehended and prosecuted for the killing.

Doolittle was a former Texas Ranger, having served in Company A of the Frontier Battalion from May 1874 until June 1876. He was single and is believed to have been buried in an unmarked grave in the area of Lexington, Oklahoma.

Denson, Shadrack Thomas
Born 1 February 1833—Died 31 March 1892
Date of incident: 14 January 1873

Denson was elected sheriff on 3 December 1869. Conflicting records indicate that General J.J. Reynolds, the U.S. Army commander of Texas during Reconstruction, had appointed Denson as sheriff on 5 February 1870. He served until 2 December 1873.

On 14 January 1873, Sheriff Denson was shot and wounded during the noon recess of the district court. He died nineteen years later from complications from that injury after having long since left the post of county sheriff.

Two brothers were involved in the incident, George Washington "Wash" and Marcus "Mark" Short. One of the pair did the shooting. When the district judge ordered the arrest of the Short brothers, three of the five Horrell boys who were present at the time (Ben, Tom and Mart), along with their companion Patrick McGinty, drew their pistols on the arresting deputies and allowed the Short brothers to escape. A posse was quickly organized, and the group composed of eight or ten men headed out of town after the pair. At the edge of town, the lawmen were met by a group of Horrell boys and effectively turned back when Ben Horrell told the posse leader Tom Sparks: "No...you can't get them." Sparks decided to have it out with the Horrells then and there but quickly backed up when Ben bailed from his horse and made ready for a fight.

Mark Short was arrested about three years later but, while in custody, was shot and killed by Sheriff Denson's son, Samuel. Samuel Denson fled to Montana to avoid the murder charge. The younger Denson eventually returned to Texas.

The sheriff, his late wife and infant daughter are buried at Sparks Cemetery.

LAREDO POLICE DEPARTMENT

Gonzales, Gregorio
Born (Unknown)—Died 20 August 1877

On 20 August 1877, City Marshal Gonzales was returning home when he was shot and killed by the notorious desperado Eduardo Dobalina. Dobalina surveyed the dead marshal for a few minutes and then coolly walked away and escaped into Mexico.

The commandant at Nuevo Laredo, Mexico, dispatched a body of cavalry to arrest Dobalina. It is unknown at this time if the murderer was ever arrested or prosecuted.

Escamilla, Juan
Born circa 1830—Died 20 July 1878

The minutes of the Laredo City Council reported the death of Officer Escamilla. No other information is known at this time.

Johnson, A.A.
Born (Unknown)—Died 19 June 1882
Date of incident: 17 June 1882

A man named "California Jim" arrived in Laredo with no property except the clothes on his back and a six-shooter that he pawned for $5.00. California Jim took a job at the Beehive Restaurant as a cook. On 17 June 1882, Jim had a falling out with the proprietor and settled up for his wages. He then reclaimed his pistol at the pawn shop and returned to the restaurant to kill the owner. The restaurateur called on Assistant City Marshal Johnson for protection. As Johnson tried to enter the establishment, Jim slammed the door shut and fired through it as he escaped. The bullet struck Johnson in the right breast and then traveled around to a point near the navel and cut a button off his trousers. The impact with the trouser button caused the bullet to turn so as to enter directly into the intestines and become lodged under the skin near the backbone. Johnson remarked that he was killed and then walked to Atlee's drugstore, where he laid down. He suffered terribly until 3:00 a.m. on 19 June, when he finally expired.

Johnson left a widow and three small children. The city council approved $48 for Johnson's funeral and $100 for his widow. His place of burial has not been located.

A former ranger named Charles S. Smith and a seventeen-year-old cowboy named Wesley DeSpain were hunting for some horses near Cibolo Station in LaSalle County when they unexpectedly came upon "California Jim." When the pair approached Jim, he shot and wounded DeSpain. Smith then shot at Jim and wounded him. The injured outlaw then shot and wounded Smith.

A sheriff's posse found all three injured men at the site of the shootout. The outlaw disclosed that his real name was John Henry Hawkins and that he was wanted in Arizona and New Mexico. He gave Smith his pistol, which had seventeen notches on the grip. Hankins died at 3:00 a.m. on 23 June and was buried at the Cibolo Station depot. Smith was taken to a hospital in San

Antonio and died on 25 June. He was buried in Flatonia in Fayette County. He was given a full ranger funeral by Captain Oglesby.

Poor young Wesley DeSpain never recovered from his wound and was institutionalized in a mental hospital, where he died at age forty.

Related case: Texas Rangers—Charles S. Smith.

Ortiz, Plutarco
Born (Unknown)—Died 21 January 1890

Assistant City Marshal Ortiz was shot and killed in a personal dispute with Juan Anthony Garcia.

Garcia claimed that Ortiz had killed his brother, Parcho Garcia, on 7 April 1886. He had sworn revenge. The men met near the Mexican Consulate, well armed with six-shooters and ready for a duel. Rather than follow through with the challenge as prearranged, Garcia simply shot Ortiz and inflicted a mortal wound.

Trevino, Theodosa
Born (Unknown)—Died 26 January 1891

At about 8:30 p.m. on the night of 26 January 1891, Officer Trevino was shot and killed on the International Foot and Tramway Bridge that linked Laredo to Mexico. He was allegedly intoxicated and was killed by Mexican police officers.

LaSalle County Sheriff's Office

Irving, Aleck
Born (Unknown)—Died 23 May 1886

Deputy Irving was accidentally shot and killed at Twobig in LsSalle County by a man named Bud Crenshaw. Deputy Irving had just returned from apprehending a Mexican man for carrying a six-shooter. He had his pistol, along with the prisoner's pistol, in his belt. He withdrew one in a joking way, claiming that it was not loaded as he cocked and dry-fired the gun repeatedly. Crenshaw, keeping up with the fun, withdrew his own pistol and, also thinking that it was unloaded, began cocking and dry-firing it as well. As it turned out, his gun was loaded. It discharged and shot Deputy Irving through the heart, killing him instantly.

Many of Irving's friends claimed at the time that Crenshaw had killed him on purpose. Deputy Irving was the son-in-law of W.A. Stewart, and old-time resident of "Peg Leg Station" in west Texas. Crenshaw would be implicated in the death of LaSalle County sheriff C.B. McKinney seven months later.

McKinney, Charles Brown "Charlie"
Born circa 1858—Died 26 December 1886

McKinney served ten years as a Texas Ranger beginning in 1876, when he enlisted in the Washington County Militia. He went on to serve with the Special State Troops and Company F of the Frontier Battalion. McKinney was a ranger lieutenant when, according to state election records, he was elected sheriff on 3 February 1883. He was reelected on 4 November 1884 and served until 2 November 1886. Other records indicate that he was elected on 7 November 1882 and was serving as sheriff when he was killed.

Sheriff McKinney was assassinated on 26 December 1886. He was shot and killed by Bud Crenshaw, the man whom he had beaten in the recent election for sheriff. Crenshaw had planned the assassination for several years and had a woman make a false report that her daughter's virtue had been violated. When McKinney arrived to investigate the crime, he spoke with Bud Crenshaw and another man named Jim McCoy. Crenshaw suddenly shot McKinney in the head with a Winchester rifle. Crenshaw and McCoy also shot at Deputy Pete Edwards. Edwards's horse became frightened and flared, so the assailant's shots missed their mark and Edwards was only slightly wounded.

Texas Rangers tracked down the two men. Crenshaw was shot and killed in an exchange of gunfire. McCoy escaped but later surrendered. McCoy was subsequently sentenced to death and was hanged on 23 August 1889.

McKinney is buried at Cotulla City Cemetery. He was survived by his wife and children.

Fly, Robert Percival
Born 18 September 1846—Died 14 June 1889

Sheriff Fly was first elected on 2 November 1886 and was reelected on 6 November 1888. He served until his death.

Using a pistol to perform the deed, Sheriff Fly took his own life on 14 June 1889. Fly was not married. No further information is known at this time.

Cope, James
Born (Unknown)—Died 25 June 1891

In the early morning hours of 25 June 1891, trouble broke out at a Mexican fandango that was being held at home near Encinal, a small station on the International Railway near Rio Grande. Constable George Reed was called to quell the disturbance, but the revelers rebuffed his efforts. Reed went for assistance and returned with Deputy Johns, as well as James Cope and Robert Carr, as possemen. As the group of lawmen approached the home where the disturbance was taking place, they were fired upon. Cope was killed instantly, and Carr was shot through the leg. One of the partygoers, a man named Blas Reyes, was also killed in the exchange.

Cope's place of burial is unknown. Some sources refer to Cope as "Cape" and to Reed as "Reid."

Tumlinson, Joseph
Born 26 May 1840—Died 29 January 1893

While traveling on a vacation to Laredo, Sheriff Tumlinson and his new young wife left the Schultz Hotel and walked about two hundred yards down the railroad tracks. Tumlinson then pulled a pistol and shot his wife. Mrs. Tumlinson was only wounded. The sheriff ran after her, caught her and shot her again—this time in the head. The second attempt was successful, and the wound was fatal. Sheriff Tumlinson then sat down on the railroad tracks and shot himself in the head. He died instantly.

It is said that the Tumlinsons were having marital difficulties and that his wife had left him for a time and moved to San Antonio. Tumlinson had married the younger Auine E. Allen in Dimmit County on 13 October 1890.

Mrs. Auine Tumlinson is buried at Encinal. Tumlinson is buried at Mount Hope Cemetery in Dimmit County, where he had been sheriff before coming to LaSalle County. The sheriff was survived by two daughters, Alta and Bell, and by his first wife, Morelda (who had passed on 1 June 1890).

LAVACA COUNTY CONSTABLE'S OFFICE

Campion, Joseph Andrew
Born circa 1837-1839—Died 17 December 1885
Date of incident: 18 October 1885

At about 2:00 a.m. on 18 October 1885, Constable Campion was attending a Bohemian dance at Witting when he was informed that a man named Frank Dickson had broken a beer glass with his pistol. Campion approached Dickson from behind and grabbed at his gun, saying, "I want your pistol." Dickson responded by striking and punching Campion, at the same time drawing his pistol and firing three times. The first shot grazed the right pocket on Campion's trousers. The second shot struck the upper part of Campion's thigh, shattering the bone. Campion fired at Dickson just as the man fired a third shot at him. The bullet passed through Campion's coat and struck a bystander named Smith, causing a large flesh wound.

After the shooting, Dickson held the crowd at bay, mounted his horse and fled the ball. Campion was taken to the Garbade Store in Witting, where Dr. Granger was summoned. On Sunday, Drs. Rabb and East operated on Campion. He was carried home on a litter by hand because his wounds were considered quite serious. Campion died two months later.

Dickson was not arrested but was later charged by indictment with the murder of Campion. He was held without bond until the Texas Court of Appeals in Galveston reversed that decision. The court set his bail at $5,000. On 16 February 1887, the case went to trial. Dickson advised the jury that he had not known that his attacker was a peace officer and that he shot in self-defense. The jury agreed with him, and Dickson was acquitted of the murder.

Before becoming an elected constable, Campion served as a deputy sheriff. He was first elected constable of Lavaca County Precinct 1 in 1880. In 1882, he lost the election but was reelected in 1884.

Campion was survived by his wife and four children. He is buried at Old Catholic Cemetery in Hallettsville, which was later relocated. His new grave site is not marked.

Stubbs, William Anthony
Born circa 1859—Died 4 August 1890

Precinct 1 constable Stubbs had stabbed and killed a man named Bob Kelly at a dance. A personal feud developed between Stubbs and the Kelly family over the years, with the Kellys swearing to kill Stubbs on sight.

On 2 August 1890, Byrd Kelly and a friend named John Smothers Jr. were in Elstner's Saloon on the southeast corner of the town square at Hallettsville. Constable Stubbs was in front of the saloon with a man named James A. Tucker when Kelly came out the side door. Words were exchanged, and Stubbs drew his pistol and collared Kelly. Kelly then drew his gun and shot Stubbs. The wound was fatal.

Several shots were fired in total, and it is reported that Smothers may have been involved in the shooting as well. During the affray, Tucker was also shot and fatally wounded. Smothers and Kelly had each fired five times, and Tucker had fired four times.

Stubbs is buried at St. Mary's Cemetery.

LEE COUNTY SHERIFF'S OFFICE

Heffington, Isaac "Bosse"
Born 28 January 1846—Died 3 December 1883

Deputy Heffington was shot and killed while in pursuit of a man who was wanted for robbery and murder. While he was searching a building, an unidentified man stepped out from behind some boxes, said something to him and then shot him.

Heffington signed a statement while on his deathbed implicating a man in the shooting, but the man was found not guilty and the case was never solved.

On 24 December 1883, an angry mob lynched three men suspected of being involved in the killing—Henry Pfeiffer, Thad McLemore and Wright McLemore. Sometime later it was reported that the real killers were two men named Fitzpatrick and Goodman.

Heffington was survived by his wife, Clarinda Holland Harrison, and their eight children.

McClenand, William
Born circa 1851—Died July 1884

Deputy McClenand was shot and killed by an unknown person at Giddings. He was survived by his wife and three children. No other information is known about the case at this time.

LEON COUNTY CONSTABLE'S OFFICE

Shotwell, William A.
Born 24 October 1853—Died 17 March 1883

On 17 March 1883, Rowe Moore and W.F. Johnston confronted Constable Shotwell at the Oakwood community. Shotwell was running from the pair when he was shot four times. His pistol had not been fired.

Moore and Johnston fled but later surrendered and hired attorneys to defend themselves. The cause of the shooting and the disposition of the charges are unknown.

Shotwell is buried at Oakwood Cemetery.

LIMESTONE COUNTY SHERIFF'S OFFICE

Pritchett (Pritchard), Ezekiel Scott (Eli or Ely)
Born circa 1814—Died July 1870

As was so often the case with newspaper reports and handwritten accounts from the nineteenth century, various sources report the spelling of this deputy's surname and given name differently.

A few days before 15 July 1870, a gang of twelve to fifteen rowdies left the county seat at Springfield bent on seeking revenge against Deputy Pritchett for some unknown reason. Pritchett lived in the Lewisville community some distance from Springfield. The men, identified as the Parson brothers, called Pritchett out of his home and then shot and killed him. His body was riddled with bullet holes.

Unbeknownst to the assailants, though, this day's gunfight had just begun. Pritchett's eighteen-year-old son John (or Tipton) Cicero Pritchett had a six-shooter. The courageous young man managed to kill one of the Parsons brothers and wound two others. The resolute youth also shot and killed another one of the assailants and wounded two more before finally being shot in the mouth with a derringer by one of the gang members.

Ezekiel Pritchett was survived by his wife, Alsey Ramsey. Pritchett's son John survived his injury and lived until 14 December 1906. No other information is known about the case at this time.

Clendennen, Robert Ned "Bob"
Born circa 1850—Died 21 May 1875

Deputy Clendennen was shot and killed while attempting to arrest a man who had just set the county courthouse on fire.

After setting the blaze, which destroyed all the county's current and historical records, Merrick Trammel returned home. When a posse that included Deputy Clendennen arrived, Trammel fled from his residence, firing at the officers as he exited. Clendennen was struck by a bullet and died at the scene. No reason was given for Trammel's successful arson assault on the courthouse.

Clendennen is buried at Hogan Cemetery in Groesbeck in an unmarked grave.

Love, John W.
Born circa 1842—Died 18 April 1877

Love was elected sheriff on 15 February 1876. Sheriff Love pursued a notorious gang led by Mitch Comon to Shreveport, Louisiana, where they had been jailed. After he won a court fight to get the prisoners released to him, the sheriff and a deputy named Dewing started back to Texas in a hack with the three prisoners.

On 18 April 1877, near Greenwood, Louisiana, the prisoners overpowered the sheriff and took his pistol. They shot him in the back and killed him. Deputy Dewing was hit in the leg but managed to return fire, wounding one of the escaping prisoners.

A posse of twenty citizens from Greenwood caught up with the killers in a nearby swamp and killed all three men.

Sheriff Love's body was returned to Groesbeck, and he is buried in Tehuacana. He was survived by his wife.

Drinkard, Levi L.
Born 23 January 1858—Died 26 October 1884

Deputy Drinkard and a posse attempted to serve a warrant on three horse thieves in Robertson County. The posse surrounded the men's cabin and ordered the occupants to come out. Drinkard read the warrants out loud and ordered the men to exit the building. Rather than surrender, the group shot and killed Drinkard and then fled the scene.

Two of the men were tried and acquitted. One was never tried.

Drinkard is buried at Old Fort Parker Cemetery in Groesbeck.

LIVE OAK SHERIFF'S OFFICE

Wilson, John W.
Born circa 1848—Died 30 August 1888

Deputy Wilson blamed Robert H. Rice for being the cause of his marital strife and pending divorce, as well as for other difficulties he cited that had taken place over the course of the preceding three years.

Rice arrived at Wimmer's Store in Oakville on the night of 29 August 1888. When asked why he had a shotgun, he replied that he was carrying it for protection because Deputy Wilson had sent word to him that he would be killed on sight. Rice said that Wilson was a deputy sheriff and was armed. Rice also inquired about getting a will and the disposal of his property in the event that Wilson should kill him.

The following day, Wilson asked a local man if he had seen Bob Rice in town. When the man confirmed that he had, Wilson said, "You go and tell Bob Rice that when he meets me…to meet me fighting." Various witnesses testified later that Wilson was a brave and dangerous man.

At about 8:00 a.m., Joseph New took his pistol to Wimmer's Store in Oakville for repair. A group of men were present, including Rice. Rice said that he would have to get a "needle" drawn for the pistol to repair it. John McGrew and Deputy Wilson were about fifteen feet from the store when Rice stepped into the doorway, spotted Wilson and fired at him. Three buckshot pellets penetrated the right side of his head, one entering at the burr of the ear, another on the side of the forehead and the third at the cheek bone. Seventeen smaller shot were scattered over the right side of Wilson's head. Wilson lived about three-quarters of an hour but never rallied enough to speak. He had left his pistol at the local hotel and was unarmed.

Sheriff Coker attempted to arrest Rice several days later at his home, but he escaped. Rice surrendered to the sheriff on 13 September. He was indicted for the murder of Wilson and held without bail. He appealed, and bail was set at $8,000. It is unknown if Rice was ever tried for the murder.

LLANO COUNTY SHERIFF'S OFFICE

Lockhart, Samuel Lee
Born 7 June 1823—Died 9 January 1858

After winning the election of 4 August 1856, Samuel Lockhart became the first sheriff of Llano County.

On 9 January 1858, Sheriff Lockhart told several men to stop gambling. As he started to walk away, one of the men, William Taylor, ran up behind him, reached around him and began stabbing him with a butcher knife. Taylor was later arrested by a deputy sheriff in Williamson County and returned to Llano County. The outcome of any charges against him are unknown at this time.

A natural granite dome near the spot where Lockhart was killed has since been named Lockhart Mountain in his honor. He is buried at Tow Cemetery. Lockhart was survived by his wife and several children.

O'Bannon, James B.
Born circa 1847—Died 22 July 1884

Deputy O'Bannon was shot and killed with his own revolver during a struggle with a prisoner.

O'Bannon was assisting a prisoner named C.C. Davis post bond. Without warning, Davis suddenly grabbed the deputy's gun. A struggle took place during which Davis shot O'Bannon twice. Davis stole a horse and fled but was apprehended in Grayson County. He was returned to Llano County to face charges of murdering O'Bannon. The disposition of the case is unknown at this time.

O'Bannon is buried at City Cemetery in Llano. He was survived by his wife and four children.

Nowlin, Thomas H.
Born circa 1863—Died 5 April 1888

Deputy Thomas Nowlin was shot and killed in San Saba County while serving a warrant issued in Jeff Davis County.

Deputy Nowlin, accompanied by a citizen, had gone to the home of Jim Jones. Jones's house was located just over the county line. When they approached the house, Jones came out with a shotgun in his hands. Because Jones was known to Nowlin, he informed him that he had a warrant for his arrest. As the two discussed the matter, Nowlin served Jones with the warrant. Jones began to read it and then suddenly raised his shotgun and fired at Nowlin, striking him full on. The citizen immediately went for help and returned with a doctor. Nowlin succumbed to his wound two hours later.

Jones was arrested and charged with Nowlin's murder. He was sentenced to twenty-four years in prison.

Nowlin had only served with the agency for one month. He was survived by his wife and son. He is buried at Old Pontotoc Cemetery.

Beeson, Benjamin Franklin "Ben"
Born circa 1847—Died October 1889

Beeson served as a deputy under Llano County sheriff J.J. Bozarth during the Mason County "Hoo Doo War." He was involved in the killing of alleged cattle rustler Henry Hoy in August 1877, which led to his indictment along with another deputy. Both deputies were acquitted.

Beeson was elected sheriff on 4 November 1884 and reelected on 2 November 1886. Commissioner Court records indicate that Beeson resigned in a dispute over use of the courthouse. His brother-in-law, Matthew Caldwell Roberts, was appointed to complete his term, which ended on 6 November 1888. Roberts did not seek reelection.

Beeson and Roberts became embroiled in a family dispute. The two former sheriffs crossed paths in downtown Llano and argued. Beeson went home and got his pistol, and both men opened fire. Beeson was killed and Roberts seriously wounded. Beeson is buried at Llano City Cemetery.

LONGVIEW POLICE DEPARTMENT

Tabler, George M.
Born 22 February 1856—Died 24 September 1886

On 1 July 1886, City Marshal Tabler and Gregg County attorney Jeff Teague were involved in an argument. At 8:40 a.m. the next morning, the two men were involved in a shooting that left Teague dead and Tabler wounded. Tabler was released on a bond of $1,500. The Tablers and Teagues were both prominent families.

On 24 September 1886, Tabler was required to go to the town of Marshall in Harrison County for a trial that involved about 150 citizens from Longview as witnesses and attendants. Trouble was expected between the Tabler and the Teague families, and officers were on alert. Tabler had breakfast at the Capital Hotel. Afterward, he walked into an office, where he was confronted by T.M. Teague. Teague's son L.L. was stationed outside. The elder Teague had a Winchester. He began shooting, and twelve to twenty shots were reportedly fired at Tabler. Tabler was hit three times in the head and once in the hip. Tabler shot and wounded both of the Teagues before dying. The Teagues posted a $5,000 bond and were later tried and acquitted.

Tabler was survived by his wife. He is buried at Greenwood Cemetery in Longview.

MARION COUNTY SHERIFF'S OFFICE

Schwab, Charles J.
Born circa 1845—Died 5 November 1890

At about 10:30 a.m. on the morning of 5 November 1890, Deputy Schwab walked into Longworth's saloon in Jefferson. As he entered the establishment, a man named Joe Howell pulled a pistol and shot him through the heart, killing him instantly. After the incident, Howell was arrested amid threats of a possible lynching. Howell gave no reason for the shooting except that he thought Schwab was coming to arrest him for carrying a pistol.

Some months earlier, it was reported that Howell was "sent to the insane asylum at Terrell and declared a lunatic." He was subsequently released and returned to Jefferson. Obviously, there seems to have been some basis for Howell having been committed to the establishment at Terrell.

Deputy Schwab had been with the agency for twenty years and at one time had served on the Jefferson police force as a lieutenant. He is buried at Oakwood Cemetery in Jefferson.

MASON COUNTY SHERIFF'S OFFICE

Milligan, Thomas S.
Born circa 1819—Died 19 February 1860

On 2 August 1858, Thomas Milligan was elected the first sheriff of Mason County. On 19 February 1860, Sheriff Milligan was killed by hostile Indians within two hundred yards of his house.

Milligan was survived by his wife and seven children.

Wohrle, Johann Anton "John"
Born (Unknown)—Died 10 August 1875

On 13 May 1875, Tim Williamson was falsely arrested for cattle rustling in Mason County by Deputy Wohrle. While Wohrle was escorting Williamson to jail, an angry mob of German cattle ranchers jerked Williamson aside and shot him to death. On 10 August 1875, Wohrle was working on his well when former Texas Ranger William Scott Cooley, the foster son of Tim Williamson, went to Wohrle's home seeking revenge. The enraged Cooley shot Wohrle six times, killing him. He then scalped Wohrle, tossed him down a well and displayed his scalp as a prize.

The killing of Deputy Wohrle was part of a larger feud called the Mason County "Hoo Doo War." Scott Cooley continued to carry out his vendetta against those who had murdered his stepfather. He was joined in this lawless endeavor by notorious outlaws William "Bill" Williams and John Peters "Johnny" Ringo. They were arrested in December 1875 but escaped and continued to terrorize the area.

On 10 June 1876, Scott Cooley died in a hotel at Fredericksburg, Texas, of what was described as "brain fever." (The term was used in those days to describe what is now more accurately called meningitis or encephalitis.)

Deputy Wohrle is buried at Gooch Cemetery.

MATAGORDA COUNTY CONSTABLE'S OFFICE

Matthews, Jerry
Born circa 1857—Died 25 September 1887

By 1887, black citizens in Matagorda County had elected a state representative, a county commissioner, two justices of the peace and Constable Jerry Matthews.

John Nuckols and Dan Kennedy, two white men who were living in the Sargent neighborhood, refused to work on the roads with a group of black men or under the supervision of a black commissioner.

Constable Matthews of Precinct 3 was ordered to summon them before Justice of the Peace A.B. Brown. Before leaving, Matthews borrowed a pistol and advised several people that he would return after serving the writs— and, if not, that he had probably met with foul play.

Matthews arrived at Nuckols's home and found him away. A man in Nuckols's employ, a desperado by the name of Stafford, met Matthews at the door. After a few words with Stafford, Matthews departed. Stafford got on his horse, overtook Matthews and shot him. He dragged the body away and hid it in a swamp. A group of about seventy-five armed black men found Matthews's body floating in a creek with a bullet wound in the head.

The crowd went searching for Nuckols and Stafford, but both men had fled the community. The sheriff was summoned and instructed the group to return to their homes. His warning went unheeded.

News of what was already being called the "Matagorda Uprising" had reached surrounding county sheriffs, as well as the governor. Several sheriffs sent posses of armed white men. The governor called out two local militias to go to Matagorda County. The posses and militias shot and killed several black men, but the alleged ringleader, Oliver Sheppard, escaped with the assistance of a white district court judge. No one was ever prosecuted for the murder of Matthews.

Very little is known about Matthews. His place of burial is unknown.

Matagorda County Sheriff's Office

Rugley, Hamilton "Ham"
Born circa 1857—Died 13 April 1881

Deputy Rugley was accidentally shot and killed by a young lady friend who playfully pointed a pistol at him and said, "I believe I will shoot you, Ham." The bullet struck him in the neck, resulting in his death in about three minutes.

McLennan County Constable's Office

Peevey, Solon B.
Born 26 December 1851—Died 17 October 1892

Apparently, local rancher Solon Peevey, who was reportedly a constable, was out riding in his buggy when he passed the home of his neighbor, W.C. "Cal" Crunk. Peevey let out a whoop, which disturbed Mr. Crunk. Crunk yelled at him in protest, because it was Sunday morning and his sleeping family had been disturbed by the clamor. Peevey got down from his buggy, and a fight soon broke out. During the encounter, Crunk fired his pistol at least three times, with the fatal bullet striking Peevey in the groin and severing a main artery. Peevey bled to death in minutes.

The newspaper reports of the day, although unsubstantiated, claimed that Solon Peevey was a constable, a former deputy sheriff and a Texas Ranger.

Crunk was arrested and charged. The disposition of the case is unknown. Peevey is buried at Robinson Cemetery.

McLennan County Sheriff's Office

Blankenship, Burwell J. "Burt"
Born circa 1844—Died 24 July 1873

Deputy Blankenship was shot and killed while riding with a posse that was searching for several inmates who had escaped from the county jail.

The inmates set up an ambush about three miles from Waco. As the posse approached, the men opened fire on them. Posse members returned fire, and in the ensuing shootout Blankenship was mortally wounded. The escaped inmates were all apprehended. The man whom the prisoners identified as Blankenship's killer, Bob Chrystal of the Moore Gang, was shot and killed on 26 July 1873 as he tried to escape from the posse a second time.

Blankenship is buried at First Street Cemetery in Waco.

Wright, Moses L. "Moak"
Born circa 1844—Died 3 March 1876
Date of incident—2 March 1876

Waco police and McLennan County deputies were advised to be on the lookout for horse thieves who were expected to pass through town.

Deputies Moak Wright and Albert Dutton and policeman Henry McGhee were watching two suspicious men. They observed them at several saloons in town and knew that the pair were armed. About midnight, the lawmen approached the duo and began questioning them. They both gave their last name as Hamilton, from Navarro County. It was later discovered that their real names were Nathaniel Branch and Augustine P. Oliver. The officers released them to confer among themselves. One the men mounted a horse and the other was preparing to mount when the lawmen decided to arrest them. Both sides drew their pistols.

Wright grabbed the man who was not yet mounted and took his pistol. The man jerked loose and snatched Wright's pistol. The mounted man shot Wright through the body. Wright and Dutton opened fire and wounded the mounted suspect, killed one of the men's horses and wounded the other horse. McGhee stumbled and never fired a shot. Both men fled the scene. Wright was carried to a drugstore, where he died about 4:00 a.m.

Branch was found hiding in a wagon and was placed in jail. His wound proved fatal, and he died about 8:00 a.m. the following day. Oliver was arrested with blood on his pistol but claimed that a fleeing man gave him the gun. Although officers identified him as having been with Branch earlier, Oliver was not charged.

Wright had served for five years with both the police department and sheriff's office. He was also a member of Fire Engine No. 1.

Wright is buried at East Waco Greenwood Cemetery. He was survived by his wife and four small children.

McLENNAN, COUNTY OF

Camp, William H. "Will"
Born circa 1848—Died 8 June 1892

McLennan County operated a convict farm (work camp) for prisoners convicted of misdemeanors. These farms were correctional facilities, with some operating under the county sheriff and some under the direction of a county agency answering to the county judge and Commissioners Court. Many of the work camps for the state and counties leased out the convicts to do work for private lessees.

On 8 June 1892, a gang of convicts was chopping cotton on the Steiner farm located near the Brazos River about twelve miles downriver from Waco. The river was swollen from flooding, and the current was swift. One of the convicts, Sam Johnson, made a break for freedom and started swimming across the river. Camp, who was a guard, and the lessee, George Oglesby, were on horseback and started following the escapee in the river. Oglesby's and Camp's horses became tangled in debris and started struggling. Oglesby managed to make it back to the bank but was too injured and exhausted to go back into the river to save Camp. Camp had his pistol in one hand and never released it as he struggled in the current. Oglesby offered to pay any of the convicts who would attempt to rescue Camp. Andy Wash went into the river in an effort to save Camp, but both he and Camp perished in the tangled and swollen waters. Their bodies were found two days later floating near each other. The escapee, Sam Johnson, made it to the other side. Seeing the tragedy he had caused, he swam back across the river and returned to the convict gang.

No personal information was discovered about Camp. The newspaper stated that he was well known. His place of burial is unknown.

McMULLEN COUNTY SHERIFF'S OFFICE

Morgan, John Tillie
Born 5 September 1851—Died 15 March 1894
Date of incident: 1 January 1894

Morgan was a deputy sheriff and deputy U.S. marshal when tragedy befell him. About midnight on the evening of 1 January 1894, he was called to

166

investigate trouble at a Mexican dance. A man named Lucio Perez had inflicted two deep wounds with a large knife to the face of a youth. When Morgan tried to make an arrest, the knife-wielding assailant fatally wounded him. Morgan ultimately succumbed to the injuries from the attack on 15 March 1894.

Morgan is buried at Hilltop Cemetery in Tilden. He was survived by his wife and ten children.

MENARD COUNTY SHERIFF'S OFFICE

Vaden, John W.
Born 22 February 1849—Died 7 October 1886

John W. Vaden was, without question, a quarrelsome character who grew even more belligerent when he was drinking. After having served as a deputy sheriff in Maverick County, he decided to open a saloon at Ballinger in Runnels County.

On 6 August 1886, Vaden was intoxicated and had armed himself with a Winchester rifle. In the midst of the drunken episode that followed, Vaden shot City Marshal Tom Hill in the foot. The wound was serious, and the foot had to be amputated. The surgery was not successful. Hill died on 8 August 1886.

Vaden quickly repaired to Fort McKavett in Menard County and obtained a deputy commission from the sheriff. On 7 October 1886, he was, once again, drunk. This time he had armed himself with a pike. Vaden began to terrorize residents and rushed at Ben Daniels with the long, sharp shaft. Daniels was a bartender who also held a commissioned as a deputy sheriff. Daniels shot and killed Vaden out of self-defense. A grand jury decided not to prosecute Daniels for the shooting.

Vaden was survived by his wife and three children. He is buried at Fort McKavett Cemetery.

Related case: Ballinger Police Department—John Thomas Hill.

Mexia Police Department

Nowlin, David T. "Tom"
Born 9 December 1849—Died 26 September 1896

On 26 September 1896, several young men, including Constable James E. Eubanks, decided to play a prank on City Marshal Nowlin. The men placed blank cartridges in his pistol. They went to Freedmantown and raised a racket. Marshal Nowlin went to quiet the disturbance. The men opened fire with blank cartridges, and Nowlin returned fire, not knowing that he was also firing blanks. Constable Eubanks pretended to be wounded. Nowlin believed that he was outgunned and returned to town to get another pistol.

As Nowlin was returning to the scene of the supposed shootout, he was told that it was all a trick. The pranksters had withdrawn to the train depot by the time he arrived. He told Eubanks that he would cut off his own arm before he would play such a hoax on a friend. Eubanks said, "Would you?" and fired two shots, striking Nowlin. Witnesses said that they saw Nowlin draw his pistol as Eubanks fired.

Eubanks was arrested and released on $5,000 bail. The city council met and declared that Nowlin was killed in the discharge of his duties and voted to hire an attorney to assist the district attorney. The disposition of the case is unknown.

Nowlin was a widower and had five small children. He was also a member of the city fire department. Nowlin is buried at Mexia Cemetery next to his wife and a daughter, who died in 1895.

Milam County Constable's Office

Norman, Francis Yewing
Born 14 June 1846—Died 27 February 1886

At about 1:00 a.m. on 27 February 1886, Precinct 7 constable Francis Norman went to Clark's Store to arrest Walter Lane on a warrant stemming from his failure to appear in court to face a charge of cattle theft in Falls County. He was accompanied by Constable M.P. Stevens and a man named Dan Campbell. Norman took the storekeeper outside to question him about the whereabouts of Lane, while Stevens and Campbell stayed inside the store. About that time, Lane rode up, armed with two pistols. Norman attempted to arrest him, and both men opened fire, killing each other.

Norman is buried at Lilac Cemetery in Sharp. He had been constable since 1878. Norman was survived by his wife and four small children.

Busby, Nathan
Born circa 1832—Died 26 April 1894
Date of incident: 24 April 1894

On 24 April 1894, Constable Busby left his beat in Rockdale to travel about two miles north of the city for dinner. About 7:30 p.m., he started back to Rockdale. Near the old York farm he arrested Yeabel Chiro for being intoxicated.

Constable Busby was walking Chiro back to town and leading his horse when Chiro suddenly turned and struck at him with a knife. The first blow missed his throat, but Chiro lunged again. His next thrust of the knife inflicted a serious wound to Busby's jaw. The constable and Chiro began to struggle. Busby discharged his pistol twice. Chiro overpowered Busby and stabbed him several times. Busby managed to throw Chiro off and escaped to a residence, where medical assistance was summoned. Busby died on 26 April 1894.

A posse was sent after Chiro, but he was successful in eluding them. In August 1894, several newspapers reported that the man had been apprehended in Kentucky, but it turned out to be the wrong person. In May 1908, it was reported that Sheriff Holtzclaw returned from Brownwood with a prisoner believed to be Chiro. The identity of that man has not been confirmed, nor is it known if Chiro was ever found and prosecuted.

Nathan Busby was elected constable for Precinct 4 in Rockdale on 8 November 1892. He had nine children. His wife, Mary, reportedly preceded him in death. Busby is buried at Old City Cemetery in Rockdale.

MILAM COUNTY SHERIFF'S OFFICE

Pool, Gabriel Leander "Lee"
Born 6 July 1858—Died 7 April 1887

On 7 April 1887, Deputies Pool, John Bickett and Frank Uccalla, along with four citizens, went to arrest Will Jacobs. Jacobs was wanted for murder.

The posse surrounded Jacobs house, which was located about twelve miles from Rockdale. Jacobs refused to surrender. Both sides opened fire. Pool was struck and fatally wounded. A posse member named Barber was also injured during the exchange of gunfire.

Although seriously wounded, Jacobs managed to escape. He was later apprehended, tried and sentenced to serve ten years in prison.

Deputy Pool is buried at Corinth Cemetery at Buckholtz.

Will Jacobs was the son of Goliad County sheriff Andrew Jacobs, who was killed in the line of duty on 5 June 1869. Will Jacobs was also involved in the killing of Guadalupe County deputy sheriff Richard "Tex" McCoy on 16 May 1881 and Deputy U.S. Marshal Frank Rhodes on 11 April 1885.

MITCHELL COUNTY SHERIFF'S OFFICE

Parks, Wayne B.
Born circa 1853—Died 29 October 1885

In October 1885, brothers Ike and Joe Adair had far too much to drink and were raising a disturbance in the gambling room located at the back of Page and Charlie's Saloon. Deputy Parks heard the noise and went to investigate. Parks walked up to Ike, who at the time was yelling. He threatened to arrest him if he did not keep quiet. Ike drew his pistol. Parks grabbed Ike's arm in an effort to make him drop the gun. While they were struggling over the pistol, brother Joe opened his long pocketknife and came up behind Parks, slashing him around his head and inflicting a serious wound. Parks drew his pistol and shot over his shoulder at Joe while at the same time attempting to keep Ike from shooting him. The deputy's bullet passed through Joe's heart, killing him instantly.

City Marshal Jim Woods came into the gambling room about that time, and Parks told him to take Ike's gun, as he did not want to hurt him.

As was the custom of the time, Parks was charged with murder and was awaiting trial at the time of his death.

The father of the Adairs was a prominent local cattleman. On 28 October 1885, Parks had accompanied a young woman to a ball in Colorado City. They left the dance about midnight, and he was escorting the woman to her home. About 1:00 a.m., as he was starting to cross a vacant lot, he was fired upon from ambush. Parks was found dead by neighbors, who heard the shot and the moaning from the injured deputy. He had been hit by ten pellets of buckshot from a shotgun, with three pellets having entered his neck, breaking the bone. The killer had obviously been lying in wait for the deputy because numerous footprints were discovered in the vicinity near a fence and under a tree. Tracks were found where one man appeared to have been waiting with two horses, while another man walked to the hiding place.

Parks had been a deputy sheriff for three years under Sheriff R.C. "Dick" Ware. His body was sent to Meridian in Bosque County, where he was buried at the city cemetery. The newspaper reported that Parks's family had been trying to persuade him to return to Bosque County because they feared that he would meet a violent death should he remain in Colorado City.

A grand jury investigated the case, and many witnesses were examined. No one was ever indicted, and no evidence was disclosed that identified the assassin of Deputy Parks.

Binnion, Joe
Born 9 February 1869—Died 14 April 1897
Date of incident: 10 April 1897

Jim Cooke's mother had asked Deputy Binnion to speak with her troubled son about returning home.

On 10 April 1897, Deputy Binnion went to the house in Colorado City where Cooke was known to be. As he stepped through the door, the young man shot at him, hitting Binnion in the bowels. Cooke then turned the gun on himself, blowing the top of his head off. Deputy Binnion fell outside and fired one shot into the room, not knowing that Cooke was already dead.

Binnion was carried home, where he eventually died on 14 April 1897. He is buried at Colorado City Cemetery.

MONTAGUE COUNTY SHERIFF'S OFFICE

Broaddus, Robert L.
Born circa 1838—Died 17 October 1876

Deputy Broaddus, along with two guards assisting him named Bud McGary and Tom Lemans, were transporting prisoner George Wilson from Collin County to Montague County. Wilson was to stand trial on misdemeanor charges. The four men were camped along Bolivar Creek in Denton County.

The two guards were preparing breakfast when Wilson grabbed McGary's pistol. He then shot and killed Broaddus. Wilson disarmed the other guard and then stole Broaddus's horse and escaped.

Newspaper accounts reported that the two guards had testified at a court of inquest that after Wilson killed Broaddus, he had offered to buy a saddle from one of them for twenty dollars. They refused but did sell Wilson a pistol for ten dollars and gave him a blanket so that he wouldn't have to ride bareback.

On 2 June 1877, the Texas governor offered a $500 reward. In November 1877, he upped the amount to $750. One source reported that Wilson was wounded and in custody of the sheriff in Yavapai County, Arizona. There are no records showing the outcome of the murder trial for Wilson.

Broaddus was survived by a brother. He is buried at Montague City Cemetery. A historic iron fence surrounds his grave.

Pollard, John Barton
Born 20 December 1854—Died 14 August 1878

Deputy Pollard shot and killed a man named "Blue" Roberts. The incident took place after Roberts had shot and fatally wounded Deputy Pollard's brother, Meredith C. Pollard.

Not long after the Roberts shooting, Deputy Pollard was reportedly ambushed and killed. Some accounts, although unconfirmed, have claimed that Pollard's killer was a Texas Ranger.

Pollard was survived by his wife, Joan Bishop, and one daughter. He is buried at Montague City Cemetery.

MONTGOMERY COUNTY SHERIFF'S OFFICE

Womack, Abner, Jr.
Born circa 1856—Died 7 April 1876

On 7 April 1876, Deputy Womack was collecting taxes in the town of Willis when he came upon a notorious horse thief named George Burrows. Womack had papers for the arrest of Burrows from a neighboring county and attempted to serve them on the man. Burrows drew his pistol and shot and killed the deputy. Burrows mounted the dead deputy's horse and escaped.

The disposition of any charges against Burrows is unknown at this time.

Morris County Constable's Office

Ledbetter, F.M.
Born circa 1856—Died 16 December 1892

Henry "Harry" Graham shot and killed a man in neighboring Titus County. He crossed into Morris County and made threats that "no little officer could arrest him."

Graham went to the town of Omaha, where Precinct 3 constable Ledbetter and Deputy Sheriff Curlee attempted to defy the challenge and arrest him. After a chase that covered several miles, Constable Ledbetter cornered Graham inside a house and ordered him to surrender. Graham pulled a pistol and shot Ledbetter. The bullet struck him in the neck, and he died within a few hours.

Graham was shot and wounded before he was eventually taken into custody at Commerce. He was convicted by a jury and sentenced to be executed at Dangerfield. On 26 May 1893, the governor granted a two-week respite while he reviewed a request filed to commute the sentence of Graham. On 7 June 1893, Governor Hogg informed Sheriff J.W. High of Morris County that he was not going to interfere with the jury's decision and that the execution could proceed. Accordingly, on 9 June 1893, Graham was executed by hanging in Morris County.

Ledbetter was survived by his wife and five children. His place of burial is unknown.

Story, Probert Peolia
Born 26 December 1855—Died 15 May 1893
Date of incident: 15 February 1893

Story was elected constable for Precinct 4 at Belden in Morris County on 15 November 1892. The old town of Belden is now the city of Naples.

On 15 February 1893, Constable Story was trying to arrest a man. He resisted. Story struck the man with his pistol. The man knocked his arm up and caused the pistol to fall to the floor and discharge. The bullet entered Story's thigh and went upward, breaking his thigh and hip bones. Constable Story died on 15 May 1893.

The disposition of the criminal charges against Story's killer are unknown.

Story is buried at Naples City Cemetery. He was survived by his wife, Zephie, and several children.

MORRIS COUNTY SHERIFF'S OFFICE

High, John W.
Born circa 1860—Died 4 December 1898

John High had been elected sheriff on 4 November 1890. He was reelected 8 November 1892 and again on 4 November 1894. He served until 3 November 1896.

On 4 December 1898, the former sheriff was in Naples when, for some unknown reason, he opened fire on a black man named Joe Thomas. He missed. Thomas fired back at High and did not miss, hitting him several times. Thomas then fled.

High died within minutes. Thomas surrendered to officers, claiming self-defense. He was jailed in Daingerfield. The disposition of the charges is unknown.

MOTLEY COUNTY SHERIFF'S OFFICE

Cook, George W.
Born circa 1856—Died 29 May 1895
Date of incident: 28 May 1895

There was a great deal of anger and hostility between County Commissioner Cook and Sheriff Joe Beckham. In June 1893, Cook and Beckham had been involved in a shootout in neighboring Childress County. That incident resulted in no injuries, but both men were indicted. Cook was acquitted and Beckham was released. Beckham was then indicted for embezzling county tax money. County commissioners removed Beckham from office. On 6 November 1894, Cook was elected sheriff.

Beckham received a change of venue to Baylor County on his embezzling charge. On 28 May 1895, Sheriff Cook traveled by train to Seymour to testify against Beckham. Beckham was waiting for Cook at the train station, where he shot the sheriff through the arm, bowels and left nipple. Cook was returned to his house in Motley County, where he died on 29 May.

Cook is buried in an unmarked grave at Matador Cemetery. He was survived by his wife and at least one child. His brother-in-law, Deputy Sheriff B.F. Harper, was appointed to fill his term of office.

Related case: Childress County Sheriff's Office—John P. Matthews.

Beckham, Joseph P. "Joe"
Born circa 1869—Died 26 December 1895

Beckham was the first elected sheriff on 5 February 1891. He was reelected on 8 November 1892 and served until he was removed from office in 1894 for embezzlement.

The county commissioners appointed J.L. Moore as sheriff, but Beckham and his deputies disarmed Moore. Childress County sheriff John P. Matthews and a posse arrested the deputies, and Beckham fled to Indian Territory. He was tracked down by Sheriff Matthews, County Commissioner G.W. Cook and a Texas Ranger. While the lawmen were attempting to get extradition papers, Beckham fled to Texas and surrendered.

A district court appointed Billy Moses as sheriff. On 6 November 1894, George W. Cook was elected sheriff. On 28 May 1895, Beckham shot Sheriff Cook at the train station in Seymour in Baylor County. Beckham fled to the Indian Territory and began a campaign of robbing and killing in Greer County.

On 26 December 1895, a posse composed of Wilbarger County sheriff R.P. Sanders, two of his deputies, Texas Ranger lieutenant Sullivan, two additional rangers and a group of cowboys surrounded Beckham and his gang. After a five-hour shootout, Beckham was finally killed.

Related case: Childress County Sheriff's Office—John P. Matthews.

NACOGDOCHES COUNTY CONSTABLE'S OFFICE

Harvell, David W.
Born circa 1842—Died 14 December 1871

Birdwell, John
Born circa 1812—Died 19 December 1871

On 14 December 1871, two black Texas state policemen, Columbus Hazlett and William Grayson, attended a justice of the peace court session in the Linn Flat community. Evidently, the pair disagreed with some of the actions of the court. The two policemen caused a disturbance and threatened to shoot one of the lawyers.

Justice Dawson charged them with contempt. An arrest warrant was issued, and Dawson gave it to Constable Birdwell to execute. Birdwell summoned a man named David W. Harvell to assist him in the arrest of the two state policemen. The constable located Hazlett nearby and arrested him. Hazlett offered no resistance and upon Birdwell's command called to Grayson in a nearby store.

When Grayson drew near, Hazlett told him that he was a prisoner. Grayson replied that he would die before surrendering. Deputized citizen Harvell then demanded that Hazlett hand over his gun. Instead, Hazlett drew his weapon and shot Harvell in the chest. Harvell did not go down immediately, however, and staggered to a nearby store and picked up a shotgun. He then fired the first barrel into Hazlett's face. Hazlett was hit by only a few pellets, but the second barrel was discharged in the direction of Grayson, wounding him. Hazlett and Grayson returned fire, twice hitting Harvell, who dropped dead on the store floor. Birdwell never had a chance to draw his weapon and was looking down the barrel of the state policemen's guns when they mounted their horses and rode off.

On 19 December 1871, Birdwell answered a knock on his door and was shot dead by Grayson and Hazlett. Arrest warrants were promptly issued for the pair. About a week later, state police lieutenant Thomas Williams rode into Linn Flat with Grayson and Hazlett. Williams negotiated with Sheriff Orton for several days over the arrest and confinement of the two state policemen. No settlement was reached, but Williams mysteriously rode away one night with the two prisoners in tow. Soon after, the head of the state police upheld the law and returned to surrender Hazlett and Grayson to the sheriff.

Grayson was convicted and sent to prison for life. Hazlett escaped from jail before his trial, fled to Arkansas and was killed by bounty hunters.

Hazlett had three children and no spouse. His place of burial is unknown.

Birdwell was survived by his wife and ten children. His place of burial is also unknown.

On 14 March 1873, Thomas Williams (now state police captain), along with three other state policemen, was killed in a shootout in Lampasas by members of the Horrell faction.

NAVARRO COUNTY CONSTABLE'S OFFICE

Craig, John N.
Born (Unknown)—Died 3 June 1890

John Craig was the constable for the precinct that included the Kerens community. On 3 June 1890, Craig went to a saloon in Kerens, intent on provoking a fight with two brothers, B.H. "Bloof" Davis and William "Will" Davis.

As he had resolved, Craig got into a confrontation with Will Davis. Will's brother Bloof attempted to break it up. A few minutes later, the fight flared up again, but this time Craig and Bloof were the parties involved. Bloof shot Craig, and either he or his brother Will cut Craig with a knife. Craig died from his wounds.

Bloof and Will Davis were convicted of second-degree murder and imprisoned. Bloof Davis was granted a new trial in August 1891, and the case was dismissed after the jury could not reach a verdict.

Craig's place of burial is unknown.

NAVARRO COUNTY SHERIFF'S OFFICE

Smithey, William J.
Born circa 1846—Died 16 December 1870
Date of incident: 10 December 1870

On the evening of 10 December 1870, Deputy Smithey and District Clerk W.B. Johnston were involved in an argument during which Johnston shot Smithey with a derringer. The bullet became lodged near his neck, and he died from his wounds six days later.

Johnston was arrested but was discharged, as the shooting was deemed to be self-defense.

Smithey was a Confederate army veteran and had served in the Fifteenth Regiment, Texas Infantry. Reportedly, he was wounded at the Battle of Yellow Bayou in 1864.

Cubley, Robert H., Jr.
Born 20 November 1862—Died 9 September 1891

Robert H. "Little Bob" Cubley Sr., a former Corsicana policeman and constable, was elected sheriff on 4 November 1890. He served until 8 November 1892. During his term of office, he employed his son, Robert H. Cubley Jr., as a deputy sheriff. Several days before the following shooting incident occurred, Sheriff Cubley had his son resign his position as deputy and move to Ennis. There had been an earlier shooting incident involving the younger Cubley and a Coriscana policeman named Rufus Highnote.

On 9 September 1891, Cubley Jr. returned to Corsicana and was seated outside the B. Marks Grocery Store with his brother, Art. Policeman Highnote and his cousin, Cal White, were standing nearby watching Cubley. Cubley rose and asked Mr. Marks for a cigar. Art went to speak to Highnote and White as they entered the store. Cubley wheeled and fired two shots at White, striking him in the arm and hand. Highnote and Cubley then exchanged fire. Cubley was struck in the lower left jaw, the side of the neck and in the left side. The mortally wounded Cubley was taken to his father's house, where he died shortly thereafter.

Highnote surrendered to the city marshal. The trial of Highnote and White lasted more than two years. Neither man was convicted of any wrongdoing.

Cubley is buried at Oakwood Cemetery.

NAVARRO, COUNTY OF

Taylor, Gideon C.
Born circa 1850—Died 23 September 1894

Taylor was shot and killed while returning to the county poor farm where he served as superintendent.

During his trip, he encountered two extremely intoxicated men, Jim and Tom Murphy. The pair had been accused of shooting a pistol earlier in the day. During his encounter with the Murphy boys, Taylor was shot and killed. Both men were arrested a short time later at a nearby home. Because there were no witnesses to the shooting, both men were acquitted.

Taylor had served with the Navarro County Sheriff's Department for two years. He was survived by his wife and seven children. He is buried at Dresden Cemetery.

NEW BRAUNFELS POLICE DEPARTMENT

Hampe, August
Born circa 1846—Died 27 January 1883
Date of incident: 26 January 1883

City Marshal Hampe was shot and killed by a man named Napoleon Pitts. The exact circumstances or motive for the killing are unclear.

Local citizens had apparently considered lynching Pitts, who was a black man. A mob of about forty angry men armed with guns and axes broke in the door of the jail at New Braunfels in an effort to get to Pitts. The undaunted jailer charged the mob single-handed, with a revolver in each hand, and drove them into the street, saying that if they returned he would open fire on them. The mob made no further attempts.

Pitts was found guilty of murder in the first degree in the killing of Marshal Hampe and sentenced to ninety-nine years in prison.

Marshal Hampe was born in Germany in 1846. He was survived by his wife, Margarethe, four sons (Ernst, Gustav, Wilhelm and August Jr.) and one daughter named Sophie.

NUECES COUNTY SHERIFF'S OFFICE

Nolan, Thomas
Born circa 1836—Died 15 August 1860
Date of incident: 4 August 1860

On 4 August 1860, Deputy Thomas Nolan and his brother, Sheriff Matthew Nolan, responded to a call concerning an armed and intoxicated man creating a disturbance. While attempting to arrest the person, John Warren, he produced a handgun from his trousers and shot Tom Nolan in the forehead. Nolan remained in a coma until his death eleven days later.

Nolan had served with the Nueces County Sheriff's Department for three years. He is buried at Old Bayview Cemetery next to his brother Matthew.

Nolan, Matthew "Mat"
Born circa 1830—Died 22 December 1864

Sheriff Nolan was talking to a horse trader named J.C. McDonald, who was sometimes called by the uncomplimentary nickname "McFox." As they talked, they were approached by two brothers, Frank and Charles Gravis. One of the Gravis brothers asked if they were Colonel Mat Nolan and "McFox." When Nolan replied that they were, one of the pair discharged a double-barreled shotgun into his back. Nolan fell mortally wounded. McDonald pursued the men. One of the Gravis brothers turned and fired at him several times. McDonald was struck by a pistol shot behind his ear. Nolan was carried into his house, where he made a dying declaration identifying the Gravis brothers.

The Gravises were cooperating with the Unionists in town. It is believed that Nolan was murdered because the Gravis faction suspected that Sheriff Nolan was going to take action against their stepfather. They were indicted but never brought to trial. Union authorities dismissed the indictment on 6 December 1866. The Gravises' stepfather was appointed sheriff, and one brother was made a deputy sheriff.

Nolan came to Corpus Christi at the age of twelve as a bugler with the U.S. Second Dragoons in 1845. He served as a Texas Ranger under John S. "Rip" Ford, fighting Indians and bandits in south Texas. Nolan was a colonel in the Confederate army at the time of his death. He had been elected sheriff on 2 August 1858, reelected on 6 August 1860 and served until 4 August 1862. He was once again elected on 1 August 1864 and served until his death.

Sheriff Nolan was survived by his wife and buried at Old Bayview Cemetery next to his brother Thomas.

Kelly, Dennis J.
Born circa 1827—Died 13 June 1870

On 13 June 1870, Sheriff Kelly walked past Thomas Burke on a downtown street in Corpus Christi. The sheriff knew that Burke was a wanted man but walked past him anyway. Burke apparently decided not to return the courtesy; he promptly shot and killed Sheriff Kelly.

Burke fled, and a $500 reward was offered for his capture. No records have been located to indicate if Burke was ever apprehended.

Kelly was appointed on 16 April 1869 by General J.J. Reynolds's Special Order No. 90 and took the oath on 30 April 1869. He was elected to the office on 3 December 1869 and served until his death.

Kelly was survived by his wife and five children. He is buried at Holy Cross Cemetery next to his wife.

Shaw, Thomas
Born circa 1852—Died September 1877

Deputy Thomas Shaw was killed while transporting a prisoner named Martin Rodriguez (alias Conequita) to jail.

Shaw and an assistant named Howell were transporting Rodriguez to the county jail in a wagon. Rodriguez's wife accompanied the men on the wagon ride. Shaw had arrested Rodriguez at Los Olmos, in northeast Brooks County.

According to the rather far-fetched account given by Rodriguez's wife, when the group reached a point about six miles from Petrolia a group of six men rode up and cut Shaw with knives, killing him. The men then released Rodriguez. The general belief is that Rodriguez had somehow managed to untie himself and that he was the one who had stabbed and killed Shaw. Shaw had sent the other man, Mr. Howell, to get fresh horses.

Shaw was survived by his mother, six brothers and sisters. His place of burial is unknown.

OLDHAM COUNTY SHERIFF'S OFFICE

McCullough, Henry W.
Born (Unknown)—Died 17 July 1882

By means of background, C.B. "Cape" Willingham was the first sheriff of Oldham County. He was elected on 12 January 1881. Sheriff Willingham appointed McCullough as constable of Precinct 1. On 1 June 1882, Willingham asked and received permission to appoint McCullough as a deputy sheriff and as city marshal of Tascosa. He was paid twenty-five dollars per month.

On 17 July 1882, Deputy McCullough attempted to arrest "Mexican Frank" Larque (also reported as "Larqus," "Larques" and "Largus") for a gambling violation at the Jenkins & Donnelly Saloon and Dance Hall in Tascosa. Larque was not going to be taken to jail, so he was not ordered to remove his pistol from his holster. While his gun was still holstered, he fired the revolver, hitting McCullough in the stomach and killing him.

Larque was quickly captured while fleeing to the New Mexico Territory. He was convicted on 12 September 1882 and sentenced to twenty-two years in the state prison.

McCullough is buried at Tascosa's Boot Hill Cemetery, apparently in an unmarked grave. Little personal information is known about McCullough. He had reportedly been on the wrong side of the law before becoming a lawman.

Orange County Sheriff's Office

Deputy, Samuel L.
Born circa 1827—About 15 May 1856

An event that would later become known as the "Orange County War of 1856" led to the death of the sheriff and a deputy.

The incident began when Deputy Samuel Deputy accused a freed black man named Clark Ashworth of butchering hogs that did not belong to him. Clark's cousin, Sam Ashworth, threatened to kill Deputy. He was charged with "abusive language by a mulatto" and sentenced to thirty lashes. He was remanded to Sheriff E.C. Glover, who was friendly with the Ashworth clan. Glover allowed Sam to escape.

Sam Ashworth and his eighteen-year-old friend Jackson Bunch ambushed Deputy and a companion on Cow Bayou while the two men were rowing their boat to Deputy's home. Ashworth and Bunch shot Deputy and beat him with the butts of their guns. Deputy died. His companion escaped and alerted authorities. The sheriff made a halfhearted search attempt.

Two factions, called the Moderators and Regulators, quickly formed after this incident. The Moderators declared the sheriff's office vacant. Sheriff Glover and his supporters organized as Regulators. The Moderators eventually captured the sheriff at a Regulator meeting and killed him.

Bunch was brought to trial for the murder of Samuel Deputy. During the trial, which took place in Beaumont, rumors spread that friends planned to rescue Bunch. As a result of the threat, people carried guns and knives into the courthouse during the trial. Bunch was convicted on 12 November 1856 and hanged two weeks later on 21 November 1856. The scaffold was so crudely constructed that the condemned youth had to climb a ladder that was then twisted and pulled out from under him.

Sam Ashworth fared somewhat better. After a period in west Texas, he fled to the Indian Territory and lived with the Choctaw tribe for several years. It is claimed, although unverified, that when the Civil War began he enlisted in the Confederate army and was killed at the Battle of Shiloh in April 1862.

Deputy is believed to have been born in Kentucky about 1827. His place of burial is also unknown.

Glover, Edward C.
Born (Unknown)—Died July 1856

John Moore and his nephew, Glover, started counterfeiting land certificates and bank notes after the Texas Revolution in 1836. Glover was arrested in 1844 for passing the bogus bank certificates, but he was never indicted. On 17 March 1856, Glover was either elected or appointed sheriff. He was friendly with wealthy freed blacks, including the Ashworth clan.

On or about 15 May 1856, Deputy Sheriff Samuel Deputy arrested Clark Ashworth for butchering a hog he did not own. Clark's cousin, Sam Ashworth, threatened Deputy and was arrested for "abusive language by a mulatto" and sentenced to thirty lashes. Ashworth was released to Sheriff Glover and allowed to escape. Ashworth and Jack Bunch later ambushed and killed Deputy. This event signaled the start of the "Orange County War of 1856."

Two factions, called the Moderators and Regulators, quickly formed after this incident. The Moderators were primarily white citizens whose purpose was to bring law and order to the county. They declared the sheriff's office vacant and ordered all mulatto families to leave the county. The sheriff and his supporters organized themselves into a group called the Regulators. Their group, headed by the sheriff, was composed of about 150 whites and free blacks. They promised to destroy the town. According to some reports, for the next six to eight weeks buildings were burned and men were killed in the streets of Orange every Saturday. The crime wave continued until the Moderators eventually captured the sheriff at a Regulator meeting place and killed him.

In early July 1856, the Moderators attacked a gathering of Regulators at John Moore's log cabin in what is now the town of Deweyville. Jack Cross, a notorious killer wanted for six murders, was riding with the Moderators. He killed John Moore. After Sheriff Glover refused to leave the county, Cross also killed him. They found a chest filled with counterfeiting plates, bogus money and land certificates. This discovery solved a counterfeiting ring that had operated for twenty years in four states. Glover's place of burial is unknown.

Fennel, James C.
Born 29 January 1853—Died 25 September 1885

Dave Anderson arrived in Orange County by train. Anderson was wanted in Nashville, Tennessee, for the 16 August 1885 murder of I.B. Buddington, who was a brakeman on the Louisville and Nashville Railway. When the brakeman tried to stop Anderson from stealing a ride on the train, Anderson killed him.

Sheriff Fennel attempted to arrest Anderson on the murder warrant from Tennessee. Anderson shot the sheriff during the arrest attempt. Fennel died about 9:30 p.m. on 25 September 1885.

Orange city marshal Davis gathered a posse and tracked down the killer. They captured Anderson and lodged him in the county jail. After dark, a torchlight mob of masked men marched to the jail and forcibly removed the prisoner "at the point of 100 cocked revolvers," according to a local newspaper report. He was quickly carried to an oak tree on First Street and hanged. After the lynching, the mob dispersed, leaving Anderson's bullet-riddled body on display.

Fennel was elected sheriff on 4 November 1884. He is buried at Evergreen Cemetery in Orange in an unmarked grave. Fennel was survived by his wife, Lucy Junker. The spelling of his surname has also been reported as "Fennell."

ORANGE POLICE DEPARTMENT

Washington, Clark
Born circa 1850—Died 4 April 1891

Clark Washington was appointed as a special policeman, which was customary at the time for black men in law enforcement.

On the night of 4 April 1891, at a hall known as the "colored schoolhouse," there was a public gathering attended primarily by black men and women. A group of citizens had turned out to hear from candidates who were running for city offices. After the speeches had concluded, all of the white citizens left, and the hall was converted to an ice cream bazaar. A man named Archie Washington, who was not related to Clark Washington, was seen with a pistol in his hands. He reportedly told someone that he would empty his gun into anyone who interfered with him. Officer Washington attempted to take the pistol away from Archie. A scuffle over the gun took place, and the participants left the hall. About thirty minutes later, Archie and the officer were seen conversing in a low tone and apparently in a cordial manner.

Officer Washington was then heard to say, "If you don't quit making so much noise I will arrest you and put you in jail." Archie, who was in the process of leaving, answered, "I guess you are a God damned liar." Officer Washington then grabbed Archie and attempted to arrest him. Archie jumped back a few feet and shot the officer twice with his pistol. When Archie fired the second time, Clark turned and ran. Archie called out after him, "Now die, you [racial expletive], die."

Washington ran a short distance and then staggered. He recovered himself and called for a doctor. He then ran into the hall, but when he reached the door, he fell mortally wounded on the floor. Officer Washington died twenty minutes later, having suffered a wound to the abdomen and a flesh wound through the left forearm.

Archie Washington was sentenced to life in prison, but his case was overturned on appeal. He was sentenced to death at his second trial. He appealed again but escaped from jail for a few days. The court dismissed his appeal, this time due largely to the escape incident. Archie Washington was sentenced to death. Accordingly, he was executed by hanging at Orange on 26 July 1892.

Officer Washington was one of the earliest line-of-duty deaths of a black law enforcement officer in Texas. He was survived by his wife, Aurena Jones. His place of burial is unknown.

PALESTINE POLICE DEPARTMENT

Cary, Dan
Born circa 1851—Died 1872

Dan Cary was a carpetbagger from New York and had come to Palestine after the Civil War. Radicals (Republicans) had elected him city marshal. Cary was said to have been a bully.

It is claimed that Cary and a man named Chris Rogers were involved in some sort of misunderstanding, the source of which is unknown. Apparently, their trouble escalated and led to Rogers killing Cary.

There are no court records of any charges having been brought against Rogers. Rogers was elected city marshal in 1874.

Cary's exact date of death and place of burial are unknown.

Rogers, Christopher "Chris" Columbus
Born circa 1846—Died 25 June 1888

Rogers lived in Palestine for most of his life. He volunteered to serve in the Confederate army at a young age, and after the war, he returned to Palestine to work in a printing office.

In 1872, he became involved in a personal dispute with the newly elected city marshal, Dan Cary. Rogers shot and killed Cary. In 1874, Rogers was elected city marshal. He served in that capacity until his death. Some have reported that he was a deputy U.S. marshal, but to date evidence to support that claim has not been located.

On 25 June 1888, Marshal Rogers was having a glass of beer with a friend named W.D. "Billie" Young when he called one of Young's friends a liar. A quarrel took place, during which Young produced a knife and cut Rogers fatally. Young was later acquitted.

Marshal Rogers is buried at East Hill Cemetery in Palestine. He is claimed to have killed nine men while serving as a lawman, adding to his tally of one before being elected.

PALO PINTO COUNTY SHERIFF'S OFFICE

Wilson, J.T.
Born (Unknown)—Died 23 January 1879

Wilson was elected sheriff on 15 February 1876 and reelected on 5 November 1878.

On 23 January 1879, Sheriff Wilson was in Austin for the sheriff's convention when he became involved in an argument with Sherman city marshal Samuel Ball. Ball shot and killed Wilson. Two bystanders were also wounded. Ball was not convicted of the crime.

Wilson is believed to be buried at Wilson Cemetery in Palo Pinto County.

In a separate and unrelated incident, Sherman city marshal Sam Ball was shot in the line of duty on 27 January 1880 and died on 2 February 1880.

Thomas, F.M.
Born circa 1858—Died 12 April 1886

On 12 April 1886, Deputy Thomas and former county treasurer John Randolph were involved in a shooting incident at Golconda. Thomas was killed in the affray. The dispute was over litigation involving the failure of the Randolph brothers' business, in which Thomas was a member.

It is unknown if Randolph was ever charged or convicted in the case.

Paris Police Department

Albright, William "Will"
Born circa 1852—Died 4 December 1874

Officer Albright attempted to arrest twenty-year-old Sam Provine and a man named McMiller at a sporting house in Paris. Provine and McMiller shot Officer Albright. The gunshots broke his neck, killing him instantly.

Provine and McMiller were arrested and held for examination. The records that would have shown the outcome of this case were destroyed in a fire at the Lamar County Courthouse.

Albright was survived by his wife and two small children. No cemetery records, or the burial location, have been located.

Pecos County Sheriff's Office

Royal, Andrew Jackson "A.J."
Born 25 November 1855—21 November 1894

Andrew Jackson Royal was elected sheriff on 8 November 1892 and served until 6 November 1894.

The controversial Royal had come to Fort Stockton from Junction City, where he had been involved in a saloon business called the Royal House with former Texas Ranger Davy Tom Carson. Royal, reportedly concerned about legal matters surrounding a shooting he was involved in with Carson in the winter of 1884, pulled up stakes and moved to Fort Stockton in Pecos County in 1889. There, in the all but abandoned town that had been bypassed by the railroad and deserted by the army, Royal bought 265 head of cattle and an

1,800-acre ranch with irrigated land seven miles west of town. He also set up a saloon business and bought the former post trader's building in town.

Royal ran for commissioner in 1890 and won, later winning a subsequent election to the post of sheriff of Pecos County on 8 November 1892.

While serving as sheriff, Royal was accused by some of using his post to terrorize those who disagreed with him. Others considered him a tough lawman who fought to establish law and order. He was defeated in the subsequent election by R.B. Neighbors.

On 24 November 1894, Royal was murdered in the sheriff's office while seated at his former desk, shot from ambush by an unknown assassin. No one was ever charged with the murder.

Royal was survived by his wife, Naomi Obedience Christmus, and seven children.

POLK COUNTY SHERIFF'S OFFICE

Rhodes, (Unknown)
Born (Unknown)—Died 25 September 1889

A Montgomery County deputy sheriff named Davis had been pursuing John Bell for cattle theft for four days. Deputy Davis was ten miles from the community of Warren on 25 September 1889 when Tyler County Precinct 2 constable Frank Walters and Polk County deputy sheriff Rhodes attempted to arrest Bell for the Montgomery County cattle theft. Bell was driving a wagon with his wife and two children when the lawmen approached him. The two lawmen were shot through the head and died immediately. Bell remained on the scene for nearly an hour and prohibited anyone from removing the dead bodies of the lawmen until he saw fit to leave. Bell took the best horse, abandoned his wife and children and fled through the Big Thicket toward the Louisiana border. Deputy Davis, Tyler County sheriff G.R. Ector and his deputy named Parker headed out in hot pursuit of Bell.

Shortly after daybreak on 27 September 1889, the lawmen got word that Bell was at a cabin nearby. As they approached, they saw Bell riding a horse ahead of them on the trail. Bell surrendered without a fight and was transported to the Tyler County jail in Woodville. Bell was reported to have been about thirty-nine years old and was rumored to have killed six men before shooting the two lawmen. There is no information at this time as to the disposition of the case against Bell.

No personal information or place of burial has been located on Deputy Rhodes.

Related case: Tyler County Constable's Office—Frank Walters.

POTTER COUNTY CONSTABLE'S OFFICE

Givens, Millard M.
Born circa 1856—Died 12 January 1889
Date of incident: 10 January 1889

Givens was appointed constable for Precinct 1 by the Potter County Commissioners Court and was referred to as the "Old Town" constable.

Constable Givens received warrants from the court for the arrest of three local men who were charged with illegal gambling. On 10 January 1889, Givens located two of the men in the back room of a saloon. The men protested being arrested. The crowd started harassing the constable, and he became uneasy. He quickly regained his composure as Sheriff James Gober and three prominent local men entered the room. Givens believed that the sheriff would back him up, so he told the two men that they would have to make bond with the magistrate. A bystander became annoyed and threatened to fight Givens. When the man started toward him, Givens drew his weapon. The sheriff told Givens to "hold up" and drew his pistol as well. While there are varying accounts concerning exactly what happened next, it appears that the sheriff's pistol accidentally discharged and that the bullet struck Givens. Givens did not return fire and collapsed on the floor. He gave a dying declaration stating that the sheriff had shot him. He died two days later.

Sheriff Gober, who was the first sheriff of Potter County and the youngest sheriff in the United States when elected in 1887, was indicted by the grand jury and released on bond. The trial commenced on 9 September 1889, the same day the sheriff's bond was declared insolvent. Gober was acquitted two days later. On 7 October 1889, no bond was approved for the sheriff and his office was declared vacant.

Very little personal information is available on Givens. County commissioners donated thirty-seven dollars to bury him. He is said to have been buried in Amarillo, but the location is unknown. He reportedly had a wife and children living at Decatur in Wise County.

PRESIDIO COUNTY SHERIFF'S OFFICE

Lindenborn, John "Johnie"
Born circa 1864—Died circa 1890—1891

Deputy John Lindenborn was reported to have been shot and killed at the mines at Shafter in 1890 or 1891. His mother took his body back to their home at Pilot Point in Denton County for burial.

It is not known if Deputy Lindenborn was married. He was survived by his father Philip, mother Friedrike and brother Thomas. No further details are known at this time.

DeLeon, Simon L.
Born (Unknown)—Died 26 July 1891

In the 1890s, Presidio County along the Rio Grande River was called the "Bloody Peninsula." It was so named for the bloodshed that was caused by outlaws and marauding bandits from Mexico. Texas Ranger sergeant Charles Fusselman, who was also a deputy U.S. marshal, was shot and killed in nearby El Paso County on 17 April 1890. Texas Ranger private John F. Gravis was shot and killed at Shafter in Presidio County on 4 August 1890.

The community once known as El Polvo is the present-day town of Redford and is located along the Rio Grande River just east of Presidio. On 26 July 1891, Deputy DeLeon was shot and killed by Nermin Lujan. Lujan fled to Mexico and was arrested at Presidio del Norte in Mexico. The newspaper reported that Lujan was given a preliminary indictment and was sent to Chihuahua for a final trial. It also speculated that Lujan would probably be placed in the army and sent to the Yucatan.

DeLeon was elected constable for Precinct 3 in Presidio County on 4 November 1890. The state election record features the notation "resigned." It appears that DeLeon resigned and assumed a position as a deputy sheriff under Sheriff S.R. Miller.

There is no personal information about DeLeon. His place of burial is unknown.

Pastrano, Toribio
Born circa 1856—Died 14 August 1891

Antonio Carrasco was a noted outlaw. He had reportedly been involved in numerous gun battles with lawmen and had killed eight men. Deputy Pastrano believed that Carrasco was involved in the murder of Texas Ranger sergeant Fusselman, which had taken place on 17 April 1890. Pastrano learned that Carrasco would be at a dance given on the Texas side of the Rio Grande River. He went alone to arrest him.

As Pastrano entered the room, Carrasco said to him, "My friend, you are an officer and wish to arrest me. Very well." As Carrasco spoke, his hand dropped to his side, and he drew his pistol. The bullet entered Pastrano's head just above the right eye, and he fell dead. Carrasco mounted his horse and crossed the river back into Mexico.

Pastrano was survived by his wife. His place of burial is unknown.

On 21 June 1892, three Texas Rangers shot and killed Antonio Carrasco's brother, Florencio, during an arrest. Another brother, Matildo Carrasco, had been shot and killed by Texas Ranger Ernest "Diamond Dick" St. Leon six months earlier. Antonio Carrasco was arrested sometime after 1892 for horse theft in Presidio County and sentenced to five years in prison. He appealed, but the case was affirmed on 8 June 1895. There is no evidence at this time that Carrasco was ever charged with the murder of Deputy Pastrano.

RAINS COUNTY SHERIFF'S OFFICE

Lindsey, Samuel E. "Sam"
Born circa 1853—Died 3 November 1886

Deputy Lindsey was shot and killed while he and other deputies were attempting to arrest two men who were wanted for stealing horses and the theft of mortgaged property. The incident occurred in Ellis County.

The posse that Lindsey was a member of was fired upon by the two men as the deputies approached the outlaws' camp. Lindsey was struck by one of the shots and was killed instantly. One outlaw was shot and killed when the posse returned fire, but the other escaped from the camp. The man who escaped was later arrested in Kaufman County.

Deputy Lindsey was unmarried at the time of his death. He is buried at Emory City Cemetery.

RED RIVER COUNTY SHERIFF'S OFFICE

Whiteman, Levi J.
Born circa 1856—Died 23 March 1891

Deputy Whiteman, Sheriff Banks and two other men in a posse were attempting to arrest three individuals on warrants for burglary, robbery, theft, arson and terrorizing the community. The alleged crimes took place about ten miles northeast of Clarksville.

The posse located the group of men at an outdoor camp in a mott of trees. Deputy Whiteman was attempting to arrest the leader of the gang, Sam Crookston, when Crookston shot Whiteman. The gunshot killed him almost instantly.

Crookston, John Toms and Kirk McGowan were all charged with the murder of Deputy Whiteman.

Whiteman was survived by his wife and five small children, all under the age of eight. He is buried at Madras Cemetery in rural Red River County.

REEVES COUNTY SHERIFF'S OFFICE

Morris, John T.
Born circa 1824—Died 18 August 1885

By means of background, Morris was born in New York and had served as a U.S. revenue agent and deputy U.S. marshal. In 1880, Morris moved his family to Erath County, where he established a reputation by killing two men while serving as a deputy sheriff. When Reeves County was organized, he was elected its first sheriff on 4 November 1884.

In 1885, Texas Ranger captain James T. Gillespie established the camp for Company E at Toyah, west of the county seat at Pecos. Captain Gillespie learned that the sheriff drank heavily and was prone to frequent outbursts. Relations between the sheriff and rangers were strained, and the sheriff had been verbally truculent to Captain Gillespie.

On 18 August 1885, Sheriff Morris left Pecos on the train to Toyah. He was drunk and belligerent, and it was believed that he came to town to kill Jep Clayton. Sheriff Morris became upset about the fact that the rangers were watching his movements. He became increasingly more intoxicated and began walking the streets with a cocked six-shooter.

Citizens complained to Captain Gillespie, who ordered Sergeant L.F. Cartwright to make an arrest and disarm the sheriff—without hurting him, if possible. Sergeant Cartwright was accompanied by rangers William S. Hughes, Frank W. DeJarnette and Thomas P. Nigh. They found the considerably inebriated sheriff at the Favorite Saloon, where Cartwright ordered him to give up his pistol and surrender. Morris fired at Cartwright but missed. He then fired a second shot at Nigh. The rangers returned fire, hitting the sheriff five times in the chest. The proprietor of the saloon was shot in both legs during the exchange. Nigh was killed instantly, but Morris was taken to the Field Hotel and died within minutes.

Morris was survived by his wife, June, and daughter, Nora.

Related case: Texas Rangers—Thomas P. Nigh.

Frazer, George Alexander "Bud"
Born 18 April 1864—Died 13 September 1896

Frazer was elected sheriff on 4 November 1890 and served until 6 November 1894. He was replaced by Daniel Murphy, who served until 3 November 1896. After losing his bid for reelection, Frazer left town in disgrace.

Frazer and his former deputy, the notorious gunman and hired killer James B. "Killing Jim" Miller, were involved in a feud of some sort. The hostility had originated while Miller was serving as Frazer's deputy and centered on the murder of a cattleman named Con Gibson and the questionable killing of a Mexican prisoner.

Miller boasted that he had run Frazer out of town and would kill him someday. On 12 April 1894, six months after losing the election, Frazer returned to Pecos on business and, as if preordained, the two men met on the street. Gunfire erupted. Frazer shot Miller in the arm and leg and then rushed in for a killing shot. Unfortunately he did not know that Miller was wearing an iron plate under his clothing and that his bullets would be deflected by the makeshift body armor. When the bullet failed to kill Miller, he ran away for good, leaving the town of Pecos to Miller.

Two years later, the bitterness had not subsided. Frazer, who was at the time working as a stable hand at the town of Toyah, was shot and killed by Miller (also known as "Deacon Jim") on 13 September 1896.

Frazer was survived by his wife, Martha "Mattie" Riggs, and one daughter, Eula Lee. His is buried at East Hill Cemetery in Fort Stockton.

The highly controversial and decidedly peculiar "Killing Jim" Miller was born on 25 October 1866. Miller, who did not drink or smoke, was a devout Methodist preacher and usually dressed in black. His favorite weapon was a shotgun. After a long and distinguished career as a gunman and hired assassin, he was lynched by an angry mob on 19 April 1909 at Pauls Valley, Oklahoma. Many believed that that he assassinated former Lincoln County, New Mexico sheriff Patrick Floyd Jarvis Garrett in 1908.

Refugio County Sheriff's Office

Sweeney, Cornelius
Born circa 1831—Died 3 December 1884
Date of incident: 24 August 1884

On 19 August 1884, someone attempted to outrage (rape) the daughter of the county treasurer. The next day, a black man named Robert Riley, who was suspected of committing the crime, was arrested by the sheriff and placed in the county jail. The sheriff placed an increased guard on Riley in anticipation of the citizens' reaction to the crime. It was believed by some that Riley had been involved in two other sexual assaults during the course of the preceding two months.

On 24 August, a group of unidentified men went to the jail, drove away the guards and attempted to break down the door. The mob threw lighted turpentine balls into the cell and shot Riley to death. A mob of black citizens had also gathered, threatening to seek retaliation if Riley was injured. During the assault on the jail, a black man named George Hawes tried to browbeat the mob members into stopping their attack on Riley. Hawes was shot "beyond recovery." Jailer Sweeney was shot in the leg as he retreated from the jail. The local newspaper alleged that Sweeney had been shot by the black mob. Sweeney died from his wound on 3 December 1884.

Sweeney, a stonemason who had been born in Ireland in about 1831, had only recently joined the sheriff's department. He was survived by his wife, Easter, and six children.

ROBERTSON COUNTY SHERIFF'S OFFICE

Hall, Zack
Born circa 1854—Died 27 January 1875

At about 7:00 p.m. on 27 January 1875, Hall was serving as the jailer for his brother, Sheriff F.M. Hall, at the county jail in Calvert. Prisoner Bonny Welborne, who was accused of stealing a horse the previous day, begged the young jailer to let him out of his cell to write a letter to his wife. When Hall released Welborne and turned his back, Welborne grabbed a pistol from a nearby bed and escaped, ordering Hall and a black prisoner not to follow him. Ignoring the warning, Hall followed the escaping prisoner. As he reached the end of the stairway, he was shot through the body.

Welborne escaped capture. He was under indictments in several counties.

Wyser, Addison D. "Ad"
Born 3 May 1844—Died 28 May 1882

At 9:00 a.m. on 28 May 1882, Deputy Wyser was the jailer on duty at the county lockup in the town of Franklin, the new county seat. Wyser was beaten to death by three prisoners who were making an escape. All three men were successful in getting away.

The prisoners had been locked up for an odd assortment of crimes. Prisoner Fred E. Waite had been charged with the theft of a drummer's valise at the Junction House in Hearne. Prisoner Watts Banks had been charged with the theft of a horse and default of payment of a gambling fine. Prisoner Dan Compton was charged with incest and for running off with his fifteen-year-old stepdaughter. Banks was also recovering in the jail after having been shot while attempting to escape from contract labor at a local farm.

Compton was convicted of murder and sentenced to life in prison. Waite asked for a severance and was convicted. He was sentenced to death. Banks was tried next, convicted and sentenced to death. That sentence was carried out on 23 March 1883 when Waite executed by hanging a half-mile outside of Franklin. On 23 April 1883, the loquacious Banks spoke for two and a half hours before a crowd of two thousand people before being hanged.

Banks had sold his body to a medical doctor and had smoked, drank and eaten up the proceeds from the sale of his remains while in jail.

Wyser was unmarried. He is buried at Franklin Cemetery in Robertson County. He was the brother of Sheriff W.Q. Wyser, who served from 1880 to 1882.

Winfrey, J.B. "Joe"
Born 28 January 1866—Died 2 July 1898

Winfrey, a prominent livery stable man and a deputy sheriff, was shot with a double-barreled shotgun by Fred Gann while he was walking down the street in Franklin. The blast hit Winfrey in the neck and killed him. Gann and E.E. Frisbee were indicted for the murder. Both men were acquitted. The motive for the murder is not known at this time.

Winfrey was survived by his wife. He had served as a constable and a deputy sheriff. He is buried at Old Franklin Cemetery. Winfrey had two brothers in public office, Dallas County commissioner R.B. Winfrey and Dallas County deputy sheriff Dick Winfrey.

Borden, David M.
Born 16 April 1846—Died 12 December 1898
Date of incident: 6 December 1898

On 6 December 1898, David Borden was run over by two boxcars that had somehow become detached from the train's engine. Both of Borden's legs were severely crushed between the knee and ankle and required amputation. Borden did not survive the surgery and died on 12 December. Newspaper articles reported Borden as a deputy sheriff and a constable. He was apparently a deputy sheriff in 1894, but no evidence was found that he was a peace officer at the time of his death.

Borden was survived by his wife, Jennifer, and nine children. He is buried at Old Franklin Cemetery. He served in the Confederate States Army in Company F of the Third Alabama Infantry.

ROCKWALL COUNTY SHERIFF'S OFFICE

Starks, Alexander C.
Born circa 1839—Died 29 September 1876

Former sheriff Starks was shot and killed in revenge for the shooting death of a man named William Cannon in April 1875. That incident had occurred almost eighteen months earlier. Cannon's son swore revenge against the sheriff for the killing of his father.

Sheriff Starks had retired from office and was in the process of selling his farm and planning on moving. A man came to the farm under the pretense that he was interested in buying it. The man, George W. Garner, then shot Sheriff Starks with a shotgun.

Garner was arrested and confessed to being hired by Cannon's son to murder Sheriff Starks for $625. Garner was sentenced to death but committed suicide before being executed.

Starks was elected sheriff on 2 December 1873 and served until 15 February 1875. He is buried at Rockwall City Cemetery.

ROUND ROCK POLICE DEPARTMENT

Hall, Augustus G.
Born circa 1852—Died 2 April 1878
Date of incident: About 26 March 1878

Near sunset on 26 March 1878, two brothers from Falls County, Alonzo and William Ross, were in Round Rock at the Blind Tiger saloon. As an interesting aside, the Blind Tiger boasted a hole in the wall through which liquor was sold to unseen patrons. One brother carried a Winchester, and the other carried a concealed six-shooter. Marshal Hall demanded the surrender of the Winchester. A bystander named Frank Lancaster who was in the room at the time also insisted that the young man surrender his Winchester. The lad was about to give up the rifle when his brother drew his revolver in defense. Hall drew his gun, a Colt Model 1851 Navy six-shooter, and the firing commenced.

Witnesses claim that about thirty shots were fired in total during this episode. Hall was hit in the left arm, near the shoulder. A young man named John Moran who was living a few miles below town and who was holding the horses belonging to the Ross brothers was shot in the left leg. One of the Ross brothers is believed to have been shot in the shoulder. One of the brothers is said to have walked down the street very leisurely while turning around every few steps to fire at Marshal Hall as he covered a distance of about one hundred yards. He then ran off in the direction of Brushy Creek.

The wound to Marshal Hall's arm was serious. The limb was amputated on 27 March, and reports indicated that he would recover. Unfortunately he did not, and he died on 2 April.

Alonzo and William Ross were indicted on 20 September for the murder. The Ross brothers posted bond. Every trial date set was delayed because witnesses failed to appear. The district court judge repeatedly had the witnesses arrested, brought before the court and fined. On 16 July 1880, the judge dismissed the case after witnesses again failed to appear.

No personal information has been uncovered about Hall, who was referred to "Captain Hall." No record of his burial has been located.

SAN ANTONIO POLICE DEPARTMENT

Fieldstrup, Frederick W.
Born (Unknown)—Died 29 May 1857

Assistant City Marshal Fieldstrup was shot and killed at the corner of Market and Alamo Streets. Fieldstrup was assigned to watch a notorious gambler named Bill Hart. When Fieldstrup approached Hart, an argument began during which both men pulled their pistols and opened fire. Both men were killed.

Wells, Van Ness
Born circa 1831—Died 22 September 1867
Date of incident: 21 September 1867

Patrolman Wells was walking back from Arsenal and South Main Streets when he came across an intoxicated man lying on the ground. He was stabbed to death by the drunkard while attempting to arrest him.

Patrolman Wells was survived by his wife, son and two daughters.

Krift, John
Born (Unknown)—Died 23 February 1880
Date of incident: 21 February 1880

On 23 February 1880, Deputy City Marshal Krift was thrown from his horse and died.

No further information has been uncovered about Krift's death at this time.

SAN AUGUSTINE COUNTY SHERIFF'S OFFICE

Hunt, James
Born circa 1863—Died 12 May 1888

At about 8:00 p.m. on 12 May 1888, Deputy James Hunt was shot and killed by George W. Wall. The bullet struck Hunt just above the heart and passed through him, exiting between the shoulders. A second bullet entered the upper part of his right hip and exited about five inches below his navel. Hunt died within minutes. During the exchange of gunfire, Wall was slightly wounded in the foot. When Sheriff B.J. Lewis attempted to arrest Wall, the man's brothers—W.C. and H.S. Wall—held the sheriff off at gunpoint. Newspaper accounts of the day make no mention of the motive behind this shooting.

Wall was reported to be a sawmill man and Hunt a stockman. Wall was tried and acquitted after he pled self-defense.

Wall was elected sheriff in 1894 and served until he was killed in the line of duty on 21 April 1900 by Curg Border during the "Border-Broocks-Wall War." Border, a former constable and city marshal, went on to be elected sheriff on 4 November 1902 but was removed from office in March 1904. Sheriff W.S. "Sneed" Noble took over the sheriff's duties and found himself caught up in the feud.

The Wall boys were enemies from boyhood of Curg (Lycurgus) Border, a relative of the powerful Broocks family. The Walls themselves had numerous relatives with plenty of backbone. In April 1900, Border shot and killed Sheriff George Wall on the streets of San Augustine. Eugene Wall retaliated by killing Ben Broocks on 2 June. On 4 June, a battle around the courthouse resulted in the deaths of Sid and Felix Roberts. Later, two more of the Wall boys were ambushed, and many of their friends and supporters quit the country. The feud was not really ended until Sheriff Sneed Nobles killed Curg Border in May 1904.

SAN ELIZARIO POLICE DEPARTMENT

Soto, Dionisio
Born circa 1835—Died 3 October 1895
Date of incident: About 30 September 1895

Officer Soto died on 30 September 1895 from wounds he received several days earlier when he was beaten by three men.

Appolonio Sierra, Jose Sierra and Severo Cordero were the threesome responsible for administering the fatal thrashing. Soto had arrested one of the men for fighting earlier that day. He had allowed the fellow to go back into a dance to retrieve his hat. When the man exited the building, he had his hat, but he also had two other men accompanying him. One of the pair asked Soto to release the suspect into their custody. When Soto refused, the men began to attack a citizen whom Soto had deputized to assist him with the arrest. As Officer Soto attempted to intervene, he was knocked from his horse and severely beaten by all three of the men.

Soto died several days later on 3 October 1895. The men fled but were later arrested.

One of the men involved, Jose Sierra, was convicted of murder and sentenced to five years in jail. Severo Cordero was reportedly scheduled for trial, but no records have been located indicating what he was charged with or if any trial ever occurred. No record was found as to whether Appolonio Sierra was ever charged.

Soto was buried at Old San Elizario Cemetery. He was reported to be single. No tombstone or marker exists, and the cemetery is now covered by a parking lot.

SAN PATRICIO COUNTY SHERIFF'S OFFICE

Timon, Hughbert (Hugh or Hubert)
Born circa 1841—Died 2 February 1880
Date of incident: 19 January 1880

Timon was appointed sheriff on 26 September 1865 by Governor A.J. Hamilton. He served until 25 June 1866. He was elected on 3 December 1869 and served until September 1872, when he failed to give a new bond. He ran again, was reelected on 8 November 1872 and served until April

1874. After a short gap in service, he was elected again on 15 February 1876 and reelected on 5 November 1878. He served until his death on 2 February 1880. Although state election records show that he served until the end of his term on 2 November 1880, Pete Hunter was appointed to complete his term of office.

Records indicate that Timon was born in Ireland in about 1841, but a family genealogy posting lists his birth year as being about 1830. Owing in part to the fact that Timon served as a second lieutenant in the Second Texas Cavalry Regiment (Second Mounted Rifles), the authors have chosen to use 1841 as his most likely birth year.

Sheriff Timon was reportedly under the influence of alcohol when he decided to execute a warrant on Andrew Hart. He was armed with a Winchester and a six-shooter when he arrived at Hart's house. While there remains some controversy as to which party fired the first shot, Hart was inside his residence with his wife when he claimed that the sheriff fired the first volley through the closed door of his home. Hart returned fire and fatally wounded Timon.

Hart tried to save Timon's life, but by the time a doctor was summoned from Corpus Christi he had already expired. It is unknown if Hart was ever prosecuted.

Timon was survived by his wife, Kate, and at least three children.

SHACKELFORD COUNTY SHERIFF'S OFFICE

Larn, John M.
Born 1 March 1849—Died 24 June 1878

By means of background, John Larn had reportedly killed a man in Colorado and a sheriff in New Mexico before he arrived at Fort Griffin in Shackelford County in 1871. He was also said to have killed three more men while on a trail drive.

By 1873, Larn was rumored to be rustling cattle while at the same time serving as a vigilante, killing and lynching suspected cattle thieves. His reputation for bringing law and order to the county was instrumental in his election as sheriff on 15 February 1876. The vigilantes continued to shoot and lynch alleged criminals.

Larn obtained a contract with the army to deliver cattle to Fort Griffin. He deputized his friend, John Selman, to assist him in stealing enough livestock to fill the order. Area ranchers soon grew suspicious of Larn and Selman. Larn resigned as sheriff on 20 March 1877 and became a deputy county hide inspector with Selman.

The Larn gang increased the level of violence and cattle rustling in the area until a band of citizens obtained a warrant in February 1878 and arrested Larn. Larn was soon released. He later shot and wounded a local rancher who had been behind his arrest. Sheriff W.R. "Bill" Cruger arrested Larn on 23 June 1878 and shackled him in a cell. The following night, vigilantes stormed the jail and shot Larn to death. Selman fled and later became a constable in El Paso County.

Larn was survived by his wife and one son. He is buried at Camp Cooper Ranch next to his infant son, who preceded him in death.

Related cases: El Paso County Constable's Office—John Selman Sr.

SHERMAN POLICE DEPARTMENT

Ball, Samuel D. "Sam"
Born (Unknown)—Died 2 February 1880
Date of incident: 27 January 1880

About 11:00 p.m. on 27 January 1880, City Marshal Sam Ball was summoned to a local sporting house to quiet down a group of intoxicated patrons. Ball ordered the men to leave, and after some protest they all did so—with the exception of a man named Alf Johnson. Ball took Johnson by the arm and escorted him outside. Johnson pulled a pistol and shot Ball in the right chest. The bullet passed through his body and became lodged near his spine. Ball grabbed the muzzle of Johnson's pistol and shot Johnson three times. Johnson fell dead on the street. Johnson's brother fired a shot at Ball's face and grazed his eyebrows.

Ball lingered in pain and eventually died on 2 February 1880.

Ball had been city marshal for two years and was survived by his wife, Lydia, and three children. He is buried at West Hill Cemetery in Sherman. Just a year earlier, on 23 January 1879, Marshal Ball had shot and killed Palo Pinto sheriff J.T. Wilson in Austin after an argument. He was not convicted.

Related case: Palo Pinto Sheriff's Office—J.T. Wilson.

Smith County Sheriff's Office

Holden, James
Born circa 1822—Died 27 September 1851

Neil, David
Born circa 1824—Died 27 September 1851

Sheriff John N. McKinley arrested Joseph Pierce, serving him with a warrant charging him with assault and intent to commit murder. Sheriff McKinley placed Pierce in the log jailhouse at Old Canton, in southeast Smith County.

Threats were made by relatives and friends of Pierce that they intended to rescue him from the custody of the sheriff. The sheriff assembled a posse to guard the jail. As anticipated, there was soon trouble. During an attack on the jail, there was a wild fight involving gunfire, knives and axes. The battle resulted in the death of Deputies David Neil and James Holden. Sheriff McKinley and posseman Thomas Brock were wounded. A bystander was killed when a bullet went through a door and struck him. Among the group of attackers, Robert Pierce and Isaac Moore were shot and killed, and Peter Crawford was severely wounded. Robert Pierce was reportedly the group member who killed the two deputy sheriffs.

Crawford was charged with the murder of Deputy Neil and Pierce was charged with assault with intent to kill Sheriff McKinley. The records also show that from 1852 to 1857 numerous unsuccessful attempts were made to locate and arrest Crawford and Pierce, who had both fled from the scene.

Holden was survived by his wife and three children. Neil was survived by his wife and two children. No cemetery records or burial location have been located for either.

Williams, Duff G.
Born (Unknown)–Died 25 August 1869

Little is known as to why Deputy Williams confronted a man named Brown and Gus Mosely. The Smith County murder indictment record dated 27 August 1869 reported, in part:

> On 26 August 1869 in Smith County…*Duff Williams acting as the special deputy sheriff of said County of Smith in the discharge of his*

duties as such deputy sheriff was feloniously and willfully attacked by Brown and Gus Mosely. Deputy Williams was shot twice with a double barrel shotgun and died instantly.

Deputy Williams was survived by his wife, Susan K., and one son. No cemetery records have been located.

Morris, Jourden Alexander
Born 15 February 1851—Died 8 October 1881

Deputy Morris approached a crowd of drunken men who were congregating in front of the saloon operated by Andrew Jackson "Andy" Harper in Lindale. He attempted to get two of the men to stop creating a disturbance. Bob Billips (or Billups) along with three brothers, Jesse, Pleasant and Warren Starnes, were in the crowd. Billips and one of the Starnes brothers told Morris that he could not arrest them. Pleasant Starnes then hit Morris in the head with some sort of object. Morris cut Pleasant Starnes with a knife. Gunfire erupted, and Morris was shot twice in the back and once in the foot by an unidentified member of the group. He died from the gunshot wounds and blows to the head.

All four men were indicted for murder. Jesse Starnes was tried, found guilty and sentenced to five years in prison. Pleasant Starnes was found not guilty. The charges against Warren Starnes were dismissed in January 1884, at the request of the Smith County district attorney. Bob Billips was never arrested or tried.

Morris was survived by his wife, Sarah, and three children. He is buried at Morris Cemetery in Smith County.

Norton, Marion D.
Born 8 March 1860—Died 18 July 1882

Deputy Norton was the victim of an unfortunate accident. While performing his duties in the sheriff's office located at the courthouse building, Norton was shot and killed. His pistol somehow fell from its holster and discharged as it struck the floor.

Norton was just twenty-two years old at the time of his death. He was not married. Norton was the son of Judge Zachariah Norton. He is buried at Oakwood Cemetery in Tyler.

SOMERVELL COUNTY SHERIFF'S OFFICE

Holley, John E.
Born 16 December 1852—Died 14 December 1892
Date of incident: 3 December 1892

On 3 December 1892, Tom Curry was attempting to avoid a fight with a man named Cal Ligon with whom he had been having a misunderstanding. Curry claimed that Ligin had attempted to strike him, so he drew his pistol. Curry claimed that someone nearby struck his arm and that the pistol discharged accidentally. In any case, the bullet struck Holley in the back near his right shoulder and passed through his body, lodging near his right breast. Holley died on 14 December 1892.

Curry was arrested and charged in the shooting. The disposition of the charge is unknown.

Holley is buried at White Church Cemetery in Glenrose. He was survived by his wife and one child.

STARR COUNTY CONSTABLE'S OFFICE

Smalley, Henry T.
Born (Unknown)—Died 9 January 1853
Date of incident: 8 January 1853

Several weeks before the shooting incident that resulted in his death, Constable Smalley and Sheriff Samuel J. Stewart had made an attempt to arrest two men, Mick Oberly and William Graham. The pair had escaped custody.

On 8 January 1853, Constable Smalley was eating supper at a restaurant when Oberly came in with a shotgun and fired at him, striking him full on and inflicting a fatal wound. Smalley died the next day.

It is unknown if Oberly was ever charged or convicted of the murder.

Smalley's place of burial is unknown.

Starr County Sheriff's Office

Campbell, Silas
Born (Unknown)—Died 1 February 1859

Several reports indicate that Silas Campbell was shot and killed in Starr County and that he was the sheriff. Although state election records indicate that John Dugan was sheriff between 1858 and 1859, it is possible that Campbell was a deputy sheriff.

Unfortunately, efforts to unravel the confusion, and to uncover information concerning the details of his death, have thus far proven unsuccessful.

Martin, John E.
Born circa 1835—Died 1 December 1881

Handy, Louis
Born (Unknown)—Died 1 December 1881

Sheriff Martin and Deputy Handy were traveling the county leaving citations and collecting taxes when they were waylaid and murdered. The incident took place about six miles below Rio Grande City at about 1:00 p.m. on 1 December 1881.

Reported as the "boldest and most outrageous crime that had occurred for a long time in this vicinity," the community was outraged. A total of four murders, including those of Martin and Handy, had taken place in the preceding month. Citizens petitioned the governor to send in Texas Rangers. Colonel Bliss, the commander at Fort Ringgold, sent army troops to accompany the citizens' posse in an attempt to pick up the trail of the wrongdoers.

Martin was appointed sheriff on 20 February 1872 and served until 8 November 1872. He was elected on 5 November 1878 and reelected on 2 November 1880. He was survived by his wife and two children.

No information is known about Deputy Handy at this time.

Rosales, Mamerti
Born (Unknown)—Died August 1886

Deputy Rosales was shot and killed by Jesus Mires. No further details are known at this time.

Ortega, Marcus
Born (Unknown)—Died 19 March 1891

On the night of 19 March 1891, Deputy Ortega was called upon to stop a disturbance at a notorious saloon in the "hell's half acre" section of Rio Grande City. When he reached the establishment, an army private named Patrick Hogan of C Troop fired a weapon at him. Ortega attempted to return the fire, but his revolver malfunctioned. Hogan fired again, hitting the deputy a second time. In the struggle that followed, Ortega managed to disarm the soldier. Hogan left, leaving his cap on the ground.

Ortega died of the wounds received in the shooting.

Friends of Deputy Ortega who were at the same saloon threatened to lynch Hogan. In the end, calmer heads prevailed.

Fern, Fred
Born (Unknown)—Died 9 December 1893

At about 11:00 p.m. on the night of 9 December 1893, the body of Deputy Fern was found near the center of Rio Grande City with a bullet hole near his right ear. His pistol was between his legs, and three rounds had been fired. The postmortem investigation concluded that Fern had taken his own life; however, many believe that he was assassinated and that the killer used Fern's own gun to kill him. The mere fact that Fern seems to have fired three shots in a suicide attempt does tend to raise suspicion of foul play.

Fern was a veteran of the "San Ignacio Raid" and was said to have been the only Anglo on the side of the *Garzaites*. A newspaper report, although unconfirmed, claimed that he was also a deputy U.S. marshal.

Solis, Yldifonso
Born (Unknown)—Died 27 June 1898

On 27 December 1898, Deputy Solis was shot and killed by a man named Juan Garza at La Gruia, about eighteen miles from Rio Grande City.

Garza was at a party and had been dancing all night. As he and his friends left, they began firing their pistols. When Deputy Solis and Constable Jacinto Rodriguez attempted to arrest them, Garza shot and killed Solis. Rodriguez returned fire and wounded Garza in the leg. Garza managed to crawl a mile to a horse and fled to a ranch. As Garza was about to cross the Rio Grande River into Mexico, he was arrested by Sheriff W.W. Shely. Three accomplices of Garza who were present at the time Garza shot Solis were also arrested.

Solis' place of burial is unknown, as is the disposition of the case against Garza.

TARRANT COUNTY SHERIFF'S OFFICE

York, John B.
Born 13 May 1825—Died 24 August 1861

By means of background, John York was elected sheriff on 2 August 1852 and reelected on 7 August 1854. He served until 4 August 1856. York returned as sheriff after being elected again on 2 August 1858 and served until 6 August 1860. William O. Yantes was reported to have been elected sheriff on 6 August 1860 and served until 4 August 1862. York's father-in-law, who was the county judge, appointed York to serve out the term of office.

There is much disagreement as to what led to the shootout between lawman York and lawyer Arch Fowler. It appears that a community barbecue was being held on 20 July 1861 at Coldspring, about a mile northeast of the public square. Due to the hot weather, a line had formed at the spring, which had a fence around it to keep out livestock. Fowler grew impatient with the wait and jumped the fence to get to the water. Sheriff York confronted him and ordered him to the back of the line. When Fowler defied him, York manhandled Fowler. Cooler heads separated the two men, and Fowler was persuaded to leave.

On 24 August 1861, Fowler and his nephew, Willie, were in Fort Worth, where they crossed paths with Sheriff York. Fowler pulled a knife and began stabbing York. York managed to draw his pistol, fire the weapon and kill

Fowler. Fowler's nephew shot and mortally wounded York. York died an hour and a half later.

Willie Fowler fled the state and enlisted in the Confederate army. He was reportedly killed during the war.

York was survived by his wife and five children. He is buried at Mitchell Cemetery in an unmarked grave.

Townsend, Richard W. "Dick"
Born (Unknown)—Died 3 April 1886

The Order of the Knights of Labor was involved in a strike against the Missouri Pacific Railroad. On 3 April, five hundred strikers surrounded the terminal in Fort Worth. Tarrant County sheriff W.T. Maddox had a posse composed of city police officers, sheriff's deputies and deputy constables.

An engine and caboose left the rail yard carrying Fort Worth officers Charles Sneed, Rufe James, John J. Fulford and Jim Thompson, along with Tarrant County special deputy sheriffs Dick Townsend and Jim Courtright. The train was stopped, and the lawmen arrested four men. Courtright then placed Townsend in charge of the men and, with Thompson and James, started back toward the engine. Four to five strikers who were concealed in a ravine and armed with Winchesters opened fire on them, hitting Fulford in both legs. The lawmen returned fire but were hampered by the fact that they were only armed with pistols. Townsend was shot in the chest and Charles Sneed in the face. Townsend died from his wound that evening.

Townsend was not married. He is buried in an unmarked grave in the Pioneers Rest Cemetery in Fort Worth. He is often misidentified as a special deputy U.S. marshal.

Courtright, Timothy Isaiah "Longhair Jim"
Born circa 1846-1847—Died 8 February 1887

Jim Courtright is best known as the legendary city marshal of Fort Worth. He served in the Civil War as a Union soldier and was recognized for his bravery. Courtright later served as an army scout and acquired the nickname "Longhair" for the lengthy hairstyle he wore that was typical of scouts of the era. Tim was mistaken for Jim, and the nickname stuck. Courtright was known for wearing two pistols in the cross-draw position with the butts facing forward.

In 1873, Courtright worked as city jailer. In 1876, he was elected city marshal by a margin of only three votes. Fort Worth was a rough cattle town, with open gambling, prostitution and vice. Marshal Courtright knew that his job depended on keeping the peace rather than strictly enforcing the laws. In 1879, Courtright ran for a fourth term and was defeated. He attempted to start a detective agency but found it more profitable to simply hire out his gun to the highest bidder or run an extortion racket than make an honest living. He moved to New Mexico but was soon accused of two murders and fled to Fort Worth, where he started another detective agency.

In spite of much public protest, he was eventually arrested. He escaped and dropped out of sight for a time. Some believe that he fled to New Mexico, although the veracity of that claim remains unproven. While there, he was acquitted of the charges in Texas and returned. After returning to Fort Worth again, he served as a deputy sheriff during the Great Southwest Railway Strike of 1886, the bitter dispute that claimed the life of Special Deputy Sheriff Dick Townsend.

Courtright was drinking heavily and using his detective agency to shake down bar owners. Although he was a friend of Luke Short's, who ran a gambling concession located upstairs over the White Elephant Saloon, Courtright tried unsuccessfully to extort money from him. In early February 1887, Short sold the establishment. On 8 February 1887, the two confronted each other outside the White Elephant Saloon. Short shot Courtright four times. The grand jury was not able to gather sufficient evidence to charge Short with the crime.

Courtright was commissioned as a deputy sheriff at the time of his death. His funeral procession was six blocks long, the largest the city had seen. Courtright is buried at Oakwood Cemetery in Fort Worth.

TAYLOR COUNTY SHERIFF'S OFFICE

Collins, Walter
Born circa 1857—Died 8 January 1884

Zeno L. Hemphill was a known gunslinger. Hemphill is alleged to have said that he wanted to kill a lawman.

In 1878, at a riotous civilian settlement below Fort Griffin in Shackleford County called "The Flat," he and some cowboys had planned to kill Special Deputies Henry Herron and Dave Barker for no reason apart from notoriety.

Deputy Herron disrupted the plot by hitting Hemphill in the head with his pistol before the man had a chance to follow through with his plan to kill the lawmen.

In 1884, Hemphill was the proprietor of the Cattle Exchange, which was a saloon and gambling hangout on Pine Street in Abilene. Deputy Collins and his brother, Frank, entered Hemphill's saloon. New gaming ordinances had recently taken effect, and they upset gambling house owners, including Hemphill. Harsh words were exchanged between the Collins brothers and Hemphill. A gunfight soon erupted. Hemphill and Walter Collins were killed outright. Frank Collins was mortally wounded and died on 14 March 1884.

Walter Collins is buried at Abilene City Cemetery alongside his brother. He was a private in the Frontier Battalion of the Texas Rangers between the years of 1878 and 1880.

Taylor Police Department

Morgan, John T.
Born circa 1857—Died 16 July 1884
Date of incident: 14 July 1884

At about 10:00 p.m. on 14 July 1884, City Marshal Morgan was involved in an altercation with local ice cream saloon owner S.E. Stiles.

Stiles opened fire on Marshal Morgan. Morgan was struck with a glancing bullet to the head, a shot to the hip and another to the groin. Stiles surrendered to local citizens because no other lawman was in town. Stiles contended that he had shot Morgan in self-defense. Morgan told witnesses that Stiles shot him without provocation. Stiles's brother, Monroe, was also implicated in the murder of Morgan. Marshal Morgan died of his wounds at 4:00 a.m. on 16 July.

The newspaper accounts claimed that most believed Morgan's death to be a coldblooded murder. Public sentiment was with Morgan. His statement before his death seems to indicate that Stiles had no cause for his actions.

Stiles was indicted for murder in the second degree and entered a plea of self-defense. On 14 January 1885, Stiles was tried and acquitted.

Very little is known about Morgan. The newspapers reported that he was originally from Alabama or Georgia and had resided for a while at Palestine, where he had a married sister. Morgan was elected city marshal of Taylor in April 1883. No burial records have been located.

TEMPLE POLICE DEPARTMENT

Hawks, Robert E.
Born circa 1856—Died 9 May 1889

Deputy Marshal Hawks was shot and killed by a man who was upset over a court-imposed fine that Marshal Hawks had attempted to collect earlier in the day. The man, Pink Wiseman, confronted Hawks in a saloon later that night and shot him to death.

Because there were no witnesses to the murder, Pink Wiseman and his accomplice, Cora McMahn, were acquitted.

Nonetheless, the citizens of Temple meted out their version of vigilante justice. On their way home from the courthouse in August 1890, a mob of angry citizens, upset with the verdict handed out by the court, beat Wiseman and McMahn and shot them to death in the street.

Deputy Hawks is buried at Evergreen Cemetery in Bloomington, Illinois.

TEXARKANA POLICE DEPARTMENT

Flint, William T.
Born 5 January 1843—Died 14–15 November 1876
Date of incident: 11–15 November 1876

There are conflicting reports as to the date of the incident and the name of the suspect. One account reported that Marshal Flint attempted to arrest a man named Lattimer (also referred to as I.D. Lattineer) on 11 November 1876. Lattimer was described as being twenty-seven years of age. A $500 reward was posted for his capture. Another account reported that Marshal Flint had been shot and killed by a desperado named Robinson but that the incident had taken place on 14 or 15 November when he had attempted to arrest the man at a sporting house. A third account claimed that Robinson was the culprit but that the incident was on 14 November. In that account, Flint is said to have been the city marshal of Texarkana, Arkansas. In any case, lawman William Flint was shot and killed sometime between 11 November and 15 November 1876.

The local newspaper reports of the day claimed that every store on the Texas side of the city closed in respect for Marshal Flint during his funeral. Flint is buried at Rose Hill Cemetery in Texarkana, Bowie County, Texas.

West, Sam
Born (Unknown)—Died 10 July 1891

Between the hour of midnight and 1:00 a.m., policeman West was shot by J.D. Gaines, a bookkeeper for the Gate City Lumber Company. West was shot through the heart and brain and killed instantly. The two men were said to have had some prior disagreement.

A shot had been fired that was heard by both West and Gaines. West said that the shot came from Arkansas. Gaines said, "No, you are mistaken, the shot was fired in Texas." West called Gaines a damned lair. Not unexpectedly, a fight soon followed. West allegedly drew his pistol and fired three times at Gaines, missing all three times. Gaines, who seemed to have been the better marksman in this affray, drew his pistol and fired at West twice, hitting him with both shots. While Gaines was arrested, the newspapers reported that public sentiment was with Gaines, giving some credence to the belief that the shooting was self-defense.

West was survived by his wife and several children. He is buried at Oakland Park Memorial Cemetery in Terrell in Kaufman County.

TITUS COUNTY CONSTABLE'S OFFICE

Tigert, Lewis
Born circa 1854—Died 31 March 1898

In perhaps the ugliest and most vulgar incident on record, a group of twenty-five men led by posseman Lewis Tigert and accompanied by Precinct 4 constable G.H. Haygood (also spelled Hagwood) went to the shack occupied by some black men in Cookville to "have some fun." Their intended "fun" in this instance was to castrate some of the young black men.

Posseman Tigert was shot and killed as they entered the shack, and posseman Walter Garrett was wounded. Lon Merrett, while defending himself, was wounded. The morning after the shooting, Constable Haygood went to the justice of the peace in an effort to obtain some papers that might explain their presence at the shack and backdated them to the day before the incident.

Merrett and another black man were arrested but were later released. Jim Tigert, Tom Tigert, Joe Marshall and Jim Denney, all of whom were white men, were arrested and charged with intent to murder. Garrett, a member of the group, later pled guilty to aggravated assault.

Tigert is buried at Concord Cemetery in Morris County.

TOM GREEN COUNTY SHERIFF'S OFFICE

White, (Unknown)
Born (Unknown)—Died 12 September 1877

The newspaper reported that Mr. White, the sheriff of Tom Green County, was shot and killed on 12 September 1877 by a merchant in Concho named Charles Frary. State election records report that Alden McIlvan was the sheriff of Tom Green County in 1877, thus White was probably a deputy sheriff.

The incident occurred in Concho, which is located in Concho County. The county was organized in 1858 but was connected to McCulloch County for judicial purposes and did not have its own sheriff until 1879. H.T. Eubank was the sheriff of McCulloch County in 1877.

Nothing further is known about White. No burial information has been located.

TRAVIS COUNTY SHERIFF'S OFFICE

Moore, Edgar Maurice Bowie
Born 1 January 1850—Died 10 November 1887

On 19 July 1878, Deputy Edgar Moore, Williamson County deputy sheriff Ahijah W. "Caige" Grimes and a group of Texas Rangers were in Round Rock to stake out the bank. An informant, Jim Murphy, reported that the Bass Gang was planning to pull off a holdup at the Williamson County Bank.

Deputies Grimes and Moore observed Frank Jackson, Sam Bass and Seaborn Barnes hitch their horses in the alley north of Georgetown Avenue and make their way toward the Kopperal's General Store. When Grimes approached one of the gang members who was purchasing tobacco, claimed by most to have been Sam, he asked him, "Do you have a pistol?" Sam replied, "I'll let you have it," at which point Sam shot him. Frank and Seaborn are also said to have opened fire. Moore, who had been waiting outside the store, began shooting as well. He wounded Sam Bass in the hand before being shot in the chest, which took him out of the affray. In all, there were six bullet holes in Moore's body.

As the gang attempted to flee from town, Seaborn Barnes was shot and killed as he made his getaway. Some claimed that he was shot by Texas Ranger George Herold, and others believed that a local citizen named

Conner fired the fatal shot. Sam Bass was also shot and fatally wounded as he fled the town. Several people have taken credit for firing that shot as well.

Almost a decade later, on 10 November 1887, Moore was shot and killed while attempting to arrest a man on a warrant. When Moore entered the man's home, he produced a rifle and a struggle took place. An unknown person, believed to have been Wilson McNeil, entered the house and shot Moore with a shotgun.

McNeil was hanged in 1905 for another murder. Moore was survived by his wife, Julia Isabelle Eans, and daughter, Sadie Bell. His grave remained unmarked for 115 years until a tombstone was put in place in May 2002. He is buried at Oakwood Cemetery.

Hornsby, Malcolm M.
Born 28 November 1841—Died 28 September 1892
Date of incident: 24 September 1892

Hornsby was elected sheriff of Travis County on 7 November 1882 and reelected on 4 November 1884. He was again elected on 2 November 1886 and served until 6 November 1888.

On the evening of 24 September 1892, the former sheriff was shot, and he subsequently died from his wounds four days later. He was attempting to quiet a disturbance at a dance near his ranch on Onion Creek about eight miles from Austin. Marcellini Lossana tried to stab Hornsby, but his son blocked the attack and was cut on the hand. Francisco Reano shot Sheriff Hornsby, piercing his right lung.

Both men were indicted for the murder, but Lossana escaped. Reano was sentenced to death; however, the governor commuted the sentence to life in prison. Lossana was arrested in Monterey, Mexico, in 1906.

Sheriff Hornsby is buried at Hornsby Cemetery in Travis County.

TRINITY COUNTY CONSTABLE'S OFFICE

Heslip, Shadrick R.
Born circa 1858—Died 22 April 1893

Constable Heslip was shot and killed at Groveton by a man named W.R. Smith while he was attempting to arrest him. He is reportedly buried at Calvary Cemetery in Nogalus Prairie.

Trinity County Sheriff's Office

Holmes, J.F.
Born (Unknown)—Died 22 April 1877
Date of incident: 11 April 1877

Sheriff Holmes was shot through the head on 11 April 1877 by Captain W.J. "John" Magee. Sheriff Holmes, who was unarmed at the time, was in the process of attempting to arrest Magee. He died at 6:00 p.m. on 22 April 1877.

The Moscow city marshal, who was accompanied by a posse of armed men, captured Captain Magee in Polk County on 26 April 1877. Magee put up a desperate resistance and would have shot the marshal had it not been for several posse members restraining and disarming him. Magee was transported to Galveston and was jailed there, pending trial, in September 1877. The disposition of the case is unknown.

Holmes was appointed sheriff on 21 February 1877 and served less than two months before being killed.

Tyler County Constable's Office

Walters, Frank
Born (Unknown)—Died 25 September 1889

Walters (also called Waters) was elected constable for Precinct 2 in Warren on 6 November 1888.

A Montgomery County deputy sheriff named Davis had been pursuing John Bell for cattle theft for four days. Davis was ten miles from the community of Warren on 25 September 1889 when Constable Walters and a Polk County deputy sheriff named Rhodes attempted to arrest Bell for the Montgomery County cattle theft. Bell was driving a wagon with his wife and two children when the lawmen approached him. The two officers were shot through the head and died immediately. Bell remained on the scene for nearly an hour and prevented anyone from removing bodies of the fallen lawmen until he saw fit to leave. He then abandoned his wife and children, took the best horse and fled through the Big Thicket toward the Louisiana border. Deputy Davis, Tyler County sheriff G.R. Ector and a deputy named Parker pursued him.

Shortly after daybreak on 27 September 1889, the lawmen received word that Bell was at a nearby cabin. As they approached, they saw Bell riding ahead of them on the trail. Bell surrendered without a fight and was transported to the Tyler County jail in Woodville. He was reported to have been about thirty-nine years old and was rumored to have killed six men before shooting the two lawmen. There is no information as to the disposition of the case against Bell.

There is no personal information on Constable Walters or Deputy Rhodes. Their places of burial are unknown.

Related case: Polk County Sheriff's Office—Deputy Rhodes.

Phillips, James K. "Polk"
Born 27 December 1843—Died 11 December 1893

Cary Geter and Monroe Jackson had apparently fought with Precinct 2 constable Phillips before. Geter paid Green Gilder and Monroe Jackson twenty-five dollars to kill Phillips. Phillips was reported to be the constable at Warren.

On the night of 11 December 1893, Jackson brought a double-barreled shotgun and a Winchester rifle from Geter's house. Gilder took the rifle and Jackson the shotgun. The pair hid near the Phillips home. As Phillips approached the gate, Jackson shot him with the shotgun, killing him.

Geter, Gilder and Jackson were all arrested. Jackson was indicted for the murder. Gilder was a witness for the state at the trial, and his testimony amounted to a confession that he and Jackson were present and acted together in killing Phillips. Gilder was then indicted for murder, convicted and sentenced to life in prison. He appealed, and the case was reversed and remanded (sent back to the lower court). The disposition of the murder charges against Geter and Jackson is unknown.

A mob tried to storm the Tyler County jail and lynch the three men, but the sheriff had already transferred the prisoners to Huntsville.

Phillips was survived by his wife and six children. He is buried at Allison Cemetery in Tyler County.

Tyler County Sheriff's Office

Bowers, John "Jack"
Born (Unknown)—Died 18 March 1891

Ed Weatherford pulled a pistol on Charlie Walker, a black man who was playing the harp in front of a group of black men and women at the train station at the Hyatt community. He then demanded that Walker begin to dance. Deputy Laurence Edwards and a citizen named John Bowers approached the men. Edwards told Weatherford to give up his pistol. Weatherford replied, "Go on, I'm not going to hurt anybody." Edwards responded, "You know I am an officer, and it is my duty." Edwards then asked Bowers to help him take Weatherford's gun.

After being warned a second time by Edwards, Bowers placed his hands on Weatherford's shoulder and was pushed back several times. Weatherford then pointed his pistol at Bowers and shot him in the stomach. Bowers put his hands over the wound to his stomach and walked away. Edwards grabbed Weatherford's right arm and left shoulder, but Weatherford reached around and shot him. When Edwards fell, Weatherford struck him on the head with his pistol two or three times. As Weatherford fled, he said, "I told you to let me alone."

Bowers died on 18 March 1891. Weatherford was convicted of murder in the second degree and was sentenced to twenty-five years in the state penitentiary. Weatherford appealed on district attorney misconduct, and the case was reversed and remanded. It is unknown if Weatherford was ever retried for the murder of Bowers.

No personal information is known about Bowers or his place of burial at this time.

Uvalde County Sheriff's Office

Daugherty, John Quincy
Born 4 December 1827—Died 18 March 1865

John Quincy Daugherty was a noted Indian fighter and early settler of the Uvalde, Texas area. He fought alongside John "Doke" Bowles in a number of encounters against hostiles. Daugherty commanded the local Minute Man organization in Uvalde and was with Bowles when he was killed in an

Indian fight in October 1859 that is described extensively in the book *Early Settlers and Indian Fighters of Southwest Texas* by Andrew Jackson Sowell.

Sheriff Daugherty was shot and killed by a gang of outlaws after he arrested one of their members. Daugherty had been with the agency for seven years. He is buried at Uvalde Cemetery.

Hewitt, Robert
Born (Unknown)—Died 27 December 1875
Date of incident: 25 December 1875

Deputy Hewitt was shot, and he eventually died from the wounds inflicted by E. Fewell and John Bowles on Christmas Day 1875.

Hewitt was attempting to arrest Fewell for disturbing the peace. Fewell drew his pistol and shot Hewitt. The wounded Hewitt managed to draw his own revolver and return fire, wounding Bowles and killing Fewell instantly. Hewitt was then shot by Bowles. Both men collapsed, seriously wounded.

Deputy Hewitt expired from his wounds two days later on 27 December. Bowles's fate is unknown.

Fisher, John King
Born circa 1854—Died 11 March 1884

King Fisher is another notorious Texan of whom much has been written. Fisher is another example of someone who crossed over the line from outlaw to lawman. Interested readers should consult the bibliography section for books containing more information about King Fisher.

Starting in 1869, when Fisher was arrested for stealing a horse, he led a life of crime. He allegedly killed half a dozen men. His numerous brushes with the law took their toll, however, and Fisher decided to live a quieter life. He married in April 1876 and bought a ranch near Eagle Pass.

In 1881, Fisher was appointed deputy sheriff of Uvalde County. He became acting sheriff in 1883 after the sheriff was indicted. Fisher turned out to be an efficient and popular lawman and made plans to run for the office in 1884.

On the night of 11 March 1884, Fisher was at the Vaudeville Variety Theater in San Antonio with his companion, noted gunman and former Austin City marshal Ben Thompson. The pair were involved in a shootout brought about by a quarrel between Thompson and the theater's owners. Both Fisher and Thompson were killed in the melee.

Fisher is buried at Pioneer Park Cemetery in Uvalde County.

Related case: Austin Police Department—Ben Thompson.

Lara, Panataleon
Born 29 July 1857—Died 28 January 1892

Deputy Lara was shot and killed at the Sabinal railway yards while attempting to apprehend two burglars. He located the men hiding in a pile of railway ties and was attempting to coerce them to return to the county courthouse with him when the pair opened fire on him. Lara was mortally wounded.

The men were arrested but escaped from the county jail without being identified. One newspaper account claimed that a deputy tried to arrest the two men several days later, but after a heated gun battle they avoided capture. It is unknown if they were ever rearrested or prosecuted.

Deputy Lara had been with the agency for just over one year. He was survived by his wife, Perfegta Ortiz.

Van Zandt County Sheriff's Office

Hunter, William Rutherford
Born circa 1857—Died 28 December 1892
Date of incident: 26 December 1892

Deputy William Hunter also worked as a salesman for Thompson and McKinney merchants in Willis Point. He was shot and killed by Henry Wills, the brother of a man named John Wills, whom he had arrested earlier in the day at Willis Point.

Hunter had found Wills in John Spires' Saloon and had recruited several men to assist with that apprehension. John's brother, Henry Wills, ran a meat market on North Commerce. On his way home, Hunter passed the shop of Henry Wills, and as he did so Henry came out and began to loudly protest the earlier arrest of his brother. Henry took off his apron, threw it into the shop and started toward Hunter. Hunter drew his pistol from his pocket. As he did so, the gun went off. The bullet missed Henry and went through the roof of the market. In the midst of the altercation, Henry's father arrived on the scene. Hunter threatened to shoot him if he interfered. Next, Henry stepped into the market. As he did so, Hunter shot him in the thigh. Henry reached over the counter, retrieved his gun and returned fire.

Henry fired three shots at Hunter, killing him. He pled self-defense and was acquitted of all charges.

Deputy Hunter was survived by his wife and five children. He is buried at Elmo in Kaufman County.

Vernon Police Department

Hammond, John L.
Born (Unknown)—Died 17 May 1890

At about 2:00 a.m. on 17 May 1890, City Marshal Hammond went to the residence of Wilbarger County sheriff J.T. Conn. The sheriff's residence was on an upper floor of the county courthouse. Marshal Hammond woke Sheriff Conn to pick up an arrest warrant. Conn went down to his office by a back stairway. Hammond accidentally fell twenty feet from the balcony at the head of the main stairway. He lived only a few minutes and did not speak.

As a mark of respect, the city council of Vernon issued a resolution regarding the accidental death of Hammond. The Knights of Pythias, of which he was a member, stated that "they will erect and present a residence to the widow."

Hammond was survived by his wife and children. He is buried at Eastview Memorial Park, Vernon.

Victoria Police Department

Sloan, Lewellen
Born (Unknown)—Died 3 January 1887

On the evening of 3 January 1887, Deputy City Marshal Sloan was at Sitterlee's Saloon in Victoria and was apparently very intoxicated. T.A. Cahill, a private night watchman at another establishment, was asked to keep Sloan out of the saloon. He did so, but Sloan soon returned, and this time he was brandishing a pistol and creating a disturbance.

Sloan was disarmed by a citizen. He appealed to Deputy Sheriff A.P. Thurmond to give him back his gun, but Thurmond refused. Cahill summoned City Marshal Henry Ragland, who then asked Thurmond to assist him with the arrest of Sloan. Ragland and Thurmond soon apprehended Sloan, who had moved to another saloon. They decided to place Sloan in the sheriff's private office until they could summon the sheriff for the keys to the jail.

The sheriff was A.P. Thurmond's uncle. Later that night, A.P. Thumond found the sheriff in a rage because Sloan had wrecked his office and burned all of his papers before escaping. The sheriff scolded his nephew at great length and fired him.

A.P. Thurmond and a citizen named R.L. Owen found Sloan and arrested him. While walking Sloan back to the jail, he began to struggle. He ran toward Thurmond with both hands up, saying, "For God's sake, Al, don't do that!" Thurmond extended his pistol to touch Sloan's chest and fired. Sloan ran away, stopped and then ran back toward Thurmond. When he did so, Thurmond shot him two more times. Owens and Thurmond fled the scene.

Thurmond was convicted of killing Sloan and sentenced to fifteen years in prison.

Ahlers, Louis W.
Born 18 December 1848—Died 8 August 1893
Date of incident: 7 August 1893

At about 10:40 p.m. on 7 August 1893, citizens heard five pistol shots fired in rapid succession. A crowd found Deputy City Marshal Ahlers lying facedown on Main Street with a bullet through his chest. An eyewitness named Louis Garza identified the suspect as a Mexican named Jim Gonzales (reported by some sources to have been named Moreno), who had been a streetcar conductor and now worked for the railroad.

Gonzales had been intoxicated and had threatened to kill Garza. Garza located Ahlers and asked him to make the arrest, but not to attempt it alone. Ahlers took Garza with him and attempted to place Gonzales in custody. Ahlers already had his pistol drawn when Gonzales went for his gun and shot Ahlers in the chest. Afterward, Ahlers's pistol was found to have been fired three times. Gonzales and a companion fled the scene and were never apprehended.

Ahlers was survived by his wife and two children. He is buried at Masonic Cemetery in Weimar in Colorado County.

WACO POLICE DEPARTMENT

Hoffman, Laben John, Jr.
Born circa 1840—Died 6 January 1871

L.J. Hoffman was a private in the Texas State Police in 1870 and was assigned to the area encompassing McLennan and Hill Counties. He resigned on 5 September 1870, when he qualified as the city marshal of Waco.

About noon on Friday, 6 January 1871, City Marshal Hoffman was in a barbershop on the southwest corner of the Square and Second Street getting a shave. An unidentified man rode up on horseback, dismounted and entered the barbershop from the rear. He examined the lathered face of the marshal, apparently to make sure it was Hoffman. He then walked behind the barber chair and shot the marshal in the back of head, killing him instantly. The man remounted his horse as he fired two shots at approaching policemen. As the assassin galloped to the bridge, he tossed the toll collector a dollar and said, "I haven't time to wait for the change," and then sped away.

Texas governor Edmund J. Davis posted a $1,000 reward for the delivery of the body of the murderer of Hoffman to the sheriff of McLennan County—dead or alive. The adjutant general of the state police reported in June 1871 that George Thomason, alias "Wild George" Thomas (name also reported as "Williams"), was mortally wounded by state policemen but had escaped. It is unknown if he died from his wounds.

Desperado John Wesley Hardin was arrested by Texas State Police for the murder of Marshal Hoffman, but he escaped after killing Private Jim Smalley on 22 January 1870.

Hoffman was born about 1840 in North Carolina. He was survived by his wife, Virginia, and two children. His place of burial is not known.

Neill, Alpheus D.
Born circa 1827—Died 6 February 1877

Officer Neill was shot and killed when he responded to a disturbance in which a man had been threatening to kill his wife and father-in-law. As Officer Neill came on the property, the man shot him.

Officer Neill had been with the agency for one year and was survived by his wife and three children.

Practically thirty years earlier, on 20 August 1850, Neill, who was at the time serving as a Texas Ranger, was traveling back to his company when he and his companions were attacked by Indians. He was accompanied by two fellow rangers, John L. Wilbarger and D.C. "Doc" Sullivan. Wilbarger and Sullivan were killed, and Neill was wounded and left for dead. He walked and crawled sixty-five miles to the nearest town. It was some time before he recovered from his injuries.

WALKER COUNTY SHERIFF'S OFFICE

Edwards, A.J.
Born circa 1825—Died 14 August 1868

A little after noon on 14 August 1868, Deputy Edwards was shot and killed by a young man named Wooten (reported by some sources to be spelled "Wooton"). Wooten fired five shots from a Colt revolver at the deputy, hitting him all five times. Wooten was the nephew of Shelby Wooten, who had reportedly been overcharged by Edwards for something a year or so earlier while he was lying sick in bed at his home.

Edwards was survived by his wife, Nancy, and four children.

Roe, William H.
Born circa 1857—Died 26 May 1888

William H. Roe had served as a deputy sheriff and jailer for Walker County sheriff W.D. Adair. He had previously been a convict camp guard in Falls County for two years and a camp guard at Huntsville, where he killed an escaping prisoner. He was tried and acquitted of that murder. In 1882, he married. Roe was elected town marshal of Huntsville but was defeated in his 1886 reelection attempt after being accused of "pandering to coloreds." Next he went into the saloon business and then went back to serving as a prison guard.

On 7 April 1886, Roe murdered his wife, Jennie, by lacing her coffee with strychnine. He was convicted of the crime and sentenced to death. Although many vigilantes wanted to lynch him, Roe was legally hanged two years later on 26 May 1888 in the town of Anderson in Grimes County. His killing by legal sentence marked the only execution in Grimes County history. Historians have claimed that Roe was the first lawman to be legally executed in Texas.

Roe is buried at Odd Fellows Cemetery at Anderson in Grimes County. Conflicting years of birth for Roe range from 1856 to 1858.

WALLER COUNTY CONSTABLE'S OFFICE

Cooper, Louis
Born (Unknown)—Died 3 December 1878

On 3 December 1878, at the community of Pattison, John O. Greer got into an argument with his uncle, Ed Greer, over some trivial matter. John pulled a pistol on Ed and threatened to kill him. Ed located Precinct 4 constable Cooper and asked for his gun. The constable refused. Ed grabbed the pistol anyway and started after his nephew. Ed fired at John but missed. John shot Ed and then shot him in the head two more times as he was lying on the ground. When John realized that Ed had the constable's pistol, he went after Constable Cooper—who was now unarmed. John fired twice at Cooper. One bullet struck him in the left lung, inflicting a fatal wound. John then robbed the train station agent of ten dollars and rode away.

John Greer had shot a man in the leg two years earlier and was wanted for various crimes in Waller and Gonzales Counties.

Greer was sent to prison for a crime other than murder. He escaped, and about six months later Sheriff McDade and Deputy Browning attempted to arrest him at Pattison on 30 March 1882. The lawmen saw Greer at the station and ordered him to surrender. As he fled, both lawmen fired at him. Deputy Browning fired two shots with a shotgun, and Sheriff McDade fired once with a Winchester. Greer and his horse were both wounded, but he still managed to escape. When a doctor was called to the house of Dave Greer the next day, lawmen followed and arrested him.

The disposition of the case against John Greer for the murder of E.B. Greer and Louis Cooper is unknown.

WALLER COUNTY SHERIFF'S DEPARTMENT

Chambers, Richard "Dick"
Born circa 1850—Died 4 April 1888

Deputy Chambers was the son-in-law of Sheriff Thomas S. McDade. Stephen W. Allchin had written a newspaper article condemning the actions of Sheriff McDade. Apparently, McDade and Allchin had had a continuing disagreement, in part involving Allchin carrying a Winchester around town.

On 4 April 1888, McDade and Chambers found Allchin at Pointer's Store and demanded a retraction. Allchin, armed with a Winchester, refused. Chambers, holding a copy of the publication, demanded that Allchin eat the newspaper and drew his pistol. More harsh words were exchanged. Chambers shot Allchin and then ran from the store before the wounded Allchin could return fire. Allchin, however, did managed to fatally shoot Chambers as he fled.

Chambers was survived by his wife and two children. He is buried at Hempstead Cemetery.

McDade, Thomas S.
Born 19 July 1829—Died 26 November 1888

McDade was elected sheriff on 15 February 1876 and reelected every successive two years until he resigned in September 1888.

The shooting of Deputy Dick Chambers on 4 April 1888 by Stephen W. Allchin, which took place in the presence of Sheriff McDade, continued the feud between the two men. Richard T. "Dick" Springfield and Jack McDade, both relatives of Sheriff McDade, soon came to Hempstead to avenge the killing of Chambers. On 19 May 1888, Allchin was shot and killed by the pair, with Dick Springfield delivering the fatal shot at close range.

On the night of 26 November 1888, less than three months after resigning as sheriff, McDade stepped out on his porch to get a drink of water and was shot from ambush by an unknown assassin. A man named Joseph M. Blasingame was suspected of being the killer and was charged with the crime. He was later found innocent on 5 October 1889.

McDade is buried at Hempstead Cemetery.

WASHINGTON COUNTY CONSTABLE'S OFFICE

Routt, George
Born circa 1863—Died 24 February 1893

Constable George Routt received word that a local merchant named George Carlisle had renewed an old dispute with him.

On 24 February 1893, the constable got his shotgun and walked back and forth on the street in front Carlisle's store, claiming that he would shoot the next person to come out. Mr. Carlisle's adopted son defiantly armed himself with a shotgun and emerged from the store to meet Routt. Apparently, a bystander called out to Routt to watch out. He wheeled around suddenly and saw young Carlisle. Both men fired almost simultaneously. Routt's shot missed, hitting the wall about a foot above Carlisle. Carlisle's shot hit Routt in the chest, killing him almost instantly.

Schley, M.H.
Born 4 January 1854—Died 1 October 1887

At about 5:00 p.m. on 1 October 1887, Constable Schley was shot and killed at Chappell Hill by Bayless Whisenant. Apparently, the two men had an argument that morning during which Constable Schley struck Mr. Whisenant. Whisenant obtained a shotgun, returned to confront the constable and shot him fatally.

Both men were well thought of in the community. Constable Schley is buried at Masonic Cemetery at Chappell Hill.

WASHINGTON COUNTY SHERIFF'S OFFICE

Maxey, Nelson
Born circa 1814—Died 19 November 1869

Nelson Maxey, a deputy sheriff and appointed constable of the precinct, was attempting to preserve order in the courtroom of Precinct 1 justice of the peace J.W. McCowan in Washington-on-the-Brazos. For reasons as yet undiscovered, Robert "Bob" Gooden and James Shapard pulled six-shooters and killed Maxey. The pair then attempted to kill the judge. Both men escaped. Military authorities tried to locate them, without success.

Very little information is known about the incident or the disposition of any case against the two shooters.

Maxey had been a deputy sheriff since at least 1860. He was survived by his wife, two daughters and one son. Descendants have indicated that Maxey was buried in Washington County, but no grave site has been located.

Thompson, William M.
Born circa 1836—Died 14 June 1870
Date of incident: 13 June 1870

Three strangers who arrived at Brenham became abusive and insulting to a black woman. A man passing by protested their treatment of the lady. The three strangers drew their pistols and told the passerby to mind his own business. The man went to Sheriff Thompson and filed a complaint, obtaining warrants for their arrest.

Several hours later, Sheriff Thompson and Deputy Crozier confronted the three individuals who were involved in the incident. One of the men has been identified by several names, including Hansboro, Handsboro, Handsborough, Hansbrow and Hertzberg.

The sheriff tapped Hansboro on the shoulder, demanding his pistol and saying, "You are my prisoner." The sheriff started to draw his gun, but Hansboro drew first. Against the advice of his colleagues, he fired a shot at the sheriff but missed. Deputy Crozier fired at Hansboro. His shot went wild. The bullet struck Sheriff Thompson in the shoulder and came out through the sheriff's left side. Hansboro then fired at the deputy, but Crozier had jumped behind a post, and the shot missed him.

Hansboro was arrested by local citizens and placed in jail. Deputy Sheriff Tesdart formed a guard to protect Hansboro from being lynched and took him to the train depot to be transferred to Galveston for safekeeping. While at the railroad station, Sheriff Thompson's grieving wife approached Hansboro with a pistol in hand, placed the weapon against his chest and pulled the trigger. The pistol misfired. The deputy quickly disarmed Ms. Thompson and hastened their departure on the train. The twice-lucky Hansboro was acquitted of the murder.

Thompson died the next day. He was survived by his intrepid wife. Thompson was elected sheriff on 3 December 1869 and served about six months. His funeral was held in Brenham, but his place of burial is unknown.

Nothing is known about the fate of Deputy Crozier or if charges were filed for the shooting of Thompson.

Stephens, James C.
Born (Unknown)—Died 15 February 1876

Deputy Stephens was shot and killed at Chappell Hill during a disagreement over an election.

Stephens was speaking out publicly against a candidate for tax collector named Captain John S. Smith. The two men had a confrontation during which Stephens struck Captain Smith in the face. Predictably, guns were drawn and the shooting soon followed. Smith fired three shots and Stephens one. Stephens was hit in the neck and head and died about sundown that day.

Garrett, William F. "Will"
Born 20 July 1850—Died 2 August 1880

Deputy Garrett received county arrest warrants for several women working at a sporting house near the passenger depot in Brenham. He executed the warrants at about 10:00 p.m. on 2 August 1880 and arrested seven of the ladies. The mayor gave Garrett his consent to use the city jail to hold the group of "soiled doves" for the night. Deputy Garrett left but learned later that the women had bonded out by the city marshal and were released.

Garrett was not pleased by this action and returned to the brothel to rearrest one of the sporting women. He entered the woman's room and was confronted by a man named W.P. Allen. An argument resulted, during which Allen shot and killed Garrett. Allen surrendered and was placed in jail. He claimed that he had acted in self-defense and that hard feelings existed between he and Garrett.

Allen was acquitted at his trial in 1881. The newspaper accounts of the day reported that Garrett was intoxicated when he confronted Allen.

Garrett was referred to as the chief deputy and a popular officer. He was unmarried and is buried at Prairie Lea Cemetery in Brenham in an unmarked grave.

WASHINGTON, COUNTY OF

Burch, James "Jim"
Born 20 August 1875—Died 10 October 1897

Washington County operated a convict farm (work camp) for prisoners convicted of misdemeanors. This convict farm was a correctional facility managed by a county judge and the Commissioners Court. Jim Burch was a guard and assistant superintendent. Before the incident, Burch had had some trouble with a black inmate and repeat offender named Bob Carter.

About 7:15 p.m. on 10 October 1897, Burch was standing under an awning on the sidewalk in Brenham when Bob Carter came around a corner with a shotgun in his hand and walking briskly. When he was only a few steps away from Burch, he raised the gun and fired. The blast hit Burch, tearing away the right side of his face and killing him almost instantly. Burch was drawing his Colt .45-caliber pistol the instant the man fired, and as he fell the gun discharged, striking the building harmlessly. Carter fled the scene.

Sheriff Teague asked for the Santa Fe switch engine to take him to the convict farm about four miles north of Brenham to get their bloodhounds to join in on the chase for Carter. Superintendent Dick Robertson at the county convict farm was Burch's brother-in-law and accompanied Sheriff Teague back to Brenham.

Groups of officers and citizens began combing the area for Carter. About 10:00 p.m., word was received that Carter would surrender to R.S Farmer, provided that the armed officers and citizens would return to town. After taking Carter into custody, Farmer and Carter took a circuitous route back, riding double on horseback as they tried to reach the rear of the jail. As the group got to within twenty steps of the rear of the building, Farmer was confronted by Superintendent Robertson and Constable R.H. Burch, who was Jim Burch's brother. Carter jumped from the horse and ran fifteen feet before Constable Burch shot him twice with a shotgun.

Sheriff Teague charged the constable with murder, but he was never convicted.

Jim Burch is buried at Prairie Lea Cemetery in Brenham. He was not married.

Constable R.H. Burch became involved in a personal dispute with a Brenham night watchman named John Lockett. Lockett shot and killed him on 22 January 1914.

WAXAHACHIE POLICE DEPARTMENT

Spalding, John H.
Born circa 1835—Died 17 December 1882

City Marshal Spalding was shot and killed while coming to the aid of a deputy city marshal who was being fired upon. He was shot in the head during the incident. The killer attempted to flee but was shot and killed by a posse member.

Marshal Spalding served with the Waxahachie Police Department for six years. He was survived by his wife. Spalding is buried at Waxahachie City Cemetery.

WEIMAR POLICE DEPARTMENT

York, Hatch
Born 14 May 1885—Died 22 January 1896

At about 6:30 p.m., Marshal York was summoned to deal with two black men from Lavaca County who had jumped the train at Schulenburg at gunpoint and had gotten off in Weimar. The two men, later identified as John Foley (aka Ira Foley) and Jim Harrison, were headed toward town when Marshal York confronted them. Harrison pulled his pistol and fired at the marshal. A running gun battle broke out, during which Marshal York was shot in the right breast and killed instantly. Foley was shot in the hip and leg and was captured. Harrison escaped. Harrison is claimed to have been a former Texas Ranger; however, no records have been found in the Texas State Archives to support that assertion.

On 24 January, twenty-eight-year-old Jurie Harrison was charged with the killing of Marshal York but had not yet been apprehended. No further information has been uncovered with regard to the outcome of any actions against Harrison. York was survived by his second wife, Pattie Holman. He is buried at Osage Cemetery.

WHARTON COUNTY SHERIFF'S OFFICE

Bythewood, Christopher Jared
Born 19 June 1850—Died 14 April 1884

Former Sheriff Bythewood was shot and killed by a man named James Watterson in a personal feud. No information was given as to the nature of their disagreement. Watterson was sentenced to five years in prison. Bythewood was appointed sheriff on 11 December 1880 and served until 7 November 1882.

Brooks, W. Clarence
Born 6 September 1845—Died 4 July 1884
Date of incident: 30 June 1884

At about 5:00 p.m. on 30 June 1884, Sheriff Brooks and his brother, Eugene Brooks, were leaving the courthouse, where they had been attending the trial of W.C. Gibbs. Sheriff Brooks had arrested Gibbs earlier, charging him with disturbing the peace.

Gibbs left the courthouse before Sheriff Brooks and his brother Eugene. He went across the street and obtained a rifle from a store and then stepped out of a doorway and fired at Eugene Brooks. The bullet struck Eugene in the left arm. Sheriff Brooks, pistol in hand, ran across the street to arrest Gibbs. As Brooks approached the store where he was hiding, Gibbs fired again. Sheriff Brooks was hit in the chest and fell, mortally wounded. He died at about 10:00 p.m. on 4 July. Eugene Brooks recovered from his wound.

Sheriff Brooks was single. He was survived by his brother Eugene and other family members in Missouri. In May 1886, family members had the body of Sheriff Brooks moved to Deepwood Cemetery at Nevada in Vernon County, Missouri. He had been appointed sheriff of Wharton County on 21 April 1884.

Dickson, Hamilton Bass
Born 4 December 1855—Died 7 February 1894

On 18 January 1894, an excursion train made an unscheduled stop near Weimar. The conductor asked Colorado County constable A. Morse Townsend and a night watchman to investigate an unruly man they had ejected from the train about two miles from the town. Constable Townsend arrested DeWitt Braddock of Flatonia and lodged him in the jail. Later that evening, Constable Townsend went to the city jail to bring some food and fresh water to the prisoner. Braddock leaned out of the cell door and, without speaking a word, plunged a knife into Constable Townsend's chest.

On the evening of 7 February 1894, Sheriff Dickson and Constable C.W. Hearte joined Colorado County sheriff J.L. "Light" Townsend in searching for Braddock at the home of Henry Moore. Upon reaching the Moore place, Sheriff Dickson, who was in the lead, came upon Braddock suddenly. Braddock immediately fired twice from his Winchester, striking the sheriff with both shots. Sheriff Townsend then fired rapidly at Braddock, killing him instantly.

Dickson lived only a short time and expired at the scene. Sheriff Townsend and Constable Hearte then began their hunt for Moore, whom they soon found hiding in a thicket. The lawmen surrounded him. Moore drew his pistol. Townsend was able to draw his gun and fire first. Hearte also fired at Moore. Moore was killed instantly.

Dickson was elected sheriff on 4 November 1890 and reelected on 8 November 1892. He had just been married to Bell Sutherland on 11 January 1894 in Jackson County.

Related case: Colorado County Constable's Office—A. Morse Townsend.

Brown, Frank
Born (Unknown)—Died 18 August 1895

On 15 August 1895, Wharton County sheriff Rabb A. Rich received notice that six convicts had escaped from the state prison farm at Matagroda County.

On 18 August, Deputy Brown arrested one of the escapees named John Stormer at a local ranch. He placed a handcuff on the prisoner and attached a rope to the saddle horn of his horse. Brown then started toward Wharton, with the prisoner walking.

Deputy Brown was found dead alongside the road. He had been shot in the back with a pistol and also with his own shotgun. Brown only carried a shotgun, so it appeared that he had failed to search the prisoner thoroughly. Stormer escaped on the deputy's horse.

John Stormer was captured near Kemp's store by citizens and was left chained to the building all night. When the sheriff reached the community where he was being held, he was told that the prisoner had escaped. Most believe that Stormer had been lynched. Brown's horse was recovered.

Brown is buried at Wharton City Cemetery. His age is unknown, and there are no dates on his tombstone that can provide a clue.

WHITESBORO POLICE DEPARTMENT

Ayers, Kirkland C.
Born circa 1850—Died 2 March 1879
Date of incident: 1 March 1879

At 4:00 p.m. on 1 March 1879, City Marshal Ayers responded to a disturbance at a store/saloon in Whitesboro. While attempting to arrest two men, Ayers was hit in the head with a chair. He died from his injuries at 1:00 a.m. the following morning.

Pat Ware and his brother, Spence, were both charged with the murder of Ayers. A Grayson County jury acquitted both brothers in April 1880.

Ayers was survived by his mother, who lived at LaGrange, Troup County, Georgia. His body was shipped by express train back to Georgia for burial.

WICHITA COUNTY CONSTABLE'S OFFICE

Mosley, Sam Abbott
Born (Unknown)—Died 22 August 1898

About 10:30 p.m. on 22 August 1898, Precinct 1 deputy constable Sam Abbott Mosley was waylaid and shot with a load of buckshot near the Fort Worth and Denver Railroad track east of Wichita Falls. Although struck by seven pellets of buckshot, Mosley managed to return fire with his pistol before he died.

On 2 September 1898, Sheriff Lee McMurty and Constable Tom Pickett arrested former deputy marshal Josh Cook and placed him in jail charged with complicity in the assassination of Mosley. During the examining trial of Cook, it was discovered that Dorsey Wilson, reported to be a local gambler, was the principal suspect. Dorsey was in the courtroom at the time and was immediately arrested.

Both Cook and Wilson were indicted by the grand jury for the murder. Even though he had not been present at the time of the shooting, Cook was convicted in Wise County of complicity in the murder of Mosley and given five years in prison. Wilson was tried for the actual murder but was acquitted.

No personal information about Mosley has been uncovered. His surname has also been reported as "Abbott," "Mosely" and "Moseley." Mosley was reported to have previously been a Wichita County deputy sheriff and assisted Texas Rangers in the arrest of one of the Joe Beckham gang.

WILBARGER COUNTY SHERIFF'S OFFICE

Musick, Uel
Born circa 1839—Died 7 December 1882

Sheriff Musick attempted to stop a fight in a saloon in Vernon. When the sheriff unwisely stepped between two brawling cowboys, he was shot and killed by one of them. Unfortunately, the name of the cowboy who did the shooting has been lost to history.

Musick was the first elected sheriff of Wilbarger County, having earned that post on 10 October 1881. He was reelected on 7 November 1882 and served until his death. He was single, and his burial location has not been located.

Stewart, Thomas "Tom"
Born circa 1856—Died 11 July 1884

Stewart was appointed sheriff on 11 December 1883 and resigned before 31 December, when a new sheriff was appointed.

Ranger J.L. Shanklin took Stewart and others, under custody, to answer to court process at the town of Graham in Young County. On 11 July 1884, they were all released and were returning home when, somewhere near Archer City, a disagreement took place. Stewart and a Texas Ranger named Hobbs got into a fistfight. Shanklin subdued the men, but Stewart threatened to kill Shanklin. The fight between Stewart and Hobbs soon flared up again. Both men were armed. Stewart went for his pistol. Shanklin warned him twice to stop. When Stewart refused, Shanklin shot and killed him.

Shanklin was acquitted of murder in Wichita Falls on 16 April 1885.

Nothing further is known about Stewart or about his place of burial.

WILLIAMSON COUNTY CONSTABLE'S OFFICE

Eanes, Charles R.
Born circa 1856—Died 31 May 1889

Precinct 2 constable Eanes was a member of a posse in pursuit of a man in a buggy who had just taken his child from his estranged wife. The man was firing his gun wildly in the air. The posse chased the man, Thomas J. Johnson, who was from Granger. Constable Eanes traveled several miles, exchanging shots with Johnson over the entire distance. Johnson finally got out of his buggy but continued firing his Winchester rifle. Eanes was struck in the face and killed. Johnson fled to Salado, where he left the child with relatives and disappeared into the brush.

Johnson was eventually arrested and sentenced to six years in jail for the murder of Eanes.

Eanes was elected constable on 2 November 1886 and was reelected on 6 November 1888. He was survived by his wife. Although he is buried in Granger, Williamson County, his grave site has not been located.

Gamble, Silas A., Sr.
Born circa 1850—Died 29 August 1898

Constable Gamble was assassinated while playing dominoes with two friends at the town of Taylor. The assailant shot Gamble with a shotgun from about thirty feet away. No one saw the actual shooter, who quickly fled the scene. About two weeks later, there was an assassination attempt on the constable of a neighboring precinct. It is believed that the two shootings were related.

Gamble was elected as Precinct 2 constable on 3 November 1896. He was survived by his wife and two children. Gamble is buried at Old Taylor Cemetery in Williamson County.

WILLIAMSON COUNTY SHERIFF'S OFFICE

Grimes, Ahijah W. "Caige"
Born circa 1851—Died 19 July 1878

Texas Rangers and lawmen were searching Texas for the Sam Bass Gang. Rangers had an informant in the gang who was sending them intelligence. The outlaws had been in the town of Round Rock several times scouting the bank. Ranger major John B. Jones, Captain Lee Hall and Privates Dick Ware, Chris Connor and George Herold were stationed around the town watching for suspicious persons. They recruited Williamson County deputy Grimes and Travis County deputy Maurice B. Moore to assist. Both men were former rangers. Apparently, Deputy Grimes did not know they were watching for the Bass Gang.

Sam Bass, Seaborn Barnes and Frank Jackson made another scouting trip but did not plan on robbing the bank until the following day. As they entered a store to buy tobacco, Deputies Grimes and Moore saw that one of the men was wearing a pistol. Grimes approached the men and asked if they were armed. The three outlaws then opened fire. Grimes was killed, and Moore was wounded. A gun battle quickly broke out that involved the three outlaws, the lawman and armed citizens. Sam Bass was mortally wounded, and Seaborn Barnes was killed. Jackson loaded Bass on a horse, and they escaped.

Bass was left under a tree outside town and was discovered the next day. He was brought back to town, where he died on 21 July. Jackson seems to have vanished into history.

Deputy Grimes was survived by his wife. He is buried at Round Rock Cemetery where, coincidentally, both Sam Bass and Seaborn Barnes are also interred.

On 10 November 1887, Travis County deputy Moore was shot and killed while attempting to arrest a man on a warrant. R.C. "Dick" Ware went on to become sheriff of Mitchell County from 1881 to 1892 and then became the U.S. marshal for the Western District of Texas. George Herold joined the El Paso Police Department.

Stanley, William J.
Born circa 1832—Died 6 August 1887

Deputy Stanley was searching for two alleged horse thieves named John Barbour and Will Whitley. The two men ambushed Deputy Stanley as he repaired the fence outside his home, shooting him a total of ten times. One of the killers was shot and killed the next month in a gun battle with two deputy U.S. marshals.

Stanley was survived by his wife and nine children.

Gunn, James Burrell
Born circa 1843—Died 24 July 1892

Deputy Gunn apparently dropped his surname and used the alias of James Burrell while serving as a Williamson County deputy sheriff.

At about 11:00 p.m. on 24 July 1892, City Marshal Brady shot Gunn while he was standing near the front door of Mankin's Saloon in Georgetown. He was killed instantly. Multiple street fights had taken place earlier in the day. Both Gunn and Brady had arrested several men. The dispute between the two men had started over a disagreement regarding which man had arrested someone named Simpkins. Brady struck Gunn with his fist. Gunn drew his pistol and fired two shots. Brady, in turn, fired three shots, one of which struck Gunn in the heart. Brady was more fortunate. One of his fingers was hit and had to be amputated.

Gunn is buried at Macedonia Cemetery in Granger. He was survived by his wife, Georgia. His brother, Will Gunn, was sheriff of Lamar County from 1884 until 1892.

Olive, John Thomas
Born circa 1844—Died 12 September 1892

Sheriff Olive was shot and killed by the Armstrong brothers while he was walking on a train platform. The Armstrong brothers are said to have shot the sheriff out of revenge. Olive had killed two of their brothers in a gunfight twelve years earlier.

Both brothers were apprehended and charged with murder. One was tried and acquitted in 1893. The charges against the other were dismissed, but he was reindicted in 1914. The case did not go to trial until 1923. Texas governor J.E. Ferguson and Secretary of State John McKay testified on behalf of the defendant. The jury found him not guilty.

Olive was elected sheriff on 4 November 1884, reelected on 2 November 1886. He served until 4 November 1888. Olive was elected a second time on 4 November 1890 and had nearly completed his two-year term when he was killed. He is buried at Taylor City Cemetery.

WILSON COUNTY SHERIFF'S OFFICE

Coy, Juan Jose
Born circa 1842—Died 25 January 1892

Deputy Coy returned from guarding a prisoner at Yoakum the previous night and gave his pistol to the bartender at the Bella Union saloon. When he returned the next day for his gun, the bartender was off duty. Shortly after attempting to retrieve his gun, he had an argument with Henry Krempkau, during which Krempkau alleged that Coy had used abusive language and threatened him with a knife. Henry's brother, Albert, fired three shots at Deputy Coy, striking him twice and hitting an innocent bystander named Ed Sarran with the third shot. One bullet from Krempkau's .44-caliber revolver hit Coy in the side, and the other hit his neck, severing a main artery and killing him. Krempkau claims that the killing was self-defense. Jacobo Coy, who was present at the time, said that both men had been drinking heavily. Albert Krempkau died before he could be tried.

Coy, then a cowboy on the Butler ranch, was accused of killing Karnes County sheriff Fate Elder and Deputies Bud Elder and Jack Bailey on 6 September 1886. He was also accused of the killing of a black man at Floresville. Coy had a murder charge pending against him at the time of his death. He is buried at Lodi Cemetery at Floresville. He left behind a wife and a child.

Juan Coy's cousin, Jacobo, was present as a special policeman in San Antonio when Ben Thompson shot and killed Jack Harris on 11 July 1882. He was also present and was slightly wounded when Ben Thompson and King Fisher were killed on 11 March 1886.

Related case: Karnes County Sheriff's Office—Sheriff Fate Elder, Bud Elder and Jack Bailey.

WISE COUNTY CONSTABLE'S OFFICE

Stevens, James B.
Born circa 1839—Died 19 December 1892

Dr. B.F. Garrison was eating his midday meal at a lunch stand at Alvord. He was reported to have been under the influence of alcohol at the time and displayed a pistol. When Precinct 2 constable Stevens asked him to hand over the gun, Garrison became angry. Constable Stevens reached for Garrison's pistol, while at the same time drawing his own gun. Garrison shot Stevens four times. The doctor mounted his horse and fled.

It is unknown if Garrison was ever arrested and charged with the murder.

Constable Stevens was with the agency for twelve years. He was survived by his wife and five children.

Martin, Akin Henry "Ake"
Born circa 1862—Died 13 November 1897

On the evening of 13 November 1897, Precinct 3 constable Martin was returning home from the circus when his pistol fell from the holster. The hammer struck a wagon wheel and caused the weapon to discharge accidentally. The bullet struck him in the cheek and passed through his brain, killing him instantly.

Martin is buried at Chico Cemetery in Wise County.

WISE COUNTY SHERIFF'S OFFICE

Coghlan, Jasper N.
Born circa 1847—Died 8 September 1889

Deputy Coghlan was shot and killed shortly after being deputized by the Wise County sheriff to assist him with the arrest of three men wanted in Parker County.

The men, two brothers and a friend, were at the home of the father of the two brothers. When the deputies arrived at the residence, the men opened fire with Winchester rifles, fatally wounding Coghlan. One man in the house was wounded in the leg by the return fire. The three shooters escaped but were eventually apprehended.

John Sherwood, the man who was believed to have shot Coghlan, was sentenced to thirty years in prison.

Coghlan had served with the agency for one day. He was survived by his wife and is buried at Garvin Cemetery in Decatur.

WOOD COUNTY SHERIFF'S OFFICE

Turner, Volney
Born circa 1828—Died 20 April 1878

Deputy Turner was shot and killed as he and several other deputies attempted to serve a warrant on a man for cattle theft.

The posse went to the home of Marion Williams in Van Zandt County to arrest him. When they arrived at the residence, they found Williams in his bed. As they attempted to make the apprehension, Williams pulled a handgun from under his pillow and opened fire, fatally wounding Turner. The other deputies returned fire. Despite being wounded five times, Williams was able to flee the scene. He was arrested a short time later.

Deputy Turner also served as a deputy city marshal for Mineola. He is buried at Mineola City Cemetery.

Williams, John P.
Born 10 March 1829—Died 7 February 1882
Date of incident: 14 July 1877

Sheriff Williams was appointed on 8 November 1872 and was elected a second time on 2 December 1873. He was reelected on 15 February 1876 and served until 2 November 1880, when he was replaced by Feilden P. Dowell.

Sheriff Williams was shot at Quitman on 14 July 1877 by a young man named Gabe Dowell. The newspaper account claimed that there had been some disagreement between the two men but did not reveal the nature of the dispute. The bullet fired from Dowell's derringer entered the lower part of Williams's chest. Although Williams initially recovered, he eventually died five years later from complications.

Gabe Dowell was the younger brother of Feilden P. Dowell, who eventually replaced Williams as sheriff. He was not charged with shooting John P. Williams.

Wagner, J.L.
Born (Unknown)—Died 10 June 1893
Date of incident: 30 April 1893

On 30 April 1893, Jailer Wagner was hit on the head by an inmate named Peter Hall. Hall had given the jailer a severe beating. Wagner died of his injuries on 10 June.

Hall was convicted and sentenced to hang. His sentence was later commuted to life in prison.

Wagner's place of burial is unknown.

Wortham Police Department

Barfield, Jackson T.
Born circa 1820—Died 3 December 1877

City Marshal Barfield responded to a disturbance at a store owned by J.J. Stubbs.

Alfred "Alf" Rushing, Frank Carter and Harv Scruggs, who were all armed with shotguns, had accused Stubbs of taking a pistol from their saddlebags, which they had left in the store a few days earlier. Marshal Barfield spoke with the men, and it seemed that he had settled the dispute. The three men mounted their horses, and Marshal Barfield had turned to walk away just as Alf Rushing fired his shotgun. The blast struck the marshal in the back, killing him instantly. The three men attempted to escape, but a posse of citizens gave chase wounding and capturing Carter.

Court records show that Rushing, Carter and Scruggs were all charged with murder, but their files are missing and the disposition of the charges is unknown. Rushing was reported to have been at large as late as 1898, with a $1,000 reward outstanding for his arrest and detention.

Barfield is buried at Crouch Cemetery in rural Limestone County.

Powers, Charles
Born (Unknown)—Died 23 September 1878

On 21 September 1878, Frank Polk—who lived at the Pisgah Ridge community in Navarro County about eight miles northwest of Wortham— was arrested by City Marshal Charles Powers for a misdemeanor. Polk was a noted desperado who was a companion of John Wesley Hardin.

Polk was released on bond and stayed in town until 23 September. Shortly before his trial, he rode out of town. Marshal Powers and Constable Wingfield rode after him and arrested him. He was brought back to town and paid his fine. Polk again left town but returned about 6:00 p.m. He then rode back and forth in front of the store of Mayor W.M. Seely, who was also a Freestone County deputy sheriff. Polk dismounted outside the store and took his Winchester rifle with him. Powers and an unnamed assistant city marshal approached Polk and told him to surrender his weapon. Mayor Seely then came out onto the street armed with a Winchester rifle. Polk started backing up, with the lawmen following him; then he suddenly fired at

Powers. Powers returned fire as he fell. The assistant city marshal shot Polk two times, and Seely fired seven shots, hitting Polk three times. Both Powers and Polk died instantly.

In spite of considerable effort on the part of former sheriff Sonny Sessions and the Freestone County Historical Society, nothing further has been learned about Charles Powers. No place of burial has been located.

YORKTOWN CITY MARSHAL'S OFFICE

Stonebraker, William Brashears
Born (Unknown)—Died 15 August 1887

On 15 August 1887, Stonebraker, who was the Yorktown city marshal, and two cowboys named Schneider and Polschinzski drove some cattle to pasture at the Rutledge Ranch in DeWitt County. Ranch hand Milam Odom said that he would prepare supper, and a fire was built. Polschinzski and Schneider then sat down near the fence and were conversing with Stonebraker when a shot was fired. Stonebraker fell, exclaiming, "Oh, God! I am killed!" Both men fled on horseback to get help at a nearby ranch.

Odom found Stonebraker lying on the ground, and when he went to get help, he was struck in the thigh and slightly wounded. Odom alerted Karnes County sheriff W.L. Rudd, who went to the ranch and found Stonebraker dead. Stonebraker had been pierced by five pellets of buckshot.

The following day, Texas Ranger lieutenant Grimes arrested John Peace, who was a Rutledge ranch employee. Peace had been threatening to kill Stonebraker for months and only days earlier had accused him of taking his feather bed.

Peace was convicted of first-degree murder and sentenced to a life term in the penitentiary. Stonebraker is reportedly buried at Yorktown North End Cemetery.

YOUNG COUNTY SHERIFF'S OFFICE

Cox, Harvey Staten
Born circa 1839—Died 15 September 1864

Sheriff Cox and four other officers came across a group of Indians while they were on patrol near Graham. Fearing the Indians to be hostile, Cox told the other men to leave. Cox mounted his horse and attempted to head out at full speed but had forgotten that he had tied the animal off to a tree. When the horse reached the end of the tether and stopped abruptly, Cox was thrown from the saddle. Now on foot, with no means of escape, Cox was at the mercy of the Indians and was promptly killed.

Cox was elected sheriff on 1 August 1864 and served only forty-five days.

Kirk, Richard "Dick"
Born (Unknown)—Died 21 February 1876

Young County had been reorganized in 1874, and Sheriff Richard Kirk became the first sheriff after the revision. He took office on 20 September 1874.

Sheriff Kirk was shot and killed at Fort Belknap while attempting to arrest a buffalo hunter and known desperado who appropriately went by the named of "Buffalo Bill." "Buffalo Bill" had been drinking at a saloon called Holly's. As Kirk approached the man and attempted to serve him with an arrest warrant, Bill shouldered a .50-caliber buffalo rifle and fired, mortally wounding the sheriff. Kirk was able to return fire, striking Bill in the collarbone and killing him.

Although no evidence has been found to confirm it, "Buffalo Bill" is assumed to have been buried at the Belknap civilian cemetery. His true identity remains a mystery.

Kirk is buried at Oak Grove Cemetery in Graham. He was survived by his mother and siblings. Sympathetic citizens named the highest point in the county Mount Kirk in the sheriff's honor.

Murphee, Sam R.
Born circa 1855—Died 1 January 1882

On 1 January 1882, Deputies Sam Murphee and Dave Melton went to the jail to feed the prisoners. The three McDonald brothers—Peter, Nick and Middleton—managed to get out of their cell and took Deputy Melton hostage. The inmates shot Murphee as he was running down the stairs in the jail trying to escape. His wounds were fatal.

Citizens on the Graham town square heard the shots and armed themselves with guns from the general store. In true Old West style, conjuring up visions of the 7 September 1876 raid on the Northfield, Minnesota bank by the James and Younger gang, a heated gun battle broke out between outlaws and citizens. When the shooting had ceased and the smoke had cleared, Peter, Nick and Middleton McDonald were all dead. Melton had also been shot through the mouth during the affray, but he survived.

The McDonald brothers are buried at Old Eastside Cemetery in Graham.

Murphee is buried at Oak Grove Cemetery in Graham.

Wallace, Marion DeKalb
Born circa 1842—Died 24 December 1888
Date of incident: 17 December 1888

On Monday, 17 December 1888, before 2:00 p.m., Sheriff Wallace and Deputy T.B. Collier went to the Denson farm to arrest Boone Marlow. The officers held a warrant for him on a charge of murder in Wilbarger County. When Deputy Collier ordered Marlow to throw up his hands, Marlow fired a shot from his Winchester rifle at the lawmen. The shot struck Sheriff Wallace below the heart, mortally wounding him. Marlow escaped from the scene.

Wallace died from the bullet wound one week later on 24 December 1888.

The Texas governor offered a $200 reward for Boone Marlow, dead or alive. The citizens of Young County added another $1,500 to the pot. In January 1889, Boone Marlow was shot and killed at a place appropriately called Hell Creek, which is located in the Indian Territory. Three men brought Marlow's body back to Graham, where the reward was promptly and gratefully paid.

Wallace was elected sheriff of Young County on 4 November 1884. He was reelected on 2 November 1886 and again on 6 November 1888. He was survived by his wife and son. Wallace and his wife are both buried at Oak Grove Cemetery in Graham.

Related case: United States Marshals Service—Sam Criswell.

Horton, John T.
Born 19 November 1850—Died 20 March 1894

John Horton, a local liveryman, was deputized to assist the sheriff in serving a warrant on a man named John English. During the arrest, English began to resist and shot Horton. The wound was fatal. English and a friend, John Willingham, escaped but later surrendered to a posse.

John English was convicted of murder and sentenced to thirty-five years in prison. His father was the sheriff of Grimes County, Tennessee.

Horton is buried at Oak Grove Cemetery in Graham.

Chapter 2

State, Federal and Other Agencies

Southern Pacific Railroad Police Department

Elsberry, John Luckie "Dick"
Born 22 April 1854—Died 16 August 1895

On 16 August 1895, two robbers entered the general store of Kelsey & Co. at Valentine in Jeff Davis County. Asleep inside the store were U.S. Customs Inspector Everett Ewing Townsend, store employee John J. Edgar (also the postmaster) and railroad brakeman W.B. Martin. The armed men took $325 from the safe. Unbeknownst to the robbers, a witness saw the men wearing bandanas pulled up over their faces and carrying rifles as they had entered the store.

The witness ran to the railroad section house and summoned Elsberry, the railroad company's experienced night watchman and a former senior captain of railroad watchmen at El Paso. Elsberry told the witness to go to the saloon and get more help. The posse, led by Deputy Sheriff Poole, surrounded the store. Elsberry went to the back door and knocked. Edgar opened the door, and Elsberry asked, "Is that you Edgar? Who is with you?" Edgar replied, "Martin, Townsend and two other gentlemen, whom I don't know."

Elsberry knew that the "two other gentlemen" remark was suspicious, so he fired one round to warn the robbers and alert the men around the store. The two robbers fled out the back door, directly toward Elsberry, firing at him as they ran. The posse of eight citizens also opened fire. The men heard a cry of pain. "Oh my God! I'm shot!" Upon investigation, Elsberry was found with a bullet hole through the body inflicted by one of the robber's using a .40–.82 Winchester rifle. He died at the scene within minutes. The two robbers escaped into the night.

Texas Rangers were summoned and arrived the next day. Eventually, two brothers, Tom and S.L. Holland, were arrested and indicted. Tom produced an alibi, but S.L. Holland was convicted of the robbery and sentenced to fifteen years in prison. He stood trial on 17 January 1896 for the murder of Elsberry. Defense attorneys argued that S.L. Holland was present at the robbery but that the posse killed Elsberry with "friendly fire." The jury acquitted him. He appealed the robbery conviction and was later acquitted. The crime remains legally unsolved.

Elsberry was survived by his wife and three children. He was reportedly buried in Valentine, but no grave site has been located. He also served as a private detective in Houston from 1889 to 1890.

TEXAS & SOUTHWESTERN CATTLE RAISERS ASSOCIATION

The Texas & Southwestern Cattle Raisers Association, which is the oldest and largest organization of its kind in the United States, was launched at Graham, Texas, on 15 February 1877 under the name Stock Raisers' Association of North-West Texas. Cattlemen in Oklahoma, New Mexico and the Indian Territory were invited to join. The call for the initial meeting was made in the fall of 1876 by a few leading cattlemen. Among them were James C. Loving and C.C. Slaughter. The immediate objective was to systematize the "spring work" and to curb cattle rustling. The association was incorporated in 1882. By 1893, the distribution of its membership had spread to such an extent that the name was changed to Cattle Raisers Association of Texas. The present name was adopted in 1921, when the organization merged with the only other cattlemen's group remaining in Texas, the Panhandle and Southwestern Stockman's Association, which had been founded in 1880.

Grissom, George Bingham
Born 7 April 1856—Died 5 July 1892

On 5 July 1892, the train arrived at Clarendon in Donley County. On board were Constable J.F. Green, D.A. Peel and G.B. (Bingham) Grissom, who was an inspector for the Stock Raisers' Association of North-West Texas. The three men went into a saloon. Potter County sheriff R.M. Worden was already in the saloon and was unarmed. Green had arrested one of the Bell clan and sent him to prison for cattle theft, thus a feud of sorts already existed between Green and the Bell clan. R.W. "Bob" Bell and his brother, Eugene, were also in the saloon. Bob Bell opened fire on Green. A stray bullet hit Inspector Grissom and killed him. Green shot seven times and killed Bob Bell before he, too, died. Eugene Bell was arrested. It is unknown if he was ever convicted of any charge.

The newspaper reported that Green had killed a black man six weeks earlier in Clarendon while he was attempting to arrest him. Green was a well-known lawman, having served as a Texas Ranger and with other area law enforcement agencies for the past sixteen years.

Grissom is buried at Bolivar Cemetery at Sanger in Denton County.

Related case: Donley County Constable's Office—James Frederick Green.

Peeler, Thomas Madison "Tom"
Born 15 January 1848—Died 18 May 1897

Cattle inspector Tom Peeler was in a saloon in the county seat of Pleasanton talking to some friends. He casually mentioned Atascosa County constable W.C. Harrell's name in connection with some occurrence he was detailing. Constable Harrell was sitting behind him, although his presence and proximity were unknown to Peeler. Harrell jumped up and, in a very angry manner, rushed at Peeler. Harrell pushed a cocked pistol in Peeler's face with one hand while he struck him with the other. Peeler told Harrell that he was unarmed. The two lawmen engaged in a fight during which Harrell severely beat Peeler on the head with his six-shooter. Afterward, Peeler made threats that he would get even. Harrell filed a complaint against Peeler for arson, but Peeler was acquitted. After his acquittal, Peeler filed a complaint against Harrell for malicious prosecution.

The case was scheduled for trial before the justice of the peace at Campbellton for the afternoon of 18 May 1897. Harrell, along with several of his friends, arrived armed. As soon as the opening of court was announced, Peeler started down the alley to go round in front of the courtroom. Harrell started to the courtroom at the same time. As Peeler reached the sidewalk in front of the court building, Harrell, who had approached him within eight or ten feet, drew his pistol and fired. The bullet struck Peeler's hat band, almost in the center of his forehead. Witnesses testified that Peeler never saw Harrell and that not a single word was spoken by either party before the shooting took place. Peeler fell to the ground and died in a few seconds. Harrell and some of his witnesses testified that just before Harrell fired Peeler made a movement with his right hand toward his hip pocket, as if to draw a weapon. The justice of the peace, county attorney, sheriff and other officers testified that they thoroughly searched the body of Peeler and did not find so much as a pocketknife on his person.

Constable Harrell was convicted and sentenced to thirty years in prison for second-degree murder.

Peeler was survived by his wife, Alice Jane Irvin, and seven children. His place of burial is not known.

Chapter 3
Texas Rangers

Literally thousands of books and articles have been written about the Texas Rangers. The Texas Rangers have played a colorful, but often controversial, role in the development of the republic and state of Texas.

In 1823, Stephan F. Austin hired ten experienced frontiersmen as "rangers" to conduct punitive expeditions against bands of Indians on the frontier. On 24 November 1835, the Republic of Texas Congress established a specific force known as the Texas Rangers. Rangers served as scouts and carried out other tasks during the Texas Revolution. When Mirabeau B. Lamar assumed the presidency of the republic in December 1838 from the Indian-friendly Sam Houston, Lamar used the rangers in an all-out war to eradicate the Native Americans. Texas was annexed into the United States in 1845, and the Mexican-American War followed in 1846. Ranger scouts assigned to General Zachary Taylor proved to be a ruthless and lethal fighting force.

From 1848 to 1861, the U.S. Army was supposed to defend the Texas frontier, as well as the border with Mexico, but the Texas Rangers were still deployed to deal with marauding Indian tribes and Mexican bandits. During the Civil War, the protection of the settlements was left mostly to men ineligible for military service. Texas was under military occupation from 1865 to 1873, and the state was a largely a lawless place. Republican governor Edmund Davis created the highly controversial Texas State Police (1870–73), but when the Democrats returned to power, the state police force was abolished.

Before 1874, Texas Ranger ranging companies were local militias, organized to defend the frontier and border. Although the men in these militias were not lawmen in the modern sense, the authors feel that recognizing the service and sacrifice of these citizen volunteers warrants their inclusion in any comprehensive book about Texas lawmen.

In 1874, the Texas legislature created the Special Force of Rangers under Captain Leander H. McNelly and the Frontier Battalion of Rangers under Major John B. Jones. Order was brought to the lawless areas of the state, and the final Indian battles were fought. In 1901, the Texas legislature reorganized the rangers into a state police force, strictly assigned to law enforcement. In 1935, the Texas Highway Patrol and Texas Rangers were merged into the Texas Department of Public Safety.

REPUBLIC OF TEXAS, 1835–1845

Castleman, Benjamin
Born (Unknown)—Died June 1835

On 1 June 1835, Indians killed a settler and his son near present-day Bastrop. A ranger company found a friendly Caddo chief and his son who were riding shod horses. Suspecting them to be the killers, the rangers executed them.

Major William Oldham and Captain John York raised a company of volunteers from Washington-on-the-Brazos. The group became involved in a fight with the Indians who had actually stolen the horses and burned their village. When the ranger company camped that night, a nervous sentry thought he saw Indians, and during the confusion Castleman was accidentally shot and killed. He was a victim of friendly fire.

Williams, John
Born circa 1789—Died 11 July 1835

The Robertson's Colony, Mounted Riflemen, was organized on 12 June 1835 under the command of Captain Robert Morris Coleman.

On 2 July, Captain Coleman and his eighteen-member ranging company crossed the Brazos River to engage Tawakoni Indians in present-day Limestone County. On 11 July, the rangers came upon about one hundred Indians, mainly Tawakonis. They had concealed themselves and were waiting for daylight to attack the village when barking dogs alerted the Indians to the rangers' presence. In the battle, Private Williams was killed, and four other rangers were wounded. The rangers killed several Indians before withdrawing.

Williams was married and had six children.

The Tawakoni Indians, a Wichita group probably originally from central Kansas, were found in 1719 living on the lower Canadian River in Oklahoma. The Tawakonis and related groups were pushed southward into Oklahoma and Texas, and in the latter part of the eighteenth century their chief range seems to have been between the sites of present Waco and Palestine.

Hornsby, Moses Smith
Born circa 1804—Died circa 3 September 1835
Date of incident: 1 September 1835

On 31 July 1835, five ranging companies gathered at Fort Parker on the Navasota River and organized a battalion. They elected John H. Moore as their colonel. Moore's company of La Grange volunteer rangers were taken over by Captain Michael R. Goheen.

On 1 September, the rangers saw two Indians on foot flee into a thicket. Several men went to capture them and managed to kill one of the Indians. Private Hornsby fired at the remaining Indian but missed. The Indian shot Hornsby in the shoulder and in the arm.

Hornsby refused to have his arm amputated and died a day or two later. He was buried by his fellow rangers near Brushy Creek, west of present-day Round Rock.

Frost, Robert
Born (Unknown)—Died 19 May 1836

Frost, Samuel
Born (Unknown)—Died 19 May 1836

Parker, Benjamin
Born (Unknown)—Died 19 May 1836

Parker, Silas Mercer, Sr.
Born (Unknown)—Died 19 May 1836

When the provisional government of Texas created a corps of Texas Rangers in October 1835, Silas Parker was selected as one of three superintendents.

On 19 May 1836, a war party consisting of hundreds of Comanche and Kiowa Indians approached Parker's Fort in present-day Limestone County. The fort was defended by ten rangers under the command of Captain James Parker, but only four rangers (Silas and Benjamin Parker, Samuel Frost and his son Robert) were in the fort at the time of the attack. When Benjamin Parker left the fort to speak with the Indians, they speared him to death. James Parker's daughter was captured, and when Silas Parker left the fort to defend her he was killed and scalped. Samuel and Robert Frost were killed defending the women and children. In total, five women and children were taken captive. Other settlers were brutally killed and wounded. The most notable captive was Silas Parker's daughter, Cynthia Ann, who married a Comanche chief. Their son, Quanah, became a Comanche war chief.

Quanah Parker was born in about 1852, the firstborn son of Comanche chief Peta Nocona and the captive Anglo girl Cynthia Ann Parker. Quanah Parker was the last chief of the Quahadi Indians. Cynthia also had another son, Pecos "Pecan," and a daughter, Topsana "Prairie Flower."

In December 1860, Cynthia Ann Parker was recaptured in the "Battle of Pease River" by Texas Rangers. With Nocona's death, his band split. Quanah joined the Destanyuka band, where Chief Wild Horse took him under his wing. He left and formed the Quahadi "Antelope Eaters" band with warriors from another tribe. The Quahadis eventually grew in number, becoming the largest of the Comanche bands—and also the most notorious.

Quanah was among the Comanche chiefs at Medicine Lodge. Though he did not give a speech, he did make a statement about not signing the treaty. His band remained free, while other Comanches signed. Quanah was in charge of one group of warriors at the Second Battle of Adobe Walls. The incident was his closest brush with death. He was shot twice during the battle.

Through wise investments, Quanah Parker became perhaps the wealthiest American Indian of his day. He embraced much of white culture and was well respected. Parker went on hunting trips with President Theodore Roosevelt, who often visited him. He had five wives and twenty-five children and founded the Native American Church. Parker died on 23 February 1911 at Fort Sill, Oklahoma.

Robinett, (First Name Unknown)
Born (Unknown)—Died 22 August 1836

Robinson, Thomas J.
Born (Unknown)—Died 22 August 1836

A ranging cavalry company commanded by Captain John G.W. Pierson engaged a group of Comanche Indians on Coleto Creek near Victoria. Rangers Robinett and Robinson were killed, and two others men were wounded.

Childers, James Franklin "Frank"
Born 11 February 1818—Died 7 January 1837

Clark, David
Born circa 1789—Died 7 January 1837

Company A of the Battalion of Mounted Riflemen under the command of Captain Thomas H. Barron was stationed at Fort Milam near present-day Falls County. Sergeant George B. Erath, ten rangers and three civilian volunteers had led a scout that located Indians camped at a bend on Elm Creek.

Just before daylight on 7 January, the rangers approached the camp on foot. They were forced to rush their attack when dogs guarding the Indian's camp spoiled their surprise assault.

The Indians soon discovered that they had numerical superiority and moved to outflank the rangers. Privates Clark and Childers were wounded during the battle. Sergeant Erath found the wounded Clark but left as he saw a dozen Indians approaching. When the rangers returned later, they found that Clark had been scalped and his hands cut off. The body of Childers was discovered sitting against a tree, dead from a gunshot wound. Historians have labeled this battle the "Fight at Elm Creek."

Clark enlisted in Colonel Burleson's Ranging Corps of Mounted Riflemen, serving in Captain Hill's company on 3 July 1836. He served until 11 September 1836, when he transferred to Captain Barron's Company B. On 1 January 1837, he transferred to Company A.

Clark was reportedly from Lincoln County, Missouri, and was the son of Captain Christopher Clark. Childers was reported to have been born in Pendleton, Kentucky.

Faulkenberry, David
Born circa 1790—Died 28 January 1837

Faulkenberry, Evan
Born circa 1815—Died 28 January 1837

Anderson, C. Columbus
Born (Unknown)—Died 28 January 1837

Fort Houston in present-day Anderson County was under the command of Captain Squire Haggard, who organized a company of Tennessee volunteers called Jewell's Company on 19 September 1836.

On 28 January 1837, Privates Abram Anglin, David Faulkenberry, his son Evan Faulkenberry, Benjamin W. Douthit, James Hunter and Columbus Anderson went to search for hogs in the Trinity River bottoms. Hunter and Douthit returned to the fort to get a canoe. About thirty Indians attacked the remaining four rangers. Anderson and David Faulkenberry were fatally wounded and swam across the river, but both died from their wounds. Although Evan Faulkenberry was reportedly killed, his body was never recovered. Anglin was wounded in the battle. He also swam the river and managed to escape.

The twice-lucky Anglin had also survived the massacre at Parker's Fort on 19 May 1836.

Martin, Philip C.
Born (Unknown)—Died in the spring of 1837

Fort Houston in present-day Anderson County was abandoned in 1841 or 1842. A fort previously named Coleman's Fort and Fort Colorado was renamed Fort Houston.

Captain Micah Andrews Company C of the Battalion of Mounted Riflemen were tracking Indians near the fort. Lieutenant Nicholas Wren took fifteen volunteers mounted on the best horses to locate the Indians before dawn. They surprised the Indians. During the battle, Martin was shot in the head and killed. He was buried at Fort Houston.

Martin was from North Carolina. He was a member of Captain William Sadler's Company of Mounted Rangers, or Houston's Company, organized on 1 January 1836 for three months. He was reported as a private in the

Second Regiment, Texas Volunteers, First Company Infantry, which fought at the Battle of San Jacinto on 21 April 1836. Martin also served in Companies A and C of the Ranger Battalion.

Bailey, Jesse
Born circa 1810—Died 6 May 1837

Cullins, Aaron
Born circa 1800—Died 6 May 1837

Farmer, David McCandless
Born (Unknown)—Died 6 May 1837

Hughes, John
Born (Unknown)—Died 6 May 1837

Neal, Claborne
Born (Unknown)—Died 6 May 1837

Captain Daniel Monroe decided to abandon Fort Smith and move Company B of the Battalion of Mounted Riflemen to Fort Fisher. He sent Ranger Privates, Bailey, Cullins and Farmer, along with Neal and Hughes, who were citizen-volunteers, to Nashville to get wagons and teams to move the ranger company and families to the new location.

On 5 May 1837, Indians killed Neal's father outside the town. On 6 May, Comanche Indians followed the wagons back toward Fort Fisher and attacked them at Post Oak Springs in present-day Milam County. All five men were killed in what historians now called the "Post Oak Massacre."

Barnes, James
Born (Unknown)—Died 10 May 1837

McLean, Daniel
Born circa 1784—Died 10 May 1837

Sheridan, John
Born 5 April 1796—Died 10 May 1837

Following the killing of five rangers several days earlier at Post Oak Springs, raiding Indians stole one hundred horses near present-day Houston County. Sheridan and his brother-in-law McLean organized a posse since there was no active ranger company in the area.

Sheridan was a former ranger. Both he and McLean were veteran Indian fighters. Barnes was an early settler and joined the posse. The posse encountered Indians on 10 May 1837 at Mustang Ridge near the present-day town of Elkhart in Anderson County. All three men were killed. Sheridan's wife recovered the bodies of her husband and brother-in-law.

A state historical marker indicates that McLean came to Texas in 1813 to assist in freeing Mexico from Spain. He returned in 1824 to settle on San Pedro Creek in Augusta. Mclean was buried at his home. Sheridan had settled on Silver Creek and is buried near his home. It is unknown where Barnes is buried.

Coryell, James
Born 26 March 1803—Died 27 May 1837

Company A of the Battalion of Mounted Riflemen was stationed at Fort Milam and was under the command of Captain Tom Barron. On 27 May 1837, Privates Coryell, Alfred Berry, Sam Burton, Michael Castleman and Erza Webb went to Perry Creek and were enjoying themselves, eating some honey that they had found. The men were soon attacked by Caddo Indians. Coryell was killed as he tried to fight back. The rangers fled back to the fort. When they returned, they discovered that Coryell had been scalped.

Coryell came to Texas from Ohio. Later, Coryell County would bear his name. The Texas Historical Commission recently discovered a distinct grouping of rocks with a grave shaft underneath in Falls County that may mark the previously unidentified burial site of the Texas Ranger James Coryell.

Blair, Jesse
Born (Unknown)—Died 10 November 1837

Bostwick, Alexander
Born (Unknown)—Died 10 November 1837

Christian, James
Born (Unknown)—Died 10 November 1837

Cooper, Joseph
Born (Unknown)—Died 10 November 1837

Joslen, James
Born (Unknown)—Died 10 November 1837

Miles, Alfred H.
Born (Unknown)—Died 10 November 1837

Nicholson, Wesley
Born (Unknown)—Died 10 November 1837

Nicholson, William
Born (Unknown)—Died 10 November 1837

Sanders, William
Born (Unknown)—Died 10 November 1837

Scheuster, Lewis F.
Born (Unknown)—Died 10 November 1837

First Lieutenant A.B. Vanbenthuysen, Second Lieutenant Alfred H. Miles and sixteen rangers from Bowyer's Company of the Harrisburg Mounted Gunmen reached a rock formation in the hills near the headwaters of the West Fork of the Trinity River known to the Indians as the "Stone Houses." They were trailing a band of about 150 Indians who were driving a herd of stolen horses. The Indians charged the rangers, who sought protection in a ravine. The combat was at close range, and a great many Indians were killed during the attack. The initial offensive also cost the lives of Privates Cooper, Bostwick, Sanders and William Nicholson.

The Indians set the prairie grass on fire, and Lieutenant Vanbenthuysen decided that the only escape for his men was on foot through an open prairie. Second Lieutenant Miles and Privates Scheuster, Joslen, Christian, Blair and Westley Nicholson were killed while trying to escape through the burning field.

Only eight rangers managed to break out, and three of them were wounded during the engagement. The rangers reported that they had killed about fifty Indians. The remaining rangers walked seventeen days through the wilderness to reach the closest settlement.

Lieutenant Miles was a veteran of the Battle of San Jacinto in 1836 and was involved in the capture of Mexican general Antonio López de Santa Anna. Christian and Sanders were also veterans of the ranger service. Nothing is known about the other five men.

The Texas Historical Commission placed a marker at the site of the Battle of the Stone Houses recognizing the sacrifice of these Texas Rangers. The rock formation is located about ten miles south of Windthorst on Highway 61 in present-day Archer County.

Bullock, Julius
Born (Unknown)—Died 12 October 1838

Carpenter, John W.
Born 25 September 1806—Died 12 October 1838

Scott, Thomas M.
Born (Unknown)—Died 12 October 1838

Wilson, John
Born (Unknown)—Died 12 October 1838

In the summer of 1838, the fledgling Republic of Texas was tested by rebel forces from northern Mexico, who were stirring up the Indian tribes to continue the war against the white settlers. This disturbance was called the "Cordova Rebellion," named for Nacogdoches *alcalde* Vincente Cordova, who was largely responsible for the rebellious activity. Later, it became known as the "Cherokee War."

On 12 October 1838, Major Leonard H. Mabbitt of the First Battalion, Third Brigade, left Fort Houston with a force of rangers to pursue a band of Indians and Mexicans who were being led by two of General Cordova's lieutenants. About six miles from the fort, the rangers were attacked. Private Carpenter, a San Jacinto veteran who had joined only a week earlier, pursued a Caddo chief into the woods. The ranger and the chief were found later and apparently had killed each other. Privates Bullock, Scott and Wilson were also killed during the battle. Two other rangers were wounded.

The four dead rangers from Captain Squire Brown's Mounted Gunmen were transported back to Fort Houston and buried in unmarked graves.

Hall, James
Born (Unknown)—Died 17 December 1838
Date of incident: 16 October 1838

On the morning of 16 October 1838, Major General Rusk and Major Babbitt, who together had a combined force of about 260 rangers, were attacked by an estimated 150 to 600 Indians and Mexican rebels. No rangers were killed during the battle, but thirteen were wounded, including Private Hall from Captain James Bradshaw's Mounted Riflemen. Hall died from his wounds on 17 December 1838.

He is buried in an unmarked grave in the fort's cemetery.

The Texas Historical Commission erected a centennial marker at the site of the Kickapoo Battlefield on Highway 19 south of the town of Frankston in northeastern Anderson County.

Haslett, Joseph
Born (Unknown)—Died 18 October 1838

Haslett served as a surgeon under Colonel Samuel W. Sims of the First Regiment, Fourth Brigade of the Mounted Gunmen. The company was organized from 6 September 1838 to 7 January 1839. It was reported that Haslett died on 18 October 1838. The circumstances of his death are not known.

Cage, Benjamin F.
Born (Unknown)—Died 20 October 1838

Conrad, Peter
Born (Unknown)—Died 20 October 1838

Green, (First Name Unknown)
Born (Unknown)—Died 20 October 1838

King, (First Name Unknown)
Born (Unknown)—Died 20 October 1838

Lee, Robert M.
Born circa 1814—Died 20 October 1838

McClung, Dr. Henry G.
Born (Unknown)—Died shortly after 20 October 1838
Date of incident: 20 October 1838

O'Boyle, Daniel
Born (Unknown)—Died 20 October 1838

Pickering, John
Born (Unknown)—Died 20 October 1838

In October 1838, a band of Comanche Indians killed five surveyors at Leon Creek near San Antonio. Captain Cage and twelve volunteers started in pursuit. The group included General Richard G. Dunlap and Judge Joseph L. Hood. The rangers quickly became engaged in a fight with more than one hundred Comanche warriors. Cage, O'Boyle and Lee were killed almost immediately. The rangers fled back toward town, and Dr. McClung, Conrad, Pickering, Green and King were all killed. General Dunlap, Judge Hood, Robert Patton and Alexander Bailey were wounded. On 20 October, settlers retrieved their bodies. They were buried in a mass grave near present-day Milam Square in San Antonio.

Cage and Pickering were veterans of the Battle of San Jacinto. Conrad was a cavalryman under Deaf Smith. Lee was reported to be twenty-four years old and from Connecticut.

Judge Hood was elected sheriff of Bexar County on 1 May 1837 and died in the "Council House Fight" on 19 March 1840.

Lakin, Calvin
Born (Unknown)—Died 4 December 1838

Captain Edward H. Tarrant commanded a company of mounted riflemen from 6 September 1838 to 7 January 1839. He reported that Private Lakin died on 4 December 1838. The circumstances of his death are not known.

Breedin, Robert Hamet
Born (Unknown)—Died 14 January 1839

Captain Joseph Daniels commanded the Milam Guards from 15 November 1838 to 14 February 1839. The company was sent to protect settlers in the Brazos River area. Captain Daniels reported that Sergeant Breedin was accidentally killed while on duty on 14 January 1839 by Private Patrick D. Cunningham. Breedin was buried along the river. He was reportedly from Mobile, Alabama.

Barton, Hale
Born (Unknown)—Died 16 January 1839

Dorsey, L.
Born (Unknown)—Died 16 January 1839

Eaton, Alfred P.
Born (Unknown)—Died 16 January 1839

Fullerton, William
Born (Unknown)—Died 16 January 1839

Haigwood, Henry
Born (Unknown)—Died 16 January 1839

Henry, Hugh A.
Born (Unknown)—Died 16 January 1839

Marlin, William N.P.
Born (Unknown)—Died 16 January 1839

McGrew, G. Washington
Born (Unknown)—Died 16 January 1839

Plummer, Jacob
Born (Unknown)—Died 16 January 1839

Powers, Andrew Jackson
Born (Unknown)—Died 16 January 1839

Sauls, Charles
Born (Unknown)—Died 16 January 1839

Ward, Cyprus L.
Born (Unknown)—Died 16 January 1839

Webb, Andrew Jackson
Born (Unknown)—Died 16 January 1839

Indians attacked the Morgan family on the upper Brazos River on 1 January 1839 and killed six people in what was called the "Morgan Massacre."

On 14 January, Indians attacked the fortified homestead of John Marlin. The Marlin clan was able to kill a number of Indians and force them to retreat. A volunteer ranging company of fifty-two local men was organized, and Benjamin Franklin Bryant was elected the captain. On 16 January, the ranging company went to the Morgan place and ran into the Indians. Captain Bryant and Chief Jose Maria were wounded. As the Indians began to retreat, the volunteers became disorganized. Some men were mounted, and others were on foot. The Indians recognized their confusion and charged the force of Texans, routing them. Eleven men were killed outright. Sauls and Marlin suffered wounds that would ultimately prove fatal. Five other men were also wounded in the fight.

Historians have labeled this battle "Bryant's Defeat." A centennial marker bearing the politically correct title "Indian Battlefield" is located on State Highway 6 south of Marlin in Falls County.

Wilson, George
Born (Unknown)—Died circa 15 February 1839
Date of incident: About 12 February 1839

Captain William Eastland was elected captain of the La Grange Company Volunteers on 21 January 1839. On January 25, Lipan Apaches alerted the rangers that there was a camp of Comanche Indians nearby. Colonel John H. Moore assumed command of the two companies that had been under Captain Eastland and Captain Noah Smithwick from Bastrop.

On about 12 February, the rangers were camped along the San Gabriel River. The weather was extremely cold, and the men were nearly hypothermic. One of the friendly Indians in camp accidentally knocked over a rifle. The weapon discharged, and the shot mortally wounded Private Wilson of Eastland's company.

The men took Wilson to the Colorado River and constructed a boat to transport him to Austin. He died on the second day and was buried alongside the river.

Martin, Joseph S. "Joe"
Born (Unknown)—Died February–March 1839
Date of incident: 15 February 1839

On 15 February 1839, Colonel John H. Moore, along with Captains Noah Smithwick and William M. Eastland, led rangers and Indian allies to the banks of the San Saba River to attack a Comanche camp. In what historians would later call "Colonel Moore's Comanche Raid," seven rangers were wounded and one ranger was killed. Private Martin of Smithwick's Bastrop Rangers was shot in the back and paralyzed. Martin pleaded with Captain Smithwick to shoot him, but he was carried off the battlefield and transported to his home in Bastrop. He died several weeks later.

Blakey, Edmund J.
Born circa 1810—Died 25 February 1839

Burleson, Jacob Shipman
Born circa 1803—Died 25 February 1839

Walters, John B. "Jack"
Born circa 1815—Died 25 February 1839

Gilleland, James
Born circa 1779—Died 7 March 1839
Date of incident: 25 February 1839

A band of two to three hundred Comanche warriors were raiding communities in central Texas near present-day Bastrop. Twenty-five volunteers organized a ranging company and elected Jacob Burleson as their captain.

The ranging company spotted the Indians near Brushy Creek. As they dismounted, the Indians charged. Captain Burleson went to assist a young ranger and was shot in the back of the head. His brother, Colonel Edward Burleson, arrived at the scene with an additional thirty rangers and joined the fight. Privates Blakey and Walters were shot in the head and killed outright. Private Gilleland was shot in the neck. He survived for ten days and died on 7 March. Colonel Edward Burleson reported that the rangers had killed about thirty Indians in this fight, which historians have named "the Battle of Brushy Creek."

Gilleland was a forty-year-old clergyman. In the spring of 1835, he organized the first Methodist congregation in Austin's Little Colony in an unfinished store belonging to Jesse Holderman. Jacob Burleson was survived by his pregnant wife and two children. His wife had a son two months after his death, and the child was named after him.

The Texas Historical Commission erected a marker commemorating "the Battle of Brushy Creek" on State Highway 95, four miles south of Taylor, naming the four men killed in the battle.

Bird, John
Born circa 1795—Died 26 May 1839

Gay, Thomas
Born circa 1810—Died 26 May 1839

Hall, Hiram Metcalf C.
Born circa 1802—Died 27 May 1839
Date of incident: 26 May 1839

Nash, Jesse E.
Born (Unknown)—Died 26 May 1839

Weaver, William H.
Born (Unknown)—Died 26 May 1839

Continuing Indian raids on the upper Brazos, Trinity and Colorado Rivers caused citizens to petition the Congress of the Republic of Texas for help. On Sunday, 26 May 1839, Captain John Bird and thirty-five rangers encountered Indians chasing a herd of buffalo and tried to capture them. The rangers decided to dismount and retreat along a creek when more Indians arrived. Private Hall remained on horseback and was mortally wounded. The Indians summoned help, and soon two hundred hostiles surrounded the rangers. The Indians charged and killed Privates Gay and Nash and First Sergeant Weaver and wounded two other rangers.

Captain Bird attempted to rally his men and was shot through the heart with an arrow. Comanche war chief Buffalo Hump and twelve warriors charged, and the war chief was killed. The Indians then withdrew. The rangers carried the three wounded men to Fort Smith, where Private Hall died the next day. The dead rangers were buried in one large coffin on the banks of the Little River. Privates Hall and Nash were members of Bird's Rangers. Privates Gay and Weaver were members of Evan's Company of Travis Spies.

In 1936, Texas Centennial markers were placed in Temple and Bell Counties honoring "Bird's Victory." Bird was born in Tennessee and was married with four children when he arrived in Texas in 1830. He had fought with Andrew Jackson in the War of 1812, against the Comanches in 1832 and against the Mexicans during the Texas Revolution in 1836. Hall was survived by his wife, Lydia Margaret Holder, and three children. Gay was survived by his wife, Eleanor, and six children.

Morales, Pedro Flores
Born (Unknown)—Died June 1839
Date of incident: 18 June 1839

On 6 June 1839, Colonel Henry W. Karnes organized an expedition to locate Comanche Indian raiders west of San Antonio. Captains Louis Franks and Juan Seguin commanded the Mounted Volunteers.

On 18 June, Private Morales was accidentally shot and mortally wounded. Captain Seguin later reported that he died during the campaign. Since the companies disbanded on 23 June, it is presumed that Morales died before that date.

Anderson, Joseph S.
Born (Unknown)—Died 15 July 1839

Crane, John
Born 21 September 1789—Died 15 July 1839

Crowson, Henry P.
Born (Unknown)—Died 15 July 1839

Day, John
Born (Unknown)—Died 15 July 1839

Rogers, Dr. Henry M.
Born (Unknown)—Died 15 July 1839

In June 1839, relations between the Cherokee Indians and the Texans were deteriorating. President Lamar wanted the Cherokees removed from the state for conspiring with Mexican rebels. He ordered more than one thousand troops, ranging companies and Indian allies to be readied for combat.

The July peace talks with Chief Bowles broke down over the Texan's firm demand that the Indians leave the state unarmed. On 15 July, a fight that would later be called "the Cherokee War" began at a place called Battle Creek. Private Crowson was killed in the fight. Private Crane was mortally wounded during the affray and died shortly after. Both men served in Captain Harrison's Mounted Riflemen. Privates Day of Captain Howard's Company D and Dr. Rogers of Captain Tipps's Nacogdoches Volunteers were also killed. Eight men were also wounded in this battle that lasted only fifteen minutes. Private Anderson of Captain Mark Lewis's Company from Woodlief's Mounted Volunteer Regiment was wounded and reportedly died.

Crane and Rogers were buried near the battlefield. It is believed that Day and Crowson were buried there, as well. Crane was survived by his wife, Mary Delozier, and nine children. Day was a former member of the Gonzales Rangers in 1829 under Captain Matthew "Old Paint" Caldwell.

Ewing, John
Born (Unknown)—Died 16 July 1839

Martin, George F.
Born (Unknown)—Died 16 July 1839

Thompson, John S.
Born (Unknown)—Died 16 July 1839

Tutts, Martin
Born (Unknown)—Died 16 July 1839

After the fight at Battle Creek, Chief Bowles and his warriors moved farther up the Neches River to the village of Delaware chief Harris. As Colonel Burleson's Texas army troops approached, they were fired upon. Private Tutts of Captain S.W. Jordan's Infantry Company C was killed. The Texans burned the Indian village. The fighting was difficult and exhausting in the summer heat. During the battle, Private Ewing from Captain G.H. Harrison's Houston County Rangers, Private Thompson from Captain Madison Smith's Mounted Company and Private Martin from Captain Jackson Todd's Nacogdoches Company were killed. Twenty rangers and militiamen were wounded. The eighty-three-year-old Chief Bowles displayed considerable bravery. As the Indians retreated, the chief was shot and wounded. As the old chief tried to sit up, Captain Bob Smith shot him in the head and killed him.

It has been reported that Cherokee chief Big Mush and about one hundred Indians were killed.

Big Mush, who was known to his own people as Gatunwali, was a principal diplomat or "war chief" of the Cherokee Indians. In 1836 and 1837, Big Mush found himself caught between the majority of Cherokees who wanted to negotiate a permanent home for the tribe and the smaller band of militants who wanted to form an alliance with Mexico to overthrow the Republic of Texas.

O'Neill, Timothy
Born (Unknown)—Died 26 July 1839

On 26 July 1839, Second Lieutenant O'Neill of Captain Adam Clendenin's Company B of the First Regiment of Infantry left Fort Lamar to scout west of the Neches River. His scouting party was attacked by Indians, and O'Neill was killed.

O'Neill was reportedly from New York and had previously served as a ranger in the Milam Guards. He was buried at the fort.

Mindiola, Marino
Born (Unknown)—Died 28 October 1839
Date of incident: 22 October 1839

Sisty, William R.
Born (Unknown)—Died 26 October 1839

Colonel Henry Karnes was in charge of two ranging companies that were organized on 8 September to scout for Comanche Indians. Jose Maria Gonzales, a former colonel in the Mexican army, was elected captain of the Mounted Volunteers from San Antonio. William F. Wilson was elected captain of the Galveston Mounted Gunmen.

On 22 October, Private Mindiola of Captain Gonzales's company was shot and wounded when another ranger's rifle became snagged on a tree limb and discharged. He was carried on a litter as the rangers changed camps. On 26 October, another accident occurred when Fourth Corporal Sisty of Captain Wilson's company was fatally wounded when another ranger accidentally discharged his rifle. He died shortly thereafter.

Sisty was buried the next day near the Guadalupe River. On 28 October, Mindiola died from his wound and was buried at the same location.

Earle, John J.
Born (Unknown)—Died 11 November 1839

Whepler, Phillip
Born (Unknown)—Died 11 November 1839

Colonel John C. Neill of the First Regiment of Mounted Gunmen led an expedition between the Trinity and Brazos Rivers.

On 25 October 1839, they attacked an Indian village in present-day Hill County. The Texans continued to pursue the fleeing Indian tribes and engaged them again on 5 November near Comanche Peak. On 11 November, on Richland Creek, Privates Earle and Whepler of Captain Henry Reed's Company G from Robertson County left the camp and were killed by Indians. Both men were from Nashville on the Brazos.

Nashville was on the southeast bank of the Brazos River, two miles below the mouth of Little River and about five miles northeast of Gause in what is now Milam County.

The town was founded in 1835. Immediately after the Texas Revolution, Nashville was considered by the Texas Congress as a possible site for the capital of the republic. The town served as county seat of Milam County from 1837 to 1846, but after the state legislature made Cameron the Milam County seat in 1846, Nashville began to decline. Construction of the Houston and Texas Central Railway at nearby Hearne in 1868 delivered the fatal blow, and the post office at Nashville was discontinued in 1868.

Lynch, John L.
Born (Unknown)—Died 25 December 1839

In December 1839, Colonel Edward Burleson initiated the Northwestern Campaign with the Frontier Regiment of the Texas army and its Indian allies. The army was ordered to drive the Comanches and other hostile Indian tribes farther away from the settlements. A mounted ranger spy company led by Captain Matthew "Old Paint" Caldwell located a Cherokee village on the Colorado River.

On 25 December, the army engaged the Indians in battle and seized the village as the warriors escaped. The only Texan casualty was Private Lynch of the company of Mounted Volunteer Scouts. Lynch had previously served as captain of Company A Battalion of Mounted Riflemen from 28 November 1837 until 20 February 1838. He had also served with Burleson's volunteers at the Mill Creek fight against Cordova's rebels on 29 March 1839. Lynch logged additional service as captain of a detachment of spies from 25 June to 25 August 1839 during the Cherokee War.

Anderson, David
Born (Unknown)—Died 4 January 1840

Lesley, Tiba
Born (Unknown)—Died 4 January 1840

During Colonel Edward Burleson's Northwestern Campaign, two privates from Captain Adam Clendenin's Infantry Company B deserted. Privates Anderson and Lesley left the camp on 2 January 1840 and were found dead on 4 January. It appeared they had been killed by Comanche Indians.

Douglass, Henry
Born (Unknown)—Died 28 February 1840

L'Estrange, Richard
Born (Unknown)—Died 28 February 1840

The First Regiment of the Texas army was moving companies toward San Antonio in anticipation of the upcoming March peace talks with the

Comanche Indians. Company A under the command of Captain William D. Redd and Company I under the command of Captain Benjamin Y. Gullen were camped at Mission Jose, just outside San Antonio.

On 14 February, several men were sent to Gonzales for supplies. During their return trip on 28 February, the men were attacked by Indians. Privates Douglass and L'Estrange were killed, and Private C.A. Root of Company A was wounded.

Dunnington, William M.
Born (Unknown)—Died 19 March 1840

Kaminsky, Frederick
Born (Unknown)—Died 19 March 1840

Whitney, Robert G.
Born (Unknown)—Died 19 March 1840

In January 1840, the government of the Republic of Texas demanded the return of all captives held by the Indian tribes and an immediate halt to all raiding of white settlements. On 19 March 1840, a party of Penateka Comanches came to San Antonio for a hearing by Texas commissioners.

The Indians brought some captive Mexican children and a sixteen-year-old white girl named Matilda Lockhart. Lockhart had been captured on 9 December 1838. She had been mutilated, and her nose had been partially burned off. She told the commissioners that other white hostages were being held. The Comanches argued that those captives were outside of their control.

Texas soldiers entered the Council House and attempted to detain the assembled Comanches. A fight broke out, and thirty-five Indian men, women and children were killed, with twenty-seven taken captive. Seven Texans were killed, including Lieutenant Dunnington, Private Kaminsky of Company A, Private Whitney of Company E and Sheriff Joe Hood.

Related case: Bexar County Sheriff's Office—Joseph Hood.

Bell, Dr. (First Name Unknown)
Born (Unknown)—Died 9 August 1840

Mordica, Benjamin H.
Born (Unknown)—Died 9 August 1840

Wolf, Gotlip (DeWolf)
Born (Unknown)—Died 12 August 1840
Date of incident: 9 August 1840

The conflict known as "the Great Commache Raid" that penetrated deep into south Texas was, in part, launched out of revenge for the deaths of the Indian chiefs at the "Council House Fight" on 19 March 1840.

On 6 August 1840, about five hundred warriors under Chief Buffalo Hump seized Victoria. On 8 August, they seized Linnville. As the massive Comanche war party headed north, it was heavily laden with stolen property, horses and hostages. On 9 August, the band of hostiles passed between Captain Clark L. Owen and his Texian volunteer company and Captain John J. Tumlinson and his Cuero and Victoria volunteer company. Captain Owen sent a three-man scouting party that included John S. Menefee, Dr. Bell and a man named Nail. Near Arenosa Creek in present-day Jackson County, the men encountered Comanche Indians and were attacked. Bell was killed and Menefee was seriously wounded. Captain Tumlinson and his rangers engaged the Comanches. Private Mordica was also killed. He had enlisted the day before the fight.

On 12 August, two hundred rangers and Tonkawa allies attacked about one thousand Comanches. The unit called the Mounted Volunteer Border Guards, led by Captain James D. Cocke, operated under the command of Captain George Howard of the First Regiment in San Antonio. The company was organized on 18 June in Houston for the defense of Austin. During the battle, the Border Guards dismounted to fight a small group of Comanches. When they saw the larger war party approaching, they retreated. Private Wolf fell behind and was killed.

Harrell, Garrett
Born (Unknown)—Died 16 October 1840

Private Harrell was attached to Captain Thomas J. Rabb's Fayette County Company of Texas Rangers, an ad hoc ranging company that elected its own officers.

On 16 October 1840, the rangers were camped along the Concho River in present-day Tom Green County. Private Harrell developed a sore throat and died from a choking spell.

Taylor, Leonard
Born (Unknown)—Died 14 February 1841

On 14 February 1841, Private Taylor of Company E was on surveying duty when he was shot and killed by another ranger who mistook him for an Indian.

Understandably, there were questions about the shooting being accidental. Private Taylor was in uniform, and the shooting took place in broad daylight at a distance of thirty feet.

Taylor was under the command of Lieutenant Robert R. Scott of the First Regiment of Infantry.

Denton, John Bunyard
Born 27 July 1806—Died 24 May 1841

General Edward H. Tarrant was the northern commander of the Fourth Militia Brigade of the Texas Militia. Denton served as a captain in this militia. On 4 May 1841, a ranger company called the Red River Volunteers was raised in Fannin County and elected James Bourland as their captain.

Denton was a veteran Indian fighter, preacher and lawyer enlisted as a private, but he was the captain in charge of scouts. On 14 May, the company of seventy to eighty men departed on what historians would later call "the Village Creek Expedition."

On 24 May, the rangers charged an Indian village near present-day Tarrant County, taking the inhabitants by surprise. The rangers did not know that there was a series of villages along the creek and that they were vastly outnumbered. Captain Denton requested permission to take a ten-man patrol farther down the creek to investigate. As he did so, Captain Henry Stout arrived. When the men reached a thicket and entered the creek, they were ambushed by a group of Indians. Stout was shot through the arm, and his clothes were pierced by bullets. Denton was hit by three bullets and died instantly. Captain Bourland and twenty men returned later and recovered Denton's body.

Captain Denton was survived by his wife and six children. His body was buried and exhumed twice. It was finally buried on the courthouse lawn at Denton in 1901.

Slein, John
Born (Unknown)—Died 24 July 1841

Captain John Coffee "Jack" Hays had formed a group of Bexar County Minute Men consisting of twenty-five volunteers and ten to fifteen Lipan and Tonkawa scouts. Slein was a merchant who enlisted as a private on 23 June 1841 and saw action with Captain Hays during a battle with Comanches at Uvalde Valley on 29 June.

The company was tracking a large number of Commache Indians near the Llano River when they were discovered on 24 July. Captain Hays and about twenty-four men rode ahead and confronted about fifty Comanches, who were creating a delaying action to allow the main camp to escape. Hays and Private John Trueheart were wounded, and Private Slein was killed. Hays claimed that eight to ten Comanches were killed.

One author has reported the name of the casualty as John Flin rather than John Slein.

Smith, Abram Trigg
Born circa 1798—Died 5 August 1841

On 9 June 1841, Robertson County Minute Men under the command of Captain Eli Chandler raided an Indian village near the Cross Timbers. They captured fourteen prisoners and rescued one Mexican hostage. The hostage knew a lot about the various Indian tribes and their locations and agreed to act as their scout. Captain George Erath and his Milam County Minute Men, as well as volunteers from Travis County, joined Chandler for a combined force of about 120 men.

On 5 August, the ranger companies moved up the Brazos River but found no trace of any Indian settlement or camp. During their wait for the arrival of supplies, Indians were seen near the camp. Captain Erath and twenty men went to track them and came upon a party of either Cherokees or Kickapoos, who opened fire at close range from atop a rock cliff. During the exchange, Private Smith was killed and several other men were wounded. Ranger sniping killed two Indians and may have wounded others. Hearing the gunfire, another ranger squad quickly responded, bringing reinforcements from the main ranger camp to join the fight.

Smith's brother and nephew served on the same expedition and carried his body away from the battlefield. He is buried in an unmarked grave. Smith had enlisted on 2 August 1841 and served only three days. He was survived by his wife and six children.

In 2005, Texas Rangers and family members honored Private Smith's service to the state with a memorial ceremony and marker at the Fort Belknap Cemetery in Young County near where he was buried in 1841.

Heard, George W.
Born (Unknown)—Died 22 August 1841

Heard had enlisted as a private on 20 July 1841. He served in the Robertson County Minute Men under Captain Eli Chandler during the battles in early August that had claimed the life of Private A.T. Smith.

The company returned to Franklin on 17 August. Captain Chandler ordered a scouting party on 21 August. The eight-man patrol was led by Private Heard. On 22 August, when they were about fourteen miles from Franklin, the patrol was attacked by Indians. Heard was struck by three bullets and killed. The seven remaining rangers realized that they could not hold out and returned to the camp for reinforcements. When Captain Chandler and the rangers found Heard's body, he had been scalped and mutilated. His head and hands had been severed. Heard is buried in Franklin.

McPherson, James
Born (Unknown)—Died 8 September 1841

In May 1841, Mexican soldiers raided Refugio and killed several people, robbing the town and taking hostages. On 14 May 1841, McPherson enlisted as a private in Captain Alanson T. Miles's San Patricio Minute Men and served through 30 June 1841. The company did not see any serious action. On 12 July, McPherson reenlisted. Captain Miles was demoted to private on 25 August, and Private William J. Cairnes was promoted to captain.

On 8 September, Private McPherson is reported to have drowned in the Nueces River.

Sowell, Joseph
Born (Unknown)—Died 28 November 1841

Sowell enlisted as a private in Captain Daniel R. Jackson's Fannin County Rangers on 28 March 1840. He served until 28 September 1840.

In July 1841, a band of Coushatta Indians were accused of attacks on settlers in present-day Grayson County. They were also thought to be responsible for the deaths of Daniel Dugan Jr. and William Kitchens. On 6 July, Captain Sowell mustered the Fannin County Minute Men to operate in north Texas until 26 September. On 14 November, Coushattas attacked the Dugan home again and killed a man named Hoover. Captain Sowell organized a company of Minute Men who crossed the Red River into the Indian Territory and killed ten to twelve Coushattas.

About 28 November, a band of about twelve Coushattas sought revenge by raiding a tavern and inn at Old Warren that was owned by Captain Sowell and a ranger named John Scott. The men were alerted as the Indians were stealing the horses. Sowell was struck by an arrow and mortally wounded. Scott killed one Indian with a shotgun as they fled.

Clubb, David (or Samuel)
Born (Unknown)—Died October–November 1841
Date of incident: October–November 1841

Bird's Fort was constructed on the Trinity River in present-day Fort Worth and was operational by mid-October 1841. Robert Sloan was leading a scouting detachment of Red River militiamen when they were attacked by Indians at a small lake on the Elm Fork of the Trinity River. Private Clubb was killed in that exchange.

Clubb was from Illinois and had fought in the Black Hawk War of 1832. The Red River County Minute Men were commanded by Captain William Becknell. Sloan's name, but not Clubb's, appears on the muster roll.

In 1854, famous Texas cattleman John Simpson Chisum located his livestock operation along Clear Creek, which has its mouth at the Elm Fork of the Trinity River near the site of Bird's Fort and the fight of November 1841. Clear Creek runs in a shoestring fashion before ultimately tapering off into Williwalla Creek northwest of Rosston in Cooke County.

Rattan, Wade Hampton
Born (Unknown)—Died 25 December 1841

Silkwood, Solomon
Born (Unknown)—Died December 1841

Major Jonathan Bird was ordered to construct a new fort along the Trinity River in present-day Fort Worth. On 19 September 1841, Colonel Daniel Montague mustered a twenty-nine-man company under the command of Captain Alexander W. Webb. Rattan was appointed quartermaster and commissary for the company.

Captain Webb sent a wagon to the Red River settlements for supplies. When the supply wagon did not return on time, Webb, along with Privates Rattan and Silkwood, went to look for the wagon. On 25 December, they encountered Indians on the Elm Fork. Rattan was killed while cutting down a tree that contained a beehive from which he had planned on taking honey. Webb and Silkwood killed one of the Indians and escaped to the fort. Rattan's body was recovered and returned to the fort for burial. He was survived by his brothers, John and Littleton Rattan, who had participated in the Village Creek fight in 1841.

It was snowing and very cold that December. Silkwood became ill and died from exposure after returning to the fort.

Jett, Stephen
Born 11 February 1813—Died 18 September 1842

Mexican troops invaded the Republic of Texas in March 1842. General Woll captured San Antonio on 11 September. Captain John Coffee "Jack" Hays's Bexar County spy company of frontier volunteers was organized on 13 September 1842. They soon joined Colonel Matthew Caldwell's forces to attack the Mexican army at Salado Creek.

Private Jett was killed and ten rangers were wounded in the fight. The Mexican army crossed back into Mexico on 29 September. Ranger muster rolls indicate that Jett had previously enlisted in Captain Hays's spy company at San Antonio on 10 January 1841 and served until 10 May 1841.

Fohr, Peter
Born (Unknown)—Died 8 June 1844

Captain John Coffee "Jack" Hays left his headquarters at San Antonio on or about 1 June 1844 with fifteen men on a scout in the hills to the north and west. The group was looking for a Comanche war party led by Yellow Wolf that had recently been raiding in Bexar County. On 8 June, the rangers spotted a band of Comanches estimated at between forty to two hundred warriors. The rangers slowly followed the Indians, who were concealed in the heavy brush. Attempts to bait the rangers into a charge were ignored. Finally, the entire Indian force rode forward in line of battle to draw the rangers into an attack. The rangers soon found themselves engaged in hand-to-hand combat with the warriors.

Two counterattacks on their flanks were repelled. The Indians fled and were pursued for three miles as the rangers laid down heavy fire from their new Colt repeating revolvers. At the end of the hour-long battle, the Indian casualties were estimated at between twenty to fifty killed or wounded, with Yellow Wolf among the slain.

Most reports indicate that the rangers lost only one man, that being Private Fohr. Four additional rangers had been seriously wounded. Another report indicates that a ranger private named Mott was also killed.

There is little personal information about Fohr except that he enlisted in San Antonio on 10 January 1841. His place of burial is unknown.

Historians later named this fight "the Battle of Walker Creek." Although much controversy exists concerning the veracity of the claim, by some reports it was the first time the rangers used the new five-shot Colt Paterson model revolvers in combat. Others contend that the Colt Paterson was first used during "the Fight at Bandera Pass" or at an unnamed engagement in the Uvalde Canyon. More recent research tends to support the claim that it was during this battle that the Patterson Colt first drew blood on the Texas frontier.

A Comanche who had taken part in the battle later complained that the rangers "had a shot for every finger on their hand."

EARLY STATEHOOD, 1846–1860

Harris, E.
Born (Unknown)—Died 28 April 1846

Hastings, H.H.
Born (Unknown)—Died 28 April 1846

Prostoski, Joseph
Born (Unknown)—Died 28 April 1846

Radcliff, Edward S.
Born (Unknown)—Died 28 April 1846

Robinson, J.
Born (Unknown)—Died 28 April 1846

Waters, William
Born (Unknown)—Died 28 April 1846

Mexico warned the United States not to annex Texas in 1845. Nonetheless, the annexation passed the Congress. It did not, however, define the state boundaries.

Texas and the United States both claimed the Rio Grande River. Mexico believed that the Nueces River was the international boundary. President Polk ordered General Zachary Taylor to establish a U.S. presence along the Rio Grande River. When General Taylor requested volunteers to act as scouts and spies for his regular army, Samuel H. Walker, a former ranger and U.S. scout, enlisted as a private and was mustered into federal service in September 1845.

On 21 April 1846, Captain Walker formed his own company of mounted rangers to serve under Taylor. On 28 April, Walker led a 75-man patrol that was attacked by a force of 1,500 Mexican soldiers. The rangers panicked and fled. Walker and 12 rangers remained to engage the enemy. Seriously outnumbered, they had to withdraw after only fifteen minutes of fighting. Sergeant Radcliffe and 15 to 18 rangers remained at the Port Isabel base camp and were caught off guard when the Mexican army attacked.

Accounts vary as to the number of dead, but First Sergeant Ratcliffe and Privates Harris, Prostoski, Robinson and Hastings were positively identified as having lost their lives in the encounter. Hastings was reported to have been a visitor at the camp.

Walker was killed during a battle at Huamantla, Tlaxcala, Mexico, on 9 October 1847.

O'Bryant, C.P.
Born (Unknown)—Died 18 September 1846

Private O'Bryant was reported to have died on 18 September 1846 at Elm Station. He was assigned to Captain Andrew Stapp's Company of Texas Mounted Volunteers.

Milligan, Little
Born (Unknown)—Died 30 November 1846

Private Milligan was reported to have died on 30 November 1846 in Corpus Christi. He was assigned to Captain Mabry B. Gray's Company of Texas Mounted Volunteers.

Murphy, Benjamin W.
Born (Unknown)—Died 2 December 1846

Private Murphy was reported to have died from as a result of an accidental shooting while en route to Mexico. He was assigned Captain H.E. McCulloch's Company of Smith's Battalion of Texas Mounted Volunteers.

Tumlinson, Josiah
Born (Unknown)—Died 3 December 1846

Private Tumlinson was reported to have died on 3 December 1846 at San Marcos. He was assigned to Captain H.E. McCulloch's Company of Smith's Battalion of Texas Mounted Volunteers.

Rhew, William
Born (Unknown)—Died 18 December 1846

Private Rhew was reported to have died on 18 December 1846 at San Antonio. He was assigned to Captain John H. Conner's Company of Smith's Battalion, Texas Mounted Volunteers. The ranger muster rolls indicate that Rhew enlisted on 24 November 1844 in the Corpus Christi Rangers under Captain H.C. Davis and was discharged on 28 January 1845. He reenlisted in the same company on 28 January 1845 and was discharged on 28 February. He apparently reenlisted on 28 February 1845 under Captain P. Bell with no discharge date noted.

Trammel, Benjamin
Born (Unknown)—Died 20 December 1846

Private Trammel was reported to have died on 20 December 1846 at Austin. He was assigned to Captain John J. Grumbles's Company of Smith's Battalion of Texas Mounted Volunteers.

Crayton, James
Born (Unknown)—Died 4 January 1847

Private Crayton was reported to have died on 4 January 1847 at Laredo. He was assigned to Captain John J. Grumbles's Company of Smith's Battalion of Texas Mounted Volunteers.

Chambliss, Simon
Born (Unknown)—Died 5 January 1847

Private Chambliss was reported to have died on 5 January 1847 at San Antonio. He was assigned to Captain H.E. McCulloch's Company of Smith's Battalion of Texas Mounted Volunteers.

The ranger muster rolls indicate that a "Solomon Chambless" enlisted on 14 September 1838 and served until 13 March 1839 as an orderly under Captain N.T. Journey of the Fannin County Mounted Rangers.

Hudson, David
Born circa 1819—Died 10 January 1847

Private Hudson was reported to have died on 10 January 1847 in Austin. He was assigned to Captain Shapley P. Ross's Company of Smith's Battalion.

Hudson was born in Tennessee and was not married. The ranger muster rolls indicate that a "David Hudson" enlisted on 10 March 1939 in the Bastrop Rangers under Captain M. Andrews and served until 10 June 1839. He reenlisted in the Bastrop Rangers under Captain N. Merrill on 19 June 1839 and served until 10 September 1839.

Roberts, Thomas
Born (Unknown)—Died 17 January 1847

Private Roberts was reported to have died on 17 January 1847 at San Gabriel. He was assigned to Captain Shapley P. Ross's Company of Smith's Battalion.

The ranger muster rolls indicate that a "Thomas F. Ross" enlisted on 14 January 1839 in the Mounted Rangers under Captain M.R. Roberts and served until 13 April 1839.

Willingham, Eli Washington
Born 22 February 1827—Died 20 January 1847

Private Willingham was reported to have died on 20 January 1847 at Independence. He was assigned to Captain Shapley P. Ross's Company of Smith's Battalion. Willingham was born in Georgia and was not married.

Neil, Perry
Born (Unknown)—Died 21 January 1847

Private Neil was reported to have died on 21 January 1847 at San Gabriel. He was assigned to Captain Shapley P. Ross's Company of Smith's Battalion.

Fulcher, Solomon Frank
Born circa 1824—Died 31 January 1847

Private Fulcher was reported to have died on 31 January 1847 at Austin. He was assigned to Captain Shapley P. Ross's Company of Smith's Battalion. Fulcher was born on Arkansas City, Arkansas.

Fulcher was not married. His last place of residence was Burleson County.

Brooks, Augustus
Born (Unknown)—Died 3 February 1847

Private Brooks was reported to have died on 3 February 1847 at Corpus Christi. He was assigned to Captain Mabry B. Gray's Company of Texas Mounted Volunteers.

Connell, Richard
Born (Unknown)—Died 4 February 1847

Private Connell was reported to have died on 4 February 1847 near Austin. He was assigned to Captain John J. Grumbles's Company of Smith's Battalion of Texas Mounted Volunteers.

Cummings, Wiley
Born (Unknown)—Died 10 February 1847

Private Cummings was reported to have died somewhere along the Guadalupe River on 10 February 1847. He was assigned to Captain Mabry B. Gray's Company of Texas Mounted Volunteers.

Warring, Thomas
Born (Unknown)—Died 13 February 1847

Private Warring was reported to have died on 13 February 1847 at San Antonio. He was assigned to Captain Shapley P. Ross's Company of Smith's Battalion.

Ross, Angus
Born (Unknown)—Died 18 February 1847

Private Ross was reported to have died on 18 February 1847 near Austin. He was assigned to Captain John J. Grumbles's Company of Smith's Battalion of Texas Mounted Volunteers.

Soleus, Charles B.
Born (Unknown)—Died 18 February 1847

Private Soleus was reported to have died on the Nueces River. He was assigned to Captain John H. Conner's Company of Smith's Battalion of Texas Mounted Volunteers.

Crabtree, Job
Born circa 1828—Died 1 April 1847

Private Crabtree was reported to have drowned in the Rio Grande River on 1 April 1847. He was assigned to Company C under Captain George W. Adams of Chevallie's Battalion, Texas Mounted Volunteers.

According to family genealogists, Crabtree was escorting a wagon train to Oregon in 1846 when he and a man named John Constable disappeared. Apparently Crabtree enlisted in the Texas Rangers. Crabtree was not married.

Gregg, Ellis
Born (Unknown)—Died 16 or 18 April 1847

Private Gregg was reported to have died on 16 or 18 April 1847 at San Patricio. He was assigned to Captain Shapley P. Ross's Company of Smith's Battalion.

Keese, William W.
Born (Unknown)—Died 15 April 1847

Private Keese was reported to have died on 15 April 1847 at San Antonio. He was assigned to Captain H.E. McCulloch's Company of Smith's Battalion, Texas Mounted Volunteers.

Koch, Henry
Born (Unknown)—Died 18 April 1847

Private Koch was reported to have died on 18 April 1847 at Castroville. He was assigned to Captain John H. Conner's Company of Smith's Battalion, Texas Mounted Volunteers.

Harney, John
Born (Unknown)—Died 12 June 1847

Private Harney was reported to have died on 12 June 1847 at Pedernales. He was assigned to Captain John H. Conner's Company of Smith's Battalion, Texas Mounted Volunteers.

Mills, M.J.
Born (Unknown)—Died 26 July 1847

Private Mills was reported to have died on 26 July 1847 at Smith's Station. He was assigned to Lieutenant E.S. Wyman's Company of Smith's Battalion, Texas Mounted Volunteers.

Gunter, R.H.
Born (Unknown)—Died 27 June 1847

Private Gunter was reported to have died at the Rio Grande River on 27 June 1847. He was assigned to Captain H.E. McCulloch's Company of Smith's Battalion of Texas Mounted Volunteers.

Tidwell, Peter
Born (Unknown)—Died 4 August 1847

Private Tidwell was reported to have died on 4 August 1847 at Austin. He was assigned to Captain Middleton T. Johnson's Company of Bell's Mounted Regiment of Texian Volunteers.

Rainbolt, John P.
Born (Unknown)—Died 21 August 1847

Private Rainbolt was reported to have been accidentally killed on 21 August 1847 at Camp Arbuckle. He was assigned to Company H of the First Regiment, Texas Mounted Volunteers under the command of Captain James S. Gillett.

Coonrod, William J.
Born (Unknown)—Died 8 September 1847

Private Coonrod was reported to have died on 8 September 1847 at Waco Village Station. He was assigned to Captain Middleton T. Johnson's Company of Bell's Mounted Regiment, Texian Volunteers.

Cundiff, Charles E.
Born (Unknown)—Died 20 September 1847

Private Cundiff was reported to have died on 20 September 1847 at Waco Village Station. He was assigned to Captain Middleton T. Johnson's Company of Bell's Mounted Regiment, Texian Volunteers.

Darnell, Dewitt C.
Born (Unknown)—Died 26 September 1847

Private Darnell was reported to have died on 26 September 1847 at Waco Village Station. He was assigned to Captain Middleton T. Johnson's Company of Bell's Mounted Regiment, Texian Volunteers.

Johnston, Joshua W.
Born (Unknown)—Died 30 September 1847

Private Johnston was reported to have died on 30 September 1847 at Waco Village Station. He was assigned Captain Middleton T. Johnson's Company of Bell's Mounted Regiment, Texian Volunteers.

Barber, John Hutcheson
Born circa 1830—17 October 1847

Family genealogists claim that John Barber joined a ranger company at age fourteen. He served three years until he died of "Winter Fever" on 17 October 1847 at Post Hamilton Valley at age sixteen. The family has recorded that he served under Colonel Hugh Smith, but it is more likely he was assigned to Company D under the command of Captain Samuel Highsmith of the First Mounted Volunteers.

Barber was not married. His father, William James Barber Jr., died a few months later while serving in the same company.

Considering his reported age of sixteen at the time of death, John Barber should qualify for special recognition as the youngest Texas Ranger to die while in service. In terms of age, he is listed ahead of L.B. "Berry" Smith, who was seventeen when he was shot and killed by Mexican bandits on 12 June 1875. However, Ranger L.B. Smith's death was clearly line of duty related, thus he retains the distinction of being the youngest Texas lawman killed in the line of duty during the 1800s.

Jennings, Henry L.
Born (Unknown)—Died 10 November 1847

Private Jennings was reported to have died on 10 November 1847 in Laredo. He was assigned to Company H under Captain James S. Gillett of the Texas Mounted Volunteers. According to family genealogists, he was born in Missouri.

Calvert, James
Born (Unknown)—Died 11 November 1847

Private Calvert was reported to have died on 11 November 1847 at Enchanted Rock. He was assigned to Company D under the command of Captain Samuel Highsmith of the Texas Mounted Volunteers.

Reed, Thompson
Born (Unknown)—Died circa November or December 1847

Lieutenant Reed was reported to have died at Camp Arbuckle. He was assigned to Company H under Captain James S. Gillett of the Texas Mounted Volunteers.

Runnolds, B.F.
Born (Unknown)—Died 12–14 December 1847

Private Runnolds was reported to have been killed in a personal affray at Camp Medina on 12 or 14 December 1847. He was assigned to Captain William G. Crump's company, under the command of Lieutenant Colonel P. Hansbrough, Bell's Mounted Regiment, Texian Volunteers.

Gilbert, Richard S.
Born (Unknown)—Died 18 December 1847

Rattan, Littleton P. "Lit"
Born 12 January 1809—Died 18 December 1847

Littleton and his brother, Daniel, enlisted on 26 April 1847 at San Antonio for federal service under Captain James B. Gillett. They completed their enlistment on 2 June 1847. Gillett later formed Company H of the Texas Mounted Volunteers, and both men reenlisted on 5 June 1847. Richard S. Gilbert apparently enlisted at the same time. Privates Gilbert and Littleton Ratton were reported to have died on 18 December 1847.

Ranger muster rolls indicate that Littleton Rattan enlisted in the spring of 1841 as a lieutenant under Captain J. Bourland. Several other Rattan's also served at the same time. Littleton was born in Madison, Illinois, and is claimed to have had six children by two wives. Family genealogists claim that he was killed by Indians near Laredo.

The State of Texas erected a historical marker in Delta County that reads:

Littleton Rattan
A native of Illinois and a veteran of the 1832 Black Hawk War, Littleton
Rattan (b. 1809) came to Texas with family members in 1839. He

established a farm at this site in Delta County and also served as a Texas Ranger in three area militia companies in the Republic of Texas area. Later, during the Mexican War, he served under legendary Ranger Jack Hays. Rattan was killed on December 18, 1847 in battle with native Americans, but the details of his death, including the location of the battle, and his grave site remain unknown, He is remembered for his contributions to the safety of pioneers in Delta County and throughout the State.

Wells, Joseph
Born (Unknown)—Died 22 December 1847

Private Wells was reported to have died on 22 December 1847 at Camp Nueces. He was assigned to Company E under the command of Captain James S. Sutton of Bell's Mounted Regiment, Texian Volunteers.

Harrison, Benjamin
Born (Unknown)—Died 25 December 1847

Private Harrison was reported to have died on 25 December 1847 in Laredo. He was assigned Captain Mirabeau B. Lamar's company of Texas Cavalry. This company was mustered into service as U.S. Volunteers in the U.S. Army.

Green, Jamson
Born (Unknown)—Died 31 December 1847

Private Green was reported to have died on 31 December 1847 at Laredo. He was assigned Captain Mirabeau B. Lamar's company of Texas Cavalry. This company was mustered into service as U.S. Volunteers in the U.S. Army.

Barber, William James, Jr.
Born 14 April 1805—Died 21 January 1848

Private Barber was reported to have died of "Winter Fever" in camp on 21 January 1848 at Enchanted Rock. He was assigned to Company D under the command of Captain Samuel Highsmith of the First Mounted Volunteers.

Family genealogists claim that he died on 22 January 1848 and is buried in an unmarked grave along Grape Creek near Fredericksburg. Barber was born in Ireland and is said to have had eleven children.

James Barber's son, John Hutcheson Barber, also served as a Texas Ranger and died of fever on 17 October 1847.

Holmark, Ansburry M.
Born (Unknown)—Died 2 January 1848

Sergeant Holmark was reported to have died on 2 January 1848 in San Antonio. He was assigned to Captain William G. Crump's Company, Bell's Mounted Regiment of Texian Volunteers. Ranger muster rolls indicate that A.M. Holmark enlisted as a private on 28 September 1838 in the First Regiment of Mounted Gunmen under the command of Captain S. Brown and that he was discharged on 28 December 1838.

Jobe, James Lawrence
Born circa 1822—Died 6 or 25 January 1848

Private Jobe was reported to have died on either 6 or 25 January 1848 at Enchanted Rock. He was assigned to Company D under the command of Captain Samuel Highsmith of the First Mounted Volunteers.

Family genealogists differ on his date of death, with some reporting 6 and others 23 of January 1848. They also are divided on his date of birth, with entries ranging from 1816 in Kentucky to 1822 in Cherokee, Texas. He was married but had no children.

Couzens, Thomas
Born (Unknown)—Died 11 January 1848

Lieutenant Couzens was reported to have been killed by Lipan Apaches near Laredo on 11 January 1848. He was assigned to Company H under Captain James S. Gillett, Texas Mounted Volunteers. The ranger muster rolls indicate that a "Thomas Cousin/Cousins" enlisted four times as a ranger private between 1838 and 1840.

Captain Gillett's son, James B. Gillett, served as a ranger and sheriff. Later in life, he wrote an account of his exploits as a lawman and chronicled the history of the Texas Rangers.

Viveon, Thacker
Born (Unknown)—Died 30 January 1848

Private Viveon was reported to have died on 30 January 1848 at San Antonio. He was assigned to Captain William G. Crump's Company of Bell's Mounted Regiment, Texian Volunteers.

Deckert, John
Born (Unknown)—Died 11 February 1848

Private Deckert was reported to have been accidentally killed at Camp Nueces on 11 February 1848. He was assigned to Captain James S. Sutton's Company of Bell's Mounted Regiment, Texian Volunteers.

Williams, Thomas
Born (Unknown)—Died 31 March 1848

Private Williams was reported to have died on 31 March 1848 at Camp Arbuckle. He was assigned to Company H of the First Regiment, Texas Mounted Volunteers under the command of Captain James S. Gillett.

Snee, James
Born circa 1818—Died 21 April 1848

Private Snee was reported to have died on 21 April 1848 at McCulloch's Station. He was assigned to Captain H.E. McCulloch's Company of Bell's Mounted Regiment, Texian Volunteers. Snee enlisted in Travis County on 25 October 1847 at age thirty and was reported to have "died in service" after five months and twenty-six days.

Guthrie, William Andrew
Born circa 1819—Died 24 April 1848

Private Guthrie was reported to have died on 24 April 1848 at San Patricio. He was assigned to Captain James S. Sutton's Company of Bell's Mounted Regiment, Texian Volunteers. Family genealogists record that he died on 22 April at Jackson. Guthrie was born in Missouri.

Cox, M. (or Don)
Born (Unknown)—Died 16 May 1848

Corporal Cox was reported to have died on 16 May 1848 at Camp Medina. He was assigned to Captain William G. Crump's Company of Bell's Mounted Regiment, Texian Volunteers.

The ranger muster rolls indicate that a "Hugh Cox" enlisted as a private in a Minute Man company under the command of Captain J. Sowell on 14 August 1842.

Connor, William
Born (Unknown)—Died 7 June 1848

Private Connor was reported to have died on 7 June 1848 at Camp Llano. He was assigned to Captain Samuel Highsmith's Company of Bell's Mounted Regiment, Texian Volunteers.

O'Hair, Michael
Born (Unknown)—Died 9 June 1848

Private O'Hair was reported to have died on 9 June 1848 near Kaufman Station. He was assigned to Captain Middleton T. Johnson's Company of Bell's Mounted Regiment, Texian Volunteers.

Jones, John A.
Born (Unknown)—Died 23 June 1848

Private Jones was reported to have died on 23 June 1848 at Sulphur Springs. He was assigned to Captain William G. Crump's Company of Bell's Mounted Regiment, Texian Volunteers.

Pritchett, Edley
Born (Unknown)—Died 1 July 1848

Private Pritchett was reported to have died on 1 July 1848 at Hickory Creek Station. He was assigned to Captain William F. Fitzhugh's Company of Bell's Mounted Regiment, Texian Volunteers.

Turley, Elish
Born circa 1825—Died 11 July 1848

Private Turley was reported to have died on 11 July 1848 at McCulloch's Station. He was assigned to Captain H.E. McCulloch's Company of Bell's Mounted Regiment, Texian Volunteers. He enlisted on 25 October 1847 at Red River at age twenty-three and served eight months and fifteen days.

Pelham, Thomas E.
Born (Unknown)—Died 12 July 1848

Private Pelham was reported to have died on 12 July 1848 at Hickory Creek Station. He was assigned to Captain William F. Fitzhugh's Company of Bell's Mounted Regiment, Texian Volunteers.

Trimmer, Beverly
Born (Unknown)—Died 17 July 1848

Private Trimmer was reported to have died on 17 July 1848 at Bosque Station. He was assigned to Captain Shapley P. Ross's Company of Bell's Mounted Regiment, Texian Volunteers.

Wethers, James W.
Born (Unknown)—Died 27 July 1848

Private Wethers was reported to have died on 27 July 1848 at Hickory Creek Station. He was assigned to Captain William F. Fitzhugh's Company of Bell's Mounted Regiment, Texian Volunteers.

Halton, Reuben B.
Born (Unknown)—Died 5 August 1848

Private Halton was reported to have died on 5 August 1848 at Waco Village Station. He was assigned to Captain Middleton T. Johnson's Company of Bell's Mounted Regiment, Texian Volunteers.

Weatherford, John
Born (Unknown)—Died 12 August 1848

Private Weatherford was reported to have died on 12 August 1848 at Camp Arbuckle. He was assigned to Company C under Captain Hiram Warfield of Bell's Mounted Regiment, Texian Volunteers.

Harrison, W.B.
Born (Unknown)—Died 17 August 1848

Private Harrison was reported to have been killed in a personal affray on 17 August 1848 at San Patricio. He was assigned to Captain James S. Sutton's Company of Bell's Mounted Regiment, Texian Volunteers. Ranger muster rolls indicate that "Wood Harrison" enlisted on 28 November 1844 as a private in Captain H.C. Davis's Corpus Christi Rangers and was discharged on 28 January 1845. He reenlisted the same day and was discharged on 28 February 1845.

O'Neal, William
Born (Unknown)—Died 29 August 1848

Private O'Neal was reported to have died on 29 August 1848 at Corpus Christi. He was assigned to Captain James S. Sutton's Company of Bell's Mounted Regiment of Texian Volunteers.

Hack, Isaac
Born (Unknown)—Died 29 August 1848

Private Hack was reported to have died on 29 August 1847 at the Sabinal River. He was assigned to Company C under Captain Hiram Warfield of Bell's Mounted Regiment, Texian Volunteers.

Mangum, Nathaniel H.
Born (Unknown)—Died 5 September 1848
Date of incident: 4 September 1848

Private Mangum was reported to have been wounded by Lipan Apache at the Leon River on 4 September 1848. He died the next day at Camp Leon. He was assigned to Captain Hiram Warfield's Company of Bell's Mounted Regiment, Texian Volunteers.

Pendergrass, Nathaniel D.
Born (Unknown)—Died 6 September 1848

Private Pendergrass was reported to have died on 6 September 1848 at Camp Leon. He was assigned to Captain Hiram Warfield's Company of Bell's Mounted Regiment, Texian Volunteers.

Blackwell, James
Born (Unknown)—Died 11 October 1848

Private Blackwell was reported to have died on 11 October 1848 at Kaufman Station, Texas. He was assigned to Company B of Captain Joseph M. Smith's Company of Bell's Mounted Regiment, Texian Volunteers.

Shultz, Robert
Born (Unknown)—Died 20 or 25 October 1848

Private Shultz was reported to have died on 20 or 25 October 1848 at Brazos Santiago. He was assigned to Company E of the First Texas Mounted Volunteers.

Deer (Dier), John Wesley
Born (Unknown)—Died Fall 1848

Warfield's Company of the First Regiment of Texas Mounted Volunteers was stationed on the Seco River above D'Hanis in Medina County. The members' enlistment was about to expire, and they decided to make a scout into the Sabinal Canyon, about twenty-five miles away.

The thirteen men were led by First Lieutenant Knox and Second Lieutenant Kaisey. The rangers set up camp near the present-day town of Utopia in Uvalde County. Indians were spotted in the distance. The night was cold, and the rangers made a fire despite the risk. Private Deer was placed on guard duty. As his time on duty ended, he approached the fire and kicked up a blaze. A single shot rang out, and Deer was fatally wounded in the heart. He fell against Lieutenant Knox and Private Josiah Cass.

The Indians charged and the rangers returned fire. Private John Sadler was wounded by an arrow but was able to kill the Indian who had shot him. The Indians withdrew, leaving eight of their dead behind. Deer was reportedly the youngest ranger in the group. His body was lashed to a horse and brought to the camp for burial.

Knox was elected sheriff of Bexar County on 2 August 1852 and served until 4 August 1856.

Tolbert, John F.
Born (Unknown)—Died 17 December 1848

Private Tolbert was reported to have been killed in a private affray on 17 December 1848 on the Brazos River. He was assigned to Captain John H. Connor's Company of Bell's Mounted Regiment, Texian Volunteers.

DeMay, Charles
Born (Unknown)—Died 5 January 1849

Private DeMay was reported to have died at Hickory Creek Station on 5 January 1849. He was assigned to Captain William F. Fitzhugh's Company of Bell's Mounted Regiment, Texian Volunteers.

Masters, James
Born (Unknown)—Died 7 February 1849

Private Masters was reported to have died on 7 February 1849 at Hickory Creek Station. He was assigned to Captain William F. Fitzhugh's Company of Bell's Mounted Regiment, Texian Volunteers.

Johnson, Isaac W.
Born (Unknown)—Died 20 October 1849

Isaac Johnson became the captain of the Goliad Rangers, Texas Mounted Rangers, on 7 July 1849.

On 20 October 1849, Johnson was killed in a personal feud in Goliad County.

Reed, John A.
Born circa 1810—Died 1 January 1850

On 1 January 1850, Private Reed fell from a boat and drowned while crossing the San Antonio River. He served under First Lieutenant R.E. Sutton, who commanded the Goliad Rangers, Texas Mounted Rangers.

Reed was survived by his wife, Hester Ann Collom, and at least six children.

Bryant, Charles Grandison
Born circa 1803—Died 12 January 1850

By means of background, Bryant, an architect and military adventurer, had been a well-known builder in Maine and was rising through the ranks of the local militia. He and two fellow militia officers opened a school to train volunteers for the Canadian Rebellion of 1837. Bryant was arrested in July 1838 for breaking the neutrality laws but jumped bail to prepare for the invasion of Canada. The invasion failed. He was deeply in debt and fled to Galveston. He later told people that he escaped the day before his execution in Canada. He served in the Texas Militia during the Mexican invasion of Texas in 1842.

By 1849, Bryant was a major in the Texas Rangers and the mustering officer and commissary for three companies called to respond to Indian depredations on the western frontier. These ranger companies included the commands of Captains John S. "Rip" Ford, John G. Grumbles and Charles M. Blackwell. Major Bryant had official business in Austin and left Corpus Christi on horseback on 12 January 1850. After crossing Chocolate Bayou, ten miles from the Nuestra Señora del Refugio Mission, he encountered a raiding party of Lipan Apaches. In the skirmish that followed, Bryant was killed.

In recognition of his service, the Texas legislature awarded his heirs 640 acres of land in Montague County.

Bryant was survived by his wife and six children. His place of burial is unknown. Bryant's son, Andrew Jackson Bryant, was wounded during a Texas naval engagement against Mexico in 1843. Later that year, while en route to New York for medical treatment, he drowned when the ship he was traveling aboard sank.

While serving as adjutant, John S. Ford acquired the lasting nickname "Rip." When sending out official notices of deaths, he included "Rest in Peace" at the start of each message. He later shortened the salutation to "R.I.P."

Gillespie, William
Born (Unknown)—Died 29 May 1850

A ranger company of about seventy men under the command of Captain John S. "Rip" Ford located a band of Comanche warriors who had been raiding settlements. One Comanche warrior was wounded twice in the charge and was left for dead. As Private Gillespie passed the wounded warrior, the man revived. Gillespie started to shoot the warrior with his pistol, but his horse flared and the shot went wild. The warrior shot Gillespie in the side with an arrow that penetrated his left lung.

Fellow rangers moved Gillespie to a shade tree. He was unable to ride a horse, so the men constructed a litter for him. He died that night about eight hours after being wounded. Gillespie was buried with honors near Agua Dulce.

Sullivan, D.C. "Doc"
Born (Unknown)—Died 20 August 1850

Wilbarger, John Lemon
Born circa 1830—Died 20 August 1850

In May 1850, Captain John S. "Rip" Ford granted Privates Sullivan, Wilbarger and Neill leave to take care of some legal business. After their leaves expired, the men met in San Antonio Viejo to travel together. Along their journey, they discovered that about thirty Indians were tracking them. The rangers had good horses and could have escaped, but they decided to stand and fight. As the Indians advanced, one had a long-range rifle and fired at the rangers. The bullet struck Sullivan in the body. The other men lifted him from his horse and tied him to a tree. Sullivan told the other two rangers not to stay with him, saying, "I am killed...you can do me no good... make your escape." He was correct, as moments later a shot fired by one of the Indians struck him in the head and killed him.

Wilbarger ran toward their foes. Evidence discovered later indicated that he killed two or three of the Indian attackers before he fell. Neill had inadvertently fastened his weapons to the pommel of his saddle. When he mounted his horse, he ran under the rope of Sullivan's mount and was dragged off the saddle. The Indians caught up with the animal and now had Neill's weapons.

During the fight, Sullivan received at least eight wounds and eventually fainted from loss of blood. After the Indians left, Neill managed to extract several arrows from his own body. He had been stripped of his clothes and left naked in the blistering sun.

Neill walked and crawled sixty-five miles to San Patricio. A group of citizens returned to the scene of the fight to bury Sullivan and Wilbarger. Wilbarger's body was reinterred at the Texas State Cemetery in 1936. The location of Sullivan's body is unknown.

Alpheus D. Neill later became a Waco police officer. On 6 February 1877, he was killed in the line of duty.

Barton, Samuel Baker
Born (Unknown)—Died 27 January 1851

Lackey, William
Born (Unknown)—Died 3 February 1851
Date of incident—27 January 1851

On 27 January 1851, Lieutenant Edward Burleson Jr. and his ranger detachment were en route from San Antonio to Fort McIntosh in Laredo when Burleson spotted three Indians near the Nueces River. The group of warriors were riding on horseback about a mile away. The rangers had been warned that the Comanches were on the warpath, stealing horses and cattle from ranchers in the Nueces Valley.

Burleson selected nine rangers to ride toward the group of three Indians and sent the rest of his detachment on to Laredo. As they approached, the rangers noticed that the Comanches were not trying to escape. The three mounted warriors stopped and turned around, revealing thirteen more warriors on foot who were armed with lances, tomahawks and bows and arrows. The rangers mistook Burleson's orders and dismounted. They quickly found themselves engaged in a hand-to-hand fight with the warriors in an open area devoid of vegetation. Burleson was grazed by an arrow that pinned his hat to his head. He managed to kill the chief of the group, which disoriented the remaining Indians.

There were four Comanches killed and nine wounded in this fight. Private Barton was wounded three times. His injuries proved fatal, and he died on his feet, grasping the horn of his saddle. The rangers suffered five men wounded, including Private Lackey.

Rangers carried Barton to a hill and buried him. Lackey was transported to a settlement and died a week later from an arrow wound to his lungs.

One newspaper article regarding the incident reported that Barton had been living in Laredo. Nothing further is known about Lackey.

Drennan, Thomas
Born circa 1826—Died 16 July 1851

The ranger muster roll indicates that Drennan enlisted at Austin on 5 November 1850 at age twenty-five as a private in the Texas Mounted Volunteers. A second, and conflicting, entry notes that Drennan enlisted as a sergeant on 5 May 1851 at Fort Merrill. He was reported to have died of an illness on 16 July 1851. Drennan's commander was Captain Henry E. McCulloch. No other information is known at this time.

Willis, Henry J.
Born circa 1816—Died 15 September 1851

On 15 September 1851, Private Willis of Captain H.E. McCulloch's Company of Texas Mounted Volunteers was reported to have been killed by Indians near the San Saba River. He had enlisted at age thirty-five on 5 November 1850 in Austin.

McMahan, Michel
Born circa 1811—Died 4 January 1853

Forty-two-year-old McMahan enlisted on 10 September 1852 at Brownsville as a private in the Texas Mounted Volunteers under the command of Captain G.K. Lewis. The ranger muster roll indicates that he died in a hospital on 4 January 1853. No other information is known at this time.

Lane, William H.
Born circa 1830—Died 17 January 1853

Lane enlisted in Austin as a second lieutenant at age twenty-three on 18 August 1852. He served in the Texas Mounted Volunteers under the command of Captain Owen Shaw. The ranger muster roll indicates that he died on 17 January 1853. No other information is known at this time.

Wood, Robert
Born (Unknown)—Died March 1855

Ranger muster rolls record Robert Wood as having enlisted as a private in the Texas Mounted Volunteers in October 1854. He was under the command of Captain P.H. Rogers and was reported to have been discharged in December 1854. Wood apparently reenlisted.

A newspaper article dated 14 April 1855 reported that

> *Robert Wood, one of the members of Captain Rogers's company of rangers, was accidentally killed in camp. His pistol falling from his belt into the fire where he was cooking, he attempted to catch it, when the load went off and*

passed into his chest. Mr. Wood is from Washington County, and his horse was valued at $175 when he enlisted.

His place of burial is unknown.

Records indicate that Captain Rogers commanded Company F of the Texas Mounted Volunteers from 8 November 1854 to 21 March 1855. Because the company disbanded on 21 March, Wood was apparently killed before that date. The Texas State Historical Commission and Archives have no record of his service.

Lee, Andrew J.
Born circa 1835—Died 8 March 1855

Lee enlisted on 14 December 1854 in Company C of the Texas Mounted Rangers at age nineteen. He was under the command of Captain William R. Henry. Lee was discharged on 6 March 1855. The ranger muster roll noted that he died on 8 March 1855. The circumstances of his death are unknown.

Clopton, William H.
Born (Unknown)—Died 3 October 1855

Holland, H.K.
Born circa 1831—Died 3 October 1855

Jones, Willis E.
Born circa 1831—Died 3 October 1855

Smith, Augustus
Born circa 1824—Died 3 October 1855

After continuous raiding into Texas by Indians from Mexico, Governor Elisha M. Pease authorized James H. Callahan to form a company of state rangers. Captain Callahan's company of 110 pursued a war party of Lipan Apaches that had been raiding across the Rio Grande River. As the rangers approached Escondido Creek, a barrage of gunfire erupted from a distant timberline. A force of 600 to 700 Mexican troops, and Indians, had been concealed there.

Captain Callahan halted his forces and ordered them to form a skirmish line. He then ordered a charge against the Indian's position. Privates Clopton, Smith, Jones and Holland were killed in the encounter. Six rangers were seriously wounded. Private Jones's body was recovered, but the other dead rangers had to be left on the battlefield.

Two hundred additional Mexican infantry soon arrived on the scene. Captain Callahan retreated to Piedras Negras, a Mexican town across the river from Eagle Pass. The U.S. Army forces at Fort Duncan in Eagle Pass had strict orders not to cross the border. When Callahan heard that an additional one thousand Mexican troops were said to be en route, he retreated across the border into Texas.

Clopton enlisted as a private on 20 July 1855 at Curry Creek under the command of Captain James Callahan, Texas Mounted Rangers. He lived in Comal County before his enlistment. His place of burial is unknown.

Holland enlisted as a private at age twenty-four on 15 September 1855 at Leona River under the command of Captain Nat Benton, Texas Mounted Rangers. His place of burial is unknown.

Jones enlisted as a private at age twenty-four on 15 September 1855 at San Antonio under the command of Captain William R. Henry of Company C of the Texas Mounted Volunteers. He was the son of Uvalde County judge William E. Jones. His younger brother, Frank Jones, later became a celebrated ranger captain and was killed in the line of duty at El Paso on 30 June 1893.

Smith enlisted as a private in the Texas Militia Volunteers in San Antonio on 1 October 1854 at age twenty-eight. He served until 17 February 1853. Smith reenlisted in the Texas Mounted Rangers in Bexar County on 20 July 1855 at age thirty-one and served two months and twenty-nine days before his death. His place of burial is unknown.

Earbee, William "Bill"
Born circa 1834—Died 9 May 1858

On 5 February 1858, Earbee enlisted as a private in a Company of Rangers in Austin under the command of Captain John S. Ford. Ford's command had been created to pursue hostile Indians in North Texas. On 5 May 1858, Earbee was accidentally killed when his gun discharged while he was tying it to his saddle.

Earbee was twenty-four years of age and had been residing in Bastrop. He had served three months. His place of burial is unknown.

Nickel, Robert
Born circa 1837—Died 12 May 1858

Robert Nickel enlisted in Bosque County as a private on 10 January 1858 at age twenty-one. He was under the command of Captain John S. Ford. John R. Nickel also enlisted as a private the same day and was most likely his brother.

An engagement that historians later titled "the Battle of Antelope Hills" (also known as the Canadian River Campaign) involved Captain Ford and a force of more than one hundred rangers. Indian Agent and Captain Shapley P. Ross and his contingent of more than one hundred friendly Indians from the Brazos Reservation accompanied Ford's men.

At 7:00 a.m. on 12 May 1858, Captain Ross and the Indian allies swept into a small Comanche campsite, where they killed or captured nearly everyone in the encampment. Two Comanches escaped on horseback. Their retreat led the ranger force into the main Comanche camp at Little Robe Creek near the Canadian River. The rangers now faced about six hundred Comanches. They strategically moved their Indian allies to the right and front of the main force in an attempt to convince the Comanches that they were facing other Indians who lacked modern weapons. Comanche war chief Iron Jacket approached and was killed in the initial barrage.

The fighting continued until about 1:00 p.m., when there was a lull in the activity. Privates Oliver Searcy and Nickel were pursuing a group of retreating warriors when they came upon a large contingent of Comanches who were coming from another encampment to reinforce the embattled group. Searcy told Nickel not to gallop but rather to halt occasionally and fire at the Comanche party in an effort to hold the Indians in check. Nickel's horse began to run, and he was unable to rein it in. Charging hostile warriors lanced him to death. Searcy was rescued by friendly Indians. Lieutenant Nelson tried to recover Nickel's body but was turned back by a large force of hostile Comanches.

Captain Ford later reported that Private Nickel and an unnamed Waco Indian were killed during the battle and that Private George W. Paschal Jr. was wounded. He also reported that seventy-six Comanches killed and many wounded. The Waco Indian and Nickel's place of burial are unknown.

Chief Iron Jacket was born circa the late 1780s. Iron Jacket (Po-hebitsquash, Pro-he-bits-quash-a or Po-bish-e-quasho in Comanche) was a Comanche chieftain and medicine man whom the Comanches believed had the power to blow bullets aside with his breath. His name probably resulted from his habit of wearing a Spanish coat of mail into battle, which protected him from most light weapons fire.

Wright, Marshall
Born circa 1836—Died December 1858

Wright enlisted as a private at age twenty-two at Camp Runnels on 15 July 1858. Ranger muster rolls have two entries for the July enlistment. One indicates that Wright was discharged on 14 November 1858. The other entry records that he was not discharged until 4 April 1859. There is no notation of his death on either record. His commanding officer was Captain William N.P. Marlin of the Texas Mounted Rangers.

A newspaper report dated 29 December 1858 claimed that Wright and J.W.D. Hill were involved in an affray at Fort Belknap in Young County during which Wright was killed and Hill wounded in the thigh. The article does not mention Wright as being a ranger. Captain Marlin's company was organized from 24 February to 15 November 1858 and then from 24 February to 4 April 1859. If the second enlistment is correct, then Wright may have survived the shooting.

Thompson, Jonathan
Born (Unknown)—Died 27 February 1859

Private Thompson was killed by accidental gunfire. He had been attached to the Texas Mounted Volunteers under the command of Captain James Bourland. Thompson enlisted in Gainesville.

Gould, Jessie
Born (Unknown)—Died 24 March 1859

Private Gould was attached to the Texas Mounted Volunteers. He had enlisted at Gainesville on 2 July 1859. Gould was under the command of Captain James Bourland. The ranger muster roll reports that he died on 24 March 1859.

Estes, Smith
Born (Unknown)—Died 15 July 1859

Private Estes died from an unidentified disease at Camp Estes on 15 July 1859. He was under the command of Captain John Henry Brown of the Texas Mounted Rangers, Texas State Troops.

Jackson, Samuel A.
Born circa 1826—Died 13 November 1859

Jackson enlisted on 14 December 1854 at age twenty-eight at San Antonio as a first lieutenant under the command of Captain William R. Henry. He was placed under arrest on 23 January 1855 for unstated charges and was discharged on 14 March 1855. He reenlisted as a second lieutenant on 10 October 1857 in the Texas Mounted Volunteers under the command of Captain G.H. Nelson and was discharged on 28 December 1857 with no service recorded. His third enlistment occurred on 18 October 1859 when he joined as a first lieutenant under the command of Captain William G. Tobin and served until his death.

On 13 November 1859, Jackson was in Matamoras, Mexico, located across the border from Brownsville, when he was allegedly intoxicated and was thrown from a carriage and killed.

Fox, John
Born (Unknown)—Died 16 November 1859

Grier, Thomas
Born (Unknown)—Died 16 November 1859

McKay, William
Born (Unknown)—Died 16 November 1859

Milett, Nicholas R.
Born (Unknown)—Died 16 November 1859

On 28 September, Juan N. Cortina and sixty to one hundred men rode into Brownsville intent on seeking revenge for numerous grievances. The bandits killed a local merchant and a constable named George Morris. Cortina's men attempted to break into the jail and release prisoners held there. Cameron County jailer Robert L. Johnson refused to release the prisoners and instead fired at the group, killing one of the raiders. Johnson and a citizen were killed in the exchange of gunfire that followed. Cortina later withdrew to Mexico.

This raid marked the beginning of what would later be called the "Cortina War." The fighting, which lasted less than three months, would eventually lead to the deaths of six rangers.

Texas governor Runnels authorized Captain William G. Tobin to raise a company of one hundred rangers from San Antonio to quell the lawlessness in Brownsville. On 16 November, a detachment of thirty rangers under the command of Lieutenant John Littleton spotted a band of Cortina's men about a mile from Palo Alto. He pursued them into the chaparral. The rangers dismounted, tied their horses to some scrubby mesquite and charged into the dense brush.

In the vicious fight, which lasted only thirty minutes, Privates Grier, McKay and Milett were killed. Four other rangers were badly wounded, including Lieutenant Littleton. Private Fox surrendered to Cortina's men and was executed. The day after the Palo Alto fight, the rangers rode to the scene, where they discovered the stripped and mutilated bodies of their dead comrades. The fallen men were given a proper burial on the battlefield.

Ranger muster rolls were found for Captain Tobin's enlistment at San Antonio; for McKay, who joined on 18 October; and for Grier, who enlisted on 25 October 1859.

Lieutenant (later Captain) John Littleton was sheriff of Karnes County from 1857 to 1860 and in 1866. He was murdered during the Sutton-Taylor Feud on 3 December 1868. Nueces County sheriff Mat Nolan— who discovered the bodies of rangers Fox, Grier, McKay and Milett—was murdered on 22 December 1864.

Herman, David
Born (Unknown)—Died 14 December 1859

In a continuation of the Cortina War, Texas Rangers under the command of Major John S. Ford and Captain Tobin joined regular U.S. Army troops under Major Samuel P. Heintzelman in pursuing Cortina's men along the Rio Grande River. Both the U.S. Army and the Cortina bandits had artillery pieces. On 14 December 1859, Private Herman of Tobin's

Company of Texas Mounted Volunteers was mortally wounded. On 27 December, the final battle was fought at Rio Grande City, where Cortina's forces were defeated.

Herman is buried on the Jesus Leon Ranch. Army major Heintzelman furnished the rangers with his fife and drum players for the burial ceremony of the fallen ranger. All that is known about Herman is that he had enlisted at San Antonio.

Woodruff, Fountain B.
Born circa 1837—Died 4 February 1860

The final engagement in the Cortina War occurred on 4 February 1860. Cortina and his men appeared at La Bolsa, a large bend on the Rio Grande about thirty-five miles above Brownsville where Cortina attempted to capture the steamboat *Ranchero*. During the fight, Private Woodruff was mortally wounded. He handed his revolver to a fellow ranger and said, "Take it...I shall never be able to use it again."

Woodruff was born in Lowdes, Alabama. While all accounts list his given name as Fountain, that may have been his middle name. His given name has also been recorded as Benjamin, Berrymore, Berryman and Barrymon.

Juan Nepomuceno Cortina was a Mexican folk hero, born on 16 May 1824, in Camargo, Tamaulipas. His aristocratic mother was one of the heirs of a large land grant in the lower Rio Grande Valley, including the area that surrounded Brownsville. The family moved to that land when Cortina was still young.

In the Mexican-American War of 1846–48, Cortina served as a part of an irregular cavalry unit during the battles of Resaca de la Palma and Palo Alto. After the war, he returned to the north bank of the river, where he was indicted at least twice by a Cameron County grand jury for stealing cattle. His political influence among Mexicans prevented him from being arrested.

In time, Cortina came to hate a clique of judges and Brownsville attorneys that he accused of expropriating land from Mexican Texans unfamiliar with the American judicial system. He became the leader of many of the poorer Mexicans who lived along the banks of the river.

The incident that ignited the first Cortina War occurred on 13 July 1859, when Cortina saw Brownsville city marshal Robert Shears brutally arrest a Mexican-American who had once been employed by Cortina. Cortina shot the marshal in the impending confrontation and rode out of town with the prisoner. Early on the morning of 28 September 1859, he rode into Brownsville again, this time at the head of some forty to eighty men, and seized control of the town. Five men, including the city jailer, were shot during the raid.

In May 1861, Cortina started the second Cortina War by invading Zapata County. He was defeated by Confederate forces. On 5 May 1862, during the French occupation of Mexico, Cortina helped to defend San Lorenzo at Puebla.

After being promoted to general of the Mexican army of the north, Cortina appointed himself governor in 1866 but immediately relinquished the office to General Tapia. He fought in numerous battles and witnessed the execution of Emperor Maximilian.

Cortina returned to the border in 1870, and forty-one residents of the Rio Grande Valley, including a former mayor of Brownsville, signed a petition asking that he be pardoned for his crimes because of his service to the Union during the Civil War. The petition failed in the Texas legislature on its second reading in 1871. In subsequent years, stockmen in the Nueces Strip accused Cortina of leading a large ring of cattle rustlers. He died in Atzcapozalco on 30 October 1894.

Martinez, Tiophilo
Born circa 1835—Died 10 September 1860

Martinez was a member of Captain W.C. Dalrymple's First Company of Texas Mounted Volunteers stationed at Liberty Hill. On 10 September 1860, Martinez was killed by a man named Joe Bannion. Ranger muster roll records his discharge as 13 October 1860. Martinez was twenty-five years of age when he enlisted.

McLeod, John D.
Born circa 1834—Died 29 October 1860

Muster roll and payroll records indicate that twenty-six-year-old McLeod enlisted as a private on 3 October 1860 at Waco for a twelve-month term. He served under Captain L.S. "Sul" Ross's Mounted Rangers. He was stationed at Fort Belknap. His record is marked "killed" with no explanation.

The Texas State Historical Commission and Archives have no records of McLeod's service. This is not an uncommon phenomenon, as records were often lost, poorly preserved or incorrectly transcribed and interpreted.

Lane, James Martin, Jr.
Born 24 February 1838—Died December 1860
Date of incident: Nine days earlier

On 5 December 1860, the Palo Pinto County Volunteers was organized by Captain J.J. "Jack" Cureton and headquartered at Fort Belknap. On 18 December, an expedition of seventy men under Captain Cureton, forty men under Captain L.S. Ross and twenty U.S. Army soldiers battled Comanche Indians at the Pease River. Chief Pete Nocona was killed, and his Anglo wife, Cynthia Ann Parker, was captured. Ms. Parker had been taken captive on 16 May 1836.

The exact date of the Fight at Yellow Wolf Creek, located near present-day Nolan County, is unknown. It apparently occurred near the end of December 1860. Captain Cureton and thirty to forty men were on scout when they confronted a band of Comanche Indians. The rangers charged and killed several of the hostiles. Private Lane was shot with an arrow that penetrated his intestines. He was transported back to Old Fort Chadbourne, where he died nine days later.

Lane is buried at Fort Chadbourne Cemetery in Coke County. He was single. His father was a ranger in 1841 from Robertson County.

Lane's brother, Alf, was a ranger in Company G of the Frontier Regiment. Alf Lane was the brother-in-law of Charles Goodnight. On 15 July 1864, Alf Lane was moving cattle when he was killed by Comanche Indians near Fort Belknap.

CIVIL WAR, 1861–1865

Texas seceded from the Union on 1 February 1861. During the time that Texas was involved in the Civil War—beginning on 2 March 1861 and ending on 2 June 1865 when Confederate general Edmund Kirby Smith surrendered the Army of the Trans-Mississippi—more than seventy thousand Texans served the Confederacy. Many served as soldiers and sailors, but some continued to serve the state as Texas Rangers.

The entries listed in this section reflect Texas Rangers who died while involved in battles with various Indian tribes, in feuds or during encounters with outlaws. An effort has been made to separate and exclude those incidents that relate specifically to military engagements associated with the Civil War.

Wright, James E.
Born circa 1825—Died 27 February 1861

Private Wright was reported to have been killed while on a scout on 27 February 1861. He was a member of the Northern District, under the command of Colonel Henry E. McCulloch. The company was organized on 5 February and disbanded on 19 March 1861.

Davidson, Sidney Green
Born circa 1832—Died 23 June 1861

McCarthy, Andrew J.
Born (Unknown)—Died 23 June 1861

Ranger payroll reports indicate that Davidson enlisted in a ranger company as a lieutenant on 20 March 1860. He was reportedly discharged on 14 April 1860. Davidson served in Company K of the First Texas Cavalry, which was organized in Bell County in 1861.

Reports claim that Davidson was a captain in Company F of the First Regiment, Texas Mounted Rifles, under Colonel Henry E. McCulloch when he was killed by Comanche Indians at the headwaters of the Colorado River in north Texas on 23 June 1861. Private McCarthy of Company D, under the command of Captain James B. "Buck" Barry, was also reported to have been killed.

Texas State Historical Commission and Archives have no record on Davidson's service. McCarthy had previously enlisted at age twenty-one at San Marcos on 20 January 1860 in a ranger company under the command of Captain Ed Burleson and was discharged on 7 September 1860.

Sidney Davidson was survived by his wife, Mary Elizabeth Kuykendall.

McKee, James
Born (Unknown)—Died 27 June 1861
Date of incident: 26 June 1861

Kelly, William
Born (Unknown)—Died 26 June 1861

Captain James B. "Buck" Barry commanded Company D of the First Regiment of Texas Volunteers, First Regiment of Texas Mounted Rifles.

On 26 June 1861, ten rangers led by Corporal Thomas J. Erkenbreck were on the road between Camps Cooper and Jackson when they were attacked by about forty Indians armed with rifles. After a five-hour battle on the prairie, the rangers suffered two casualties. Privates McKee and Kelly were killed. Six other rangers were wounded.

One conflicting report claimed that only one unnamed soldier was killed.

Freeman, Erasmus G.
Born (Unknown)—Died 5 July 1861

Freeman was a private in Company K of the First Regiment of the Texas Mounted Rifles under the command of Captain Travis H. Ashby. He was murdered on 5 July 1861 by a deserter named Charles A. Williams at Holiday's Creek.

Connelly, Harrison R. "Tips"
Born (Unknown)—Died 29 July 1861

Lynn, Jerome C. "Bud"
Born (Unknown)—Died 29 July 1861

Weatherby, Thomas C.
Born (Unknown)—Died 29 July 1861

Company C of the First Mounted Rifles, which was under the command of Captain James B. "Buck" Barry, was engaged in a battle with Indians that left several men wounded. Two days later, on 29 July 1861, Captain Barry sent twelve rangers back to get the pack mules that had stampeded during the fight. The men were attacked by about one hundred Indians near the Little Wichita River. Privates Connelly, Lynn and Weatherby were killed. The main company of about thirty rangers charged and wounded the chief. The Indians withdrew, suffering about seven casualties.

McFarland, James D.
Born (Unknown)—Died 5 August 1861

Ranger records indicate that Lieutenant McFarland died on 5 August 1861. He was assigned to Company H of the First Texas Mounted Rifles under the command of Captain James M. Homsley at Camp Jackson. The company was organized on 6 May 1861.

Mayes, James N.
Born (Unknown)—Died 23 September 1861

Private Mayes was reported to have died of typhoid fever at Camp Cooper on 23 September 1861. He was assigned to Company D of the First Texas Mounted Rifles under the command of Captain James B. "Buck" Barry.

McCarver, W.P.
Born (Unknown)—Died 27 September 1861

Private McCarver of Company G of the First Texas Mounted Rifles under the command of Captain Thomas C. Frost was reported to have died of bilious fever at Camp Colorado on 27 September 1861.

Owen, Solomon
Born (Unknown)—Died 23 October 1861

Private Owen of Company C of the First Texas Mounted Rifles under the command of Captain James B. "Buck" Barry was reported to have died on 23 October 1861 at Camp Cooper.

Rhodes, Andrew J.
Born (Unknown)—Died 13 February 1863

On 13 February 1863, Private Rhodes drowned when his horse fell while crossing a river. He was assigned to Forty-sixth Texas Frontier Cavalry Regiment under the command of Colonel James E. McCord.

Roberts, Isaac Van
Born circa 1840—Died October 1863

In October 1863, Company E, a Border Battalion of the Frontier Regiment under the command of Captain F.M. Totty was stationed at Camp Brushy near the present-day town of Forestburg in Montague County. A Comanche war party of about twenty-five braves was raiding in Montague County and was headed back to the Indian Territory with kidnapped children, stolen cattle and horses. Lieutenant Roberts and his eight rangers took an Indian trail and came upon the Comanches. Roberts dismounted, but his men did not. After they exhausted their ammunition supply, the rangers retreated on horseback. Roberts could not escape. He was hit by several arrows, killed and scalped.

Roberts's family lived near Roberts' Spring. Indians went to the spring to get water and came upon two of Roberts's younger brothers. The father came out and killed one Indian. Captain Totty brought Roberts's body to his home, where he was allegedly buried at McGee Cemetery. Roberts was a second lieutenant from March 1862 until June 1863 and served under Captain John Salmon, Company B, Erath County, Frontier Regiment. The Texas State Archives and the Ranger Hall of Fame and Museum do not list Roberts as a lieutenant.

Vatne, Johan Johansen
Born (Unknown)—Died 17 December 1863

Private Vatne was reported to have been killed while on a scouting patrol. He was assigned to the Forty-sixth Texas Frontier Cavalry Regiment.

Maxwell, R.H.
Born (Unknown)—Died 15 March 1864

Private Maxwell died on 15 March 1864 in Jack County. He was assigned to Captain E.M. Orrick's Company B of the First Frontier District. The circumstances surrounding his death are not known at this time.

Maupin, Perry
Born (Unknown)—Died 25 March 1864

Sageser, J.A.
Born (Unknown)—Died 25 March 1864

On 25 March 1864, Privates Maupin and Sageser died in Cooke County. They were both members of Captain James O. Hill's Company of the First Frontier District. No details of their deaths are known at this time.

Gonsolas, J.J.
Born circa 1843—Died 25 April 1864

On 25 April 1864, Private Gonsolas was murdered by Border Regiment troops in either Cooke or Fannin County. Gonsolas served under First Lieutenant Thomas Smith's Company from Jack County, First Frontier District. The ranger muster roll indicate that Gonsolas was "[t]aken by Col. Bourland's men & killed April 25th." Colonel James Bourland commanded Bourland's Texas Cavalry Regiment, also known as "Border Battalion" and "Border Regiment."

Still, Washington
Born—(Unknown)—Died 28 April 1864

Private Still was hanged on 28 April 1864 in Wise County. He was a member of Captain J.M. Hanks's Company B of the First Frontier District.

Strong, James R.
Born circa 1832—Died 6 May 1864

Private Strong was assigned to Captain J.J. "Jack" Cureton's Company A of the First Frontier District. He died on 6 May 1864 in Stephens County.

Strong, who was originally from South Carolina, had come to Texas from Monroe, Indiana. It is believed that he served in the Sixteenth Regiment, Indiana Infantry, during the Civil War.

Strong was survived by his wife, Caroline, and five children.

Young, Harve F.
Born (Unknown)—Died 14 July 1864

On 14 July 1864, Private Young of Company D of the Border Regiment died in Gainesville in Cooke County. No other information is known at this time.

Gilbert, Singleton
Born (Unknown)—Died 9 August 1864

Gilbert, Tom
Born (Unknown)—Died 9 August 1864

Keith, Burton
Born (Unknown)—Died 9 August 1864

During the Civil War, communities in Texas frequently found themselves under attack from raiding Indian tribes. Texas State Troops were assigned for their protection. Major George B. Erath's Second Frontier District covered Eastland, Callahan and Shackelford Counties.

On 8 August 1864, Lieutenant Gilbert of Company Number One sent out a patrol of eight men led by Corporal James L. Head. The following day, they found Indian tracks and followed them to near Ellison Springs. Lieutenant Gilbert arrived with twelve to sixteen troopers, who now faced thirty to thirty-five hostile Indians. He ordered a frontal assault.

During the fighting, Gilbert was mortally wounded. Accounts of this battle vary, with one source claiming that an unnamed ranger was killed. Another report alleged that Private Burton Keith was killed and that one civilian volunteer named Tom Gilbert was also killed. Three rangers were wounded. The Indians suffered no casualties and escaped.

The Texans continued to pursue the Indians and recovered eighteen of the fifty horses they had stolen at Stephenville. The rangers later engaged the band of warriors, killing two Indians and recovering seventy-three horses.

No personal information is known about Gilbert or Keith.

Judd, J.L.
Born (Unknown)—Died 11 September 1864

Sergeant Judd was accidentally shot by a sentry in Brownsville. He had been assigned to Captain D.M. Wilson's Company under the command of Colonel John Ford. The Texas State Archives does not have a record of his service or Captain Wilson. This is not an uncommon phenomenon, as records were often lost, poorly preserved or incorrectly transcribed and interpreted. His place of burial is unknown.

Peveler, William R.
Born 9 September 1834—Died 26 September 1864
Date of incident: 13 September 1864

In 1860, the five Peveler brothers served as rangers in a Minute Men company for Young County.

The primary purpose of the Minute Men force was to control the Indian depredations that were taking place in the region. Three of the Peveler brothers enlisted in the army of the Confederate States of America. James M. Peveler served in Morgan's Cavalry Division. William R. Peveler served as a captain in the same unit. Francis M. Peveler completed his service with Company F, Harris's Texas Cavalry. A fourth brother is reported to have also served. All of the brothers survived the war, with the exception of William Peveler.

Although reported as a captain as late as 1864, it appears that he was a second lieutenant when he and four other men were surrounded by a band of about fifty Indians on 13 September 1864 while on a mission to purchase horses. The attack took place about ten miles north of Graham near Salt Creek Prairie. Peveler was mortally wounded and died on 26 September.

Peveler was reportedly assigned to Company G of the Frontier Regiment, Forty-sixth Texas Cavalry Regiment, when he was killed. He is buried at Peveler Cemetery in Young County.

Blue, Erastus
Born (Unknown)—Died 13 October 1864

Jones, J. "Sim"
Born (Unknown)—Died 13 October 1864

Neatherey, Robert
Born (Unknown)—Died 13 October 1864

Snodgrass, Henry I.
Born (Unknown)—Died 13 October 1864

Walker, J.G.
Born (Unknown)—Died 13 October 1864

A combined Comanche and Kiowa force of seven hundred warriors entered Texas and were led by Little Buffalo. On 13 October 1864, the war party was divided into smaller groups and attacked settlers near Fort Belknap in Young County. Twenty rangers from Company D of the Texas Border Cavalry Regiment under Lieutenant N. Carson Sr. clashed with three hundred Indians. Five rangers were killed (Sergeant Jones and Privates Blue, Neatherey, Snodgrass and Walker). The Indians withdrew with seven captives and killed seven settlers.

Neil, Ambrose H.
Born (Unknown)—Died 28 November 1864

On 28 November 1864, Lieutenant Neil of the Forty-sixth Texas Frontier Cavalry Regiment died as a result of an infection from an unidentified wound he had received. No other information is available at this time.

Barnes, R.S. "Sam"
Born (Unknown)—Died 8 January 1865

Bible, Noah A.
Born (Unknown)—Died 8 January 1865

Burke, John
Born (Unknown)—Died 8 January 1865

Cox, M.
Born (Unknown)—Died 8 January 1865

Culver, William H.
Born (Unknown)—Died 8 January 1865

Dyers (Byers), J.B. "Jake" (or "Joe")
Born (Unknown)—Died 8 January 1865

Epperson, G.M.
Born (Unknown)—Died 8 January 1865

Etts, William
Born (Unknown)—Died 8 January 1865

Everett, Albert E.
Born (Unknown)—Died 8 January 1865

Gibbs, Noah
Born (Unknown)—Died 8 January 1865

Giddens, James R.
Born (Unknown)—Died 8 January 1865

Gipson, Francis
Born (Unknown)—Died 8 January 1865

Gillintine, John O.
Born (Unknown)—Died 8 January 1865

Gillintine, Nick W. (N.M.)
Born (Unknown)—Died 8 January 1865

Gillintine, William M.
Born (Unknown)—Died 8 January 1865

Harris, George
Born (Unknown)—Died 8 January 1865

Latham, B.D.
Born (Unknown)—Died 8 January 1865

Love (Land), W.M.
Born (Unknown)—Died 8 January 1865

Mabray (Mabry), James S.
Born (Unknown)—Died 8 January 1865

Maroney, P. Nelson
Born (Unknown)—Died 8 January 1865

Parker, Tom
Born (Unknown)—Died 8 January 1865

Persons, William
Born (Unknown)—Died 8 January 1865

Steene (Stein/Steele), John D.
Born (Unknown)—Died 8 January 1865

Stuart, J. (Isaac Anderson "Jack")
Born (Unknown)—Died 8 January 1865

Wray, S.M. (S.W.)
Born (Unknown)—Died 8 January 1865

Wylie, W.L.
Born (Unknown)—Died 8 January 1865

The "Dove Creek Fight" was a controversial showdown between a combined force of Confederate soldiers and Texas Rangers under Captain George B. Erath's Second District of the Texas Frontier Organization and a large village of Kickapoo men, women and children trying to immigrate to Mexico during the final days of the Civil War.

Texas scouts mistook the friendly Indians for a hostile war party of Comanches or Kiowas. The Kickapoos were camped at Dove Creek, which is near the Middle Concho River about twenty miles from present-day San Angelo.

A state militia force of about 325 men from Bosque, Comanche, Coryell, Erath and Johnson Counties gathered under Captain S.S. Totten. About 160 Texas Confederate troops of the Frontier Battalion were dispatched under Captain Henry Fossett.

Countless mistakes were made by the feuding Confederate army officers and state militia commanders. Battle plans were hasty, reconnaissance was poor and no effort was made to determine if the Indians were a friendly tribe or not.

It was estimated that about four hundred to six hundred warriors were concealed in a heavy thicket. In the opening moments of the battle, the Indians killed numerous attackers, including Captain Gillintine and sixteen enlisted men. When the battle ended at dusk, more militiamen and soldiers were found to have been killed and wounded. Texans reported between twenty and one hundred Kickapoo casualties, but after the Indians reached the safety of Mexico and assessed their losses, they claimed that they had lost only fourteen.

The consequences of this ill-advised, unwarranted and poorly planned attack on friendly Kickapoo Indians who were simply trying to escape the violence of the Civil War would haunt Texans along the Mexican border for years. In retaliation, the once friendly Kickapoos now made a habit of mounting frequent raids into Texas.

Many of the numerous accounts of this battle are conflicting and vague. Due in large part to poor recordkeeping and the confusing aggregation of Texan forces, exactly who was killed during this battle remains something of a mystery to this day. The correct spelling of the surnames of those known to have been casualties is equally unclear. Some men were seriously wounded and died some time later. The following roster of fatalities includes rangers, civilian volunteers and Confederate soldiers. A variety of sources have been used to compile this account containing the names of participants that most sources have reported as casualties:

- Captain R.S. "Sam" Barnes and Privates Noah Bible, Albert E. Everett, John D. Steene and S.M. Wray of Barnes's Company of the Second Frontier Regiment.
- Sergeant J. Stuart of Cathey's Company.
- Captain William H. Culver of Culver's Company.

- Privates M. Cox and Tom Parker of Cunningham's Company.
- Captain Nick W. Gillintine (mortally wounded) and Privates John Burke, John O. Gillintine and William M. Gillintine (mortally wounded and died 1867–68) of Gillintine's Company.
- Lieutenant B.D. Latham, Sergeant W.M. Love and Privates Francis Gipson, George Harris and P. Nelson Maroney.
- Private James S. Mabray of the Second Frontier District was mortally wounded.
- Corporal G.M. Epperson and Private W.L. Wylie of Company A of Fossett's Battalion were reported to have been killed.
- The Frontier Regiment of the Confederate army reported that Lieutenant James R. Giddens of Company D was killed and that Private J.B. "Jake" Dyer of Company G was mortally wounded. Three other names have appeared on some reports—Civilian volunteers William Etts and Noah Gibbs and William Persons of Coryell County.

RECONSTRUCTION, 1865–1873

There are practically as many opinions regarding the post–Civil War Reconstruction era in Texas as there are authors. Earlier accounts tend to emphasize the unreasonable influence and control imposed on the state by Federal troops and the impact of carpetbaggers brought in to take over much of the state and local governance. Chaos often resulted, and neighbors who had lived together peacefully were pitted against one another in dozens of local feuds and racially motived hostilities. A case can be made that racial tensions in Texas were far greater as a result of Reconstruction than they were before it. Nonetheless, contemporary authors tend to portray the period in more of a "it could have been much worse" manner, placing emphasis on only the unfortunate racial aspects of the discontent and downplaying the turmoil that resulted from installing biased and inexperienced administrators to govern local affairs. In any case, a decade of confusion, violence and turmoil resulted that had long-lasting and wide-ranging implications.

Willis, Matthew Shook
Born 8 June 1845—Died 4 April 1865

On 4 April 1865, Private Willis of Company A of Fossett's Battalion died when he fell from his horse at Camp Colorado.

Dunn, N.F.
Born (Unknown)—Died 20 November 1866

Ranger muster roll reports show that Dunn enlisted as a private in the First Company of the Minute Men in Parker County under the command of Captain L.L. Tackitt on 20 October 1865. He was discharged on 22 June 1866. Dunn's file notes that he was "killed 20 November 1865." The Texas State Archives does not have a record of his service. This is not an uncommon phenomenon, as records were often lost, poorly preserved or incorrectly transcribed and interpreted.

His place of burial is unknown.

Clark, Alvin A.
Born circa 1846—Died 29 June 1866

Clark joined the Second Parker County Minute Men Company on 26 April 1866 at Weatherford for an enlistment period of three months and nine days.

Captain Hartford Howard and his ranger company were pursuing Indians who had killed several citizens and stolen livestock in the county. Private Clark and seven citizens were on patrol when they were attacked by hostile Indians near Springtown. Clark was killed during the engagement, and two citizens were wounded. The newspaper reported that none of the Indians was injured. The Indians traveled down the Brazos Valley as far as Comanche Peak in Johnson County, stealing horses, and then they started back north.

Clark's place of burial is unknown. He was twenty years old when he enlisted.

Singleton, J.S.
Born circa 1849—Died 3 November 1870

Singleton enlisted in Company B of the Frontier Forces on 8 September 1870 under the command of Captain A.H. Cox. On 3 November 1870, Privates Singleton and Frank Holmes got into an argument. Holmes shot Singleton in the back four times, killing him instantly.

There is no record of the disposition of any charges against Holmes. Singleton's place of burial is unknown.

Texas Rangers

Biediger, Lorenzo
Born circa 1846—Died 6 December 1870

Richarz, Walter
Born circa 1846—Died 6 December 1870

Riff, Joseph R.
Born circa 1847—Died 6 December 1870

In the summer of 1870, the State of Texas created the Frontier Forces in an effort to protect the remote western counties from raiding Indian tribes. German-born Captain Henrich Joseph Richarz organized Company E of the Frontier Forces at San Antonio on 9 September 1870. The unit was composed of volunteers who were primarily from Medina County.

Captain Richarz, along with fourteen rangers and three volunteers, left Fort Inge in Uvalde County to scout for Indians who had been conducting raids about one hundred miles from the post. Before making camp, a rider from Fort Duncan arrived and advised the rangers that a force of five hundred Indians were moving in their direction. The rider also told the captain that a patrol led by Dr. J.E. Woodbridge had encountered Indians about twelve miles from the Rio Grande River.

On 6 December 1870, Dr. Woodbridge, who had suspended his practice to serve as a ranger officer, was leading a patrol of fourteen men when he met an estimated seventy Comanches. The Comanches formed two lines on a slight rise and soon managed to flank the rangers. The rangers put up a stubborn resistance, using their Winchester repeating rifles to wound several attackers. Woodbridge himself was struck in the head and unhorsed in a hand-to-hand encounter. Several rangers came to his rescue. During the exchange, Private Biediger was killed. Three rangers who were some distance from the fight heard the sounds of heavy firing and returned, striking the flank of the surprised Comanches and killing a chief. The Comanches withdrew back into Mexico.

On that same day, another band of Indians killed Privates Walter Richarz (son of Captain Richarz) and Joseph Riff at a creek about sixteen miles from Fort Inge. Evidence at the scene indicated that the two rangers put up a fierce fight. Lieutenant Xavier Wanz departed from Fort Inge with the reserve force to track the Indians who had killed Richarz and Riff, but the raiders had already escaped into Mexico. On 8 December, Captain Richarz received word of the death of his son Walter and Private Riff.

All three rangers were from Medina County and had enlisted on 9 September 1870. They served for two months and twenty-seven days before their deaths. Richarz was twenty-four and single. He is buried at Rudinger/Richarz Cemetery at D'Hanis in Medina County. Biediger was twenty-four and single. He is buried at St. Louis Cemetery at Castroville in Medina County. Riff was twenty-three and married. He is also buried at St. Louis Cemetery.

Swift, Albert M.
Born circa 1835—Died 27 December 1870
Date of incident: 14 December 1870

Swift enlisted on 14 December 1854 at age nineteen. He joined Company C of the Mounted Volunteers and served for three months until he was discharged on 14 March 1855. At about age thirty-five, Swift reenlisted on 1 October 1870 for one year in Captain H.R. Biberstein's Company L. He was discharged on 31 October 1870 by Governor E.J. Davis. On 5 November 1870, he once again enlisted in Company F of the Frontier Forces of the Texas Rangers and served until his death less than two months later.

The Texas Ranger Hall of Fame and Museum reports that Swift was killed by Indians on 27 December 1870. This information is incorrect. The monthly return of Company F for December 1870 states that "A.M. Swift left sick in hospital at Fort Griffin, Texas Dec. 14, 1870." The monthly return also mentions the severe weather, snowstorms, lack of shelter and medical attention that the rangers had to endure. There is correspondence relating to how several of their horses and mules froze to death as a result of the brutal weather conditions. The muster roll for Company F for the period of 5 November 1870 to 15 June 1871 states that "A.M. Swift died at Fort Griffin, Tex. Dec. 27, 1870." The Texas State Archives records that Swift must have been a casualty of the weather conditions or that he died from some illness possibly contracted in connection with the extreme weather.

Very little personal information is known about Private Swift apart from the fact that he is reported to have been born in either Germany or Missouri between 1835 and 1837.

Goodlet, Patrick
Born circa 1830—Died 11 February 1871

Private Goodlet of Company B of the Frontier Forces died of typhoid pneumonia in Erath County on 11 February 1871. Records indicate that he was twenty-seven years old when he enlisted at Austin on 8 September 1870. Goodlet was a single man and had come to Texas from South Carolina in 1870. His place of burial is unknown.

Green, John
Born circa 1838—Died 10 July 1873

Green enlisted for one year in Company D of the Frontier Regiment of Mounted Troops at age twenty-three in February 1862. In 1870, he reenlisted as a private in the Minute Men organized in Blanco and Llano Counties under Captain Alexander "Buck" Roberts. On 13 October 1871, he again enlisted as a private in the Provisional State Troops in Groesbeck under James Snowball. He was discharged on 20 October 1871. On 1 September 1872, he enlisted as a first sergeant in Company V of the Minute Men at Medina County under the command of George Hanby.

Cesario Menchaca enlisted as a private in Company V of the Minute Men on 1 September 1872 and was discharged on 14 July 1873. Ranger muster rolls report that he deserted one day later, on 15 July.

The rangers were camped near Helotes in Bexar County watching for Indian activity. First Sergeant Green had posted Private Menchca on guard duty. Menchaca stayed on watch all night and never called for a relief. The next day, Sergeant Green ordered the camp moved to a point farther west. While saddling up, Menchaca suddenly shot and killed Sergeant Green with his Winchester rifle. Another ranger attempted to arrest Menchaca, but he escaped on foot while trying to shoot the man.

The disposition of any charges against Menchaca is unknown.

While the ranger muster roll reports that Green died on 14 July, newspaper accounts put the date of his death as Sunday, 10 July 1873. His 1862 enlistment documents indicate that he was born in Germany. Green's place of burial is unknown.

FRONTIER PERIOD, 1874–1901

George, Phillip S.
Born circa 1860—Died 22 January 1874

George enlisted in the Jack County Rangers on 3 December 1873 under the command of Captain S.W. Eastin. Ranger muster rolls report that he died of pneumonia on 22 January 1874 after one month and nineteen days of service. George's place of burial is unknown.

Jones, Henry
Born (Unknown)—Died 22 March 1874

Jones enlisted in the Jack County Rangers on 31 December 1873 under the command of Captain S.W. Eastin. The ranger muster rolls report that he died on 22 March 1874 after three months and nineteen days of service. The cause of death is unknown. According to one report, Private Jones was wounded on 10 July and died on 12 July at Lost Valley.

The Texas Ranger Hall of Fame and Museum reports that Jones was a private in Company C of the Kendall County Minute Men and that he died during the Lost Valley Indian fight on 12 July 1874. That record appears to be incorrect. His rank was also reported as an eighth corporal. Such inconsistencies are commonplace when researching the oftentimes incomplete, scant and illegible records of the ranger force.

No other information is known at this time. His place of burial is unknown.

Osgood, Joseph F.
Born (Unknown)—Died July 1874

Osgood enlisted as a private in a company of frontiersmen in Nueces County on 29 June 1874 under the command of Captain Warren Wallace. Ranger muster roll for the period of 29 June to 28 July report Osgood as being "dead." He probably died in early July 1874. No cause of death was indicated.

Bailey, David W.H.
Born (Unknown)—Died 12 July 1874

Glass, William A. "Billy"
Born 21 July 1854—Died 12 July 1874

On 2 May 1874, the Frontier Battalion of the Texas Rangers was created to defend Texas citizens against Indian raids. On 10 July, Major John B. Jones joined with Captain G.W. Stevens of Company B and moved with them to a camp in Young County. The rangers received word that a band of Comanches attacked the Loving Ranch and killed several cowboys on 20 May and 10 July.

On 12 July, a detachment of about thirty rangers followed an Indian trail for fifteen miles into the Lost Valley between Belknap and Jacksboro in Jack County. Unbeknownst to the rangers, they had picked up the trail of a band of fifty Kiowas led by Chief Lone Wolf and his medicine man, Maman-ti. Lone Wolf had been fighting with U.S. troops since 1856. His son and nephew were killed by troops from the Fourth Cavalry on 10 December 1873 in Edwards County.

Some Comanches joined the Kiowas, and the group grew to about 150 warriors. The Indians ambushed the rangers, wounding Privates Lee Corn, George Moore and Billy Glass. A sniping battle occurred, during which Glass was caught lying in the open between the two sides. Glass called out, "Don't let them get me. Won't some of you fellows help?" Several rangers ran out and brought Glass back to the gully from which they had been firing.

Glass later died from his wound. Wounded rangers were calling for water, but the nearest stream was a mile away. Private Mel Porter decided to ride to the stream. Private Bailey volunteered to go with him. The rangers could see Bailey seated on his horse covering Porter while he got water. About twenty-five Kiowas moved in on them. Bailey called to Porter to flee. The two rangers took off in different directions. Porter barely escaped. Private Bailey was cut off and surrounded. He was levered off his horse by an Indian with a lance. Lone Wolf himself chopped Bailey's head to pieces with a brass hatchet-pipe and then disemboweled him. Satisfied that he had avenged the deaths of his son and nephew, Lone Wolf ordered his band to retreat.

At 3:00 a.m. the next day, the rangers, accompanied by army troopers, returned to recover Bailey's horribly mutilated body.

After evading federal troops and conducting several more raids, Lone Wolf surrendered to the U.S. Army at Fort Sill, Oklahoma, on 26 February 1875. He died shortly after his release from prison in 1879.

There is very little personal information about these two rangers. Both men enlisted in Company B in Wise County on 16 May 1874. Glass had an earlier enlistment of four months in the Wise County Rangers from 26 November 1873 through 26 March 1874. Both men were buried at Cambren Cemetery in Jack County.

Cliff, W.H.
Born circa 1851—Died 23 September 1874

Texas Ranger private W.H. Cliff joined Company E of the Frontier Battalion on 6 June 1874 at Brownwood. He was twenty-three at the time of his enlistment and had come to Texas from Hopkins County, Kentucky.

Another muster roll for Company E, dated 12 November 1874, shows that W.H. Cliff died on 23 September 1874 but does not indicate the cause of death. However, a letter from captain William Jeff Maltby to Major John B. Jones Maltby reported that at about 3:00 a.m. a wall of water several feet high rolled down the valley of Home Creek, where the camp was located. A guard put out an alarm, and the rangers tried to cut the horses loose and climb trees. When the water subsided, the surviving rangers found that Private Cliff, seven horses and one pack mule had drowned. Captain Maltby sent an escort to retrieve Cliff's body and return him to Camp Colorado in Coleman County. Cliff was reportedly "buried with honours of war"; however, his grave has not been located.

He was survived by his parents, Joseph and Miranda Cliff, of Hanson, Hopkins County, Kentucky.

Smith, L.B. "Sonny" or "Berry"
Born circa 1858—Died 12 June 1875

On 12 June 1875, Texas Ranger captain L.H. McNelly requested twenty-two volunteers to intercept a band of Mexican bandits at Palo Alto Prairie, a few miles from Brownsville in Cameron County. D.R. Smith and his son, Berry, were the oldest and youngest rangers in the company, respectively. D.R. requested that his son be allowed to stay in camp with him. He told Captain McNelly that Berry was an only child and that if he were killed his mother would grieve to death. Berry protested and told the captain that every boy's mother in the company would grieve if they were killed.

The rangers soon engaged the bandits and fought in mortal hand-to-hand combat across the prairie. The men killed sixteen of the Mexicans without suffering the loss or injury of a single ranger. As they were regrouping, they saw ranger Spencer J. Adams near a Spanish pond in a field of grass that stood six to eight feet high. Adams advised Captain McNelly that he and Berry had spotted a Mexican combatant who had been shot during the fight crawling away into the stand of grass. Berry volunteered to dismount and go in after him. Adams stayed on his horse to see over the foliage and prevent the outlaw's escape. Adams reported that the bandit shot and killed Smith. The rangers surrounded the pond, shooting into the grass and killing the outlaw.

The bodies of the Mexican bandits were taken to Brownsville and stacked in the town square. At 3:00 p.m. on 13 June 1875, McNelly had Smith's body taken under military escort to the city cemetery, where the ranger was given a full military funeral. Sadly, no marker exists to recognize the heroism of young ranger Smith.

Smith enlisted with his father in the Washington County Volunteer Militia at Austin in Travis County on 25 July 1874 and served ten months and eighteen days. His age at the time of his death was said to be sixteen to eighteen. The City of Brownsville Record of Interments indicates that he was seventeen. Smith is the youngest Texas Ranger killed in the line of duty and the youngest recorded line-of-duty death of a lawman in the state of Texas.

Much controversy remains concerning Smith's given name and nickname(s)—even between the authors. Smith was apparently called "Sonny" and "Berry." It is claimed that Captain McNelly reported his name as Benjamin. His father referred to him as "Berry" in a heartfelt letter to his wife (Sarah P. Smith) telling her of their son's death. Berry's companion, S.J. Adams, who was with him when he died, refers to him only as "L.B." in his letter of sympathy to Mrs. Smith. A study of family genealogy does not reveal any solid clue concerning his given name.

Hendricks, A.R.
Born (Unknown)—Died 27 December 1875

Hendricks was a Confederate army veteran who joined the Frontier Battalion of Captain McNelly's Washington County Volunteers on 25 July 1874 and served honorably until 31 March 1875. In September, he married the widow of William Kelly. Kelly had been killed by a posse under Bill Sutton during the Sutton-Taylor Feud. Unfortunately, Hendricks had fallen in with Bill and Jim Taylor, as well as Mason Arnold, in the revenge killing of former Cuero City marshal Reuben "Rube" Brown on 18 November 1875.

On 27 December, Jim Taylor, Arnold and Hendricks were in Clinton and had stabled their horses at Martin V. King's stables. King was also a DeWitt County jailer. Deputy Dick Hudson, a Sutton supporter, gathered a posse and confronted the outlaws. When the outlaws tried to reclaim their horses, they discovered that the stable was locked. The posse descended on the men and killed Taylor, Arnold and Hendricks.

Hendricks was survived by his wife, Elizabeth Jane Kelly Hendricks. He was buried at the "Old Taylor Cemetery" on the Guadalupe River.

Related case: Cuero City Marshal's Office—Reuben "Rube" Brown and DeWitt County Sheriff's Office—Martin V. King.

Sims, W.H.
Born 8 October 1828—Died 31 August 1876

Sims was the commanding officer of Company O in Burnet County from 9 March 1873 to 13 August 1873. His rank was reported as both captain and lieutenant.

On 31 August 1876, Sims along with his wife and children were near Morgan Creek in the Burnet County when they were awakened by the presence of five or six men who had entered their tent. Sims reached for his gun but was overpowered and forcibly taken outside by the intruders. The men were masked, and their bodies were painted. Sims and his wife begged the men not to kill them, but to no avail.

Sims's body was found about three quarters of a mile from their camp, hanging from a tree. He is buried at Dobyville Cemetery.

Mortimer, Conrad E.
Born circa 1840—Died 13 December 1877

McBride, John E.
Born (Unknown)—Died 17 December 1877

The El Paso Salt War began in the late 1860s. It was a political struggle between Anglo entrepreneurs desiring to acquire title to the salt deposits at the foot of Guadalupe Peak (one hundred miles east of El Paso) and Tejano citizens wanting the salt flats to remain open to the public. Feelings between the two groups erupted into open warfare in 1870. In 1872, Charles Howard tried to claim ownership of the salt flats, an act that outraged local citizens, who seized Howard and released him on bond only if he would leave the state.

On 10 October 1877, Howard returned and killed a rival political leader. On 11 November 1877, Lieutenant John B. Tays took command of newly organized Detachment of Company C. Howard was arraigned for the murder and freed pending trial.

Howard was guarded at an adobe house the rangers used as quarters in San Elizario. The Tejanos gathered, roped Howard's associate and former El Paso County sheriff Charles Ellis and dragged him through the streets, slashing him to death with knives and mutilating his corpse.

On 13 December, John Atkinson, an ex-El Paso police lieutenant and San Elizario businessman, managed to get through the citizen militia and into the ranger quarters with a trunk containing about $11,000. Second Sergeant Mortimer was walking between the buildings when a single shot from a sniper's rifle struck him and passed through his body. Mortimer staggered a few steps and then collapsed in the middle of the road. Tays ran into the street and carried Mortimer inside. Mortimer died just before sundown that day. The rioters charged the building several times but were beaten back.

On 17 December, Tays met with the Tejano junta leaders, who advised the rangers to surrender Howard or they would blow up the ranger quarters. Howard was not fooled by guarantees of his safety and, against Tays's advice, agreed to surrender to save the rangers. Atkinson offered the mob the $11,000 to save Howard and First Sergeant McBride, who continued acting as Howard's agent in San Elizario after his enlistment. The junta agreed and swore to uphold their end of the agreement. Atkinson returned to the ranger quarters with a flag of truce and told the rangers that Tays had ordered them to surrender. They agreed. This is the only time in the history of the Texas Rangers that they were forced to surrender.

Tays was not aware of the surrender agreement, and when he saw the rangers file out and be disarmed he was furious. The junta decided to execute Howard, Atkinson and McBride despite guarantees not to harm them. Each man was shot by a firing squad. Their bodies were stripped, mutilated and thrown into a well. A mob among the insurgents then wanted to kill the twenty or so rangers, but the junta military commander regained control and the rangers were released on 18 December. Four days later, rangers and a sheriff's posse (actually New Mexican mercenaries) descended on San Elizario, killing four or five men and wounding several others until the U.S. Army put a stop to the rampage. The leaders of the insurgents and many of their followers fled to Mexico.

Some of the participants were arrested and later escaped. Some were indicted, but none was ever brought to trial.

A key discovery based on more recent research by historians such as Paul Cool asserts that it would be incorrect to call the local citizenry involved in this affray a "mob." This was simply the standard nineteenth-century Texan reference to angry Tejanos, picked up and repeated by every Texas historian afterward. All of the primary evidence indicates that the citizens were highly organized into a junta, town councils and an armed force with leaders and subordinates—much like the Minute Men of 1775. They had a long history of local self-rule and military self-defense, since Spain, Mexico, the Republic of Texas and the United States never effectively extended power to their towns.

No personal information is known about either Mortimer or McBride.

Related case: El Paso County Sheriff's Office—Charles Ellis.

McCarty, Timothy J. "Tim"
Born circa 1851—Died 2 January 1878
Date of incident: 1 January 1878

On the evening of 1 January 1878, Ben Johnson and George Stevenson, who were serving as teamsters for the rangers, left the camp to attend a dance in town. Stevenson borrowed a pistol from Private McCarty.

Once in town, the two teamsters were confronted by a group of local men who were discharged soldiers from the Tenth Cavalry stationed at the fort. The two teamsters returned to the ranger camp and reported that the men had taken McCarty's pistol. Lieutenant Reynolds told Sergeant McGee and Private McCarty to go back to town and get the pistol. They did so.

As McGhee and McCarty approached the dance hall, the men closed the door and denied the rangers entry. McGhee ordered the men to return the pistol and surrender. He covered the front door while McCarty guarded the back door. Anticipating further trouble, George Stevenson was sent back to the camp to get Lieutenant Reynolds. Reynolds returned with Privates Tom Gillespie and Dick Harrison. The men in the dance hall again refused to surrender to Reynolds. He then ordered the dance hall cleared of all women and gave the men five minutes to surrender.

The mood inside the dance hall started to transform as the women began to scream and the men became tense. One of the fellows poked McCarty's pistol out of the window, muzzle first, and said, "Here...come get your damned pistol." As McCarty stepped forward and gripped the gun, the man holding it pulled the trigger. The bullet struck McCarty just below the heart, inflicting a serious wound.

The rangers opened fire, killing three men. One man managed to escape in the confusion.

McCarty lingered until 1:20 a.m. on 2 January, when he finally expired.

McCarty was buried at Fort McKavett, twenty miles southwest of Menard in Menard County. McCarty had first enlisted as a private in Company F on 4 June 1875. He later reenlisted as a private in Company A on 10 September 1877.

Frazier, Samuel
Born circa 1845—Died 31 January 1878

Frazier enlisted in Company C on 21 November 1877 under the command of Lieutenant John B. Tays at El Paso. He was discharged on 31 January 1878. Frazier died later the same day in a personal disagreement. His death may have been a suicide.

Ruzin, A.A.
Born (Unknown)—Died 10 August 1878

In 1878, the Trans-Pecos region of far west Texas was still the domain of the Western Apaches. Company C was commanded by Lieutenant John B. Tays, the ill-fated commander who had surrendered to a mob during the El Paso Salt War siege at San Elizario in December 1877. Ranger major John B. Jones had not relieved or censured Tays over the incident. Tays resigned in March 1878 but reenlisted as a lieutenant.

On 10 August 1878, Lieutenant Tays was on a scouting expedition when he approached a group of springs. He divided his men into two groups of six rangers each to get water. As the first group of rangers rounded some rocks, they encountered a band of ten or twelve Indians who were riding away from the water holes. Both sides were startled. The Indians headed for the rocks, and five of the six rangers dived into a nearby gully. The sixth, Private Ruzin, chose to stand upright and fight like a "gentleman." He was quickly cut down with a bullet to the brain.

Two horses were shot. No other rangers were killed or wounded in the fight, nor were any Indians reported to have been killed or wounded. The Indians stole Ruzin's Winchester and pistol along with five ranger horses before making their escape.

Little is known about Ruzin. By all accounts, he was said to have been a Russian nobleman. His pay record indicates that he had enlisted as a private on 1 June 1878. Ruzin was reportedly buried on the battlefield, and a wooden marker was placed on his grave. According to legend, Indians passing by the burial place would desecrate the marker.

Anglin, William B.
Born circa 1850—Died 29 June 1879

Ranger captain June Peak and Company B were having trouble with Indian raids on area ranches. The captain dispatched Corporal Douglas and six rangers, including Private Anglin, to locate the Indians.

About twenty-five miles northwest of Fort Concho, the rangers met a rancher who told them that he had observed Indians in the area. On 28 June 1879, the rangers and the rancher came upon the Indians' horses and staked out their camp. Douglas charged the horses, cutting them loose while coming under heavy fire. Two ranger horses and the rancher's horse were wounded. The rangers tried to circle the Indian camp but had no success. They then seized eight Indian horses but, in so doing, lost their pack mules and supplies. Under cover of darkness, the Indians struck the rangers' camp. They were successful in beating back the advancing hostiles.

As dawn broke on 29 June, the rangers found the Indians heading due west and followed them for about one hundred miles. They eventually spotted two of their stolen pack mules atop a slight rise. Not seeing any Indians, the rangers split up and approached the animals from two sides. Anglin rode in close before the other rangers were ready. He was hit by a volley of fire from the concealed hostiles. Although wounded, Anglin managed to free himself from his now dead horse but was soon killed when the Indians let loose a second volley of gunfire.

Two more ranger horses were killed. Douglas ordered his men to pull back. The Indians were well concealed and had plenty of ammunition. Without benefit of sufficient horses and supplies, Douglas ordered his men back to camp.

On the return trip, the rangers met a patrol from the Tenth U.S. Cavalry. Douglas sent two mounted rangers with the troops to guide the soldiers in the recovery of Anglin's body.

Anglin is buried on the Magee Ranch in Midland County near where the fight had taken place the preceding day. He had enlisted in Company B on 1 June 1875.

Bingham, George R. "Red"
Born circa 1845—Died 4 July 1880

Noted cattle thief, outlaw and killer Jessie Evans was released from jail in New Mexico on 19 March 1879. Accompanied by a small band of his loyal followers—most thought to have been former members of the Seven Rivers Gang—the group made its way to southwest Texas and settled in the Fort Davis, Marfa and Alpine vicinity.

Evans and his colleague, John Selman, set up a rather efficient and profitable cattle butchering operation at Fort Davis that was made all the more profitable by the fact that the cattle they were processing had all been stolen from local ranchers.

Evans's gang terrorized the area for some time, until Presidio and Pecos County officials sent a dispatch to Governor Roberts requesting his help. Sergeant Edward A. Sieker and eight ranger privates arrived at Fort Stockton on 6 June 1880 to respond to the disturbance. After three fruitless weeks of searching, an informant tipped off the rangers to the hiding place of Evans and his gang in the Chinati Mountains southwest of Fort Davis.

On 4 July 1880, Sergeant Sieker and Privates Samuel A. Henry, Davy Tom Carson, R.R. "Dick" Russell, L.B. Caruthers and George "Red" Bingham, along with their Mexican guide, were spotted by the gang. A running gun battle resulted, with dozens of shots being fired as the rangers pursued the outlaws across about two miles of rough country. The outlaws finally reached a rock ledge and could go no farther. Carson's horse was hit by two rounds, and his hat was practically shot off when another round pierced the brim.

In a desperate charge across open ground, Ranger Carson shot outlaw George Graham in the side with his carbine. The impact of the bullet knocked him to the ground. Wounded but unwilling to quit the fray, Graham rose to continue firing. Sergeant Sieker quickly fired at Graham. The shot struck him in the head and killed him instantly. During the gun battle, Private Bingham was shot and killed. Bingham's colleagues did not see the shooting take place, nor did they observe Jessie Evans fire the killing shot as the wounded Bingham desperately tried to lever another round into his now jammed Winchester carbine. Sieker later said, "I should have killed them all." Evans was sentenced to prison, but he later escaped and was never heard from again.

Bingham was about twenty-eight years old at the time of his death. He enlisted in Company D on 1 September 1878. Bingham is reportedly buried at Fort Davis, but his grave site has not been located.

More than a decade later, Private Davy Tom Carson was shot and killed at the Benton Weston Saloon at the corner of Mountain and Water Streets in Kerrville on 21 April 1893. John Selman eventually became an El Paso County constable. He killed Deputy U.S. Marshal Baz Outlaw on 5 April 1894 after Outlaw killed ranger Joe McKidrict. On 19 August 1895, Selman killed John Wesley Hardin. On 6 April 1896, Deputy U.S. Marshal George Scarborough killed Constable Selman.

Williams, J.H.
Born circa 1859—15 September 1881

Williams enlisted in Company B on 1 September 1879 and served under Captains June Peak, Ira Long and S.H. McMurray. He was discharged on 13 September 1881, just two days before he was shot and killed at Big Spring in Howard County.

Williams had gone to Big Spring on business. There he met a number of cowboys. The men were all drinking heavily. The cowboys had gone to a sporting house, where they were shooting off their guns when Williams was shot in the chest. He staggered out, claiming that a man named McGhee had shot him. Before he died, Williams said that the shooting was an accident.

There is another account of the same incident, but under slightly different circumstances. In that version of the story, Williams was going from tent to tent, lighting a match at each entrance and apparently looking for someone. It seems that he decided to bed down in the tent of Mrs. Buchanan and sat down on the end of her daughter Olive's bed with two other men. McGhee suddenly pulled out a pistol and fired, hitting Williams.

McGhee escaped but was later arrested.

Ware, W.L.
Born (Unknown)—Died 8 March 1882

Ware enlisted on 11 January 1882 in Company A under the command of Captain George Baylor.

In a letter dated 12 March 1882, Captain Baylor wrote to Adjutant General H.W. King:

> *I have been a good deal occupied lately with various matters pertaining to the Co. and by Ware's sickness. He was taken whilst in town with pneumonia and disease of the heart & died in 4 days. We gave him every attention we could but the complication of heart disease made it impossible to save him…I have another sick man in camp Jack Parker a young Texan who I fear is dangerously ill with pneumonia. We have mumps in the camp, but so far have been lucky enough to escape small pox.*

Ware died of pneumonia at Ysleta in El Paso County on 8 March 1882.

Parker, A.J. "Jack"
Born circa 1862—Died 15 March 1882

Parker enlisted on 9 January 1882 in Company A at Ysleta in El Paso County under the command of Captain George Baylor.

In a letter dated 14 March 1882, Captain Baylor wrote to Adjutant General H.W. King:

> *Yesterday I found Parker so ill from pneumonia that I had him removed to town as Dr. McKinney said he could not receive the attention he needed in camp. So I rented a room for a month for $12.00 pr mo as cheaper & better than any other place. As the men who waite [sic] on him can sleep in the same room. I will have to get the nurses board in Town. Dr. Taylor U.S.A. was called in as consulting physician. He thinks he has a chance for life by close watch…& good nursing. I am afraid he will die…I have come back from the death bed of poor Jack Parker. It seems so sad to see a mere boy, he is not 20, striken [sic] down in only a few days. We did all we could for the poor fellow, but he seemed very much depressed from the first by Ware's sudden death, & said he would die.*

Parker died of pneumonia on 15 March 1882.

Smith, Charles S.
Born circa 1856—Died 25 June 1882
Date of incident: 22 June 1882

At the age of sixteen, Smith got into a fight with his first cousin and accidentally killed him. Later, he drifted to south Texas, where he worked as a cowboy around Cotulla and Laredo. At the age of twenty-three, Smith killed a man in a fight in Webb County and was arrested by Texas Rangers. Smith pled self-defense and was acquitted. Ranger captain L.H. McNelly is claimed to have told Smith, "If you like to shoot people, why don't you join the Rangers?" On 1 April 1880, he enlisted in Captain T.L. Oglesby's Special Forces Company. Smith was discharged on 21 September 1881.

On 17 June 1882, a man named "California Jim" had a falling out with his boss at a café and returned to kill him. The owner called on Laredo assistant city marshal A.A. Johnson for protection. As Johnson tried to enter, "California Jim" slammed the door shut and fired through it as he escaped. Johnson was mortally wounded and died on 19 June.

A reward of $500 was offered for "California Jim." Posses from Webb and LaSalle Counties began a search. On 22 June, Smith and a seventeen-year-old named Wesley DeSpain were hunting for some horses near Cibolo Station (later known as Millet Station and then simply as Millet) in LaSalle County when they spotted a man walking along the top of a brushy ridge near the depot. When Smith and DeSpain were within thirty yards, "California Jim" opened fire at them. His first or second bullet struck DeSpain in the side. The shot hit him near his spine and knocked him from his horse.

Smith dismounted and fired his Winchester three times at the desperado. One bullet struck the outlaw at the joint of the hip, crushing the bone and passing through his bowels and then ranging up and lodging against the skin on the other side. "California Jim" was down but was partially hidden by the brush. The outlaw rose to a sitting position, fired one last shot and then fell back. His shot hit Smith just below the knee, ranging up through the fleshy part of his leg and entering the chest. "California Jim" lingered until 3:00 a.m. on 23 June and then died.

Before he passed, Jim apologized to Smith and offered him his Colt .45 with a 7.5-inch barrel and seventeen notches on the grip. He said that his real name was John Henry Hankins and that there was a reward for his capture in Arizona. He also said that he was wanted in New Mexico as well.

Hankins is buried in a plain pine box under a mesquite tree near the Cibolo Station.

Smith was taken by train to Santa Rosa Hospital in San Antonio, where he died on 25 June. His body was shipped to Fayette County, where he was given a full Texas Ranger funeral by Captain Oglesby. Smith is buried at the family cemetery with his Winchester and wearing his six-shooter and his hat. DeSpain never fully recovered and went mad in 1890. He was institutionalized and died at age forty.

Related case: Laredo Police Department—A.A. Johnson.

Tardy, R.L.
Born (Unknown)—Died 15 February 1883

Tardy enlisted in Company A on 1 December 1882. He died of pneumonia on 15 February 1883 at Ysleta in El Paso County. He was under the command of Captain G.W. Baylor at the time. His place of burial is unknown.

Sparks, John C.
Born circa 1841—Died 9 April 1883
Date of incident: 6 April 1883

Sparks served as a captain in Company C, having enlisted at Clay County on 21 September 1876. He was discharged on 30 November 1877.

Sparks was shot and killed while attempting to make a citizen's arrest of the Fuller brothers near the town of Corsicana in Navarro County.

His killer, J.G. Fuller, was arrested by Deputy R.H. Cubley but was not indicted. On 18 April 1883, the Fuller brothers went before Justice Walton, and the decision to indict was reversed.

There is some conflicting evidence claiming that Captain Sparks may have accidentally shot himself with his own gun, which would tend to validate Justice Walton's decision to drop the indictment.

Stapleton, William
Born (Unknown)—Died 11 November 1883

Stapleton enlisted in Company A of the Frontier Battalion under Captain George W. Baylor. He deserted in the fall and was reported to have been stabbed to death in a drunken quarrel near Villalerio on the Mexican Central Railroad.

One ranger record lists his enlistment as being on 1 December 1882 and his discharge as 28 February 1883, after three months of service. Another record indicates that he enlisted on 1 August 1882. Such inconsistencies are commonplace when researching the oftentimes incomplete, scant and illegible records of the ranger force.

Warren, Benjamin Goodin "Ben"
Born circa 1843—Died 10 February 1885

Private Warren obtained warrants for the arrest of several men who had cut barbed wire fences around ranches so that they could graze their cattle on property belonging to others.

As Warren was sitting in a hotel office in Sweetwater talking with friends, a shot was fired from outside. The bullet struck him in the head, killing him instantly.

The three men who had originally been charged with fence cutting (C.W. Boyett, W.J. Wood and Neil Boyett) were also charged with Warren's murder. Two of the men were convicted and sentenced to life in prison. One of the convictions was overturned. It is not known if the third man was ever charged.

Warren had served as a Texas Ranger for only ten months. He was survived by his expectant wife and eight children. His ninth child was born eight months after his murder. Warren is buried at Old Fort Chadbourne Cemetery in Coke County.

Wood, J.G.
Born (Unknown)—Died 13 May 1885

Wood enlisted in Company C on 28 April 1885 under the command of Captain George Schmitt. The rangers were troubled with fever and sickness, caused by high water from recent heavy rains. Many men had become sick from exposure and from having to swim the flooded rivers. After only fifteen days of service, Private Wood became ill and died.

Captain Schmitt received a very terse letter from Captain John O. Johnson of the adjutant general's office in Austin regarding expenses incurred by the company while on recent duty in Fredericksburg. The letter criticized Schmitt for the cost incurred to bury Private Wood. Captain Schmitt's reply, dated 13 June 1885, reads in part:

> *I don't make any unnecessary Expence and do not allow any men to make any, and if the State can not pay any expence to live decently I will have to quit. I am not to blame for the expence of Wood, I was not in camp when he died, he died while in the service of the State and if only one day, the State are compelled to pay the burial Expence…I stopped $16.00 all pay due him as part of payment on burial Expence and the balance to be paid by the State is only $26.05. Lieutenant Grimes contracted & bought coffin & C. and it was my duty to settle it.*

On 22 June, a second ranger, Private William M. Bohanon, became ill with typhoid fever. He died just over a week later on 2 July. No further information is known about Private Wood.

Sieker, Frank E.
Born (Unknown)—Died 31 May 1885

Frank Sieker enlisted in Company D on 23 September 1884 under the command of his brother, Captain L.P. Sieker.

On 31 May 1885, Private Sieker was a part of a scouting patrol searching for escaped convicts along the Rio Grande River north of Laredo in Webb County. The rangers spotted two men on horseback who were leading a third horse. They started in pursuit when the two men began to run. The rangers gave chase but ran into slippery creek banks where some of the rangers were thrown from their horses. Only Privates Sieker, Aten and Riley remained mounted.

Riley charged forward to arrest the men. They opened fire, and Riley was wounded. Aten opened fire with his rifle and Sieker with his pistol. One man was wounded and rode off.

The two rangers exchanged shots with the remaining man, resulting in Sieker being wounded. The wounded shooter also escaped.

When the remainder of the party arrived, the rangers found Sieker dead, having been hit once in the heart. Sergeant Lindsay chased the wounded outlaw to a nearby village. The local deputy sheriff said that he would arrest the men.

The rangers and the deputy sheriff brought the two prisoners to the Webb County jail and turned them over to Sheriff Darrio Gonzales. Soon a group of men saying they were deputies arrested the rangers for assault.

A local merchant posted bail and had the rangers released, but in the meantime Sheriff Darrio Gonzales had already turned the two suspects loose. They immediately fled to Mexico.

Frank Sieker's body was transported to Eagle Pass in Maverick County, where he was buried.

Bohanon, William M.
Born circa 1856—Died 2 July 1885
Date of incident: 22 June 1885

Bohanon enlisted as a private in Company C on 11 November 1883 under the command of Captain George Schmitt. As a result of heavy rains and high water, the rangers had been troubled with fever and illness during the summer of 1885. On 13 May 1885, a new recruit, Private J.G. Wood, died from illness after serving for only a brief time. Captain Schmitt received a very terse letter from Captain John O. Johnson of the adjutant general's office in Austin regarding expenses incurred by the company while on recent duty in Fredericksburg. In his reply, which gives some indication of conditions, Schmitt related that "several men were sick with fever from exposure and from having to swim the rivers." He went on to say that "one sick man, Bohanon, was not expected to live."

Private Bohanon became ill with typhoid fever on 22 June and died on 2 July. He was reportedly buried in Pearsall, Frio County.

Nigh, Thomas P.
Born circa 1857—Died 18 August 1885

Thomas Nigh enlisted in the ranger service on 17 July 1883. He served until his death two years later.

In 1880, J.T. Morris moved his family to Erath County, where he established a reputation by killing two men while he was serving as a deputy sheriff. When Reeves County was organized, he was elected its first sheriff on 4 November 1884. In 1885, Texas Ranger captain James T. Gillespie established the camp for Company E at Toyah, west of the county seat at

Pecos. Gillespie learned that the sheriff drank heavily and was prone to frequent outbursts. Relations between the sheriff and rangers were strained, and the sheriff had been verbally abusive to Gillespie.

On 18 August 1885, Sheriff Morris left Pecos on the train to Toyah. He was drunk and belligerent. It was believed that he had came to town to kill Jep Clayton. Sheriff Morris was so upset about the fact that the rangers were watching his movements that he became increasingly more intoxicated and began walking the streets of town with a cocked six-shooter.

Citizens complained to Gillespie, who ordered Sergeant L.F. Cartwright to arrest and disarm the sheriff, without hurting him if possible.

Cartwright accompanied rangers William S. Hughes, Frank W. DeJarnette and Thomas P. Nigh in an attempt to disarm Morris. They found the considerably inebriated sheriff at the Favorite Saloon. Cartwright ordered Morris to give up his pistol and surrender. Morris responded by opening fire at Cartwright. He missed and then let loose a second shot at Nigh. The rangers returned fire, hitting Morris five times in the chest. The proprietor of the saloon was shot in both legs during the exchange. Nigh was killed instantly. Morris was taken to the Field Hotel and died within minutes.

Nigh was survived by his young wife and two small children. He was reportedly buried by the rangers in Toyah.

Related case: Reeves County Sheriff's Office—J.T. Morris.

May, George B.
Born (Unknown)—Died 24 September 1886

May enlisted in the ranger service in Company C on 22 April 1885 and served until 25 October 1885. He enlisted in Company B on 9 April 1886. Sterling Price was a policeman in Weatherford in 1880 and enlisted in Company B on 10 March 1886. Company B, under Captain S.A. McMurry, was transferred to Quanah in Hardeman County.

On 24 September 1886, Price and May were in the ranger camp outside of town when they became involved in an altercation over Price having placed his coffeepot on the same fire as May's coffeepot. May kicked Price's pot and drew his pistol. Price, who was unarmed, went to his tent to get his pistol. Price shot and killed May, apparently for nothing more than a breach of campfire or culinary etiquette.

Price was arrested but was never convicted of a crime. Price, along with Donley County deputy sheriff J.F. Green, was involved in another shooting death in Quanah while at a sporting house on 26 May 1888.

Price continued to serve as a ranger until September 1889. He later became a Dallas policeman, police chief and detective. He died in 1924 while still serving as a detective.

Moore, James H. "Jim"
Born (Unknown)—Died 31 March 1887

A posse of rangers from Company F, along with a group of sheriff's deputies, had been searching for five days in the heavy thickets near Hemphill in Sabine County for an outlaw family named Conner. The posse split up near dawn. One group wandered into an ambush that had been set up by Willis Conner and his three sons, Bill, Fred and John.

The Conner gang opened fire. The rangers returned fire, killing Bill Conner. Private Moore was shot through the heart and killed almost instantly. Captain William Scott, Sergeant John Brooks and Private John Rogers were all shot and seriously wounded. Fred Conner was wounded but escaped. More than one hundred rounds were fired in a matter of minutes at a distance of less than fifty feet.

Fred Conner was later shot and killed while resisting arrest on 25 October 1887. Willis Conner and a grandson were killed during an arrest attempt on 15 November 1887. John Conner was never heard from again. John Brooks and John H. Rogers later became celebrated ranger captains.

Private Moore appears to have been in ranger service since 1875 in Companies B, C and D. He is buried at Hemphill Cemetery in Sabine County. His tombstone reads "James H. Moore, Texas Ranger Killed by Outlaws, March 31 1887."

King, James W. "Jim"
Born circa 1856—Died 11 February 1890
Date of incident: 4 February 1890

James King enlisted in Company F on 1 December 1882 under Lieutenant Charles B. McKinney. He served until 1 March 1883. King also enlisted from 1 June 1884 to 31 August 1884, again from 1 September 1887 to 30 November

1887 and from 23 March 1888 to 4 September 1889. In 1889, Captain Frank Jones asked King to go undercover in Zavala County in south Texas.

King was dismissed from ranger service on 4 September 1889. For reasons no one can explain, King returned to Zavala County and told a group of cattle rustlers that he was an honorably discharged ranger. On 4 February 1890, King was assassinated near Loma Vista.

Two years later, George W. Rumfield and William "Will" Speer were charged in his death. Neither man was ever convicted.

King is buried at Loma Vista Cemetery in Zavala County.

Fusselman, Charles Henry Vanvalkenburg
Born 16 July 1866—Died 17 April 1890

Fusselman enlisted in Company D in Duval County on 25 May 1888 at age twenty-one. On 18 May 1889, he was promoted to corporal. On 4 June 1889, Corporal Fusselman killed a man he was attempting to arrest in Marathon. The pair were involved in an intense gun battle during which fifteen shots were fired in less than twenty minutes. Fusselman shot the man eight times. On 19 June 1889, Fusselman was appointed a deputy U.S. marshal. He offered to resign his ranger commission, but Captain Frank Jones allowed him to retain both commissions simultaneously. By November 1889, he had been promoted to the rank of sergeant.

On 17 April 1890, Fusselman was in El Paso to attend court. While at the sheriff's office, a rancher named Barnes came in to complain that some bandits had stolen a number of his cattle. The deputy sheriff could not leave the office, so Fusselman agreed to accompany Barnes and a sixty-year-old former lawman and ranger named George Herold to pursue the rustlers. The men quickly captured one of the rustlers who was serving as the lookout for the bunch. The three men found the cattle and assumed the rustlers had fled. This hypothesis turned out to be incorrect. They were soon ambushed.

The rustlers killed Fusselman during the gunfight. Herold and Barnes had to flee. After the incident, a posse was formed in pursuit of the rustlers, but they were unable to locate them.

Ultimately, Geronimo Parra, a well-known rustler along the Mexican border, was identified as the man who had killed Fusselman. Captain John R. Hughes, who had replaced Captain Jones when he was killed in the line of duty on 30 June 1893, learned that Parra was jailed in New Mexico.

Hughes asked Sheriff Pat Garrett (the same Pat Garrett who had killed Billy the Kid in 1881) to deliver Parra to Texas in return for a prisoner named Pat Agnew whom Garrett wanted and the rangers were holding. The prisoner swap finally took place on 6 October 1898, eight years after Fusselman's death.

Parra was convicted and sentenced to hang. He was executed on 5 January 1900.

Charley Fusselman had been involved in numerous shootings and scrapes with bandits. He had been promoted to the rank of sergeant in the Texas Rangers and had been given an appointment as a deputy U.S. marshal. Amazingly, he was only twenty-three years old when he was killed. Fusselman is buried at Lagarto Cemetery in Live Oak County. The canyon in the Franklin Mountains in El Paso County where Fusselman was killed now bears his name.

Gravis, John F.
Born circa 1868—Died 4 August 1890

Gravis enlisted in Company D under the command of Captain Frank Jones on 24 February 1890. He was sent to the Trans Pecos area in far west Texas.

The Shafter settlement in Presidio County was a mining town, and there had been a number of disturbances there in recent months. On 4 August 1890, a fight broke out during a dance at a private residence in Shafter. Gravis was at the dance when the wild gunfight erupted, during which several people were killed. Gravis was shot and killed instantly during the incident. Captain Jones arrived with several rangers and began rounding up suspects. He returned to Marfa with seven men in custody and charged them with murder. Other rangers and a civilian posse brought in another dozen men.

Rangers later arrested three men fleeing to Mexico. While one newspaper account in September 1890 reported that a man was to be tried at Marfa for the murder of Private Gravis, it is unknown if anyone was ever convicted.

Gravis served for a little more than five months before he was killed. His body was shipped to his home at Laredo in Webb County. His place of burial is not known.

Doaty (Doughty), Robert E.
Born circa 1858—Died 22 March 1892

In the early 1890s, Catarino Garza formed a small army in south Texas that became known as the *Garzistas*. The aim was to overthrow Mexican president Porfirio Díaz.

Garza was a Texas resident who was well known as a newspaper editor and charismatic orator. Despite having almost one thousand men under his command, his three attempts to invade Mexico failed and caused President Díaz to complain that the United States had failed to enforce its neutrality laws. The *Garzistas'* activities challenged the U.S. Army on the federal level, as well as Texas Rangers and county officers locally. In February 1892, Garza slipped out of the United States and fled to Central America. His group of soldiers then became bandits and as such were wanted men.

On 20 March 1892, rangers from Company E captured several bandits and killed one. On 22 March, Private Doaty was with seven or eight rangers when they came upon a band of *Garzistas* about twenty miles below Pena, on the Duval-Starr county line. Doaty was shot in the head and killed instantly.

Ranger enlistment papers indicate that Doaty joined on 1 March 1892 in Alice and served for only twenty-one days before he was killed. While his enlistment papers show his name as "Doaty," his surname was spelled "Doughty." There were countless mistakes made in the records of this era. Many of the men who served as rangers were only marginally literate or were often completely uneducated. The records often reflect the writer's interpretation of the spelling of the enlistee's name from hearing it spoken.

Doughty was apparently not married, because his mother, Elizabeth Gravis, signed for his pay of twenty-two dollars. His place of burial is unknown, but he was most likely laid to rest near his mother and stepfather in the family plot in Duval County at the San Diego cemetery.

Carson, Davy Thomas "Tom" (or "D.T.")
Born 22 December 1852—Died 21 April 1893

Carson was born in Texas. He migrated to Newton County, Kansas, where he served as a constable or deputy sheriff. By November 1871, Carson was employed as a deputy for Sheriff John W. "Brocky Jack" Norton in Abilene, Kansas. After Carson shot a bartender, both he and Norton were dismissed from office.

Carson enlisted in the ranger service on 1 September 1878 and resigned on 31 August 1882. He was involved in the capture of Jessie Evans and his gang in the Chinati Mountains near Presidio in July 1880. During the fight that took place during the capture of Evans, ranger George R. "Red" Bingham was shot and killed along with one member of the Evans gang.

In 1883, Carson got into the saloon business with Andrew Jackson "A.J." Royal, who owned the Royal House Saloon in Junction City. On a bitterly cold night in the winter of 1884, Carson and Royal were locking up the saloon at closing time when Carson suspected a man named Jim Stout of drawing a gun. Carson shot and killed him. Both Carson and Royal were indicted for the murder but found not guilty.

On the night of 21 April 1893, former Texas Ranger Carson was involved in an altercation with a man named Bill Holman (or Holiman/Holliman) at the Benton-Weston Saloon in Kerrville. The episode turned ugly, and Holman shot and killed Carson for reasons still unknown.

The body of Carson was returned to his home in Junction City. Definite evidence as to the location of his burial continues to elude researchers.

Related cases: Pecos County Sheriff's Office—Andrew Jackson "AJ" Royal and Texas Rangers—George R. "Red" Bingham.

Schmid, Frank Louis, Jr.
Born 18 October 1866—Died 17 June 1893
Date of incident: 16 August 1889

Schmid enlisted in the ranger service on 23 June 1886 in Company C at Laredo but was transferred on 1 September 1886 to Company D, which was commanded by the famed captain Frank Jones.

In 1888, tensions in Fort Bend County erupted into what historians would later call the Jaybird-Woodpecker War, a feud between two political factions for the control of Fort Bend County. The Jaybird bloc represented most of the wealth and about 90 percent of the white population. They were the regular Democrats who sought to rid the county of the Republican government that had gained control during Reconstruction. The Woodpeckers, numbering about forty persons, also claimed to be Democrats but were the officials and former officials who held office as a result of the black vote for the Republican ticket. In this unfortunate feud, former friends, neighbors and relatives became bitter enemies.

Governor L.S. Ross ordered rangers to Richmond, the embattled county seat, to head off further hostilities between the Democratic Jaybirds and the Republican Woodpeckers. Sheriff J.T. Garvey was a leader of the Woodpeckers.

A showdown arrived on 16 August 1889 when the Jaybirds faced off against the Woodpeckers in front of the courthouse. Sheriff Garvey and a crowd of armed men warned the rangers to get out of the way, telling them that the disagreement was none of their business. Sergeant Ira Aten and Privates Schmid and Alex McNabb, all mounted, attempted to block the path of the feuding groups. Their efforts were unsuccessful and gunfire erupted. Private Schmid was wounded in the right thigh. When the shooting finally ended, four people were dead, including Sheriff Garvey and his uncle, former sheriff J.W. Blakely.

Schmid's wound worsened, but he continued on the ranger rolls while having to pay his own medical expenses. Numerous surgeries and treatments failed. He requested, and received, a clerk's job at the state treasury.

On 29 March 1893, the state legislature passed a bill reimbursing Schmid for $584.50 in medical bills. On 17 June 1893, Schmid died from his wound. He never married and is buried at Bellefontaine Cemetery in St. Louis, Missouri.

Related cases: Fort Bend County Sheriff's Office—Tom Garvey and J.W. Blakely.

Jones, Franklin "Frank"
Born 12 June 1856—Died 30 June 1893

Jones first enlisted on 1 September 1875 in Lieutenant Ira Long's Company A when he was only nineteen years old. He served until 31 August 1876. On 25 November 1876, he enlisted in Lieutenant Pat Dolan's Company F. That period of service ended at Uvalde on 17 August 1877. On 28 July 1881, he enlisted in Captain Dan Robert's Company D in Kimble County and continued in the service until he was discharged at Kimble County on 22 February 1882. On 1 September 1882, Jones reentered the service when he was enlisted by Lieutenant Lamar P. Sieker, then commanding Company D. Rising rapidly in the ranks, he was made lieutenant in 1884 and assumed command of the company in 1885. On 1 May 1886, he was promoted to captain.

Captain Jones, Corporal Kirchner and Privates Tucker, Aten and Saunders, as well as El Paso County deputy sheriff Bryant, obtained a warrant for the arrest of Jesus-Maria Olguin and his son, Severio, for cattle rustling. The Olguin clan were known outlaws and lived in a sort of no man's land on Pirate Island, which was situated in the middle of the Rio Grande River between Texas and Mexico across from El Paso County. While Mexico claimed jurisdiction over the disputed island, parts of the island were in Texas. The rangers would later claim that they did not realize that they were in Mexico until after the gun battle.

The lawmen saw two Mexican riders flee, dismount and enter some adobe building in the town of Tres Jacales, Mexico. As Captain Jones and his men approached, gunfire erupted from inside the buildings and from the surrounding brush. Jones was wounded in the thigh and fell from his horse. He straightened out his leg and continued firing. Private Tucker came to his assistance, but Jones told the other men to save themselves. Seconds later, he was riddled with bullets and died.

The vastly outnumbered lawmen returned to Texas to summon assistance. El Paso County sheriff Simmons went to Juarez, Mexico, to request the return of Captain Jones's body. Mexican authorities filed a diplomatic protest but did return the body several days later. The Olguins were reportedly wounded and arrested by Mexican authorities, but they were never prosecuted.

Captain Jones had sent a letter to ranger officials six weeks earlier requesting additional men due to the large number of bandits in the area. He is buried on his father-in-law's ranch. In 1936, he was reburied at Ysleta in El Paso County, and a state historical marker was erected. Jones was thirty-seven years old and was survived by his wife and two daughters.

Woods, J.W.
Born (Unknown)—Died 30 November 1893

On 1 September 1883, Woods enlisted as a private in Company B under the command of Captain John H. Rogers. Pay records show Woods still attached to Company B as late as 29 February 1884.

On 1 January 1893, Captain Rogers formed Company E and recruited Woods. Rogers's biography reported that Woods was promoted to corporal in March 1893, but ranger payrolls indicate that he was a private during this enlistment.

In the summer of 1893, the sheriff of Menard County requested assistance from the rangers with cattle thefts. Captain Rogers assigned Woods to work undercover, and Woods went to work at a local ranch.

In July 1893, Woods simply vanished. His body was never recovered, and no one was ever prosecuted for what the rangers concluded was his murder. On 30 November 1893, the rangers declared him dead because no one had collected his paycheck since July. There is no personal information available about Woods.

McKidrict, Joseph W. "Joe"
Born circa 1871—Died 5 April 1894

Private McKidrict was in El Paso to testify in court. Baz Outlaw was a former ranger sergeant in Company D who was dismissed for excessive drinking. Outlaw had been involved in numerous shootings and was considered a dangerous man when intoxicated. Outlaw was able to get a commission as a deputy U.S. marshal for the Western District of Texas. Private McKidrict and Outlaw were acquaintances.

On 5 April 1894, Outlaw was inebriated, fired his pistol and was creating a disturbance in a sporting house. He started chasing the madam, who began blowing her whistle to alert the police. Private McKidrict and El Paso County constable John Selman Sr. responded. McKidrict asked Outlaw why he had fired his pistol. Without uttering a reply, Outlaw shot McKidrict in the head, killing him instantly. Outlaw also fired at Constable Selman, nearly striking him in the face. Selman returned fire, hitting Outlaw in the chest. Outlaw in turn shot the constable in the leg. Outlaw died later that night from his wounds.

Constable Selman was put on trial for killing Outlaw. The judge instructed the jury to find him not guilty.

On 19 August 1895, Selman shot and killed the infamous desperado John Wesley Hardin. While awaiting trial for that murder, Selman was shot and killed by Deputy U.S. Marshal George Scarborough on 5 April 1896, two years to the day after the shooting deaths of McKidrict and Outlaw.

McKidrict is buried at Oakwood Cemetery in Austin, Texas. His tombstone incorrectly states his age as thirty-two and his year of death as 1893.

Related cases: El Paso County Constable's Office—John Selman; United States Marshals Service—Baz Outlaw.

Hooker, Walker Lee
Born 15 July 1869—Died 28 August 1894

On 28 August 1894, Private Hooker and several rangers were on a scout when Hooker decided to ride to a nearby ranch and get a fresh horse. When he did not return, search parties began looking for him. Due to heavy rains and flooding, the creeks as well as the Nueces River were over their banks, and it was feared that he had drowned. On 15 September, his body was recovered in LaSalle County.

Hooker was assigned to Company F of the Frontier Battalion under the command of Captain J.A. Brooks, stationed in Cotulla. He is buried at Hico Cemetery in Hamilton County.

Breaux, Oscar J.
Born circa 1868—Died 29 August 1898

St. Leon, Ernest "Diamond Dick"
Born circa 1859—Died 31 August 1898
Date of incident: 29 August 1898

Ernest "Diamond Dick" St. Leon was one of the most colorful Texas Rangers to have served during this era and the last Texas Ranger to be killed in the line of duty in the nineteenth century.

St. Leon was reportedly born in Canada and was raised in San Antonio. He served in the U.S. Cavalry some time from about 1885 to 1886. St. Leon took his oath of enlistment on 30 November 1890 with Company D of the Frontier Battalion. He earned the nickname "Diamond Dick" for his flashy style of dress and the diamond stickpin that he always wore on his shirt that had been a gift from his mother.

St. Leon was eventually dismissed from Company D as a consequence of his drinking. He became a detective and continued to remain in contact with Ranger captain John Hughes. St. Leon is known to have worked with Hughes on a number of cases. In 1889, the Fronteriza Mining Company hired St. Leon as a guard, and he was involved with rangers in the capture of a gang of outlaws.

St. Leon reenlisted in Company D on 1 May 1896. On 29 August 1898, Private St. Leon went to Socorro, about sixteen miles below El Paso, in search of a fugitive. The justice of the peace called on St. Leon to arrest

John Collier and Bob Finley for forcibly taking two stray horses out of the town impound. St. Leon arrested the men as requested but discovered that the pair actually owned the horses. He asked the judge to release the men. After the men left town, St. Leon heard gunshots. The judge warned St. Leon not to follow the men in the dark, but St. Leon deputized a local dentist named Oscar Breaux and went in pursuit.

St. Leon and Breaux got to the Lemaire Ranch ahead of the cowboys and waited. Breaux dismounted. Three men on two horses approached, and St. Leon advised them to surrender. The men opened fire, striking Breaux in the right ear and killing him instantly. St. Leon was shot through the left arm, with the bullet becoming lodged in his left lung.

Collier, Finley and John Ray went to the town of Clint and surrendered themselves to justice of the peace. Ray was suffering from a wound in the right thigh, and Finley's horse had been wounded in the neck.

Ranger captain Hughes later brought the three men to El Paso and placed them in jail, charging them with the murder of Dr. Breaux and the assault on St. Leon. None of them was ever convicted of murder.

On 31 August 1898, St. Leon died of the wounds. He is buried at Concordia Cemetery in El Paso. St. Leon was survived by his wife.

Dr. Breaux was from New Orleans, where he had family. He had arrived in Socorro about three months earlier, having made the change of climate for health reasons and to set up a medical practice. His place of burial is unknown.

Chapter 4

Texas State Penitentiary

Before a central state penitentiary was established in Texas, local jails housed convicted felons. The Congress of the Republic of Texas defeated bills for a penal institution in both 1840 and 1842. In May 1846, the first legislature of the new state passed a penitentiary act, but the Mexican-American War prevented implementation of the law. Finally, on 13 March 1848, the legislature passed the act that established the Texas penitentiary system. On 1 October 1849, the first prisoner, a convicted horse thief from Fayette County, entered the partially completed Texas State Penitentiary at Huntsville.

In February 1867, the prison board leased 100 prisoners to the Airliner Railroad and 150 to the Brazos Branch Railroad. For most of the next forty-five years, the state contracted out vast numbers of Texas prisoners to private employers, including railroads, mining companies and plantations. Other convicts remained at the Huntsville and Rusk Penitentiaries.

In 1927, the Texas State Penitentiary became the Texas Prison System. In 1957, the name was changed to the Texas Department of Corrections. In 1989, the state legislature changed the name again, to the Texas Department of Criminal Justice.

Butler, James Monroe
Born circa 1853—Died 25 May 1882

Guard Butler was struck by a train and killed while supervising a prison work crew on the Missouri Pacific Railroad tracks in Fort Worth.

An engineer operating one of the trains backed a locomotive up too rapidly, striking several railroad cars and causing them to derail. One of the derailing cars struck Guard Butler, causing the fatal injury.

Butler is buried at Earle's Chapel Cemetery in Cherokee County.

Boudreaux, S.
Born (Unknown)—Died 23 April 1883

Leonas, John
Born (Unknown)—Died 24 April 1883
Date of incident: 23 April 1883

The black men and women living on the Lake Jackson plantation, located about seven miles south of Brazoria, were having a festival. Two white convict guards from the state prison farm named S. Boudreaux and John Leonas were in attendance. The two guards started creating a disturbance, drew their pistols and fired them.

The guards had directed their gunfire at a black man named Jim Wright, whom they missed nine times. Wright, who was apparently the better marksman, turned and fired twice at Leonas, striking him with both shots. Leonas died the next day. Boudreaux continued to fire at Wright, who returned fire and shot Boudreaux in the bowels. Boudreaux was mortally wounded, and it was reported that he would not survive.

Very little is known about either man, including the correct spelling of their surnames. Leonas is believed to have been John C. Lonis, who was born in 1821. S. Boudreaux may have been Sylvanie Boudreaux, born in 1840.

Taylor, George W.
Born circa 1825—Died 15 March 1884

Sergeant Taylor was employed at the East Texas Penitentiary near Rusk in Cherokee County as the "Outside Sergeant" or "Dog Sergeant," in charge of the bloodhounds used to chase escaping convicts. Every day he supervised the squads of three or four convicts, each with a convict guard, who were sent to work in the coal fields near the prison.

Near sundown on 15 March 1884, the convict squads were marching back to the penitentiary when prisoners T.W. Wallace, John Kennedy and G.W.

Miller overpowered a guard and seized his twelve-gauge double-barreled shotgun. Another guard opened fire and wounded Wallace in the elbow, but the three convicts made their escape into the woods.

Sergeant Taylor, Assistant Superintendent (Captain) F.P. O'Brian and a group of guards that included his son William Taylor, Hiram Newman, John J. Dial and Joe Summers started trailing the escapees with a pack of bloodhounds. The dogs cornered the prisoners near a creek, but the darkness and thick brush made it difficult to see the men across the stream. As the guards approached the baying dogs, a shotgun blast struck and wounded Guard Newman and his horse. Guard Taylor and Captain O'Brian returned fire with pistols in the direction of the shotgun blast.

The escapees had now fired two shots from the double-barreled shotgun they had taken from a guard earlier. Assuming that the men were now out of ammunition, Sergeant Taylor called out to the guards: "Don't shoot anymore boys, they have no more loads and we will get them now." Sergeant Taylor called on the convicts to "put down that gun." Unbeknownst to Sergeant Taylor, Wallace had purchased twenty-one shotgun shells from a source outside the prison. One of the convicts fired another blast that struck Sergeant Taylor in the chest and knocked him off his horse. The guards returned fire but the convicts escaped.

Taylor's son found his father lying dead in a clearing near the creek.

It is not known if Kennedy or Miller were ever captured and prosecuted. Wallace remained at large until May 1885, when he returned to the prison. He was convicted and sentenced to life.

Taylor was survived by his wife, Mollie Welch, as well as two daughters (one by a prior marriage). His place of burial is unknown.

Epperson, Joe
Born (Unknown)—Died 29 April 1889

Epperson was a guard at the convict coal camp at Alto in Cherokee County. On 29 April 1889, he was captured by three convicts, disarmed and killed by one of the men whose name was James Roach. Roach had snatched a pistol away from another guard, which he then used to commit the murder.

After the killing, Roach and another convict named Spears, who was also from Parker County, along with a convict named Ellis Bybee from San Saba County, made their escape with horses and weapons. A posse quickly apprehended Spears and Bybee in Leon County.

The Texas Prison Museum records indicate that Roach and Bybee were convicted of first-degree murder and sentenced to death. Outgoing governor Joseph Sayles pardoned Roach and Bybee on 25 December 1902. The disposition of the Spears case is unknown.

Virtually nothing is known about Epperson. One newspaper article reported that he was from Henderson County.

Williamson, Benjamin "Riley"
Born circa 1832—Died 30 June 1890

In the early morning hours of 30 June 1890, guard Benjamin Williamson took a squad of six convicts out on a work detail at the Butterfield Coal Camp (managed by Texas Prison System as a work camp). The camp was located about sixteen miles south of Rusk in Cherokee County. Guard Williamson was found with several bullet wounds to his head. The convicts he was guarding had shot him and fled with his weapon.

Other convicts had also escaped and had managed to secure additional weapons from guards and civilians. A former guard at the prison named Walter Freeman, who had been fired for negligence, was found to have furnished firearms to the escapees who were responsible for killing Williamson.

Freeman was charged with the murder of Williamson and for inciting a riot. He fled the state but was arrested shortly afterward at Little Rock, Arkansas. Freeman was taken back to Texas, where he posted bond and immediately fled the state again. He was arrested once again near Princeton, Kentucky, on 30 June 1891 and was transported back to Texas. In July 1891, Freeman was convicted of inciting a riot and insurrection and sentenced to six years in prison. On 27 June 1892, he attempted to escape and was shot by a guard. According to reports at the time, he was not expected to live.

Williamson is believed to be buried at Arnold Cemetery in Forest in Cherokee County. He had ten children.

Goodwin, Jesse F.
Born circa 1869—Died 16 July 1890
Date of incident: 14 July 1890

Fourteen days after the murder of the guard, Williamson, two convicts at the same Butterfield State Coal Camp near Alto in Cherokee County (managed by the Texas Prison System as a work camp) shot and mortally wounded Guard Goodwin.

Prison guards and convicts were all out on work details, and Goodwin had been left behind in charge of the camp hospital. One of the convicts in the hospital had been supplied with a pistol, presumably by someone on the outside. When Goodwin entered the hospital, the convict leveled his pistol at the guard and demanded the guard's weapon. Goodwin refused to surrender his gun, so the convict shot him. As Goodwin tried to escape and ran outside the tent, a trustee fired a shotgun at him, hitting him with buckshot in the legs and hip.

The two convicts fled to the woods with the weapons. One was shot and killed by a posse of guards. The disposition of the other prisoner is unknown.

Goodwin died two days later. His father and sister were at his side. His body was returned to Hempstead in Waller County for burial.

Jackson, James "Joe"
Born (Unknown)—Died 15 December 1890

On 15 December 1890, George Jarvis, manager of the Retrieve State Prison Farm at Angleton in Brazoria County, sent guard Jackson (referred to in the newspaper as "Joe") to the express office at Oyster Creek Station to pick up a package containing about $300. Jackson was seen at the office at about 4:00 p.m. About 9:00 p.m., a man opened the gate of the prison farm and discovered Jackson lying dead on the ground.

An investigation revealed that Jackson had been shot in the face with a shotgun. The money was missing. Brazoria County sheriff Yerby and Magistrate Fackney conducted an inquest at the scene. A prominent merchant at Oyster Creek had seen Jackson, and in a conversation with him Jackson had asked how far a man named Bill Davidson was in advance of him. Upon learning Davidson's whereabouts, Jackson immediately spurred his horse to a gallop, saying that he and Davidson were going to hunt ducks and that he wished to catch him. This was the last time Jackson was seen alive.

A search warrant was issued for Davidson's house. Blood was found splattered on his boots. Soot on the soles of his shoes matched material from the ash pile outside the prison gate. Davidson was found in Brazoria City, where he was drinking and spending money freely. He had been seen repeatedly at the express office, asking about the package that Jackson had gone to pick up.

Davidson was placed in jail awaiting an examining trial. It is unknown if he was ever prosecuted for the crime.

Williams, R.L.
Born (Unknown)—Died 12 December 1893

Guard Williams was shot and killed by a fellow guard named S.M. Evitts at Sugarland in a personal dispute over a saddle. No other information is known about this incident.

Cury, W.M.
Born (Unknown)—Died 1 October 1894

Guard Curry accidentally shot himself with a shotgun loaded with buckshot. The incident took place near Burlington in Milam County.

Curry was reported to have been a young man. He is buried at the old City Cemetery in Rockdale.

Milburn, S.L.
Born circa 1868—Died 21 March 1897

Milburn was employed as a convict guard. On 21 March 1897, he was on the sidewalk at Luling in Caldwell County when he was attacked and beaten. His injuries were so severe that he died shortly afterward at the convict camp. Milburn's head was crushed at the base and over his left eye. A large rock covered with blood that was found at the scene is thought to have been the weapon used in the beating.

Lawmen discovered that Milburn had been to some nearby cabins used by black prostitutes. He got into an argument with a black man named Frank Houston. Houston was arrested, tried, convicted and sentenced to nine years in prison. He appealed and was granted a new trial. The district attorney dismissed the case on 10 April 1899.

Milburn was said to have been from Coriscana in Navarro County, where he had a brother and sister. He is buried at the Luling city cemetery, but his grave site has not been located. Milburn's surname has also been reported as "Wilburne" and "Wilkins."

McCarley, S.A.
Born circa 1875—Died 27 June 1897

McCarley was employed as a guard at the Koppe Convict Farm in Brazos County. The convict camps were under the control of the Texas State Penitentiary.

Between 1:00 a.m. and 3:00 a.m. on 27 June 1897, McCarley was shot and killed by a man named Will Little. Little had gone to a house on the Burleson County side of the Brazos River where McCarley was spending the night and called for him. Little tried to force open the door. McCarley looked out the window, and Little fired a double-barreled shotgun at him. The blast struck McCarley in the head, killing him almost instantly. Little fled and hid under a bed in another house. Deputy sheriffs eventually located him and took him into custody, charging him with murder.

Little was an inmate at the convict farm. He had been sentenced to the state penitentiary in 1892 and was later discharged. He was convicted of first-degree murder in Burleson County on 27 May 1898 and sentenced to life in prison on 7 June 1898. A notation in his file states that he died in prison, but records indicate that he was pardoned on 6 December 1914.

Such inconsistencies and conflicting information can be frustrating for researchers but, regrettably, are commonplace.

McCarley was described as about twenty-three years old, single and formerly a guard at the White Convict Farm in Brazos County. He was reported to have been buried at Wellborn in Brazos County. His grave site has not been located.

Parsons, H.D.
Born circa 1846—Died 26 July 1898

At 11:30 p.m., Parsons was working as the night prison guard at the Donovan Convict Farm, located seven miles from Eagle Lake in Colorado County. He was called to the grated window of a cell and asked to bring some medicine to a man who claimed to be sick. As he brought the medication and placed it on the jamb, a convict grabbed his hand and jerked him against the grating. Another convict grabbed Parson's pistol from his belt and killed him.

The convicts, four in all, then took a bench and knocked the window out of their cell and escaped. One of them attempted to ring the alarm bell in spite of the fact that he was being threatened by another prisoner who was armed with Parson's gun.

The fleeing convicts crossed the river and headed for Scull Creek bottom while being tracked by a posse using bloodhounds. At about 1:30 a.m. on 17 August 1898, one of the escapees, Dr. J.K. Miles, was arrested near Mayfield in Milam County by the sheriff and a posse of guards. Dr. Miles had been sent to prison from Polk County about two years earlier to serve a ten-year sentence for bigamy. Superintendent Whatley had sent Miles to the Donovan Convict Farm as a surgeon and physician, and he was serving in that capacity when he escaped.

Miles denied being involved in the murder of guard Parsons. It is unknown if he was charged with the murder. The Texas Prison Museum records indicate that Miles was discharged on 22 November 1904.

Parsons was the son of General George Parsons of Washington, D.C. He was about fifty-two years old at the time of his death. His place of burial is unknown. In 1880, he was living in Bellville, Austin County, with his wife and three children.

Miller, Frank
Born circa 1879—Died 7 October 1899

Miller was a black convict guard on a Texas Trunk construction train in Dallas. The train was stationed at the corner of Commerce Street and the Trunk Railroad.

Miller was examining his double-barreled shotgun when it accidentally discharged. The shotgun was loaded with no. 6 shot. The contents of both barrels struck him in the chest and left arm. He was taken to the city hospital but lived only a few hours.

W.R. Bowen was in charge of the construction train and said that Miller, who was about twenty years old, was born and raised in Kaufman County and had been employed for about one month. It was reported that he had no living relatives. An inquest was held and determined that the shooting was accidental.

Miller's place of burial is unknown.

Chapter 5

Texas State Police

During Radical Republican rule after the Civil War, Texas was lawless and chaotic. The Texas legislature passed the Police Act of July 1870 authorizing the formation of the Texas State Police with a force of 257 men. In spite of that mandate, the force never grew to more than about 200 men at its peak. The state police was authorized to arrest offenders in cases where local law enforcement officers failed to do so. Adjutant General James Davidson was appointed chief of the state police but was paid no more than his men.

The Texas state policemen came from all walks of life. Some were black, some Hispanic and some Anglo. Many had fought in the Civil War, either for the Union or the Confederacy. Some were excellent lawmen and some were criminals. Most were Republicans. Despite what some believe was the general success of the state police, the fact that the force employed black men and was controlled by Governor Edmund J. Davis made it unpopular. Adjutant General Davidson embezzled $37,000 and disappeared. Though his crime cannot be blamed on the police, his association with the force contributed to their lack of popularity. On 22 April 1873, the law authorizing the state police was repealed. Former policeman Leander H. McNelly and at least thirty-six other state policemen became Texas Rangers.

Contemporary studies of the state police describe them as having been politically oriented and corrupt. However, in many cases, the evidence does not substantiate that claim. More recent research seems to indicate that Texas historians of the Reconstruction era may have allowed their bias against Republican organizations to influence their summaries and writing.

Popular political views of the day often manage to creep into the interpretations of historians who are dealing with events that occurred during a decidedly different era. On balance, both arguments seem to have some validity. Thus it is difficult to categorically support one version or the other. As is generally the case, it is best for the informed reader to be the judge.

Smalley, Jim
Born circa 1847—Died 22 January 1871

On 6 January 1871, the notorious outlaw John Wesley Hardin was arrested in Longview. He was charged with stealing a horse and with the murder of Waco city marshal Laben J. Hoffman. Texas State Police lieutenant E.T. Stakes, Private Jim Smalley and a volunteer named L.B. Anderson were transporting Hardin to McLennan County to stand trial. They camped for the night in Freestone County. Hardin had been searched, but apparently he had hidden a pistol under his arm attached to a string. Although there are conflicting accounts of the events that followed, it appears as though Hardin shot and killed Private Smalley while Lieutenant Stakes and Anderson were gathering wood. Hardin then escaped.

Although Hardin was never charged with the murder of Private Smalley, the governor offered a $1,100 reward for his capture. He was later convicted of the murder of Brown County deputy sheriff Charles M. Webb on 26 May 1874 and sentenced to prison.

Hardin was killed by El Paso County constable John Selman Sr. on 19 August 1895.

Texas Adjutant General Service Records indicate that Jim Smalley was paid for a period of three months and twenty-two days as a private in the Texas State Police, Second District, from 1 October 1870 until 22 January 1871. Smalley was a twenty-four-year-old black man from Mississippi. His place of burial is unknown.

Related cases: Brown County Sheriff's Office—Charles M. Webb; DeWitt County Sheriff's Office—Jack Helm; El Paso County Constable's Office—John Selman Sr.; Texas Rangers—Joe McKidrick; Texas State Police—Green Paramore; and Waco Police Department—Laben J. Hoffman.

Bell, General
Born circa 1850—Died 25 February 1871

Private Bell, a black man, arrested a freedman named Drew. Drew was charged with horse theft in Falls County. Joseph Miller, another freedman, had furnished Drew with a pistol. While Private Bell was bringing the prisoner to town, Drew shot him in the small of his back. The bullet passed through the region of the kidneys, inflicting a fatal wound that resulted in Bell's death fifteen hours later.

Bell was born in Alabama about 1850 and was a private in the First District of the Texas State Police. He enlisted on 27 July 1870 and served until his death. His place of burial is unknown.

Steen, Robert
Born circa 1829—Died 27 April 1871

On 27 April 1871, Private Steen, a black man, attempted to stop T.C. "Code" Brown from firing his pistol inside a saloon at Hearne in Robertson County. Brown was the son of Green Brown, of the law firm Brown & Wilkerson. As Private Steen stepped up to talk to Brown, the man shot him and then shot him again after he had fallen to the ground wounded.

Brown fled the scene. Texas State Police captain Leander H. McNelly was sent to investigate the crime. His report to the adjutant general on 3 May 1871 identified the killer as Brown.

There is no evidence that Brown was ever arrested or tried for the murder of Private Steen.

The roster for the Third District of the Texas State Police indicates that Steen was commissioned on 8 July 1870 but not accepted until 10 August 1870 (which is when his oath is dated). He was dismissed on 30 November 1870 and reinstated on 1 December 1870. Steen had served slightly more than eight months. His place of burial is unknown.

Briggs, Edward W. "Ed"
Born (Unknown)—Died 22 May 1871

There is very little information known about this case. Private Briggs was shot at a house in the suburbs of Waco in McLennan County. The bullet entered below his nose and ranged upward, becoming lodged under his cheekbone. The man who shot him was arrested but not charged.

When the Texas State Police was abolished, his records indicated that he had been killed in the line of duty. His place of burial is unknown.

Werner, August
Born (Unknown)—Died 14 August 1871

Late in the evening of 14 August 1871, Ben Yoast had a disagreement with a freed black man in Bastrop. His intoxicated father, Frank Yoast, rode up, drew his pistol and demanded a fair fight. The elder Yoast threatened to shoot anyone who interfered.

Two citizens intervened and separated Yoast's son and the black man. Bastrop County sheriff Jung and two Texas state policemen arrived and attempted to arrest Frank Yoast. Private August Werner and a citizen fired at Yoast. Yoast fired back three times, having only three chambers of his revolver loaded at the time. One shot struck Werner, killing him. The other two shots had no effect, striking the clothing of Jung and the other policeman.

Adding to the confusion at the scene, a woman named Halter, who was subject to hemorrhage of the lungs, came out of her nearby home and fell dead on the steps from internal bleeding. Contributing further to the pandemonium, one of Private Werner's bullets struck and wounded a bystander. Frank Yoast fled the scene.

Ben Yoast appeared in District Court of Bastrop, charged with two counts of carrying deadly weapons and assault to kill and murder. No records exist as to whether Frank Yoast was ever charged with the murder of Private Werner.

The German-born Werner was a farmer before joining the state police. He was married and had children. Werner was commissioned as a private on 12 November 1870 in the Third District. Werner was transferred to the Fourth District to work out of Bastrop. He resigned on 11 February 1871 and was reinstated on 7 August, only to be killed seven days later. His place of burial is unknown.

Paramore, Green
Born circa 1845—Died 6 October 1871

There were thirty special policemen assigned as auxiliary officers throughout the state.

Special Policeman Paramore, who was a black man, and another officer named John Lackey went to a general store at Nopal in Gonzales County to arrest the infamous outlaw John Wesley Hardin. Officer Paramore went inside, while Lackey remained by the back door. Paramore told Hardin that he was under arrest and demanded that he hand over his two pistols. Hardin complied. As he began to hand over the guns to Paramore butt first, Hardin did a maneuver known as a "border roll," whirling the pistols around in his hands and firing. Paramore was shot in the head and was killed instantly. Officer Lackey opened fire, but Hardin shot him four times before fleeing. Lackey survived his wounds.

Hardin was never convicted of the murder of Private Paramore. Paramore was survived by his wife and three children. His place of burial is unknown.

Related cases: Brown County Sheriff's Office—Charles M. Webb; DeWitt County Sheriff's Office—Jack Helm; El Paso County Constable's Office—John Selman Sr.; Texas Rangers—Joe McKidrick; Texas State Police—Jim Smalley; and Waco Police Department Laben J. Hoffman.

Grigg, William
Born circa 1842—Died 12 October 1871

Very little information is known about this case. Private Grigg was killed while in a sporting house in Wise County. When the Texas legislature abolished the state police, its records indicated that Grigg had died in the line of duty, a rather curious entry considering the nature of his death.

Private Grigg's killer remains unidentified, and no further facts regarding the incident have come to light. Grigg's place of burial is unknown.

Stewart, John Americas
Born circa 1841—Died 16 May 1872
Date of incident: 15 May 1872

On 22 July 1871, two men named Barnes and Kimble robbed and killed Joseph Philpot. The pair were arrested and held in the Williamson County jail in Georgetown.

On 7 October 1871, Kimble escaped. On 15 May 1872, Texas State Police captain J.M. Redmon, Private Stewart and Travis County special deputy sheriff Day left Cooke County and entered the lands of the Chickasaw nation (present-day Oklahoma) accompanied by five Chickasaw Indians. The group had an arrest warrant for Kimble. They located him, along with his brother and a woman, traveling in a wagon. When the officers attempted to arrest Kimble, a gun battle quickly broke out.

Kimble jumped from the wagon and shot Private Stewart, mortally wounding him. He also shot Deputy Day in both thighs. After firing four or five times, Captain Redmon killed Kimble's brother and wounded two of the friendly Chickasaw Indians. Kimble was arrested. Stewart died the next day from his wounds.

Stewart was married and had two children. He enlisted in the Texas State Police in December 1871 and served only five months. He was elected tax collector of Burnet County in 1865 after serving in Colonel Burford's Regiment, Nineteenth Texas Cavalry, in the Civil War. Stewart is buried with Odd Fellow honors, but the exact location is unknown.

Barnes and Kimble were convicted of the murder of Philpot in October 1871. They were sentenced on 7 March 1873 to be hanged, with that sentence to be carried out on 11 April 1873. The execution was delayed. On 14 April 1873, both Barnes and Kimble were executed by hanging at Austin.

Apparently, no action was brought against Captain Redmon for recklessly wounding the two Chickasaw Indians.

Williams, Thomas G.
Born circa 1845—Died 14 March 1873

Daniels, James M.
Born circa 1826—Died 14 March 1873

Cherry, Wesley
Born circa 1837—Died 14 March 1873

Melville, Andrew
Born circa 1848—Died 10 April 1873
Date of incident: 14 March 1873

On 14 January 1873, Sheriff Shadrack T. Denson of Lampasas County was shot and wounded. When the district judge ordered the arrest of brothers George Washington "Wash" and Marcus "Mark" Short, three Horrell brothers drew pistols on the deputies and allowed the Short brothers to escape. Local authorities asked Governor Davis to send state police officers to maintain order.

Texas State Police captain Williams and seven state policemen were sent to Lampasas on 14 March 1873 to arrest the Horrells. They were also charged with enforcing the new law against carrying a firearm in town. The group of officers saw a man named Bill Bowen carrying a pistol and entering Jerry Scott's saloon. Captain Williams left four state policemen outside and took Privates Daniels, Cherry and Melville with him as he went inside to arrest Bowen. When Williams told Bowen that he was under arrest, Mart Horrell told Bowen that he did not have to submit to arrest. Captain Williams drew his pistol, fired and wounded Mart Horrell. Gunfire erupted from the ten or more men inside the small barroom. Williams and Daniels were killed instantly. Cherry made it outside before being killed. Melville was mortally wounded and ran to a local hotel. Tom Horrell was also wounded in the exchange. The remainder of the Horrell sympathizers came out shooting as the four remaining state policemen (Henry Eddy, Ferdinand Marshal, Sam Wicks and W.W. Wren) fled back to Austin. Melville died on 10 April 1873.

In October 1876, Tom, Mart and Merritt Horrell were acquitted of the killing of the four state policemen. The state failed to produce any witnesses to the shooting, and it was determined that the state policemen had fired first. The jury members reached this verdict without leaving their seats.

Some believe that this incident spoke to the lawlessness and deteriorated state of affairs in Lampasas at the time. Others hasten to point out that Captain Williams, by all accounts, was the one who initiated the gunfight over an arrest for a relatively trivial offense. In addition, he did so in a setting where bitterness was bound to lead to a confrontation. Further, there are reliable reports that Williams had been drinking heavily in the hours preceding the encounter at Lampasas. At the very least, historians are sharply divided about the factual interpretation of this incident.

Williams, Daniels, Cherry and Melville were buried at Oak Hill Cemetery in Lampasas. Melville's grave has a marker, but no grave site or marker has been located for Daniels and Cherry. Williams was reinterred and buried at Texas State Cemetery.

Chapter 6
United States
Customs Service

Hammonds, George T.
Born circa 1842—Died 18 December 1868

Phelps, William H.
Born circa 1849—Died 18 December 1868

On 18 December 1868, at the village of Clarksville near the mouth of the Rio Grande River in Cameron County, a group of bandits from Mexico crossed the river into Texas. The gang of outlaws also included two black men. The bandits seized a citizen and held him captive. Three of the men approached the small customshouse and found Acting Deputy Collector R.R. Ryan standing outside. They spoke to Ryan in Spanish, but he did not understand them. One bandit pointed his pistol at Ryan and began struggling with him until Ryan was knocked unconscious. Next the group of outlaws entered the customshouse and found the night inspector of customs, Phelps, sitting on a cot. Without a word they all fired at him. The men then used knives to mutilate his body. Ryan revived and fled on foot in a hail of gunfire.

The bandits then went to the house of Captain James Selkirk and tried to lure him to the door, but his daughter refused them entry. Mounted Inspector Hammonds heard the gunfire and went to investigate. When he entered Captain Selkirk's house, he learned that they had no guns in the house, so he left to get assistance. In the process of doing so, he was shot in both legs. Hammonds crawled back into the house, but the bandits dragged him outside screaming, "Kill him, kill him!" Hammonds replied, "I am already killed." The already wounded Hammonds was shot and stabbed to death in front of the Selkirk home. After exchanging gunfire with other citizens who had come to aid Hammonds, the bandits fled into Mexico.

Inspector Hammonds was twenty-six years old. He was survived by his wife and one child. Hammonds had just written to his family, who were expected to arrive on the next steamer from New Orleans. Inspector Phelps was only nineteen years old and was reportedly from West Virginia. Customs officers from the United States and Mexico attended the funeral. Both men were buried locally, but the grave sites have not been located.

DuPont, Frank
Born (Unknown)—Died 16 June 1869

Very little is known about this incident. The United States Department of the Treasury reported that on or about 16 June 1869, Inspector Dupont was killed by Mexican smugglers near Brownsville. His body was found in the Rio Grande River. DuPont was the third U.S. customs inspector killed in Texas during the six-month period preceding this incident.

Spalt, John H.
Born circa 1860—Died 6 November 1898

Colorados y Azules ("Reds and Blues") was a color classification system used to designate political parties in south Texas to assist illiterate or Spanish-speaking voters in the use of English language ballots from the 1870s to about 1920. The system was associated with "boss rule."

During the second half of the nineteenth century and the first part of the twentieth, boss rule was a prevalent pattern of political organization in Texas. An exclusive organization of politicians dominated the political life of a city by manipulating the votes of large numbers of immigrants. The bosses resorted to bribery and coercion, but they also won the support of the hard-pressed newcomers by providing informal welfare services and limited opportunities for upward mobility.

Voters were assembled in an open area or business, typically the day before the election. They were often given barbecue and liquor, as well as cash, in exchange for their vote. Such politics in Texas often lead to bloodshed. In Starr County, which is located along the Texas-Mexican border, the "Blues" (Republicans) were challenging the "Reds" (Democrats), who had held power since 1868. W.W. Shely, a former Texas Ranger who had served as sheriff since 1884, was the leader of the Reds. The sheriff deputized more than one hundred special officers to guard the voting places and work for the Democratic ticket. Twenty-five complaints were filed with state and federal authorities, including illegally smuggling mescal (a distilled alcoholic beverage made from the maguey or agave plant that is native to Mexico).

Mounted Customs Inspector Spalt was going to his home after having made a seizure of mescal when he met two men suspected of smuggling. While attempting to search the pair, Fred Marks, special deputy sheriff and Democratic candidate for county clerk, intervened. Spalt was a prominent Blue but apparently was just doing his law enforcement job when Marks shot him twice in the back. The wounds would prove fatal. Marks was arrested and jailed in the guardhouse at Fort Ringgold. Spalt, who knew that he was not going to live, made a dying declaration to Commissioner E.E. Neal. Spalt died at 8:30 p.m. Several days later, Joe Magena, a Red, was shot and killed by a Blue special deputy at an election dance. The disposition of any case against Marks is unknown.

Spalt was reported to have been thirty-eight years old and born in Germany. He also operated a local mill. Spalt was survived by his wife and young daughter. His place of burial is unknown.

Wallace, Richard W. "Dick"
Born circa 1857—Died 30 November 1899

The town of Presidio, a border community in the Big Bend area of the Rio Grande River between Eagle Pass and El Paso, was known as the "Bloody Peninsula."

At about 8:00 p.m., U.S. Customs deputy collector Wallace was killed while he was transporting a prisoner and contraband goods about twenty miles north of Presidio. Four men ambushed Wallace when he passed a dangerous place about two hundred yards from the Rio Grande River near the Spencer Ranch. During the ambush, Wallace was shot and killed. His attackers escaped into Mexico, taking with them the prisoner and contraband goods. Wallace was found lying in a pool of blood a few hours later by Mr. Spencer, who had gone to search for him. He had been shot in the head with a Winchester.

Records indicate that Wallace is buried at the city cemetery in San Antonio, but his grave site has not been located. The newspaper reported that Wallace was a well-known black Republican politician in Presidio County. He had been appointed a deputy customs collector for the Saluria District five months earlier, with headquarters in Presidio.

Wallace holds the distinction of being the last lawman killed in the nineteenth century.

Chapter 7
United States Marshals Service

Council, W.G.
Born circa 1832—Died 26 December 1866

On 26 December 1866, W.G. Council of Navasota in Grimes County was waylaid and shot with a double-barreled shotgun as he passed through the gate and entered the yard of his own home. Twelve or more pellets penetrated his legs above the knees. He died a few hours later.

Council was acting deputy U.S. marshal for the Western District of Texas. At the time of his death, he had in his hands thirty or more writs from the U.S. court in Austin. His neighbors said that he had no enemies and that there was no reason for his murder except his service as a marshal.

Council was born in Virginia. He was survived by his wife and two children. His place of burial is unknown.

Schefsky, C.R.V.
Born circa 1830—Died 7 September 1870

The U.S. marshal for the Western District of Texas was required to hire deputies to assist in the taking of the 1870 Federal Census. Schefsky was appointed as a deputy U.S. marshal to take the census in Bastrop County, where he lived.

Schefsky's buggy was observed near Friskville Road, about four miles from Bastrop. When searchers examined the vehicle, they discovered the body of Schefsky. He had apparently been beaten to death. The census rolls, along with his money and gun, were missing.

It is not known if anyone was ever arrested or charged with the murder. Schefsky was survived by his wife, Johanna. His place of burial is unknown.

Hillebrand, Herman J.
Born 28 February 1842—Died 22 September 1870

In 1790, the United States Congress required the U.S. Marshals Service to take the census every ten years. The position of assistant deputy U.S. marshal was created, in part, to facilitate the census taking. U.S. Marshal Thomas Purnell of the Western District of Texas appointed Hillebrand to perform the census duties in Fayette County.

Newspaper accounts of the day report that Hillebrand sustained an injury to his leg while engaged in taking the census. He died from the injury on 22 September 1870 (although another source shows his date of death as 19 September 1870).

Hillebrand is buried at Hillebrand Cemetery in Fayette County.

Griffin, Frank
Born circa 1849—Died 6 October 1872

Brothers Thomas and James Flynn were wanted for a series of post office robberies in the vicinity of Galveston.

On 6 October 1872, U.S. Marshal Thomas Purnell and a posse that included Deputy Marshal Griffin went to arrest the two men. The lawmen knocked on the door and announced themselves. As Griffin entered the house, he was hit with sixteen pellets from a shotgun blast. He died within minutes. Purnell and the posse opened fire, and a gun battle took place. Purnell ordered the house set on fire. As anticipated, the blaze caused the Flynn brothers to surrender.

There is no record of the Flynn brothers ever being tried for the murder. Marshal Griffin was buried the next day in Galveston.

Knight, Charles J.
Born (Unknown)—Died 25 April 1873

On 22 July 1872, indictments were issued in Bastrop County under the Ku Klux law against a group of desperadoes (the Ku Klux Klan Act of April

1871 permitted the president of the United States to suspend the writ of habeas corpus in cases of secret conspiracy). Grand jurors and witnesses had reportedly been threatened. One witness was shot and killed. U.S. Marshal Thomas Purnell of the Western District of Texas had sent his son, along with Tom Williams and Mr. Platt, to execute the writs.

Deputy Marshal Knight worked under Marshal Purnell and was serving warrants when he mysteriously disappeared. The U.S. attorney general's office stated that Knight was assassinated in Bastrop County, where he was seeking to arrest Ku Klux Klan members who were killing blacks.

Nothing further is known about the case.

Greene, Maston Reynolds "Boss"
Born 14 October 1843—Died 12 May 1877

Greene was the city marshal at Comanche and a Texas Ranger captain before being appointed a deputy U.S. marshal under Thomas Purnell of the Western District of Texas.

On 12 May 1877, Deputy Marshal Greene and a man named Hill left Comanche in pursuit of two brothers, Dee and James Bailey, who were counterfeiters "pushing the queer" around the town. Greene caught up with the Bailey brothers and arrested them. Dee Bailey tossed over the saddlebags containing the counterfeit money—about ten dollars worth. Jim Bailey, still mounted, gave his pistol to Mr. Hill. Greene had failed to notice the Winchester rifle belonging to Dee Bailey that was still in Dee's saddle scabbard.

Greene's horse flared, and Dee Bailey pulled the Winchester rifle from the scabbard. Greene fired once from his Colt revolver, grazing Dee Bailey in the head and dislodging a lock of hair and hide. Dee Bailey fired twice from his Winchester, hitting Greene in the lower jaw on his second shot. The first shot had gone wild and missed its mark. The .44-caliber bullet traveled upward into Greene's cheekbone. As Greene fell from the horse, Dee Bailey shot him again, this time in the foot. The Bailey brothers made good their escape.

Mr. Hill fled without making any attempt to aid Marshal Greene. Greene crawled to a nearby house and died at 7:30 p.m. that evening. He is buried at Oakwood Cemetery in Comanche.

The Bailey brothers were eventually captured and incarcerated. On 19 September 1883, they appeared in the District Court of Comanche and were granted bail. A mob of angry citizens from Comanche took the two Bailey brothers from jail and lynched them from a post oak tree.

On 6 March 1884, the state dismissed the case against the Bailey brothers, citing that the two men were already "deceased."

Anderson, William H.
Born circa 1840—Died 8 November 1878

William Collins was a member of the Sam Bass Gang that robbed the train at Mesquite in Dallas County on 10 April 1878. Collins was arrested later that month and posted bond. He fled Texas, and a bench warrant was issued.

Anderson was appointed a deputy U.S. marshal in 1872 and was assigned to the Western District of Texas. He tracked Collins to Pembina, North Dakota. While staking out the post office, Collins entered. Anderson ordered Collins to surrender. A struggle occurred during which Anderson shot Collins through the hand and in his shoulder. Collins returned fire, with his second shot hitting Anderson in the chest. Both men died at the scene.

Anderson was survived by his wife and two children. He is buried at Greenwood Cemetery in Dallas.

Crowell, Lorenzo C.
Born circa 1858—Died 10 January 1879

Crowell was elected sheriff of Kinney County on 23 June 1875 and reelected on 15 February 1876. He served until 5 November 1878, when Stillwell Russell, the U.S. marshal for the Western District of Texas, appointed him a deputy U.S. marshal. During the course of his duties as a deputy marshal, Crowell contracted smallpox. Even though he was extremely sick, he continued to help other victims of the disease.

On 10 January 1879, Crowell died of the illness. Contemporary newspapers reported that "while in the strict performance of his duty Crowell contracted a fatal case of smallpox, resulting in his untimely end."

Crowell was originally from Maine and moved to Fort Clark, Texas, after the Civil War. He was survived by his wife and two young children. Crowell is buried at the Ballantyne family cemetery at Brackettville in Kinney County.

Wright, Buck
Born circa 1860—Died 8 November 1884

Deputy Marshal Wright was killed under perhaps the most unusual circumstances imaginable. While at a celebration of the election in Luling in Caldwell County, an anvil exploded, showering the crowd with heavy metal fragments. A piece of the exploded anvil was propelled through a saloon window about twenty yards away and struck Deputy Marshal Wright, killing him. Another young man in the same saloon was so severely injured by another fragment from the exploding anvil that newspaper accounts of the day claimed that he was not expected to live.

For the benefit of the uninformed, anvil shooting (or firing) is the sport of placing a charge of gunpowder under a large anvil and seeing how far into the air one can launch the heavy object. The sport was popular during the late 1800s and was frequently practiced at celebrations such as the Fourth of July. Although not confined to the state of Texas, this unusual and somewhat bizarre form of entertainment was, and still is, widespread among Texans.

Gosling, Harrington Lee "Hal"
Born 2 June 1851—Died 21 February 1885

Gosling was appointed the U.S. marshal for the Western District of Texas on 22 May 1882. Two outlaws, Charles Yeager and James Pitts, were arrested for robbing post offices and other crimes. They were tried, convicted and sentenced to life in prison at a trial in the U.S. District Court in Austin. Family and friends conspired to free them on the train back to the jail in San Antonio. The conspirators agreed in advance that they had to kill Marshal Gosling.

The prisoners were handcuffed together and were seated facing each other at the window. James Pitts's eighteen-year-old wife and Yeager's sister were allowed to sit next to them on the train. Marshal Gosling was warned of an escape attempt but imprudently took no special precautions. Only Deputies John Manning and Fred Loring accompanied him. A number of family and friends had also boarded the train, including Pitts's grandmother.

At a point about four miles from New Braunfels, one or both of the women handed the prisoners each a pistol. Pitts ordered the officers to surrender. Marshal Gosling was hindered in drawing his own weapon by the fact that he was wearing his pistol in a shoulder holster under his vest.

Gunfire broke out in the cramped boundaries of the railroad car. Pitts shot Gosling behind the left ear, and Yeager shot him in the back. Gosling collapsed on Manning, who was then himself shot twice. The injured Manning rose and shot Pitts twice. The conductor then opened fire, shooting and killing the wounded Pitts's grandmother. Deputy Loring opened fire. He wounded Yeager's sister and shot Yeager twice as he and Pitts jumped from the train and fled. Pitts died from four wounds, and Yeager was arrested later by a posse. One can only imagine the mayhem in the smoke-filled confines of that railroad car with bullets flying in every direction. It seems that the only person who escaped injury that day was the conductor.

Charles Yeager and the conspirators were never convicted of the murder of Marshal Gosling. Yeager was sent to federal prison in Illinois on the original conviction. He was pardoned on 25 December 1903 after eighteen years in prison.

Marshal Gosling is buried at the Knights of Pythias cemetery in San Antonio. He was survived by his wife and two small sons.

Rhodes, Frank
Born circa 1851—Died 11 April 1885

Will Jacobs's father, Andrew, was sheriff of Goliad County. He was killed in the line of duty on 5 June 1869. Jacobs and his cousin, Alfred Allee, killed a man in 1877 but were acquitted. Jacobs was next involved in the killing Guadalupe County deputy sheriff Richard "Tex" McCoy on 16 May 1881.

Deputy Marshal Rhodes and Allee became involved in a dispute over stolen cattle and altered brands. The men had a close relationship before the dispute. Rhodes eventually pistol-whipped Allee, who threatened to get even. On 11 April 1885, Rhodes crossed paths with Jacobs and Allee at Gabe Hans's saloon in Pearsall in Frio County. The encounter proved fatal, as the two cousins shot and killed Rhodes.

Both men were charged with murder. Allee stood trial and was acquitted. Jacobs became a fugitive. A Milam County posse attempted to arrest Jacobs on 7 April 1887. Deputy Sheriff Gabriel Leander "Lee" Pool was killed. Jacobs was indicted for the murder of Pool. Jacobs was arrested in Frio County on 24 September 1888. He was released on bond.

Will Jacobs was tried and found guilty in Milam County of a lesser charge and sentenced to ten years in prison. He was released on 18 March 1897 and faced numerous charges over the murder of Deputy McCoy.

Related cases: Goliad County Sheriff's Office—Andrew J. Jacobs; Guadalupe County Sheriff's Office—Richard "Tex" McCoy; and Milam County Sheriff's Office—Gabriel Leander "Lee" Pool.

Niggli, Ferdinand "Fred"
Born January 1849—Died 31 August 1885
Date of incident: 25 August 1885

Niggli was elected sheriff of Medina County on 15 February 1876 and was reelected on 5 November 1878 and again on 2 November 1880. He served until June 1882, when he resigned to accept appointment as a deputy U.S. marshal for the Western District of Texas.

On 25 August 1885, Deputy Marshal Niggli was attending the "St. Louis Day" celebrations at Castroville in Medina County when he became intoxicated. When Sheriff Thumm attempted to speak to him, Niggli pointed his pistol at the sheriff.

Later that night, the sheriff and a deputy returned to find a sobered-up Niggli sitting in a chair and smoking a cigar. As Thumm approached, Niggli rose from his chair. Apparently out of retaliation for the fact that Niggli had pointed a gun at him earlier in the day, Thumm opened fire at Niggli. One shot entered his left arm, passed through his shoulder and into his neck. The wound was fatal, and Niggli died on 31 August.

Thumm was arrested and released on bond. While still under charges, he ran again for sheriff and was reelected. Thumm finally went to trial and, on 27 March 1887, was acquitted. He later killed a man inside the county courthouse. On that occasion, he was convicted and sentenced to twenty-five years but was pardoned after serving fifteen years.

Marshal Niggli is buried at Lutheran Cemetery in San Antonio.

Bryant, Vince Morgan "Vint"
Born circa 1852—Died 30 March 1886

On 30 March 1886, at about 5:00 p.m., J.D. Hodges, Frank and Vint Bryant and Bob Richardson, proprietors of the Rock Saloon in Ranger, were engaged in a shootout. Richardson was killed instantly, and both Frank and Vint Bryant were mortally wounded. Vint Bryant was a deputy marshal under U.S. Marshal Cabell of the Northern District of Texas. The affray grew out of an argument over an old debt.

Bryant appears to have been a widower and had three children. His place of burial is unknown.

Carleton, John
Born circa 1837—Died 5 November 1887

Deputy Marshal Carleton of the Western District of Arkansas and three possemen were serving warrants in the southern part of the Indian Territory.

They decided to serve one more warrant in Denison, Texas, before returning to Fort Smith, Arkansas. The lawmen were searching for John Hogan, who was wanted for selling whiskey in the Indian Territory. Carlton and Deputy Lawrence spotted Hogan at a woman's house. When Carlton entered the dwelling and announced that he was a federal officer, Hogan shot him in the side. He died at 6:30 p.m. after telling doctors to relay to his wife that "he died happy."

On 6 November, lawmen in Fort Worth located Hogan hiding in a railroad car and arrested him. Hogan was convicted and sentenced to life in prison.

Carleton's body was shipped to Hackett, Arkansas, for burial.

Criswell, Sam
Born circa 1854—Died 19 January 1889

Criswell worked as a posseman for Deputy U.S. Marshal Ed W. Johnson of the Northern District of Texas. In February 1888, Johnson was lodging in Wichita Falls when he got into an argument with a cowboy that ended with him killing the man. Johnson was wounded and had his right arm amputated. Fortunately, he was able to return to work afterward.

On 25 August 1888, Marshal Johnson and a posse consisting of Sam Criswell and Dink Allen traveled into the Indian Territory in pursuit of some horse thieves. The lawmen caught up with their quarry and arrested Boone Marlow and Lewellyn "Epp" Marlow. They later picked up Charles and Alf Marlow in Fort Sill. George Marlow was soon captured and brought to Graham in Young County for trial. All of the brothers were released on bail.

On 17 December, Young County sheriff Marion Wallace received a warrant for the arrest of Boone Marlow for the murder of a man named James Holdson. Holdson had killed a man in Wilbarger County. Sheriff Wallace and Deputy Thomas B. Collier headed out to the Marlow place to arrest Boone.

Boone resisted and shot Sheriff Wallace in the hip and Deputy Collier in the head. Collier's wound was superficial. He managed to arrest George, Charles and Alf Marlow and transport them to county jail. Boone Marlow got away. Sheriff Wallace's wounds were fatal, and he died on 24 December.

The Marlow brothers escaped custody but were soon recaptured. After several attempts were made to break them out of jail, the U.S. marshal decided to transport them to a more secure facility at Weatherford in Parker County. Deputy Marshal Johnson formed a seven-man posse that included Sam Criswell to transport the prisoners using two wagons. While en route, the posse was ambushed just outside the town of Graham. Sam Criswell, Alf Marlow and Epp Marlow were killed. Two members of the mob who ambushed them were also killed. George and Charles Marlow escaped but were later arrested. Boone Marlow was killed resisting arrest in the Indian Territory.

Related case: Young County Sheriff's Office—Marion Wallace.

Pitts, William
Born (Unknown)—Died 30 November 1890

Pitts was a deputy U.S. marshal for the Eastern District of Texas, which included the southern part of the Indian Territory.

Pitts received information that three Indians were smuggling liquor into the Indian Territory from Texas. He set up surveillance and stopped a wagon being driven by three men who identified themselves as Isam Frazier, Lige Woods and Jim Allen. When Pitts said that he suspected them of liquor smuggling and began to search the wagon, a confrontation took place. Pitts's pistol was ripped from his holster, and he was shot in the stomach with his own gun. He died within minutes.

Allen and Wood were acquitted of the shooting. Frazier was convicted of manslaughter and sentenced to a long prison term.

Wise, George
Born circa 1860—Died 30 October 1891

Garcia, Calixto
Born circa 1873-1876—Died 30 October 1891

Deputy Marshal Wise of the Western District of Texas was stationed at Laredo in Webb County. He was advised that a smuggler named Francisco Flores would pass at a certain place with a shipment of illegal goods from Mexico.

At about 2:00 a.m. on 30 October 1891, Wise appointed Calixto Garcia and Fernando Salazer to assist him and stationed the men at different points near a house one block northeast of School House Plaza. At 4:30 a.m., Flores leisurely approached the house from the direction of the plaza. Wise drew his pistol and ordered him to stop. Flores stated, "I will." He stopped and laid down his bundles of goods. However, upon rising, he stabbed Wise in the stomach with a large dagger. Wise managed to fire two shots at Flores. He then called out to Garcia that he was killed and told Garcia to catch his murderer. Wise staggered toward Salazer and said, "Help me, I am wounded."

Garcia gave chase, and as he closed the distance, Flores stabbed him as well. The blade on the dagger entered his chest about one inch below the left nipple. Garcia died instantly. Garcia's body was carried to his home.

Wise was conscious until he died about 8:00 a.m. that same morning. Flores, a naturalized U.S. citizen and a native of Nuevo Laredo, Mexico, fled into Mexico. The bundles were found to contain ten gallons of mescal (a distilled alcoholic beverage made from the maguey plant that is a form of agave).

Wise was survived by his wife and two children. Over time, a building was constructed on the site of his burial in Laredo. Wise was one of the first members of the Laredo Fire Department in April 1883. He was a Laredo city policeman as of May 1890 and a Webb County deputy sheriff as of November 1890.

Very little is known about Calixto Garcia. He was reportedly survived by his wife and three children. A newspaper account of the day claimed that Garcia had recently been married and was from one of the city's oldest families. Garcia is buried locally, but the location is unknown.

Glover, Rufus B.
Born circa 1856—Died 31 January 1892

In September 1891, Catarino Garza formed a small army in south Texas called the *Garzistas*. Their purpose was to overthrow Mexican president Porfirio Díaz. Garza made three unsuccessful attempts to invade Mexico, which caused President Díaz to complain to the U.S. authorities that they were not enforcing neutrality laws. Texas Ranger companies joined the Third Cavalry of the U.S. Army under the command of Captain George Chase in pursuit of Garza and his revolutionaries along the Texas-Mexico border. Captain Chase sent three deputy U.S. marshals—Lino Cuellar, Juan Moreno and Rufus Glover—to scout ahead of his troops.

Near dusk on 31 January 1892, the three deputy marshals were ambushed at Soledad Wells, which is located on William Hubbard's ranch near Benavides about twenty-five miles from San Diego in Duval County. Glover was shot in the back and fell dead from his horse. The two other deputy marshals escaped. Glover's brother, the marshals and U.S. troops went to the scene to recover his body and found a pile of spent cartridges behind a ledge of rocks near where Glover had fallen.

On 23 February 1893, about thirty-five miles from Rio Grande City, Starr County sheriff W.W. Shely and ranger lieutenant Lowe attempted to arrest Ensiblo M. Martinez (with the curious alias, Mangas De Aqua, "sleeves of water") for the murder of Glover. He resisted arrest and was shot and killed. When the officers examined his body, Martinez was found to be wearing Marshal Glover's leggings.

Glover had been elected three times as the district and county clerk of Duval County, Texas. He is buried in Duval County. Glover was survived by his wife, one child and a brother.

Related case: Texas Rangers—Robert E. Doaty.

Smith, Thomas Calton "Tom"
Born 27 September 1846—Died 4 November 1892

Thomas Smith's father was the sheriff of Fort Bend County from 1852 to 1856. Tom Smith later served as a Fort Bend County deputy sheriff and was involved in the Jaybird-Woodpecker War in which Sheriff J.T. Garvey and others were killed in a conflict on 16 August 1889. Smith also served as the city marshal of Taylor, a deputy U.S. marshal for the Western District of Arkansas and a cattle detective involved in the Johnson County War in New Mexico. He returned to Texas in 1892 and became a deputy U.S. marshal for the Eastern District of Texas, operating out of Paris. His territory covered Texas and southern part of the Indian Territory.

Smith, along with Deputy Marshals Booker and Tucker, left Gainesville for the lands of the Chickasaw nation in the Indian Territory. The three lawmen boarded a northbound Santa Fe train. About 11:00 p.m., when they were just inside Indian Territory, the three deputy marshals entered a passenger car that was reserved for black men and women while on their way to the smoking car. One of the black passengers took offense at white men in their sleeping car and pulled a pistol, shooting Smith through the heart, killing him. Deputies Booker and Tucker pulled their pistols and killed the assailant.

It was reported that the killer was Commodore Miller, who was wanted in Dallas County and was in the process of escaping to the Indian Territory.

Smith was survived by his wife, Sallie, and their four children. He is buried at Taylor Cemetery.

Outlaw, Bazel Lamar "Baz"
Born circa 1857—Died 5 April 1894

Much has been written about the notorious Baz Outlaw. Interested readers should consult the bibliography section for information on books containing more detailed information about the life of this controversial lawman.

Numerous accounts refer to Outlaw's given name as "Bass," but most believe that his first name was Bazel or Bazzell. More recently, historians contend that his given name was simply Baz. For purposes of this condensed biographical sketch, the name "Baz" has been used.

Baz Outlaw became a Texas Ranger on 11 August 1885, enlisting in Company E at Toyah. Records indicate that he was working as a special agent as early as February 1884. He was promoted to a sergeant, but when he was discovered drunk on duty at Alpine, he resigned on 18 September 1892. Outlaw later obtained an appointment as a deputy U.S. marshal under U.S. Marshal Dick Ware on 26 January 1893 but was continually reprimanded for drinking.

On 5 April 1894, when Outlaw was in El Paso, he got drunk and fired a shot into Tillie Howard's sporting house. When challenged by Constable John Selman Sr. and Texas Ranger Joe McKidrick, Outlaw shot McKidrick in the head. He then shot at Selman, missing but almost blinding the constable. Selman quickly returned fire and shot Outlaw in the chest. Outlaw fired two more times and seriously wounded Selman. Outlaw was led to a nearby saloon, where he died four hours later.

Baz Outlaw is buried at Evergreen Cemetery in El Paso.

Related cases: El Paso County Constable's Office—John Selman; Texas Rangers—Joe McKidrick.

McHenry, John
Born (Unknown)—Died 26 December 1895

Lem Young was wanted on several charges, including assault with intent to kill and a lesser charge of theft of hogs.

Deputy U.S. Marshal C.R.V. Hamilton and posseman John Slaughter pursued Young and captured him in the lands of the Choctaw nation near Caddo in the Indian Territory. Hamilton and Slaughter were taking the prisoner to Atoka but, due to high water, had to spend the night at a cabin. Deputy U.S. Marshal McHenry gathered a posse and went to the shack to serve Young with a warrant. McHenry and Hamilton became involved in an argument that eventually escalated into a gun battle. McHenry and Young were both killed.

Hamilton and Slaughter were charged with the murder of McHenry and released on bond. Opinions differed as to who was at fault. The two deputy marshals had a history of ill feelings between them. The disposition of the case against Hamilton and Slaughter is unknown.

Rankin, John T.
Born circa 1853—Died 27 November 1897

On 27 November 1897, at about 1:00 p.m., Austin policeman James "Jim" Grizzard heard that former U.S. marshal Rankin was hunting for him. When he saw Rankin walking toward him and hesitate, Grizzard drew his pistol and fired. Grizzard alleged that Rankin tried to draw his gun first.

Grizzard fired four times, with the final shot killing Rankin. A doctor examined Rankin's body afterward and said that three, or perhaps all four, of the shots were fired from the rear.

The trouble between the two men was said to have stemmed from a political difference. Rankin was involved in the forthcoming municipal elections. Grizzard denied the existence of any strife between the two men. An examining trial reported that Rankin was unarmed and that the pistol found on him had been placed there after the shooting. The final disposition of the case against Grizzard is unknown.

Rankin was elected sheriff of Fayette County on 7 November 1882 and reelected on 4 November 1884. He served until 17 June 1886, when he resigned. He was survived by his wife and a twenty-year-old son. Rankin is buried at Oakwood Cemetery in Austin.

Chapter 8
Unidentified
Lawmen

CUERO POLICE DEPARTMENT

Unknown Man
Born (Unknown)—Died 1886

The *Dallas Morning News* of 5 April 1891 reported that Sim McGrue was arrested for the murder of a deputy city marshal in Cuero in 1886. No other information has been uncovered about this case at this time.

MAVERICK COUNTY SHERIFF'S OFFICE

Unknown Posseman
Born (Unknown)—Died 2 August 1880

On 1 August 1880, five of the prisoners confined in the county jail overpowered the jailer and made their escape, taking with them several pistols belonging to the guard. Information was received by Sheriff H.J. Yarrington as to the whereabouts of the escapees. He summoned five men to assist in making the arrest and proceeded to where the men were said to be hiding.

Early in the morning on 2 August, while trailing the prisoners through a dense cane thicket, the party of lawmen was suddenly fired upon. One of the possemen, whose identity is unknown, was killed. The person doing the shooting was not seen, but the sheriff and posse fired a volley in the direction from which the shots had been fired. It is not known if anyone was hit in the return fire.

The attention of the posse was called to one of the men, who had jumped into the river and was trying to escape to the other side. Numerous shots were fired at the man while he was still in the water. He finally held up his hands and surrendered. While the posse was heading back to the cane thicket to recover the body of the man killed in the skirmish, they unexpectedly came across a wounded prisoner. When he was discovered, the man was sitting in the thicket with a pistol in his hand and trying to shoot at them. He was shot and killed instantly.

Three of the prisoners succeeded in making good their escapes. One was a black man named Rollins, charged with murder. The others prisoners were Mexicans who were charged with smuggling.

TRINITY COUNTY SHERIFF'S OFFICE

Unknown Deputy
Born (Unknown)—Died 10 March 1874

On 10 March 1877, two men from Louisiana swore out warrants for horse theft against Amos Walker. Walker was an alleged accomplice with his brother in the murder of Green Butler in Galveston County on 19 May 1872.

An unnamed deputy was sent out with a posse of eight men to make the arrest. The posse surrounded the house, and the deputy advanced. Walker opened fire and killed the lawman. The posse members returned fire and believed that they had killed Walker. They had not, and Walker fled the house and escaped.

Although there are no fewer than fifty newspaper articles about this incident and the associated trials, none of the accounts of either the *Galveston Daily News* or the *Dallas Morning News* ever mentions the deputy's name.

TEXAS RANGERS

Unknown, "Paddy"
Born (Unknown)—Died 1 April 1844

A ranger private identified only as "Paddy" was reported to have died on 1 April 1844 at Nueces Canyon. He was under the command of Captain

Unidentified Lawmen

John C. "Jack" Hays's Frontier Ranging Company, Corps of Rangers. The company was organized on 25 February and served until 25 April 1844.

Four Unknown Rangers
Born (Unknown)—Died June 1844

Reports indicate that four rangers (names unknown) were killed fighting Indians near Corpus Christi.

Unknown Ranger
Born (Unknown)—Died 25 January 1851

On 19 January 1851, Lieutenant Andrew J. Walker of Captain Ford's company took nineteen rangers to scout the Arroyo Gato (Cat Creek) north of Laredo. They found a cache of supplies and horses thought to have been left by Comanche Indians raiding into Mexico.

On 25 January, the rangers saw seventeen Comanches returning with stolen horses and goods and decided to attack. In the fierce hand-to-hand combat, one ranger (name unknown) was reported to have been killed and one was wounded. The Comanches left four dead on the field. One captive Mexican boy was returned to his parents.

Unnamed Waco Indian
Born (Unknown)—Died 12 May 1858

On 12 May 1858, an engagement that later became known as "the Battle of Antelope Hills" (also known as the Canadian River Campaign) involved Captain Ford and a force of more than one hundred rangers. Indian Agent and Captain Shapley P. Ross and his force of more than one hundred friendly Indians from the Brazos Reservation accompanied Ford's men.

Captain Ford reported that an unnamed Waco Indian was killed during the battle. He also reported seventy-six Comanches killed and many wounded.

The Waco Indian's name and place of burial remain a mystery.

Unknown Ranger
Born (Unknown)—Died 19 July 1863

An unknown Texas Ranger assigned to the Forty-sixth Texas Frontier Cavalry Regiment was killed fighting Comanches on the Clear Fork of the Brazos River.

Unknown Ranger
Born (Unknown)—Died 24 July 1863

On 24 July 1863, rangers under Captain M.B. Lloyd of Company E of the Frontier Regiment left camp Cooper with fourteen men. They traveled up the Clear Fork of the Brazos River, where they confronted a party of Comanche Indians. An unnamed ranger was killed in the fighting, and four rangers were wounded.

Four Unknown Rangers
Born (Unknown)—Died 23 December 1863

In what historians would later label "the Cooke County Raid," more than three hundred Comanche Indians crossed the Red River from the Indian Territory into Texas on 21 December 1863. The band was on a stealing and killing spree.

On 23 December, two ranger companies composed of about fifty-five men under Captains John T. Rowland of the Frontier Regiment and Captain Samuel P. Patton of the Border Regiment confronted the Comanche war party near Potter's Settlement. The rangers charged, but their efforts proved to be unsuccessful. Four unnamed rangers from Company G under the command of Captain Rowland were killed. Fifteen settlers were also killed, and several more were taken captive.

TEXAS PENITENTIARY SYSTEM

Unknown Guard
Born (Unknown)—Died March 1882

Newspaper accounts of the day claimed that convicts killed a guard on a train near Big Spring. Texas Rangers reportedly killed two of the escapees and captured two others.

Unidentified Lawmen

Unknown Guard
Born (Unknown)—Died 6 July 1885

According to newspaper reports of the day, an accident of some sort occurred on a convict train in Hays County. An unnamed guard was killed by an escaping convict. The convict was recaptured.

Unknown Guard
Born (Unknown)—Died July 1887

According to newspaper reports of the day, an unnamed guard was killed by escaping convicts in Columbus.

Texas State Police

Unnamed Posseman
Born (Unknown)—Died 9 July 1871

On 8 July 1871, Charles Smith of Guadalupe County waylaid and killed Fayette Durham. The following day, he shot and killed Turner Youngman.

Texas state special policeman Peter Haynes, a black man, organized a six-man posse to arrest Charles Smith at the home of James Smith. James Smith refused to surrender the suspect and opened fire on the posse. One unnamed posseman was killed outright. The posse returned fire, killing James Smith. Charles Smith fled to Seguin and obtained a writ to arrest the policemen and his posse on the grounds that they had no warrant for his arrest.

The newspaper noted that Smith killed three men but was able to get a writ to arrest the policeman and the posse. It is likely that the unnamed state police posseman was a black man.

Appendix

Memorials

The criteria for inclusion on the national, state, sheriff's and various local memorials vary. Some names may be enrolled on one or more of the memorials and not on others. Some of the cases listed in this book have not yet been thoroughly researched or may lack sufficient information to be included at this time. Others cases may qualify for inclusion on one or more of the memorials in the future.

A notation of "On File" means that the case has been submitted to the memorial for action but that no action has been taken as yet. "Ineligible" means that, for some reason, the memorial has not accepted the lawman's case. A "Deferred" notation means that the memorial has considered the case but that it has been held because it does not meet that memorial's criteria.

NATIONAL LAW ENFORCEMENT OFFICERS MEMORIAL (N)

The National Law Enforcement Officers Memorial Foundation, Inc., manages the national memorial in Washington, D.C. NLEOMF does not accept cases from Texas during the republic period (before statehood in 1846). The names of the fallen officers are engraved on the memorial walls each year, for the most part in random order. To help visitors find the names of specific officers, directories are placed at each of the four entrance points. The directory lists names in alphabetical order, by state or by federal and U.S. territory agencies. Each name is associated with a panel and line number. Panels on the west are marked (W) and the east are marked (E). The walls are numbered from one to sixty-four. The panel number is engraved at the bottom of each panel. Line one is at the top of each panel, so one must count down to locate the line you are looking for. For example, Panel 20-W, Line 16 refers to the sixteenth line from the top on the twentieth panel of the west wall.

TEXAS PEACE OFFICERS MEMORIAL (T)

The Texas Commission on Law Enforcement Officer Standards and Education (TCLEOSE) manages the state memorial, which is located at the state capitol in Austin. The location identifier system works as follows. The first number indicates the column number, the letter indicates the row and the last number indicates the line. For example, location 07, C, 12 means Column 7, Row C and Line 12. When facing the memorial, the north elevation is on the left of the center columns, and the south to the right.

LOST LAWMAN MEMORIAL (S)

The Sheriff's Association of Texas manages the Lost Lawman Memorial, located at its office at 1601 South IH 35 in Austin, Texas. The location identifier system is similar to that of the Texas Peace Officers Memorial. The letter indicates the column, and the last number indicates the line. For example, location 3, A, 2 would be Panel 3, Column A and Line 2.

A	National	Texas	Sheriff's
Adair, John W.B.	24-E: 24	05, D, 18	11, B, 16
Adams, John A.	16-E: 23	36, D, 01	--
Adams, John H.	37-E: 24	07, D, 14	--
Ahlers, Louis W.	42-W: 24	09, D, 11	--
Albright, William	57-E: 25	19, A, 07	--
Anderson, Columbus C.	26-W: 2	15, A, 10	--
Anderson, William H.	26-W: 2	15, A, 10	--
Anglin, William B.	2-E: 26	17, D, 16	--
Archer, Jack B.	48-W: 26	28, A, 05	--
Ayers, Kirkland C.	2-E: 25	19, A, 15	--

Memorials

B	National	Texas	Sheriff's
Bailey, David W.H.	19-E: 26	4, D, 18	--
Bailey, John M.	58-W: 27	11, D, 08	0, C, 09
Ball, Samuel D.	53-W: 22	38, B, 11	--
Barbee, William B.M.	19-W: 27	25, A, 17	--
Barfield, Jackson T.	9-W: 26	25, A, 04	--
Barton, Samuel Baker	On File	12, A, 13	--
Batts, Charlie A.	40-W: 25	13, D, 12	0, B, 05
Bell, Charles	40-W: 9	38, D, 07	--
Bell, General	On File	6, A, 14	--
Biediger, Lorenzo	55-E: 26	19, A, 13	--
Bingham, George R.	18-E: 26	20, D, 14	--
Binnion, Joe	On File	One File	On File
Bird, John	Ineligible	24, D, 11	--
Birdwell, John	On File	19, D, 18	--
Black, James H.	62-W: 22	02, C, 11	Ineligible
Blair, Jesse	Ineligible	19, D, 11	--
Blakey, Edmund J.	Ineligible	20, D, 05	--
Blankenship, Burwell J.	32-E: 23	36, D, 05	1, B, 01
Bohanon, William M.	31-E: 26	14, A, 01	--
Bostwick, Alexander	Ineligible	19, A, 03	--
Bowers, John	42-W: 27	24, A, 12	On File
Breaux, Oscar J.	On File	13, A, 15	--
Breeland, Samuel S.	42-W: 24	32, D, 03	--
Brewer, C.O.	26-W: 17	29, C, 02	--
Brigham, Joe	22-E: 43	32, B, 07	10, B, 12
Brito, Santiago A.	34-E: 26	15, B, 19	11, B, 17
Broaddus, Robert L.	57-E: 25	20, D, 13	0, C, 14
Brooks, John M.B.	On File	23, A, 02	--
Brooks, W. Clarence	49-W: 27	On File	On File
Browne, Matthew L.	46-E: 25	05, D, 07	12, A, 05
Bryant, Charles G.	On File	On File	--
Buchanan, Joseph R.	62-W: 2	38, C, 09	2, B, 05
Bullard, Joseph C.R.	34-W: 24	34, D, 01	--
Bullock, Julius	Ineligible	30, C, 18	--
Burch, James	On File	One File	--
Burleson, Jacob Shipman	Ineligible	24, D, 13	--
Burnett, W. Riley	24-W: 21	16, C, 05	--
Busby, Nathan	11-W: 24	15, A, 03	--
Butler, James Monroe	54-W: 25	17, B, 14	--

C	National	Texas	Sheriff's
Cain, Charlie D.	On File	17, A, 14	On File
Camp, William H.	49-E: 26	20, D, 12	On File
Campbell, John B.	On File	On File	On File
Campion, Joseph A.	On File	On File	--
Carleton, John	13-E: 13	12, A, 04	--
Carpenter, John W.	Ineligible	19, A, 04	--
Cherry, Wesley	34-W: 18	11, D, 19	--
Christian, James	Ineligible	22, D, 14	--
Clark, Alvin A.	On File	21, A, 13	--
Clark, David	Ineligible	26, A, 12	--
Clark, William A.	59-E: 25	19, D, 16	--
Clendennen, Robert Ned	46-W: 24	09, D, 09	11, A, 12
Clopton, William H.	On File	20, A, 16	--
Coberly, Floyd	15-E: 25	05, D, 04	11, B, 05
Coghlan, Jasper N.	37-E: 25	19, B, 11	0, D, 03
Coleman, Reuben D.	31-W: 22	01, B, 01	2, B, 06
Coleman, Robert R.	On File	On File	On File
Collins, Walter	16-W: 26	12, A, 02	On File
Conley, Robert M.	10-E: 24	32, D, 19	11, B, 06
Cooper, Joseph	Ineligible	22, D, 03	--
Courts, Carl F.	60-E: 25	28, D, 18	0, A, 03
Cox, Harvey Staten	60-E: 1	33, C, 02	5, A, 14
Craig, T.C.	11-W: 27	On File	--
Crowell, Lorenzo C.	On File	24, A, 05	--

D	National	Texas	Sheriff's
Daniels, James M.	27-E: 18	19, B, 13	--
Daugherty, John Quincy	21-W: 19	24, B, 16	11, A, 09
Davis, Henry Clay	59-W: 22	38, C, 06	2, B, 09
Day, John Sherman	23-W: 8	03, D, 07	--
Day, Rufus H.	53-E: 26	13, A, 11	0, D, 08
Deaton, Thomas J.	7-W: 22	03, C, 11	2, B, 08
DeLeon, Simon L.	52-W: 27	15, A, 01	On File
DeLisle, Leonard C.	38-E: 26	17, A, 15	On File
Deputy, Samuel L.	On File	26, D, 18	0, A, 14
Dickson, Hamilton Bass	22-E: 47	34, B, 18	6, B, 03
Doaty, Robert E.	3-E: 26	14, A, 07	--
Doolittle, George M.	34-W: 26	22, A, 17	0, C, 11

	National	Texas	Sheriff's
Drinkard, Levi L.	39-E: 24	07, D, 11	11, A, 15
Dunn, Morris T.	34-W: 23	28, B, 18	--
E	National	Texas	Sheriff's
Eanes, Charles R.	On File	32, B, 05	--
Earbee, William	On File	21, A, 14	--
Elder, Isham Lafayette	61-W: 27	32, D, 14	7, A, 11
Elder, James J.	49-W: 27	07, D, 05	0, D, 04
Elsberry, John Luckie	44-W: 27	On File	--
Epperson, Joe	36-W: 25	17, A, 11	--
F	National	Texas	Sheriff's
Fahey, Cornelius L.	49-E: 21	12, C, 18	--
Farmer, James P.	23-W: 2	05, B, 13	--
Faust, Edward	40-W: 27	On File	On File
Fenn, James E.	15-E: 3	29, C, 15	--
Fennel, James C.	On File	28, D, 10	0, B, 01
Ferguson, John T.	22-E: 35	36, D, 15	--
Fieldstrup, Frederick W.	14-E: 17	02, C, 01	--
Fitzgerald, Columbus C.	22-E: 7	09, B, 19	--
Fletcher, William E.	On File	On File	On File
Flint, William T.	On File	On File	--
Fohr, Peter	Ineligible	19, D, 12	--
Foley, C. Edward	17-E: 24	05, B, 10	--
Fox, John	6-W: 27	20, A, 10	--
Fries, John P.	13-E: 4	20, A, 03	5, B, 15
Fulkerson, James Preston	31-E: 24	30, D, 02	12, A, 02
Fusselman, Charles H.V.	62-W: 4	26, D, 14	--
G	National	Texas	Sheriff's
Gamble, Silas A., Sr.	On File	07, D, 10	--
Garcia, Calixto	53-W: 27	11, A, 05	--
Garvey, James Thomas	7-E: 2	19, B, 04	3, A, 06
Gay, Thomas	Ineligible	20, D, 01	--
Gilleland, James	Ineligible	09, C, 18	--
Gillespie, William	On File	27, A, 17	--
Givens, Millard M.	On File	19, D, 03	--
Glass, William A.	2-W: 27	20, A, 08	--
Glazner, William C.M.	On File	32, D, 10	11, A, 08

Glover, Rufus B.	On File	15, A, 02	--
Godley, James Robert	53-E: 26	18, A, 05	0, D, 11
Goode, Robert	33-W: 22	34, D, 18	--
Goodwin, Jesse F.	42-E: 26	13, A, 09	--
Gorman, Newton Samuel	--	17, B, 13	11, A, 10
Gosling, Harrington Lee	5-E: 15	23, A, 14	--
Gravis, John F.	12-E: 26	17, D, 05	--
Green, James Frederick	On File	On File	--
Green, Mat	10-E: 25	30, C, 19	0, B, 02
Greene, Maston Reynolds	3-E: 13	23, A, 12	--
Grier, Thomas	48-E: 26	19, D, 14	--
Griffin, Frank	34-W: 4	12, A, 16	--
Grimes, Ahijah W.	33-E: 20	01, C, 02	9, A, 15
Grissom, George Bingham	On File	On File	--

H	National	Texas	Sheriff's
Hagood, Robert F.	52-E: 26	16, A, 15	On File
Hall, Augustus G.	On File	32, D, 06	--
Hall, Hiram Metcalf C.	Ineligible	17, D, 09	--
Hall, James	Ineligible	19, A, 11	--
Hall, Joseph A.	On File	On File	--
Hall, William C.	46-E: 23	24, B, 18	1, B, 01
Hammond, John L.	54-E: 26	16, A, 10	--
Hammonds, George T.	On File	On File	--
Harris, Jesse Sutton	32-W: 2	28, B, 08	7, A, 10
Harvell, David W.	On File	19, D, 05	On File
Hawks, Robert E.	26-E: 23	15, B, 18	--
Hearn, A.G.	18-W: 26	14, A, 12	--
Heffington, Isaac	22-E: 7	34, B, 05	10, B, 05
Herman, David	24-E: 26	24, D, 16	--
Hill, John Thomas	On File	22, A, 07	--
Hodges, Dallas	19-W: 22	02, C, 06	--
Hoffman, Heinrich W.	21-E: 20	26, C, 04	9, B, 14
Hoffman, Laben John, Jr.	20-W: 26	11, A, 11	--
Holden, James	48-W: 27	12, A, 12	On File
Holland, Benjamin F.	57-W: 23	07, B, 09	1, A, 16
Holland, H.K.	On File	27, A, 07	--
Hood, Joseph L.	59-W: 10	01, D, 16	4, B, 10
Hope, Larkin Secrest	22-E: 59	05, C, 11	--

	National	Texas	Sheriff's
Horton, John T.	50-W: 25	07, D, 15	12, A, 11
Hoskins, H.M.	33-E: 21	04, C, 04	7, B, 17
Hunter, William Rutherford	22-E: 61	07, B, 13	1, B, 04

I	National	Texas	Sheriff's
Isbell, James	22-E: 21	33, C, 16	--

J	National	Texas	Sheriff's
Jackson, James	21-E: 26	15, A, 14	--
Jacobs, Andrew Jackson	On File	13, D, 03	7, B, 10
Johnson, A.A.	2-E: 24	07, B, 06	--
Johnson, J.D.L.	22-W: 25	13, D, 10	--
Johnson, Joseph E.	22-E: 50	36, D, 13	--
Johnson, Robert L.	40-W: 24	20, B, 14	0, B, 16
Jones, Franklin	33-W: 18	28, D, 11	--
Jones, Willis E.	On File	28, A, 16	--
Joslen, James	Ineligible	22, D, 10	--

K	National	Texas	Sheriff's
Kelly, Dennis J.	24-W: 25	26, D, 16	8, A, 08
Kelly, Patrick William	59-W: 24	24, A, 03	On File
King, William Meredith	31-E: 26	14, A, 02	4, A, 15
Kirk, Richard	11-W: 5	33, C, 10	6, A, 04
Knight, M.M.	59-W: 25	20, B, 12	12, A, 01
Krempkau, Gus	On File	11, D, 13	--

L	National	Texas	Sheriff's
Lackey, William	On File	25, A, 07	--
Lampley, Judge Edward	26-W: 27	26, D, 01	0, B, 07
Lara, Panataleon	53-W: 24	03, D, 05	9, B, 02
Lathrop, James W.	33-W: 27	On File	On File
Leary, Edgar	64-W: 27	09, D, 10	7, A, 05
Ledbetter, F.M.	63-W: 23	01, D, 08	--
Lindsey, Samuel E.	59-W: 24	05, D, 06	--
Little, Albert	23-E: 26	26, D, 02	0, D, 07
Lockhart, Samuel Lee	28-W: 24	11, B, 08	1, A, 12
Loftin, Thomas H.	27-E: 24	30, D, 11	--
Love, John W.	24-W: 24	36, D, 09	1, A, 09

M	National	Texas	Sheriff's
Martin, Joe N.	22-E: 36	06, C, 18	1, B, 17
Martin, John E.	33-W: 25	05, D, 05	12, A, 14
Martin, Samuel B.	63-W: 3	03, D, 12	1, B, 05
Martindale, John E.	10-E: 26	21, A, 05	--
Mastin, James	32-W: 25	11, B, 16	8, B, 09
Matthews, Jerry	On File	22, A, 10	--
Maxey, Nelson	33-E: 26	27, A, 15	On File
May, Robert L.	6-W: 22	10, C, 15	5, B, 10
McBride, John E.	29-E: 26	19, D, 04	--
McCarty, Timothy J.	56-E: 26	09, C, 17	--
McCoy, Richard	30-W: 27	26, D, 07	0, B, 17
McCullough, Henry W.	40-E: 25	19, A, 06	12, B, 15
McDuff, William	6-W: 19	11, C, 19	--
McGee, Thomas T.	42-W: 1	17, C, 08	5, A, 11
McHenry, John	48-W: 4	Deferred	--
McIver, John	On File	18, A, 11	6, A, 14
McKay, William	56-E: 26	17, D, 18	--
McKidrict, Joseph W.	38-W: 24	38, D, 15	--
McKinney, Charles Brown	10-E: 21	36, B, 15	8, A, 09
McMahan, James	13-W: 22	01, B, 16	2, B, 10
McMullen, William Read	40-E: 26	21, A, 12	0, D, 15
Melville, Andrew	36-W: 18	26, D, 03	--
Menn, Otto	59-E: 26	21, A, 17	0, D, 16
Meredith, Charles	30-W: 25	13, D, 15	12, A, 12
Meredith, Samuel Jackson "Sam"	1-W: 25	26, D, 04	12, A, 06
Miles, Alfred H.	Ineligible	17, D, 19	--
Milett, Nicholas R.	7-E: 26	22, D, 12	--
Miller, Frank	On File	13, A, 03	--
Miller, Nimrod Johnson	35-W: 23	11, B, 13	1, A, 14
Millican, Marcellus R.	On File	20, A, 01	--
Milligan, Thomas S.	26-W: 9	28, C, 06	8, A, 11
Milstead, Thomas E.	51-E: 24	20, B, 17	--
Mitchell, William L.	7-E: 8	05, D, 03	6, B, 12
Moad, Thomas P.	42-W: 9	34, C, 11	--
Moore, Edgar Maurice Bowie	58-E: 20	14, C, 19	10, B, 11
Moore, James H.	43-E: 26	30, D, 14	--
Morgan, David	27-E: 24	09, D, 05	12, B, 05
Morgan, John	36-E: 26	28, A, 03	On File

	National	Texas	Sheriff's
Morgan, John T.	On File	32, D, 07	--
Morgan, John Tillie	37-W: 27	22, A, 12	5, B, 16
Morgan, Parker	63-E: 26	24, A, 14	On File
Morgan, Robert	29-W: 24	07, D, 19	12, A, 03
Morris, Jourden Alexander	22-W: 27	On File	On File
Mortimer, Conrad E.	34-E: 26	17, D, 04	--
Mosley, Sam Abbot	62-E: 26	11, A, 01	--
Murphee, Sam R.	25-W: 23	13, B, 14	1, A, 03
Musick, Uel	62-E: 26	15, A, 15	0, D, 17
Mussett, Elias Tyre, Jr.	29-W: 23	11, B, 09	--
N	National	Texas	Sheriff's
Nance, Benton	26-W: 25	26, D, 06	--
Nash, Jesse E.	Ineligible	15, D, 19	--
Neil, David	21-W: 27	24, A, 10	On File
Neill, Alpheus D.	9-W: 22	36, B, 17	--
Nelms, James A.	22-E: 41	05, B, 01	--
Nelson, John D.	16-W: 27	27, A, 03	On File
Nettles, William Lafayette	30-W: 23	32, B, 18	1, A, 05
Nichols, Charles H.	47-W: 21	16, C, 10	9, B, 05
Nicholson, Wesley	Ineligible	22, D, 16	--
Nicholson, William	Ineligible	19, A, 05	--
Nickel, Robert	50-E: 26	25, A, 13	--
Nigh, Thomas P.	61-E: 26	30, D, 19	--
Nolan, Matthew	9-E: 24	05, D, 08	11, B, 12
Nolan, Thomas	29-E: 24	17, B, 11	11, B, 04
Norman, Francis Yewing	On File	34, D, 02	--
Norton, Marion D.	46-W: 27	On File	On File
Nowlin, David T.	On File	On File	--
Nowlin, Thomas H.	45-W: 27	19, B, 16	On File
Null, Charles Hendrickson	On File	32, B, 16	--
O	National	Texas	Sheriff's
O'Bannon, James B.	60-E: 23	09, B, 07	1, A, 17
Olive, John Thomas	55-E: 21	02, C, 03	9, B, 16
P	National	Texas	Sheriff's
Paramore, Green	On File	On File	--
Parks, Wayne B.	37-E: 26	15, A, 17	On File
Parsons, H.D.	46-E: 26	22, A, 14	--

	National	Texas	Sheriff's
Pastrano, Toribio	53-E: 26	14, A, 06	On File
Pate, Addison C.	64-W: 21	18, C, 04	10, A, 08
Patman, Charles	22-E: 6	30, B, 08	--
Patterson, William E.	64-W: 24	26, B, 14	--
Phelps, William H.	On File	On File	--
Phillips, Jack	--	05, D, 09	4, A, 12
Pierson, Jabez C.	39-E: 25	20, A, 04	0, A, 16
Pitts, William	26-W: 6	15, A, 06	--
Pivoda, John	On File	18, A, 09	--
Pool, Gabriel Leander	13-W: 25	38, D, 11	10, B, 16
Powers, Charles	59-W: 26	20, D, 06	--
Q-R	National	Texas	Sheriff's
Ragsdale, Thomas A.	56-W: 22	03, C, 19	2, B, 16
Rhodes, John E.	24-E: 24	32, D, 02	--
Rice, Darwin P.	21-E: 26	17, B, 15	11, A, 17
Richarz, Walter	23-E: 26	24, D, 19	--
Riddle, William H.	40-W: 14	17, B, 08	--
Riff, Joseph R.	40-W: 14	17, B, 08	--
Robertson, Marion David	8-W: 25	13, D, 17	12, B, 12
Rogers, James Bonner	49-W: 14	36, C, 13	5, A, 01
Rogers, John	16-W: 25	13, D, 09	12, A, 08
Ross, John T.	41-E: 24	11, D, 15	12, B, 16
Ruzin, A.A.	16-E: 26	15, D, 16	--
S	National	Texas	Sheriff's
Sanders, William	Ineligible	24, D, 05	--
Sanford, William Daniel	14-E: 24	26, B, 13	--
Schefsky, C.R.V.	59-E: 26	21, A, 02	--
Scheuster, Lewis F.	Ineligible	15, D, 17	--
Schmid, Frank Louis, Jr.	9-E: 24	01, D, 09	--
Schwab, Charles J.	24-W: 23	01, D, 18	11, A, 11
Scott, Thomas M.	Ineligible	22, D, 02	--
Shain, Thomas	7-W: 24	34, D, 12	11, B, 10
Shaw, Thomas	45-W: 27	On File	On File
Sieker, Frank E.	33-W: 18	34, B, 02	--
Smalley, Jim	On File	25, A, 03	--
Smith, Abram Trigg	Ineligible	19, A, 10	--
Smith, Augustus	On File	18, A, 10	--

	National	Texas	Sheriff's
Smith, L.B.	14-E: 26	28, D, 17	--
Smith, Levin P., Jr.	33-E: 26	30, D, 04	--
Smith, Thomas Calton	35-W: 7	18, A, 14	--
Snow, Richard	42-W: 10	03, B, 12	--
Soto, Dionisio	On File	11, D, 16	--
Spalding, John H.	27-W: 24	15, B, 17	--
Spalt, John H.	On File	On File	--
St. Leon, Ernest	On File	26, A, 05	--
Stafford, James Monroe	53-W: 25	28, D, 02	12, A, 15
Stallings, Eli	38-E: 25	19, A, 02	--
Stanley, William J.	5-W: 22	36, B, 03	10, A, 05
Stark, John	22-E: 18	07, B, 07	--
Starks, Alexander C.	50-W: 25	11, D, 04	On File
Steen, Robert	On File	On File	--
Stevens, Edward Alexander	On File	15, B, 13	12, B, 06
Stevens, James B.	22-E: 48	13, B, 19	--
Stewart, John Americas	On File	11, A, 07	--
Story, Probert Peolia	On File	On File	--
Sullivan, Blackstone B.	51-E: 25	32, D, 08	12, B, 04
Sullivan, D.C.	On File	18, A, 07	--
Sutton, David Ike	On File	On File	--
Sweet, Albertus	45-W: 18	01, B, 08	--
Swift, Albert M.	On File	14, A, 14	--
T	**National**	**Texas**	**Sheriff's**
Tabler, George M.	30-E: 25	24, A, 15	--
Taylor, George W.	57-W: 26	22, D, 08	--
Taylor, Gideon C.	40-W: 25	19, B, 12	On File
Tedder, William	37-W: 24	07, D, 18	--
Thompson, Jonathan	16-E: 26	On File	--
Thompson, William M.	21-W: 26	28, A, 07	4, A, 05
Townsend, A. Morse	45-W: 22	38, B, 12	--
Townsend, R.W.	36-W: 4	06, C, 12	1, A, 10
Townsend, Thomas L., Jr.	23-W: 22	04, C, 16	--
Truitt, James M.	51-W: 23	01, D, 15	1, A, 06
Turman, John Martin C.	On File	22, B, 13	9, A, 04
Turner, Volney	47-W: 25	15, D, 04	12, A, 16

U-V	National	Texas	Sheriff's
Unnamed Waco Indian	On File	24, A, 06	--
Venable, Frank W.	44-W: 24	24, B, 11	11, B, 14
Vise (Vice), George V.	22-E: 55	32, C, 13	1, A, 02

WXYZ	National	Texas	Sheriff's
Wagner, J.L.	43-E: 23	05, D, 10	11, A, 05
Wall, Lee	16-W: 22	04, C, 07	-
Wallace, Marion Dekalb	39-E: 9	09, D, 01	4, B, 03
Wallace, Richard W.	On File	13, A, 06	--
Waller, C. Lee	22-E: 15	34, C, 14	--
Walters, Frank	On File	On File	--
Walters, John B.	Ineligible	19, A, 17	--
Ward, Isaac	59-W: 25	13, D, 08	0, A, 10
Warren, Banjamin Goodin	36-W: 25	11, D, 06	--
Washington, Clark	57-W: 25	15, D, 05	--
Weaver, William H.	Ineligible	22, D, 17	--
Webb, Charles M.	11-E: 7	03, B, 14	5, B, 09
Wells, Van Ness	48-W: 8	28, C, 18	--
Werner, August	On File	14, A, 17	--
White, George	50-W: 23	36, D, 14	--
Whiteman, Levi J.	36-E: 21	01, C, 06	2, B, 13
Wilbarger, John Lemon	On File	23, A, 08	--
Wilcox, Murdock M.	46-E: 25	17, B, 18	--
Williams, Duff G.	15-W: 27	On File	On File
Williams, Henry	10-E: 13	05, C, 06	--
Williams, Thomas G.	18-E: 18	11, D, 07	--
Williamson, Benjamin	15-E: 26	27, A, 01	--
Wilson, John	Ineligible	20, D, 09	--
Wise, George	55-W: 27	12, A, 15	--
Wise, W.T.	22-W: 23	13, B, 12	--
Wolf, John W.	4-E: 23	03, D, 11	--
Wood, J.G.	On File	21, A, 04	--
Woodruff, Fountain B.	3-W: 27	19, A, 01	--
Woods, Henry Gonzalvo	18-W: 27	On File	On File
Woods, J.W.	9-E: 26	20, A, 07	--
Wright, Moses L.	On File	19, B, 17	12, A, 04
Wyser, Addison D. "Ad"	28-E: 26	03, D, 17	11, A, 14
York, John B.	63-W: 22	02, C, 09	1, B, 14
York, Hatch	22-E: 10	05, B, 15	--

Bibliography

BOOKS

Adler, Larry. *The Texas Rangers*. New York: David McKay Company, Inc., 1979.

Alexander, Bob. *Fearless Dave Allison: Border Lawman*. Silver City, NM: High-Lonesome Books, 2003.

———. *Lawmen, Outlaws, and S.O.B.s: Gunfighters of the Old West*. Silver City, NM: High-Lonesome Books, 2004.

———. *Lawmen, Outlaws and S.O.B.s*. Vol. 2. Silver City, NM: High-Lonesome Publishing, 2007.

———. *Winchester Warriors: Texas Rangers of Company D, 1874–1903*. Denton: University of North Texas Press, 2009.

Allen, Allyn. *The Real Book About the Texas Rangers*. Garden City, New York: Garden City Books, 1952.

Anderson, Gary Clayton. *The Conquest of Texas: Ethnic Cleansing in the Promised Land 1820–1875*. Norman, OK: University of Texas Press, 2005.

Ball, Larry D. *The United States Marshals of New Mexico & Arizona Territories 1848–1912*. Albuquerque: University of New Mexico Press, 1978.

Bartholmew, Ed. *Jesse Evans: A Texas Hideburner.* Houston: Frontier Press of Texas, 1955.

———. The "Hanging Tree" of Orange Texas, Cross-Cut Saw Thwarted Judge Lynch.

Borders, Gary B. *A Hanging in Nacogdoches: Murder, Race, Politics, and Polemics in Texas's Oldest Town 1870–1916.* Austin: University of Texas Press, 2006.

Breihan, Carl W. *Lawmen and Robbers.* Caldwell, ID: Caxton Printers, Ltd., 1986.

Brown, Gary. *Texas Gulag: The Chain Gang Years 1875–1925.* Plano: Republic of Texas Press, 2002.

Brown, John Henry. *Indian Wars and Pioneers of Texas.* Easley, SC: Southern Historical Press, 1978.

Bullis, Don. *New Mexico's Finest: Peace Officers Killed in the Line of Duty, 1847–1996.* Albuquerque: New Mexico Department of Public Safety, 1996 edition and 1999 edition.

Burton, Art. *Black, Red, and Deadly: Black and Indian Gunfighters of the Indian Territories.* Austin, TX: Eakin Press, 1991.

Butts, J. Lee. *Texas Bad Boys: Gamblers, Gunfighters and Grifters.* Austin: Republic of Texas Press, 2002.

Caldwell, Clifford R. *A Day's Ride From Here.* Vol. 1. *Mountain Home, Texas.* Texas, self-published, 2009.

———. *Dead Right: The Lincoln County War.* Mountain Home, TX: self-published, 2008.

———. *John Simpson Chisum: The Cattle King of the Pecos Revisited.* Santa Fe, NM: Sunstone Press, 2010.

Calhoun, Frederick. *The Lawmen: United States Marshals and Their Deputies, 1789–1989.* Washington, D.C.: Smithsonian Institution Press, 1989.

Carrigan, William D. *The Making of a Lynching Culture: Violence and Vigilantism in Central Texas 1836–1916*. Urbana: University of Illinois Press, 2004.

Carter, Robert G. *On the Border with McKenzie: Or Winning West Texas from the Comanches*. Austin: Texas State Historical Association, 2007.

Castleman, Harvey N. *The Texas Rangers: The Story of an Organization that is Unique, Like Nothing Else in America*. Girard, KS: E. Haldeman-Julius, 1944.

Clarke, Mary Whatley. *A Century of Cow Business: A History of the Texas and Southwestern Cattle Raisers Association*. Fort Worth, TX: Evans Publishing, 1976.

Collins, Michael L. *Texas Devils: Rangers & Regulars on the Lower Rio Grande, 1846–1861*. Norman: University of Oklahoma Press, 2008.

Conger, Roger N. *Texas Rangers: Sesquicentennial Anniversary, 1823–1973*. Fort Worth, TX: Heritage Publications, 1973.

Congers, Roger N., et al. *Rangers of Texas*. Waco, TX: Texian Press, 1969.

Cool, Paul. *Salt Warriors: Insurgency on the Rio Grande*. College Station: Texas A&M University Press, 2008.

Cox, Mike. *Historic Photos of Texas Lawmen*. Nashville, TN: Turner Publishing Company, 2008.

———. *Texas Ranger Tales: Stories that Need Telling*. Plano: Republic of Texas Press, 1997.

———. *Texas Ranger Tales II*. Plano: Republic of Texas Press, 1999.

———. *The Texas Rangers: Wearing the Cinco Pecos, 1821–1900*. New York: A Tom Doherty Associates Book, 2008.

Crouch, Carrie J. *A History of Young County, Texas*. Austin: Texas State Historical Association, 1956.

Cunningham, Eugene. *Triggernometry: A Gallery of Gunfighters*. New York: Barnes & Noble Books, 1996.

Davis, John L. *The Texas Rangers: Images and Incidents*. San Antonio: University of Texas Institute of Texan Cultures, 2000.

Day, Jack Hays. *The Sutton-Taylor Feud*. San Antonio, TX: Sid Murray & Sons, 1937.

De Arment, Robert K. *Alias Frank Canton*. Norman: University of Oklahoma Press, 1996.

———. *Bravo of the Brazos: John Larn of Fort Griffin, Texas*. Norman: University of Oklahoma Press, 2002.

———. *Deadly Dozen: Twelve Forgotten Gunfighters of the Old West*. Norman: University of Oklahoma Press, 2003.

———. *George Scarborough: The Life and Death of a Lawman on the Closing Frontier*. Norman: University of Oklahoma Press, 1992.

———. *Jim Courtright of Fort Worth: His Life and Legend*. Fort Worth: Texas Christian University Press, 2004.

De Arment, Robert K., and Jack DeMattos. *A Rough Ride to Redemption: The Ben Daniels Story*. Norman: University of Oklahoma Press, 2010.

De la Garza, Beatriz. *A Law for the Loin: A Tale of Crime and Injustice in the Borderlands*. Austin: University of Texas Press, 2003.

DeShields, James T. *Border Wars of Texas*. Austin, TX: State House Press, 1993.

Douglas, Claude Leroy. *Famous Texas Feuds*. Dallas, TX: Turner Publishing Company, 1936.

———. *The Gentlemen in White Hats*. Dallas, TX: Southwest Press, 1934.

————. *The Gentlemen in the White Hats: Dramatic Episodes in the History of the Texas Rangers*. Austin, TX: State House Press, 1992.

Dunn, J.B. John. *Perilous Trails of Texas*. Dallas, TX: Southwest Press, 1932.

Durham, George. *Taming of the Nueces Strip: The Story of McNelly's Rangers*. Austin: University of Texas Press, 1962.

Eckhardt, C.F. *Tales of Badmen, Bad Women, and Bad Places: Four Centuries of Texas Outlawry*. Lubbock: Texas Tech University Press, 1999.

Egloff, Fred R. *El Paso Lawman G.W. Campbell*. College Station, TX: Creative Publishing Company, 1982.

El Paso Genealogical Society. *Births, Deaths, & Marriages From El Paso Newspapers Through 1885*. Easly, SC: Southern Historical Press, 1982.

————. *Births, Deaths, & Marriages From El Paso Newspapers 1886–1890*. Vol. 2. Greenville, SC: Southern Historical Press, 1992.

————. *Births, Deaths, & Marriages From El Paso Newspapers 1896–1899*. Vol. 4. Provo, UT: Print & Mail Production Center, 2000.

Elwonger, Steve. *In the Line of Duty*. Dallas, TX: Taylor Publishing Company for the Dallas Police Department, 2002.

Ernst, Robert. *Deadly Affrays: The Violent Deaths of the US Marshals*. N.p.: Scarlet Mask Enterprise, 2006.

Etulain, Richard W., and Glenda Riley, eds. *With Badges & Bullets: Lawmen & Outlaws in the Old West*. Golden, CO: Fulcrum Publishing, 1999.

Exley, Jo Ella Powell. *Frontier Blood: The Saga of the Parker Family*. College Station: Texas A&M University Press, 2001.

Fallwell, Gene. *The Texas Rangers*. Texarkana, TX: Connell Printing, 1959.

Farber, James. *Texans with Guns*. San Antonio, TX: Naylor Company, 1950.

Fisher, Ovie Clark, and Jeff C. Davis. *King Fisher: His Life and Times*. Norman: University of Oklahoma Press, 1966.

Ford, John Salmon. *Rip Ford's Texas*. Austin: University of Texas Press, 1963.

Foster, Kevin, and Richard F. Selcer. *Written in Blood: The History of Fort Worth's Fallen Lawmen*. Vol. 1. *1861–1909*. Denton: University of North Texas Press. 2010.

Franscell, Ron. *The Crime Buff's Guide to Outlaw Texas*. Guilford, CT: Globe Pequot Press, 2011.

Fuller, Henry C. *A Texas Sheriff*. Nacogdoches, TX: Baker Printing, 1931.

Fulton, Maurice G. *History of the Lincoln County War: A Classic Account of Billy the Kid*. Tucson: University of Arizona Press, 1968.

Gatewood, Jim. *Decker: A Biography of Sheriff Bill Decker of Dallas County, 1898–1970*. Garland, TX: Mullaney Corporation, 1999.

Gillette, James B. *Fugitives Justice: The Notebook of Texas Ranger Sergeant James B. Gillett*. Austin, TX: State House Press, 1997.

———. *Six Years with the Texas Rangers: 1875 to 1881*. New Haven, CT: Yale University Press, 1963.

Gober, Jim. *Cowboy Justice: Tale of a Texas Lawman*. Lubbock: Texas Tech University Press, 1997.

Gournay, Luke. *Texas Boundaries: Evolution of the State's Counties*. College Station: Texas A&M University Press, 1995.

Greer, James Kimmins. *Texas Ranger: Jack Hays in the Frontier Southwest*. College Station: Texas A&M University Press, 1993.

Guthrie, Keith. *Raw Frontier*. Vol. 2. *Survival to Prosperity Along the Texas Coastal Bend*. Austin, TX: Eakin Press, 2000.

BIBLIOGRAPHY

Gwynne, S.C. *Empire of the Summer Moon: Quanah Parker and the Rise and Fall of the Comanche, the Most Powerful Indian Tribe in American History*. New York: Scribner, 2010.

Hardin, John Wesley. *The Life of John Wesley Hardin*. Seguin, TX: Smith and Moore, 1896.

Hardin, Stephen, MD. *Texas Rangers*. Oxford, UK: Osprey Publishing, 2000.

Harrington, Fred Harvey. *Hanging Judge*. Norman: University of Oklahoma Press, 1996.

Harris, Charles H., III, and Louis R. Sadler. *The Texas Rangers and the Mexican Revolution: The Bloodiest Decade, 1910–1920*. Albuquerque: University of New Mexico Press, 2004.

Hatley, Allen G. *Texas Constables: A Frontier Heritage*. Lubbock: Texas Tech University Press, 1999.

Horan, James D. *The Lawmen: Accounts of Eyewitnesses and the Lawmen Themselves*. New York: Gramercy Books, 1996.

Horan, James D., and Paul Sann. *Pictorial History of the Wild West*. New York: Bonzana Books, 1964.

Horton, David M., and Ryan Kellus Turner. *Lone Star Justice: A Comprehensive Overview of the Texas Criminal Justice System*. Austin, TX: Eakin Press, 1999.

Hughes, John R. *The Killing of Bass Outlaw*. Austin, TX: Brick Row Books, 1963.

Hughes, W.J. *Rebellious Ranger: Rip Ford and the Old Southwest*. Norman: University of Oklahoma Press, 1964.

Hutton, Harold. *The Luckiest Outlaw: The Life and Legends of Doc Middleton*. Lincoln: University of Nebraska Press, 1993.

Ingmire, Frances T. *Texas Rangers: Frontier Battalion, Minute Men, Commanding Officers, 1847–1900*. St. Louis, MO: Ingmire Publications, 1982.

Ivey, Darren L. *The Texas Rangers: A Registry and History*. Jefferson, NC: McFarland & Company, Inc., 2010.

Jenkins, John H., and H. Gordon Frost. *I'm Frank Hamer: The Life of a Texas Peace Officer*. Austin, TX: Pemberton Press, 1968.

Jennings, N.A. *A Texas Ranger*. Edited by Ben Proctor. Chicago, IL: R.R. Donnelley & Sons Company, 1992.

Jensen, Ann, ed. *Texas Ranger's Diary and Scrapebook*. Dallas, TX: Kaleidograph Press, 1936.

Johnson, Benjamin Heber. *Revolution in Texas: How a Forgotten Rebellion and Its Bloody Suppression Turned Mexicans into Americans*. New Haven, CT: Yale University Press, 2003.

Johnson, David. *John Ringo*. Stillwater, OK: Barbed Wire Press, 1996.

———. *John Ringo, King of the Cowboys: His Life and Times from the Hoo Doo War to Tombstone*. Denton: University of North Texas Press, 2008.

———. *The Mason County "Hoo Doo" War, 1874–1902*. Denton: University of North Texas Press, 2006.

Johnson, Dorothy. *Famous Lawmen of the Old West*. New York: Dodd, Mead, 1963.

Keating, Bern. *An Illustrated History of the Texas Rangers*. New York: Rand McNally & Company, 1975.

Kelsey, Michael, Nancy Graff Floyd and Ginny Guinn Parsons. *Miscellaneous Newspaper Abstracts—Deaths*. Vol. 1. Bowie, MD: Heritage Books, 1995.

———. *Miscellaneous Newspaper Abstracts—Deaths*. Vol. 2. Bowie, MD: Heritage Books, 1997.

Kennedy, Imogene Kinard, and J. Leon Kennedy. *Genealogical Records in Texas*. Baltimore, MD: Genealogical Publishing Company, 1987.

Kilgore, D.E. *A Ranger Legacy: 150 Years of Service to Texas*. Austin, TX: Madrona Press, 1973.

Knight, Sherri. *Vigilantes to Verdicts, Stories from a Texas District Court*. Stephensville, TX: Jacobus Books, 2009.

Knowles, Thomas W. *They Rode for the Lone Star: The Saga of the Texas Rangers*. Dallas, TX: Taylor Publishing Company, 1999.

Lackey, B. Roberts. *Stories of the Texas Rangers*. San Antonio, TX: Naylor, 1955.

Ladd, Kevin. *Gone to Texas: Genealogical Abstracts from the Telegraph and Texas Register 1835–1842*. Bowie, MD: Heritage Books, 1994.

Landrey, Wanda A. *Outlaws in the Big Thicket*. Austin, TX: Eakin Press, 1976.

Larralde, Carlso, and Jose Rodolfo Jacobo. *Juan N. Cortina and the Struggle for Justice in Texas*. Dubuque, IO: Kendall/Hunt Publishing Company, 2000.

Lavash, Donald R.. *Wilson & the Kid*. College Station, TX: Creative Publishing Company, 1990.

Marohn, Richard C. *The Last Gunfighter: John Wesley Hardin*. College Station, TX: Creative Publishing, 1995.

Martin, Charles L. *A Sketch of Sam Bass, the Bandit*. Norman: University of Oklahoma Press, 1997.

Martin, Jack. *Border Boss: Captain John R. Hughes*. San Antonio, TX: Taylor Publishing, 1942.

McCright, Grady E., and James H. Powell. *Jessie Evans: Lincoln County Badman*. College Station, TX: Creative Publishing Company, 1983.

McGinnis, Bruce. *Reflections in a Dark Glass: The Life and Times of John Wesley Hardin*. Denton: University of North Texas Press, 1996.

McGrath, Roger D. *Gunfighters, Highwaymen & Vigilantes: Violence on the Frontier*. Berkeley: University of California Press, 1984.

Metz, Leon Claire. *Dallas Stoudenmire: El Paso Marshal*. Austin, TX: Pemberton Press, 1969.

———. *John Selman: Texas Gunfighter*. New York: Hastings House, 1966.

———. *John Wesley Hardin: Dark Angel of Texas*. Norman: University of Oklahoma Press, 1996.

———. *Pat Garrett: The Story of a Western Lawman*. Norman: University of Oklahoma Press, 1974.

———. *The Shooters*. El Paso, TX: Mangan Books, 1976.

Miller, Rick. *Sam Bass Gang*. Austin, TX: State House Press, 1999.

Moneyhon, Carl H. *Texas After the Civil War*. College Station: Texas A&M University Press, 2004.

Moore, Stephen L. *Savage Frontier: Rangers, Riflemen, and Indian Wars in Texas*. Vol. 1. *1835–1836*. Plano: Republic of Texas Press, 2002.

———. *Savage Frontier: Rangers, Riflemen, and Indian Wars in Texas*. Vol. 2. *1838–1839*. Denton: University of North Texas Press, 2006.

———. *Savage Frontier: Rangers, Riflemen, and Indian Wars in Texas*. Vol. 3. *1840–1841*. Denton: University of North Texas Press, 2007.

———. *Savage Frontier: Rangers, Riflemen, and Indian Wars in Texas*. Vol. 4. *1842–1845*. Denton: University of North Texas Press, 2010.

———. *Taming Texas: Captain William T. Sadler's Lone Star Service*. Austin, TX: State House Press, 2000.

Morris, John Miller. *A Private in the Texas Rangers: A.T. Miller of Company B, Frontier Battalion*. College Station: Texas A&M University Press, 2001.

Nash, Jay Robert. *Bloodletters and Badmen: A Narrative Encyclopedia of American Criminals from the Pilgrims to the Present*. New York: Evans and Company, 1973.

————. *Encyclopedia of Western Lawmen & Outlaws*. New York: Da Capo Press, 1994.

Neal, Bill. *From Guns to Gavels: How Justice Grew Up in the Outlaw West*. Lubbock: Texas Tech University Press, 2008.

————. *Getting Away With Murder on the Texas Frontier: Notorious Killings & Celebrated Trials*. Lubbock: Texas Tech University Press, 2006.

Nicklas, Linda Cheves. *Abstracts of Early Texas Newspapers, 1839–1856*. Greenville, SC: Southern Historical Press, 1994.

Nordyke, Lewis. *John Wesley Hardin: Texas Gunman*. Edison, NJ: Castle Books, 1957.

Nunn, W.C. *Texas Under the Carpetbaggers*. Austin: University of Texas Press, 1962.

Olmsted, Charles L., and Edward Coy Ybarra. *The Life and Death of Juan Coy*. Austin, TX: Eakin Press, 2001.

O'Neal, Bill. *The Bloody Legacy of Pink Higgins: A Half Century of Violence in Texas*. Austin, TX: Eakin Press, 1999.

————. *Encyclopedia of Western Gunfighters*. Norman: University of Oklahoma Press, 1974.

————. *War in East Texas: Regulators vs. Moderators*. Lufkin: Best of East Texas Publishers, 2006.

Paine, Albert Bigelow. *Captain Bill McDonald, Texas Ranger: A Story of Frontier Reform*. Austin, TX: State House Press, 1986.

Parcedes, Americo. *With a Pistol in his Hand: A Border Ballad and its Hero*. Austin: University of Texas Press, 1958.

Parsons, Chuck. *John B. Armstrong: Texas Ranger and Pioneer Ranchman*. College Station: Texas A&M University Press, 2007.

———. *The Sutton-Taylor Feud: The Deadliest Blood Feud in Texas*. Denton: University of North Texas Press, 2009.

Parsons, Chuck, and Donaly Brice. *Texas Ranger N.O. Reynolds: The Intrepid*. Honolulu, HI: Talei Publishers, 2005.

Parsons, Chuck, and Gary P. Fitterer. *Captain C.B. McKinney: The Law in South Texas*. Austin, TX: State House Press, 1993.

Parsons, Chuck, and Marianne E. Hall Little. *Captain L.H. McNelly—Texas Ranger: The Life and Times of a Fighting Man*. Austin, TX: State House Press, 2001.

Parsons, Chuck, and Marjorie Parsons. *Bowen and Hardin*. College Station, TX: Creative Publishing Company, 1991.

Patterson, Paul E., and Joy Poole. *Great Plains Cattle Empire: Thatcher Brothers and Associates (1875–1945)*. Lubbock: Texas Tech Press, 2000.

Patterson, Richard. *Historical Atlas of the Outlaw West*. Boulder, CO: Johnson Publishing Company, 1985.

Penfield, Thomas. *Western Sheriffs and Marshals*. New York: Grosset and Dunlap, 1955.

Petersen, Paul R. *Quantrill in Texas: The Forgotten Campaign*. Nashville, TN: Cumberland House, 2007.

Pike, James. *Scout and Ranger, Being the Personal Adventures of James Pike of the Texas Rangers in 1859–1860*. Princeton, NJ: Princeton University Press, 1932.

Prassel, Frank Richard. *The Western Peace Officer: A Legacy of Law & Order*. Norman: University of Oklahoma Press, 1972.

Preece, Harold. *Lone Star Man: Ira Aten, Last of the Old Texas Rangers*. New York: Hastings House Publishers, 1960.

Pylant, James. *Sins of the Pioneers*. Stephenville, TX: Jacobus Books, 2009.

Raine, William McLeod. *Famous Sheriffs and Western Outlaws*. Garden City, NY: Garden City Publishing Company, 1929.

———. *.45-Calibre Law: The Way of Life of the Frontier Peace Officer*. Evanston, IL: Row, Peterson and Company, 1941.

———. *Guns of the Frontier: The Story of How Law Came to the West*. Boston, MA: Houghton Mifflin, 1940.

Reed, Paula, and Grover Ted Tate. *The Tenderfoot Bandits: Sam Bass and Joel Collins, Their Lives and Hard Times*. Tucson, AZ: Westernlore Press, 1988.

Roberts, Dan Webster. *Rangers and Sovereignty*. San Antonio, TX: Wood Printing and Engraving Company, 1914.

Roberts, Lou Conway. *A Woman's Reminiscences of Six Years in Camp with the Texas Rangers*. Austin, TX: Von Boeckmann–Jones, 1928.

Robinson, Charles M., III. *The Men Who Wear the Star: The Story of the Texas Rangers*. New York: Random House, 2000.

Rocha, Rodolfo. *Background to Banditry in the Lower Rio Grande Valley of Texas, 1900 to 1912*. Microform, Dallas Public Library, 1974. NC.

Romo, David Dorado. *Ringside Seat to a Revolution: An Underground Cultural History of El Paso and Juarez 1863–1923*. El Paso, TX: Cinco Puntos Press, 2005.

Rose, Victor M. *The Texas Vendetta, or the Sutton-Taylor Feud*. New York: J.J. Little, 1880.

Russell, Traylor. *Carpetbaggers, Scalawags & Others*. Jefferson, TX: Marion County Historical Society, 1982.

Samora, Julian, Joe Bernal and Albert Pena. *Gunpowder Justice*. Notre Dame, IN: University of Notre Dame Press, 1979.

Sandos, James A. *Rebellion in the Borderlands: Anarchism and the Plan of San Diego, 1904–1923*. Norman: University of Oklahoma Press, 1992.

Schoenberger, Dale T. *The Gunfighters*. Caldwell, ID: Caxton Printers, Ltd., 1976.

Scott, Bob. *Leander McNelly, Texas Ranger: He Just Keeps on Keepin' On*. Austin, TX: Eakin Press, 1998.

Selcer, Richard F. *Fort Worth Characters*. Denton: University of North Texas Press, 2009.

Shirley, Glenn. *The Fighting Marlows: Men Who Wouldn't Be Lynched*. Fort Worth: Texas Christian University Press, 1994.

Sinise, Jerry. *George Washington Arrington: Civil War Spy, Texas Ranger, Sheriff and Rancher*. Burnet, TX: Eakin Press, 1979.

Siringo, Charles A. *Riata and Spurs: The Story of a Lifetime Spent in the Saddle as a Cowboy and Ranger*. Boston and New York: Houghton Mifflin, 1931.

Sitton, Thad. *The Texas Sheriff: Lord of the County Line*. Norman: University of Oklahoma Press, 2000.

Smallwood, James M. *The Feud that Wasn't: The Taylor Ring, Bill Sutton, John Wesley Hardin and Violence in Texas*. College Station: Texas A&M University Press, 2008.

Smallwood, James M., Barry A. Crouch and Larry Peacock. *Murder and Mayhem: The War of Reconstruction in Texas*. College Station: Texas A&M University Press, 2003.

Smith, David Paul. *Frontier Defense in the Civil War: Texas' Rangers and Rebels*. College Station: Texas A&M University Press, 1992.

Smithwick, Noah. *The Evolution of a Stare or Recollections of Old Texas Days*. Austin: University of Texas Press, 1983.

Sommer, Robin Langley. *The History of the U.S. Marshals: The Proud Story of America's Legendary Lawmen*. Leicester, England: Magna Books, 1993.

Sonnichsen, Charles Leland. *I'll Die Before I'll Run: The Story of the Great Feuds of Texas*. New York: Harper and Brothers, 1951.

———. *Texas Feuds*. Albuquerque: University of New Mexico Press, 1971.

Sowell, Andrew J. *Rangers and Pioneers of Texas, With a Concise Account of the Early Settlements, Hardships, Massacres, Battles, and Wars, by Which Texas Was Rescued from the Rule of the Savage and Consecrated to the Empire of Civilization.* San Antonio, TX: Shepard Brothers, 1884.

———. *Texas Indian Fighters*. Austin, TX: State House Press, 1982.

Spellman, Paul N. *Captain John H. Rogers: Texas Ranger*. Denton: University of North Texas Press, 2005.

Spinks, S.E. *Law on the Last Frontier: Texas Ranger Arthur Hill*. Lubbock: Texas Tech University Press, 2007.

Spurlin, Charles D. *Texas Volunteers in the Mexican War*. Austin, TX: Eakin Press, 1998.

Stambaugh and Stambaugh. *The Lower Rio Grande Valley of Texas*. Austin, TX: Jenkins Publishing Company, 1974.

Steelwater, Eliza. *The Hangman's Knot: Lynching, Legal Execution, and America's Struggle with the Death Penalty*. Boulder, CO: Westview Press, 2003.

Stephens, Robert W. *Bullets and Buckshot in Texas*. N.p.: privately published, 2002.

———. *Captain George H. Schmitt: Texas Ranger*. N.p.: privately published, n.d.

———. *Lone Wolf: The Story of Texas Ranger Captain M.T. Gonzaullas*. Dallas, TX: Taylor Publishing Company, n.d.

———. *Mannen Clements: Texas Gunfighter*. N.p.: privately published, 1996.

———. *Texas Ranger Captain Dan Roberts: The Untold Story*. N.p.: privately published, 2009.

———. *Texas Ranger Indian War Pensions*. Quanah, TX: Nortex Press, 1975.

———. *Texas Ranger Sketches*. N.p.: privately published, 1972.

———. *Walter Durbin: Texas Ranger and Sheriff*. Clarendon, TX: Clarendon Press, 1970.

Sterling, Hank. *Famous Western Outlaw-Sheriff Battles*. New York: Rainbow Books, 1954.

Sterling, William Warren. *Trails and Trials of a Texas Ranger*. Norman: University of Oklahoma Press, 1959.

Sullivan, W. John L. *Twelve Years in the Saddle for Law and Order on the Frontiers of Texas*. Austin, TX: Von Boeckmann–Jones, 1909.

Summerfield, Charles. *The Rangers and Regulators of the Tanaha: or, Life Among the Lawless, a Tale of the Republic of Texas*. New York: Robert M. DeWitt, 1856.

Sutton, Robert C., Jr. *The Sutton-Taylor Feud*. Quanah, TX: Nortex Press, 1974.

Thompson, Jerry. *Cortina: Defending the Mexican Name in Texas*. College Station: Texas A&M University Press, 2007.

Thompson, Jerry, ed. *Fifty Miles and a Fight: Major Samuel Peter Heintzelman's Journal of Texas & the Cortina War*. Austin: Texas State Historical Association, 1998.

Thompson, Jerry, and Lawrence T. Jones, III. *Civil War and Revolution on the Rio Grande Frontier: A Narrative and Photographic History*. Austin: Texas State Historical Association, 2004.

Timanus, Rod. *An Illustrated History of Texas Forts*. Plano, TX: Wordware Publishing, 2001.

Tise, Sammy. *Texas County Sheriffs*. Albuquerque, NM: Oakwood Printing, 1989.

Utley, Robert M. *Lone Star Justice: The First Century of the Texas Rangers*. New York: Oxford University Press, 2002.

————. *Lone Star Lawmen: The Second Century of the Texas Rangers*. New York: Oxford University Press, 2007.

Walker, Donald R. *Penology for Profit: History of the Texas Prison System 1867–1912*. College Station: Texas A&M University, 1988.

Ward, James Randolph. *Texas Rangers 1919–1935: A Study in Law Enforcement*. T Microform, Dallas Public Library, 1972. NC.

Webb, Walter Prescott. *The Texas Rangers: A Century of Frontier Defense*. Austin: University of Texas Press, 1965.

Wellman, Paul I. *A Dynasty of Western Outlaws*. New York: Bonanza Books, 1961.

Wharton, Clarence Ray. *History of Fort Bend County*. San Antonio, TX: Naylor, 1939.

Wilbarger, J.W. *Indian Depredations in Texas*. Austin, TX: Hutchings Printing House, 1889.

Wilkins, Frederick. *Defending the Borders: The Texas Rangers 1848–1861*. Austin, TX: State House Press, 2001.

————. *The Highly Irregular Irregulars: Texas Rangers in the Mexican War*. Austin, TX: Eakin Press, 1990.

————. *The Law Comes to Texas: The Texas Rangers 1870–1901*. Austin, TX: State House Press, 1999.

————. *The Legend Begins: The Texas Rangers, 1823–1845*. Austin, TX: State House Press, 1999.

Williamson, G.R. *Texas Pistoleers: The True Story of Ben Thompson and King Fisher*. Charleston, SC: The History Press, 2010.

Yardon, Laurence J. *200 Texas Outlaws and Lawmen, 1835–1935*. Gretna, LA: Pelican Publishing Company, 2008.

Zink, Wilbur A. *The Roscoe Gun Battle: Younger Brothers vs. Pinkerton Detectives.* Appleton City, MO: Democrat, 1967.

Zoch, Nelson J. *Fallen Heroes of the Bayou City: Houston Police Department 1860–2006.* Kingwood, TX: Call to Duty Publications, 2007.

GOVERNMENT DOCUMENTS

"El Paso Troubles in Texas." House Executive Document No. 93, Forty-fifth Congress, Second Session, 69–70, 157–158, Serial No. 1809. Frederick W. Hodge Collection, Huntington Free Library, Native American Collection, Cornell University.

House Executive Document No. 81, Thirty-sixth Congress, First Session, 2ff, Serial No. 1056. Frederick W. Hodge Collection, Huntington Free Library, Native American Collection, Cornell University.

Journals of the Fourth Congress of the Republic of Texas. Vol. III. Texas State Archives, Austin, Texas.

Report to the Adjunct General of State of Texas for the Year 1872 by Frank L. Britton. Austin, TX: James P. Newcomb & Company, 1873.

"Texas Border Troubles." U.S. House Miscellaneous Document No. 64; Forty-fifth U.S. Congress, Second Session, Serial No. 1820.

NEWSPAPERS

Austin Daily Democratic Statesman. "Published list of 12 state policemen killed in service." April 17, 1873.

Dallas Morning News. Various dates.

Galveston Daily News. Various dates.

Houston Chronicle. Various dates.

San Antonio Daily Express. Various dates.

San Antonio Evening Light. Various dates.

San Antonio Express. Various dates.

San Antonio Light. Various dates.

PERIODICALS

Baenziger, Ann Patton. "The Texas State Police During Reconstruction: A Reexamination." *Southwestern Historical Quarterly* 72, no. 4 (April 1969): 473.

Block, W.T. "The Orange County War of 1856." Reprinted from Block, W.T. "Meanest Town on the Coast." *Old West* (Winter 1979): 10ff.

Caldwell, Clifford R. "Davy Thomas 'Tom' Carson—Texas Ranger." *Journal of the Wild West History Association* 2, no. 3 (June 2009).

———. "Thalis Tucker Cook—Texas Ranger." *Journal of the Wild West History Association* 2, no. 6 (December 2009).

Callan, Austin. "Sheriffing in the Old Days." *Sheriff's Association of Texas Magazine* 1, no. 1 (1930): 9–10.

Duke, J.K. "Bad Men and the Peace Officers of the Southwest." *West Texas Historical Association Year Book* 13 (June 1932): 51–61.

Field, William T., Jr. "The Texas State Police, 1870–1873." *Texas Military History* 5 (Fall 1965).

Holden, W.C. "Law and Lawlessness on the Texas Frontier, 1875–1890." *Southwestern Historical Quarterly* 44, no. 2 (October 1940): 188–203.

McConnell, Joseph Carroll. *West Texas Frontier* 1 (1933), Jacksboro, Texas.

———. *West Texas Frontier* 2 (1939), Palo Pinto, Texas.

Schuster, Stephan W. "Modernization of the Texas Rangers: 1933–1936." *West Texas Historical Association Year Book* 43 (October 1967): 65–79.

Sheriff's Association of Texas Magazine 1, no. 11. "Texas First Sheriff" (September 1932): 15.

Webb, Walter Preston. "Texas Rangers Kept Idle: Present Restraints Upon Force Brings Back Memories of Past Accomplishments of Men." *State Trooper* 7, no. 10 (June 1926): 13–14.

Wilkins, Frederick. "Texas Rangers—Life on a Scout" (2003). Texas Ranger Hall of Fame and Museum.

THESES AND DISSERTATIONS

Briscoe, Eugenia Reynolds. "A Narravtive History of Corpus Christi, Texas 1519–1875." PhD diss., University of Denver, 1972.

Caldwell, Clifford R. Unpublished manuscript. June 2010. Soon to be published in *Wild West History Magazine Journal* 4, no. 2 (February 2011).

Copeland, Ronald Craig. "The Evolution of the Texas Department of Corrections." MA thesis, Sam Houston State University, 1980.

Gunn, Jack Winton. "Life of Ben McCulloch." Unpublished MA thesis, University of Texas, 1947.

Hendricks, George David. "The Bad Men of the West." Unpublished MA thesis, University of Texas, 1938.

Nunn, William Curtis. "A Study of the State Police During the E.J. Davis Administration." Unpublished MA thesis, University of Texas, 1931.

Spiller, Phillip N. "A Short History of the San Antonio Police Department." Unpublished MS thesis, Trinity University, 1954.

Thonhoff, Robert. "A History of Karnes County." Master's thesis, Southwest Texas State College, 1963.

Ward, Charles F. "The Salt War of San Elizario, 1877." Unpublished MA thesis, University of Texas, 1932.

West, John Olive. "To Die Like a Man: The 'Good' Outlaw Tradition in the American Southwest." Unpublished PhD diss., University of Texas, 1964.

Index

About the Authors

Cliff Caldwell has continually cultivated his interest in western history since boyhood. After a stint in United States Marine Corps during the Vietnam War, and a successful thirty-five-year career working for several Fortune 500 corporations, Cliff is now retired and free to pursue his interests as a historian and writer on a full-time basis. Cliff holds a Bachelor of Science degree in business and is the author of several book and published works, including *Dead Right, The Lincoln County War, Guns of the Lincoln County War, A Day's Ride From Here* and his most recent work, *John Simpson Chisum: The Cattle King of the Pecos Revisited.*

Cliff is recognized as an accomplished historian and researcher on the American West. He is a member of Western Writers of America, Inc., the Wild West History Association, Texas State Historical Association and the Buffalo Bill Historical Center. When not deeply involved in writing, Cliff volunteers some of his time doing research for the Peace Officers Memorial Foundation of Texas and is a member and volunteer at the Museum of Western Art in Kerrville, Texas.

Cliff and his wife, Ellen, live in the Hill Country of Texas, near Mountain Home.

Ron DeLord was a patrol officer for the Beaumont, Texas Police Department from 1969 to 1972. He served as a patrol officer and detective for the Mesquite, Texas Police Department from 1972 to 1977. In 1977, DeLord was one of the founders of the Combined Law Enforcement Associations of Texas (CLEAT) and was elected its first president. After thirty years as president, he is currently serving as special counsel. He is a licensed Texas attorney, a nationally recognized police labor official and an author who is known for his leadership style and visionary ideas.

Ron has a Bachelor of Science degree in government from Lamar University (1971), a Master of Arts degree in police science and administration from Sam Houston State University (1982) and a Doctor of Jurisprudence degree from South Texas College of Law (1986). He has been a licensed Texas attorney since 1987. He graduated from the ten-week Harvard University Trade Union Program (1992).

Ron initiated the legislation to create the Texas Peace Officers Memorial on the grounds of the state capitol in Austin. He is the director of the Peace Officers Memorial Foundation, Inc., a 501(c)(3) charitable corporation dedicated to honoring the memories of Texas law enforcement and corrections officers who have given their lives in the line of duty. He volunteers his time researching historic cases for the Sheriff's, National, Texas and other state memorials.

Ron is is the author and coauthor of several book and published works, including *Police Union Power, Politics and Confrontation in the 21ˢᵗ Century: New Challenges, New Issues* (2nd edition); *Navigating Dangerous Waters: The Real World of Police Labor Management Relations*; *Working Together: A Police Labor-Management Practitioner's Guide to Implementing Change, Making Reforms and Handling Crisis*; *Police Association Power, Politics and Confrontation: A Guide for the Successful Police Labor Leader*; and *The Ultimate Sacrifice: The Trials and Triumphs of the Texas Peace Officer*.

Ron and his wife, Brenda, live in Georgetown, Texas.

"Tell the boys I died, discharging my duty, like a man."

Bryan police officer A.G. "Race" Hearn
2 February 1870

Visit us at
www.historypress.net